CW01203716

REARMING THE RAF FOR THE SECOND WORLD WAR

'A detailed and highly readable account of how the RAF became obsessed with the bomber in the decades before the Second World War, yet even after six years of continual expansion, Bomber Command was unable to mount a credible offensive against Germany in 1940. Adrian Phillips skilfully uses archival sources to show how the clash of personalities inside Whitehall combined with false orthodoxies within the Air Ministry to leave Britain with no counter to Hitler's Luftwaffe –except, almost by accident, the Spitfires and Hurricanes of Fighter Command.'
Brett Holman, author of *The Next War in the Air: Britain's Fear of the Bomber, 1908–1941*

'A compelling, sometimes shocking and always thought-provoking description of what happens when blind prejudice, bureaucratic infighting and ill-formed theories are allowed to determine defence policy, equipment procurement and the security of the nation.'
Robert Lyman, author of *A War of Empires: Japan, India, Burma & Britain, 1941–45*

REARMING THE RAF FOR THE SECOND WORLD WAR
POOR STRATEGY AND MISCALCULATION

ADRIAN PHILLIPS

Pen & Sword
HISTORY
AN IMPRINT OF PEN & SWORD BOOKS LTD.
YORKSHIRE – PHILADELPHIA

First published in Great Britain in 2022 by
PEN AND SWORD HISTORY
An imprint of
Pen & Sword Books Ltd
Yorkshire – Philadelphia

Copyright © Adrian Phillips, 2022

ISBN 978 1 39900 624 8

The right of Adrian Phillips to be identified as Author of this work has been asserted by him in accordance with the Copyright, Designs and Patents Act 1988.

A CIP catalogue record for this book is available from the British Library.

All rights reserved. No part of this book may be reproduced or transmitted in any form or by any means, electronic or mechanical including photocopying, recording or by any information storage and retrieval system, without permission from the Publisher in writing.

Typeset in Times New Roman 11.5/14 by SJmagic DESIGN SERVICES, India.
Printed and bound in the UK by CPI Group (UK) Ltd.

Pen & Sword Books Limited incorporates the imprints of Atlas, Archaeology, Aviation, Discovery, Family History, Fiction, History, Maritime, Military, Military Classics, Politics, Select, Transport, True Crime, Air World, Frontline Publishing, Leo Cooper, Remember When, Seaforth Publishing, The Praetorian Press, Wharncliffe Local History, Wharncliffe Transport, Wharncliffe True Crime and White Owl.

For a complete list of Pen & Sword titles please contact
PEN & SWORD BOOKS LIMITED
47 Church Street, Barnsley, South Yorkshire, S70 2AS, England
E-mail: enquiries@pen-and-sword.co.uk
Website: www.pen-and-sword.co.uk

Or

PEN AND SWORD BOOKS
1950 Lawrence Rd, Havertown, PA 19083, USA
E-mail: Uspen-and-sword@casematepublishers.com
Website: www.penandswordbooks.com

For Jessica, William and George

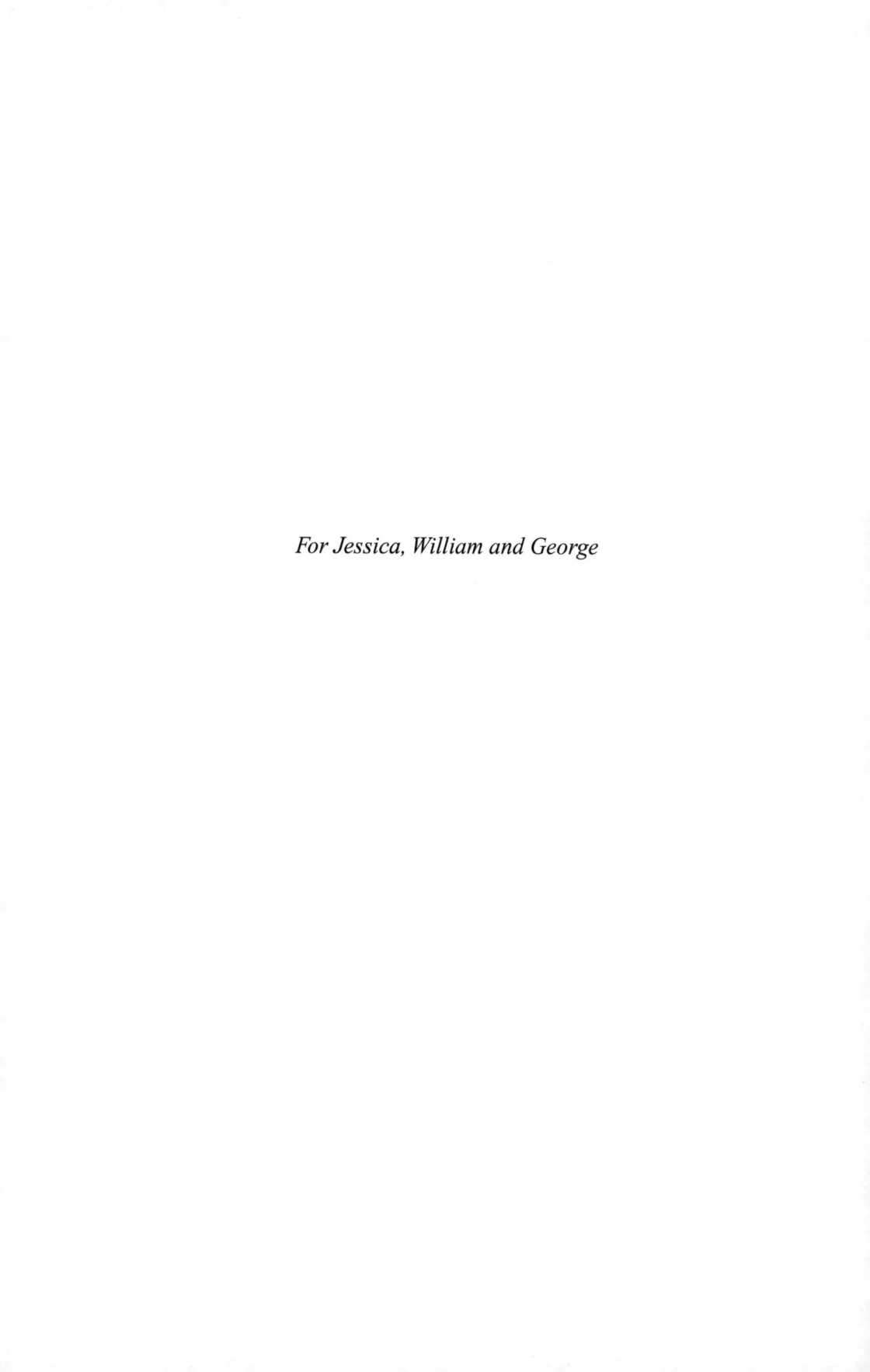

Contents

Author's Notes		ix
Dramatis Personae		x
Abbreviations and Table of Ranks		xvi
Introduction	Why the Few Were so Few	xviii
Chapter 1	A Modern Major-General	1
Chapter 2	The Prophet	10
Chapter 3	Who Squeals First?	16
Chapter 4	Rabbits	25
Chapter 5	Evasion of Responsibility	36
Chapter 6	Protection from the Slipstream	48
Chapter 7	Incalculable Potential	57
Chapter 8	The Air Defence of Great Britain	63
Chapter 9	No Longer in a Position Inferior	70
Chapter 10	A Pretty Bad Half Section – Scheme A	77
Chapter 11	A Malay Running Amok	87
Chapter 12	An Air Minister Bypassed – Scheme C	94
Chapter 13	The Man for Push and Go	101
Chapter 14	A Striking Force of Such Power – Scheme F	108
Chapter 15	An Ideal Scheme of Defence	115
Chapter 16	Horrors in the Most Intense Form	124
Chapter 17	A Striking Bomber Force Not Inferior – Scheme H	134
Chapter 18	Maximum Offensive Potential	140

Chapter 19	Swinton's Hobby	150
Chapter 20	Striking a Careful Balance – Scheme J	159
Chapter 21	The Interpreter	167
Chapter 22	Morally Sure – Scheme K	174
Chapter 23	No Reflection on Swinton's Administration – Scheme L	182
Chapter 24	A Wave of Uneasiness	190
Chapter 25	From Telephones to Warplanes	197
Chapter 26	The Doubts of Sir Edgar Ludlow-Hewitt	202
Chapter 27	An Ideal of Bombing	210
Chapter 28	As Much Damage as Possible on the Attackers	215
Chapter 29	Large Allowances Against Underestimate	224
Chapter 30	The Utmost Limit Compatible	230
Chapter 31	A Weapon We Can Use Very Effectively	236
Chapter 32	Per Astra Ad Ardua	244
Chapter 33	By This Means Alone – Scheme M	252
Chapter 34	Saturation Point – Fighters and Scheme M	264
Chapter 35	A Gross Misuse of Air Forces	272
Chapter 36	You Can Stand up to Hitler Now	280
Chapter 37	The Result of Overexpansion	285
Chapter 38	The Miracles Proposed for Them	294
Endnotes		300
Selected Bibliography		328
Acknowledgements		336
Index		338

Author's Notes

The term 'type' is used to refer to a distinct model of aircraft, such as Hawker Hurricane. The term 'class' refers to all aircraft designed to meet a specific requirement, such as 'fighter'. At the start of the 1930s the RAF used the term 'heavy bomber' almost as a synonym for night bomber. Otherwise, there was no distinction between the missions of the different classes of bombers: they were all intended to attack the enemy's cities; the distinction between 'strategic' and 'tactical' bombing only became current after the period covered by this book. When the designation 'heavy bomber' re-emerged to apply to the Short Stirling, this referred to its size and bombload; it was to do the same job as the 'medium bombers' that were being designed at the same time – the Halifax and the Manchester – and the older 'medium bombers', the Battle, Blenheim, Hampden, Whitley and Wellington. Only in retrospect did the Battle and the Blenheim become labelled as 'light bombers', in the case of the Battle after the type had been withdrawn from combat service.

The term Air Staff had no precise definition but embraces the RAF officers based at the Air Ministry in London, especially the most senior who were the service members of the Air Council, the RAF's governing body. The most senior was the Chief of the Air Staff (Air Chief Marshal Sir Cyril Newall) who had an unusually wide remit that included direct charge of the Plans, Operations, Intelligence and Signals departments. In 1939 his colleagues were the Air Member for Personnel (AVM Portal), the Air Member for Supply and Organization (AVM Welsh) and the Air Member for Development and Production (Air Marshal Sir Wilfrid Freeman) and the Deputy Chief of the Air Staff (AVM Peirse). The Assistant Chief of the Air Staff (AVM Sholto Douglas) was not a member of the Air Council. The air ministers also sat on the council as did the Ministry's head civil servant, but he had little influence on policy.

Dramatis Personae

This section aims to provide sufficient information to situate individuals within the narrative of the book. It makes no attempt to provide a balanced assessment of their careers and, still less, an exhaustive list of their titles, honours and decorations. The titles given are those held at the periods in which they are discussed. Readers seeking fuller information are directed to the relevant entries in the *Oxford Dictionary of National Biography* and *Who Was Who* respectively.

Attlee, Clement (1883–1967). Leader of the opposition Labour Party 1935–40.

Baldwin, Stanley (1867–1947). Prime minister 1923–4, 1924–9 and 1935–7. As Lord President of the Council 1931–5 he was de facto joint head of the National Government. Leader of the Conservative Party 1923–37. The dominant politician between the wars.

Balfour, Harold (1891–1988). Politician. RFC in the First World War, awarded MC and bar. Under Secretary for Air 1938–44.

Beatty, Lord (1871–1936). Royal Navy officer. First Sea Lord 1919–27. Fought a long, ruthless and underhand campaign to bring naval aviation back under the control of the Royal Navy.

Brooke-Popham, Air Chief Marshal Sir Robert (1878–1953). AOC-in-C ADGB 1933–5. Inspector General RAF 1935–7. C-in-C Far East 1940–1.

Bruce-Gardner, Sir Charles (1887–1960). Industrialist. Industrial adviser to Bank of England 1930–8. Chairman SBAC 1938–43. Trusted by Chamberlain and Wilson to run the programme of air rearmament, he was accordingly influential.

Dramatis Personae

Bullock, Sir Christopher (1891–1972). Civil servant. Principal private secretary to three successive air ministers 1919–30. Permanent Secretary to Air Ministry 1931–6. Dismissed controversially by Fisher for a breach of ethics. Part of the dysfunctional Ellington/Londonderry era at the Air Ministry.

Chamberlain, Neville (1869–1940). Politician. Chancellor of the Exchequer 1931–7. Prime minister 1937–40. Chiefly known for attempting to appease Hitler and Mussolini, but also convinced of the need to rearm.

Christie, Group Captain (1881–1971). Air attaché Berlin 1927–30. On retirement businessman and freelance intelligence operative.

Churchill, Winston (1874–1965). Politician. Secretary of State for War and Secretary of State for Air (posts held simultaneously) 1919–21. Backbench MP 1929–39. Fell out with National Government over its policy of granting limited autonomy to India. Recognized danger of Hitler earlier than most and campaigned for rearmament, especially in the air.

Cunliffe-Lister, Philip see Swinton.

Dean, Maurice (1906–1978). Civil servant. Private secretary to Ellington 1934. Private secretary to Newall 1937. Assistant Under Secretary of State for Air 1943. His book *The Royal Air Force and Two World Wars* was written with great inside knowledge.

Dowding, Sir Hugh (1882–1970). RAF officer. Rose to command a wing of the RFC. AOC Fighting Area ADGB 1929. Air Member for Supply and Research 1930, Air Member for Research and Development 1935. AOC-in-C Fighter Command 1936–40.

Ellington, Sir Edward (1887–1967) RAF officer. Various staff appointments in BEF and then RFC during the First World War. CAS 1933–7. Inspector General RAF 1937–40.

Fairey, Richard (1887–1956). Industrialist. Founder and manager of eponymous aircraft company. Chairman SBAC 1922–4.

Fisher, Sir Warren (1887–1948). Civil servant. Head of the Civil Service/Permanent Secretary to Treasury 1919–39. One of the dominant Whitehall figures between the wars.

Freeman, Sir Wilfrid (1888–1953). RAF officer. Commanded RFC wing, awarded DSO and MC in the First World War. Air Member for Research and Development 1936. Air Member for Development and Production 1938. Vice-Chief of Air Staff 1940. Chief Executive Ministry of Aircraft Production 1942–5.

Goebbels, Joseph (1897–1945). German politician. Reich Minister for Public Enlightenment and Propaganda Hitler's master propagandist

Göring, Herman (1893–1946). German politician. Commander-in-chief of the Luftwaffe amongst his various appointments

Handley Page, Frederick (1885–1962). Industrialist. Founder and managing director of eponymous aircraft company. Twice chairman of SBAC and its first president 1938–9.

Hankey, Sir Maurice (1877–1963). Administrator. Secretary to Committee for Imperial Defence 1912–38. Secretary to the Cabinet 1917–38. Member of War Cabinet as Lord Hankey 1939–42. Dominant figure in the military establishment and Whitehall between the wars.

Harris, Arthur 'Bert' (1892–1984). RAF officer. Rose to command an RFC squadron in the First World War and awarded AFC. Group captain and Deputy Director of Plans on Air Staff 1934–7. Highly influential despite comparatively junior rank. AOC-in-C Bomber Command 1942–5.

Hoare, Sir Samuel Bt (1880–1959). Politician. Secretary of State for Air 1922–9 and (briefly) 1940. Admirer of Trenchard and a major supporter during his second term as CAS.

Inskip, Sir Thomas (1876–1947). Politician. Minister for the Coordination of Defence 1936–9. Gently and unsuccessfully challenged the Air Staff policy of concentrating on bombers.

Dramatis Personae

Lindemann, Frederick (1886–1957). Scientist and politician. RFC experimental pilot and researcher in the First World War. Professor of Experimental Philosophy Oxford University. Churchill's personal adviser on science. Member of the CID committee on the scientific problems of air defence 1935–6.

Londonderry, Lord (1878–1949). Politician. Secretary of State for Air 1931–5. He and his wife were prominent figures in London society.

Ludlow-Hewitt, Sir Edgar (1886–1973). RAF officer. In the First World War became RFC brigade commander and Chief of Staff RAF in France; awarded DSO and MC. AOC RAF India 1935. AOC-in-C Bomber Command 1937. Inspector General RAF 1940.

MacDonald, James Ramsay (1866–1937). Politician. Prime minister as head of the Labour Party 1924 and 1929–31. Prime minister in 'National Government' 1931 to 1935, but dwindled to little more than the figurehead for a Conservative dominated government.

Milch, Erhard (1892–1972). German air force officer and administrator. Switched from running the Lufthansa airline to managing the build-up of the Luftwaffe. Played a greater part in the detailed running of the Luftwaffe than Göring.

Newall, Sir Cyril (1886–1963). RAF officer. Second-in-command IAF in the First World War, awarded CB and Albert Medal. AOC RAF Middle East 1931. Air Member for Supply and Organization 1935. CAS 1937.

Nuffield, Lord (1877–1963). Industrialist. Founder and owner of Morris motor company and other enterprises

Peirse, Richard (1892–1970). RAF officer. Deputy Chief of Air Staff 1937–40.

Rothermere, Lord (1868–1940). Newspaper proprietor and politician. Secretary of State for Air 1917–18. Appeaser but strong advocate of air rearmament.

Salmond, Sir John (1881–1968). RAF officer. Awarded DSO 1915. Succeeded Trenchard as commander of the RFC 1918. GOC/AOC RAF Iraq 1922–4, where he was highly successful in handling both the Turkish incursion into Kurdistan and a revolt against British rule in Iraq. AOC-in-C ADGB 1925–8. CAS 1930–3. Retired making way for his brother **Geoffrey Salmond** to succeed him as CAS. Geoffrey Salmond died within weeks of his appointment.

Sholto Douglas, William (1893–1969) RAF officer. RFC squadron commander in the First World War, awarded MC and DFC. Assistant Chief of Air Staff 1938–40.

Simon, Sir John (1873–1954). Politician and lawyer. Left Cabinet in 1916 and served as a major on the RFC staff 1917–18. Foreign Secretary 1931–5. Succeeded Chamberlain as Chancellor of the Exchequer 1937.

Slessor, John (1897–1979). RAF officer. Attained rank of major and awarded DSO and MC in the First World War. Air Staff plans directorate, worked closely with Trenchard 1928–31. OC 3 Wing RAF India 1935. Assistant Director then Director of Plans Air Staff as group captain, working closely with Newall 1937. CAS 1950–3.

Swinton, Lord (1884–1972). Politician. Born Philip Lloyd-Graeme and adopted surname Cunliffe-Lister in 1924. Secretary of State for Air 1935–8.

Sykes, Frederick (1877–1954). Air force officer, administrator and politician. Succeeded Trenchard as CAS 1918–19. Controller-General of Civil Aviation 1919–22. MP 1922–8.

Tallents, Sir Stephen (1884–1958). Publicity expert. Director General designate Ministry of Information 1935–8.

Tizard, Henry (1885–1959). Scientist, science administrator and government adviser. Experimental RFC pilot and Assistant Controller Experiments and Research during the First World War. Chairman Aeronautical Research Committee, 1933–43. Advocate of radar and other scientific aids.

Dramatis Personae

Trenchard, Sir Hugh (1873–1956). RAF officer. GOC RFC France 1916. CAS 1918. GOC IAF March 1918. CAS 1919. Commissioner Metropolitan Police Force 1931–5. Trenchard was raised to the peerage in 1930 and after retiring from government service, used the House of Lords as a platform to promote his policies for the RAF.

Watson Watt, Robert (1892–1973). Government scientist. Superintendent radio department of the National Physical Laboratory 1933. Appointed to lead development of RDF (now called radar) at Air Ministry 1935. Often erroneously considered the inventor of radar.

Weir, Lord (1877–1959). Industrialist, politician and government adviser. Founder and chairman of Weir Pumps. Controller of Aeronautical Supplies 1917–18. Succeeded Rothermere as Secretary of State for Air 1918. Adviser to Principal Supply Officers committee and member of the Defence Policy and Requirements committee 1933. Adviser to Lord Swinton as Secretary of State for Air. Amongst the very first advocates of strategic bombing, he promoted this policy and the career of Trenchard.

Wilson, Sir Horace (1882–1979). Civil servant. Personal Civil Service adviser to Baldwin then Chamberlain based at 10 Downing Street 1935–40. Head of the Civil Service 1939–42. The *éminence grise* of the Chamberlain government.

Wimperis, Harry (1876–1960). Government scientist. Director of Scientific Research, Air Ministry 1925–37. Early advocate of radar.

Wood, Sir Kingsley (1881–1943). Politician. Postmaster General 1931. Minister of Health 1935. Secretary of State for Air in succession to Swinton 1938–40.

Abbreviations and Table of Ranks

Abbreviations

ADGB	Air Defence of Great Britain
AFC	Air Force Cross
AMSR	Air Member for Supply and Research
AOC	Air Officer Commanding
AOC-in-C	Air Officer Commanding-in-Chief
AVM	Air Vice-Marshal
BEF	British Expeditionary Force
BMARC	British Manufacture and Research Company
CAS	Chief of the Air Staff
CID	Committee for Imperial Defence
DFC	Distinguished Flying Cross
DRC	Defence Requirements Committee
DSO	Distinguished Service Order
FAA	Fleet Air Arm
GOC	General Officer Commanding
IAF	Independent Air Force
MC	Military Cross
OC	Officer Commanding
RAF	Royal Air Force
RFC	Royal Flying Corps
RN	Royal Navy
RNAS	Royal Naval Air Service
SBAC	Society of British Aircraft Constructors

Table of Ranks

RAF	British Army equivalent	US equivalent
Marshal of the Royal Air Force	Field Marshal	5-star General
Air Chief Marshal	General	4-star general
Air Marshal	Lieutenant-General	3-star General
Air Vice-Marshal	Major-General	2-star General
Air Commodore	Brigadier	1-star General
Group Captain	Colonel	
Wing Commander	Lieutenant-Colonel	
Squadron Leader	Major	
Flight Lieutenant	Captain	
Flying Officer	Lieutenant	
Pilot Officer	Second Lieutenant	

Introduction

Why the Few Were so Few

Guy Hamilton's all-star, big budget 1968 movie *The Battle of Britain* is a fixture of British television, screened regularly, notably when any anniversary related to the battle passes. It strove for authenticity in a way that went beyond the clunky patriotism and simplistic vision of wartime politics that the black-and-white (in both senses) war films of the 1950s peddled. In one scene, set before the battle begins, the Commander-in-Chief of RAF Fighter Command, Air Marshal Sir Hugh Dowding, played by Laurence Olivier, tries to pour cold water on the blustering optimism of his minister. The unnamed politician wants Dowding to present a confident picture that can be given to the Cabinet, as Britain braces itself for the coming Nazi assault. The minister tells the airman that it will be possible to deliver as many as one hundred fighters a week on top of the 650 planes that the British have already and 'we have radar'. Dowding counters, 'And they have 2,500 aircraft, haven't they?' Dowding accepts that radar does give the British an advantage, but warns the minister that radar will not shoot down aircraft, so, 'the essential arithmetic is that our young men will have to shoot down their young men at the rate of four to one … if we're to keep pace at all'. The episode is fictional, but it encapsulates a legend that persists to this day: that the RAF was hugely outnumbered by the Luftwaffe in the summer of 1940. Churchill immortalized the RAF's fighter pilots as 'the Few' and the battle against a hugely superior enemy is part of the national legend.

As with any statistical exercise, it pays to dig into the numbers and a degree of exaggeration swiftly becomes obvious. The figure Dowding gave for his fighters is widely accepted, but it is a figure for serviceable aircraft available for combat.[1] The figure for Luftwaffe strength is a gross total; only about 80 per cent of German aircraft were serviceable.[2] Almost all the RAF fighters were (by then) Hurricanes and Spitfires fully capable of fighting any German aircraft; the German total included approximately 300 Junkers 87 dive-bombers, which were so vulnerable that they were quickly withdrawn from action, and perhaps 200 Messerschmitt Bf 110 twin-engine fighters which were also severely outclassed in dogfights with single-engine fighters. Moreover, the figures that Dowding and his minister discuss contain an elementary imbalance: the figure for German strength includes both fighters and bombers whilst the British figure is for fighters only. At the time of the Battle of Britain the RAF had approximately 500 bombers available for combat.[3] Thus the RAF was certainly outnumbered, but in terms of serviceable, combat effective aircraft by a far, far smaller margin than the legend.

Bringing the RAF's bombers into the equation is not merely an abstract statistical exercise. All the men who built the RAF, from its early years as an independent air force just after the First World War, starting with its long-serving commander, Sir Hugh Trenchard, would have derided the view that fighters could have defended Britain successfully as the product of pitiable ignorance of air warfare, amongst populist politicians and militarily illiterate members of the public. The RAF had been built on an unchallenged doctrine that the only way to fight the bomber was with the bomber. This doctrine was proclaimed vehemently and remorselessly for the entire period between the wars. The doctrine insisted that only the absolute minimum should be spent on fighters, anything more would waste resources that could otherwise be devoted to Britain's true defence: the bomber. The advent of radar (or RDF as it was then called) had not changed this. Indeed, there was downright scepticism towards radar at the top of the RAF and only a few of its commanders recognized that radar had transformed the potential of air defence in favour of the fighter. The Munich crisis of 1938 had forced the RAF to bow to the politicians and increase spending on fighters but it had increased spending on bombers even more. In the wake of Munich, the RAF pushed through its strategy of an all-big bomber force which featured aircraft that cost a multiple of what their predecessors did.

Throughout the 1920s and early 1930s the RAF had twice as many bombers as fighters. When it began to rearm in earnest in 1935 the men in charge of the RAF tried to push the balance even further in favour of bombers. As the threat from the Luftwaffe was seen to grow remorselessly, the RAF's response was to seek more and bigger bombers, not fighters. At one stage the RAF aimed to have more than three times as many bombers as fighters. Even more important, the size and cost of bombers rose far faster than those of fighters, Under the plans of early 1936 the RAF's bomber force was costing five times as much as its fighters did and that was with relatively modestly priced bombers compared to the very large bombers that the RAF saw as its true weapon. The historian A. J. P. Taylor sneered that the politicians who wanted the RAF to concentrate on fighters did so merely because fighters were cheaper than bombers as though military considerations are quite distinct from economic ones.[4] This slur meshes happily with the traditional image of 1930 politicians as feeble fiscal conservatives who held back from rearmament and left Britain unprepared for war because of their obsession with the budget, but it is wrong to trivialize the debate as one about money only. The Second World War was a total war in which the entire economic resources of the combatants had to be mobilized. No less an individual than Dowding understood the underlying economic reality:

> I speak of spending money, but this is only a convenient yard stick to cover expenditure of the national capital in man power, material, etc.[5]

The RAF's unflinching application of the bomber doctrine was making a huge economic choice in favour of one military technology over others. The state of Britain's defences when the Second World War came was not just the product of how much money the politicians were prepared to spend, but also what the military spent that money on. From the moment that rearmament began, it was accepted universally that the greatest threat to Britain came from Germany's strength in the air and it was the RAF that was there to deal with this threat. The RAF was the priority service and spending on it rose far faster than on the other services. It received the largest share of the extra money directed at defence.

The RAF chose to spend far more money on its bombers yet it was the RAF's fighters that won the Battle of Britain with minimal assistance from its bombers. The RAF's doctrine stated that bombers could defend against bombers, but when it came to the crunch, they could not. In the words of John Terraine, who wrote *The Right of The Line: The Royal Air Force in the European War 1939–1945*: 'Bomber Command's operational plans were quite impracticable; with its existing equipment and methods, it was simply not able to perform what it had intended and promised.'[6] This led to a:

> bleak period from 1940–43 when Bomber Command remained painfully weak for the task in hand, when its equipment – by comparison with the last phase of the war – was ridiculously inadequate, when the results that it was able to achieve were often pitiful.[7]

The official history of Bomber Command's campaign *The Strategic Air Offensive Against Germany 1939–1945* sets out in full detail everything that had to be done before the RAF was able to come close to delivering on its promises and achieving anything commensurate with the financial commitment that the government had made to rearming it. Between 1939 and 1942 the British public received extremely poor value for what it had spent to back the RAF's devotion to the bomber doctrine.

Even before the RAF was confronted with the reality of war in September 1939, albeit Phoney War, and a few months later with the challenge of defeating the full weight of the Luftwaffe's own bomber strength, the execution of the bomber strategy had run into deep difficulties. When Britain faced the threat of war over the Czechoslovakia crisis in the summer of 1938, the RAF knew it was in no condition to take on the Luftwaffe, not because it had been starved of funds, but because the expansion purchased with the extra funds was very far from complete. The first generation of modern bombers which made up the bulk of its strength did not even have the range to attack Germany. Crew training and organization had lagged behind the growth in aircraft numbers. The Air Staff was pursuing a conscious and radical strategy of re-equipping the RAF's bomber force entirely with larger and more complex aircraft; the first generations of the new bombers were a long way short of being ready for battle but the Air Staff had already turned its attention to the next generation on from these which would be ready in 1941 at the very earliest. The chief of Bomber Command since the autumn of 1937, Air Marshal Sir Edgar Ludlow-Hewitt, had almost no confidence in the ability of his force to fulfil its task and glumly foretold horrendous casualties if it tried to. The RAF's leadership was thrown back on an unheroic strategy of 'conserving the bombers', avoiding the loss of trained aircrew until the new aircraft and organization to handle them were ready. The vast force built up to defend Britain was to be used as sparingly as possible. The Air Staff knew that otherwise it would suffer badly in operations, compromising its ability to do its job as and when it was again re-equipped, this time with the kind of bombers that the Air Staff truly wanted.

The failure of rearming the RAF hurt both diplomatically and militarily. When prime minister Neville Chamberlain flew to Germany to ward off war over Czechoslovakia in September 1938, he knew how weak Britain was in the air. His fear of what war would involve was dominated by a wildly pessimistic picture of what the Luftwaffe could do to Britain. Britain had no reason to fear the other German services. The German army threatened Germany's immediate neighbours and not Britain. The Royal Navy was immensely stronger than the Kriegsmarine so the kind of sudden invasion that had troubled British imagination before the First World War was impossible. The German U-boat arm was in its infancy and the Admiralty believed that the ASDIC submarine detection system gave it the advantage. The RAF had sedulously cultivated the fear of a German knock-out blow from the air to sustain its own case for weapons. The fear of German bombers was part of the RAF's pitch for more bombers of its own. The vision of London defenceless against German bombs that inspired Chamberlain's surrender at Munich was doubly flawed. The Germans had neither the means nor the intention to launch the 'knock-out blow' he feared. When the RAF analysed how it could parry this – imaginary – threat, it obeyed the doctrine that only counterattack mattered. Chamberlain sought to avoid war because he believed it would have meant immediate defeat for Britain. He was wrong

When the Luftwaffe's bombers spearheaded the German plan to invade Britain in 1940, the RAF's bombers proved no defence at all. Their sole significant contribution to defeating the plans for Operation *Sealion*, the German invasion planned for the summer of 1940, was to inflict heavy damage on the fleet of invasion barges that would have shipped the German army to England had the Luftwaffe won air superiority, which it never did. Bombing the invasion fleet was not, as Air Marshal Sir Arthur Harris, the eventual successor to Ludlow-Hewitt as head of Bomber Command later claimed, decisive.[8] Otherwise, a handful of bombing raids on German airbases cost severe casualties for almost no result.[9]

Why the Few Were so Few

The bomber offensive against Germany's industrial heartland, in particular the Ruhr, which was finally unleashed after the Battle of France in May 1940, inflicted only very slight damage and had no effect on the Luftwaffe's strategy. The RAF had convinced itself that the Ruhr offered a vulnerable target, which could be attacked to bring German industry to its knees in matter of weeks in a triumphant demonstration of the power of its bomber force – the service's historic mission and under the Trenchard doctrine its raison d'être. The RAF exaggerated the strength of its bomber force and underestimated the effort that would be needed to achieve its goal.

Nor did the RAF's bombers achieve anything worthy of the resources devoted to them for another two years. Whilst Britain stood alone and suffered defeat after defeat at the hands of the Germans and then the Japanese, the largest component of the RAF made no contribution to the war effort. British military history is punctuated with glorious defeats which prove the endurance and valour of the British fighting man in adversity. The RAF's deeply unimpressive showing in the first battle of the Ruhr was not one of these; that crown falls to the massacre of the RAF's Fairey Battles in the opening days of the German offensive over Sedan and the Maastricht bridges in May 1940. The failure of the RAF's campaign to bomb Germany in 1940 and 1941 was not at all sublime. It was simply a tale of unmitigated failure; there was no famous commander on the opposite side who could be acknowledged as the worthy victor. The campaign was fought with inadequate resources for the task but government parsimony can only very partly be blamed for this. It was the battle that the RAF had chosen to fight. Most of the aircraft types which it had bought to fight the battle proved severely inadequate for the task. Bomber Command was crippled by weaknesses in organization, training, technology and preparation, above all as they affected navigation, that were entirely the fault of the service's leadership. The distinguished aviation historian Williamson Murray puts this with brutal simplicity, 'Considering that "strategic" bombing represented the raison d'être for the Royal Air Force, it is surprising that so little was done to prepare for this task.'[10]

Only with Operation *Millennium*, the thousand-bomber raid on Cologne in May 1942, did the bombing offensive against Germany start in earnest, under the efficient and remorseless command of Arthur Harris. He reaped the reward of having at his disposal significant numbers of the four-engine heavy bombers that had been the Air Staff's ideal since 1936. It took another year on from this for the bombers to begin to hurt Germany grievously; the devastating firestorm raids on Hamburg in July 1943 were the turning point here. The new heavy bombers were there but it took longer than expected to develop the techniques to use them to their full effect. Nor was this achieved by the RAF on its own. The US Eighth Air Force practically doubled the force attacking Germany, in a development quite unforeseen during the years of rearmament. By 1943 the war had anyway turned decisively against Germany and Britain was becoming clearly only the junior of the three major powers fighting the war against the dictators. The crushing German defeat at the Battle of Stalingrad in January 1943 marked the failure of Hitler's attempt to conquer the Soviet Union. By the middle of the year the allies had gained the upper hand in the Battle of the Atlantic. The combination of Soviet and US economic resources and manpower made allied victory inevitable.

In the summer of 1940 Britain's salvation was RAF Fighter Command, which prevented the Luftwaffe from gaining the air superiority over the invasion coast that was a precondition of a successful landing. Fighter Command also saved the reputation of the entire RAF, from the abject failure of its bombers to give protection from German bombers as well as creating a stock of capital which shielded the service from its mediocre performance until the bomber offensive got properly under way. Victory in the Battle of Britain is now part of the foundation myth of the RAF: but for the establishment of an independent air force, Britain would have lost. The historian A. J. P. Taylor recognized that this claim was specious as long ago as 1962 when he reviewed a biography that claimed that Trenchard's efforts laid the ground for the British victory in the Battle of Britain. Taylor's words are often quoted: 'The Battle of Britain was won by Fighter Command and by radar. Trenchard despised the one and knew nothing of the other.'[11]

The old saying that the Battle of Waterloo was won on the playing fields of Eton applies equally to air warfare, an industrialized form of conflict shaped by economic factors and choices present long before battle is joined and which are either immutable or take years to change. The outcome of air war depends much less on the tactical choices of commanders than either land or sea warfare. The air force with which Britain entered the Second World War had been fixed years before and it left Britain's military leaders with only a limited range of options. These air forces had been chosen on the basis of theory and not combat experience. This factor was especially acute as technology was developing so rapidly that the Air Staff was having to plan for its second, and even third, generation of modern aircraft before the first generation had even entered service. The replacements for the Battles, Blenheims, Whitleys, Hampdens and Wellingtons amongst the bombers and the Hurricanes and Spitfires of the fighter force were conceived in a pragmatic void. No one knew what the next war in the air was going to be like so the replacement generations simply magnified the effects of preconceptions and doctrine that had shaped the first generation.

As Britain rearmed through the 1930s, the RAF expanded through a series of alphabetically labelled schemes beginning with Scheme A in 1934 and concluding with Scheme M, which came up for approval in late 1938. Some were abortive so letters are missing from the sequence; some were only partly approved. They sometimes appear as a smooth progression of the increasing size of force that the RAF needed to meet the expanding threat of the Luftwaffe, but each scheme was shaped by distinct factors: intelligence estimates of German capacity, technological advances, politics and budgetary considerations. As well as the lettered schemes there was one expansion scheme that never made it into the formal alphabetical sequence, but one which was of supreme importance, but has usually escaped attention. The 'substitution scheme' set in stone the Air Staff's choice of large bombers as the best, if not only, means of accomplishing the RAF's Trenchardian mission. It is often pointed out that the Luftwaffe's arsenal never included an effective long-range heavy bomber, but it usually escapes attention that before the war the RAF had adopted the radical strategy of a bomber force that consisted of nothing but such planes. There was even one rival scheme to that of the Air Staff's. Each scheme involved a shifting cast of senior RAF officers, politicians, bureaucrats and industrialists. Practically the only common thread that ran through all of them was the Air Staff's commitment to the Trenchardian doctrine that the only true means of defence was attack. A small handful of sceptics in government and the civil service did try to resist the effects of RAF's doctrine and put up increasing but never entirely successful opposition. The story of how each scheme came to be defined and its ultimate fate provides an anchor for this narrative.

The choices that shaped the RAF as it rearmed to face the menace of Hitler led ineluctably to the bomber offensive against Nazi Germany. It is one of the most passionately debated episodes in the Second World War. This features two distinct controversies, one military, the other ethical: how effective was the offensive in the defeat of Germany; can the scale of civilian deaths and suffering be justified? This book makes no pretence to answering either. It provides a faint sidelight on the ethical question because it discusses the thinking of the RAF's commanders about bombing and it adds an unexplored dimension to the military one. Hitherto the military debate has focused on whether the RAF's bomber force could have been used more profitably on other objectives and whether the offensive was worth the losses incurred. This book describes how the RAF chose to wage the bomber offensive with large bombers in 1937 (and probably before). This choice meant that the RAF played an insignificant part in the diplomacy that led to the war and a very limited part in the war that was fought until 1942. The Battle of Britain in 1940, is of course, a shining exception that proves the rule. To apply a term from economics, there was an opportunity cost to the strategic bomber offensive against Germany. The resources that the offensive consumed were not available for anything else. It is a question of speculative counter-factual history what else might have been achieved with these resources, but it is beyond doubt that British weakness in the air is partly to blame for the defeats in France, Greece, the Western Desert and the Far East.

Chapter 1

A Modern Major-General

There is no doubt as to when the Royal Air Force was born. It came into being on 1 April 1918 as the Air Force (Constitution) Act of November 1917 combined into a single service the air components of the Royal Navy and the British Army: the Royal Naval Air Service (RNAS) and the Royal Flying Corps (RFC). Until then these had operated quite independently of each other, fully under the command of their parent services and subordinated to their operational plans. The First World War was still being fought and had reached one of its most intense moments with massive German land offensives on the Western Front. The new service held a status equal to the two older ones. It came under the military authority of the newly created Chief of the Air Staff and the political direction of a government minister, the Secretary of State for Air. These posts ranked equally with their naval and military equivalents, respectively: First Lord of the Admiralty and First Sea Lord; Secretary of War and Chief of the Imperial General Staff. The RAF was the first such fully independent air arm in the world and was to remain so for many years.

There is less certainty over the exact date of the RAF's conception. The chain of events that directly culminated in its creation had begun appropriately enough some nine months before when the German campaign of attacking the British mainland took a frightening and dangerous turn. Since 1915 Germany had been bombing Britain using Zeppelin airships. At first this had caused widespread concern, some panic but little damage. The image of the massive airships cruising over Britain had been the epitome of terrifying and unstoppable menace, but this was soon proved to be a wild exaggeration. The airships were not especially good weapons; they were slow and vulnerable to weather conditions. The British defences got the measure of the airships, shooting a number of them down in spectacular and gratifying infernos visible to many onlookers over wide areas. The first two British pilots to destroy

Zeppelins were awarded Victoria Crosses. Zeppelins proved to be one of the many blind avenues pursued in the early days of aviation. The Germans did not, though, abandon their ambition to attack the British homeland and continued their assault, but switched to fixed wing aircraft, which presented a far less imposing spectacle but were far more deadly.

In May 1917 Operation *Türkenkreuz* (Turk's Cross) was launched using purpose-built Gotha twin-engine aircraft to bomb mainland Britain, with sufficient range to reach their targets from bases in occupied Belgium. *Türkenkreuz* was considerably more successful than the Zeppelin attacks and triggered shock and a wave of fear. The first raid inflicted some 300 casualties in Kent and the second raid reached London, where it killed 162 people including 18 children at a primary school. The British reinforced fighter and anti-aircraft artillery defences, forcing the Germans to switch to night attacks, although they destroyed few of the attackers. What successes they did score were far less visible than those over the Zeppelins. By the end of the war some 800 people had been killed by German bombs. The success of the attackers and the perceived ineffectiveness of the defenders sparked a full-scale political debate over Britain's vulnerability to bombing and the best way to defeat this threat, which was to lead to the creation of the RAF.

There is even less certainty as to the true biological father of the RAF and a good field of possible candidates. The RAF came into existence because the Germans bombed London, so it could be said that it was the German officer behind this who deserves the credit. The commander of *Türkenkreuz* was Hauptmann Ernest Brandenburg and his units, the *Bogohls* or *Bombengeschwader der Obersten Heeresleitung* (Bombing squadrons of the army supreme command) as their name makes plain, came directly under Germany's top general, so the honour might equally belong to Paul Hindenburg. Trenchard's German opposite number, Wilhelm von Höppner, *Kogenluft* or *Kommandierender General der Luftstreitkräfte* is another candidate for the accolade. He was appointed in October 1916, with as his first, urgent task to begin aeroplane bombing of London.[1] The purpose of *Türkenkreuz* was unabashedly terroristic. No attempt was made to hit specific military targets, which would have been well beyond the technology of the day anyway. *Türkenkreuz* succeeded as a diversionary operation, leading to the transfer of guns and fighters from the Western Front but its most powerful effect was to bring home to the British, whose country had not experienced directly the horrors of war for 200 years, that they were vulnerable to attack. The perceived ineffectiveness of British defences triggered a serious political furore which was countered by the traditional tool of an inquiry conducted by the great and good of the land.

The government's inquiry was conducted by the South African soldier and statesman Jan Christian Smuts. It addressed two distinct topics: the immediate question of defending London and the wider issue of how Britain's air forces should be organized. Even before *Türkenkreuz* there had been widespread concern that Britain was being left behind in the air. The existence of two separate and competing air services made for inefficiency; in particular the RNAS and the RFC vied with each other for scarce aircraft manufacturing resources. Smuts concluded that the most efficient way to organize Britain's air resources was to combine the separate air arms in an autonomous air force. His vision was not solely defensive; it was anchored in a conception of the British air forces as an offensive arm, which could defend Britain by deterring Germany:

> The enemy is no doubt making vast plans to deal with us in London if we do not succeed in beating him in the air and *carrying the war to the heart of his country* [author's italics].[2]

In part, Smuts's view was shaped by Lieutenant-General Sir David Henderson, the Director General of Military Aeronautics, who persuaded him that Britain was producing so many aircraft that by 1918 it would have far more aircraft than it needed to support the British armies in France and that the excess aircraft should be formed into a powerful force to attack the German homeland directly. Henderson's forecast was far too high. This was merely the first of many instances in which dubious statistics were used to set the future of the RAF. Henderson was a strong advocate of an independent air force and probably entertained hopes of becoming the first Chief of the Air Staff. He was to be disappointed in this ambition and left the service shortly afterwards. The man who did get the job, Sir Hugh Trenchard, openly described Henderson as the 'father of the RAF'.[3]

Smuts's report applied to air warfare the military principle that the best means of attack is defence, but less appealing considerations played a strong part in the political debate. The killing of British civilians sparked loud calls for outright revenge across the political spectrum. The government lost only two Parliamentary seats in by-elections and both were to candidates calling for reprisal bombings: Noel Pemberton-Billing from the far right and Ben Tillett from the far left. The British prime minister Lloyd George promised to repay the Germans for bombing London with 'compound interest'.[4] The newspaper proprietor and wartime politician Lord Rothermere, who was to become the first air minister, was even more bloodthirsty: 'we are wholeheartedly in favour of air reprisals! It is our duty to avenge the murder of innocent women and children. As the enemy elects, so it will be the case of "an eye for an eye, a tooth for a tooth".'[5] Unhappy chance amplified a powerful voice in the chorus of reprisal seekers. The Odhams printing works in Covent Garden's Long Acre, home of the rabidly anti-German newspaper *John Bull*, was hit by a Gotha bomb with heavy loss of life. *John Bull* was the personal platform of Horatio Bottomley, MP, anti-German propagandist and large-scale swindler, who leapt on the pretext for claiming that his operation had been targeted in revenge for his scabrous attacks on the Kaiser. This was just as fraudulent as Bottomley's investment schemes.

The calls for revenge did not stop at idle political rhetoric and they were soon translated into military action. Even before the RAF was formed, the British had set up a unit dedicated to bombing Germany at the direct behest of the Cabinet. 41 Wing of the RFC was established at Ochey, in France, far away from the British armies, but close to Germany, under the command of Lieutenant-Colonel Cyril Newall in October 1917. Trenchard was summoned back to London to be personally questioned by Lloyd George on the progress at Ochey and Trenchard promised him that bombing would begin within a week. The promise was kept but it was an inevitably slow process to build the unit at Ochey, which had expanded to become VIII Brigade of the RFC. Trenchard earned enormous kudos in London when Newall's force began to bomb Germany.[6]

When the RAF came into being, Trenchard was an almost inevitable choice to lead it as the first Chief of the Air Staff (CAS). He was Britain's most successful air commander. Even though he was little known to the general public, his name would inspire confidence in the corridors of power. However, he took the job with deep reluctance as it meant giving up the operational command of the RFC in France which he had held since 1915. He was passionately devoted to the RFC which had launched him from an undistinguished beginning as an Edwardian professional soldier. He had built the RFC into a powerful component of Field Marshal Sir Douglas Haig's armies in France and was a fervent ally and admirer of his commander. Trenchard shared Haig's commitment to an offensive strategy and to the importance of the Western Front. The RFC's key task and the one which Haig prized above all, was to conduct reconnaissance of the German armies confronting the allies, which had become a vital factor in planning army operations. Aircraft could also observe and improve the accuracy of fire by artillery, which dominated the battlefields of the First World War.

The fight for air superiority over the battle area came next. Control of the skies was necessary to allow reconnaissance by the British and to prevent that of the Germans. This meant that the RFC required a balanced force of fighters to contest air superiority with the Germans and dedicated aircraft to make use of it once that superiority was assured. At the start these were reconnaissance aircraft but in the later stages of the war the RFC took on the role of actively attacking the German army on the ground. The Airco (de Havilland) DH.4 was designed as a general-purpose aircraft capable of reconnaissance, but ended up being used overwhelmingly as a bomber. Trenchard was insistent that supporting Haig's armies with a package of reconnaissance machines, fighters and bombers was the true primary mission of his force. He was utterly convinced that air warfare should be conducted offensively but his dominant focus was on the Western Front. Attacking Germany directly was a luxury activity to be conducted only as and when resources became available.[7] As head of the RFC Trenchard had neither empire-building ambitions nor abstract concepts of air warfare that required an independent air force. Tellingly enough, the most effective bomber available to Newall's force at Ochey was a purpose-designed and -built long-range bomber, the Handley Page 0/400, which proved very efficient in operation, delivering a heavy bombload reliably and beating off German fighter attacks, but it had originally been designed for the navy's RNAS and not Trenchard's RFC.

Trenchard was appointed as CAS because of his military reputation and because of his standing as a successful field commander, and not his bureaucratic skills, but he was far from being apolitically ingenuous. Like Haig, Trenchard was fully alert to the need for direct access to political support and he had brought two high-profile MPs onto his staff in France. Sir John Simon had even been a member of the Cabinet and Hugh Cecil was a member of the powerful political dynasty, a feature of British politics from the reign of Elizabeth I. Cecil's father, the Marquis of Salisbury, had been prime minister and he himself brought unreasoning savagery into the political debates that attracted his attention. Trenchard made full use of Simon and Cecil in the squalid and complex political intrigues, unpleasant even by the demanding standards of the Lloyd George government, which confronted him in his new job even before the RAF came officially into being.[8] Trenchard barely had any opportunity to fulfil the aim intended for the RAF of providing the country with a powerful organization to channel its aviation resources into combat. He was confronted by the serpentine political manoeuvres of the press baron brothers, Lords Northcliffe and Rothermere to whom the nascent RAF offered a magnificent tactical strong point in their campaign against Trenchard's patron, Haig. Trenchard fell out with Rothermere almost instantly, beginning a lifelong feud. Their supporters threw themselves into the fray with glee; Cecil treated Rothermere with high-handed venom.

Trenchard's first spell as CAS was a brutal education in the nastier aspects of politics but he was a rapid learner. The threat of resignation and resignation itself are the ultimate weapons in the arsenal of any public servant. It calls for the finest of judgement of the political landscape as well as a sufficiently important issue over which to bring them to bear. To succeed the card can only be played from a position of genuine personal strength in that landscape, independent of the office held, so that a voluntary departure is a greater loss to the administration against which it is directed than to the individual resigning. Trenchard played this trump card with devastating effect with the hand barely dealt and resigned as CAS even before the RAF officially came into existence. He was taking an immense risk because of the turn that the war took as the manoeuvres unfolded in London. The sudden and massive success of German offensives on the Western Front exposed Trenchard to the accusation that he was deserting a military post at a moment of supreme crisis, placing his own interests before his country's. Trenchard's judgement proved correct and his resignation made Rothermere's position untenable. Simon and Cecil forced the government to accept a debate on Trenchard's departure and that of Sir David Henderson, who had resigned in sympathy. Rothermere resigned immediately. Ever afterwards Trenchard held the reputation of a fine connoisseur of the resignation technique.

He had not overrated his own importance. He was too commanding and respected a military figure to be left on the side-lines with a major war still to be fought and he was persuaded to return to active service in a role that had to some extent been created especially for him. He accepted the command of what was to be known as the Independent Air Force (IAF), arguably the world's first specifically 'strategic' air force dedicated to bombing the enemy's country. He operated independently of the RFC in France which had been placed under the command of one of his most faithful lieutenants, Sir John Salmond. The IAF was a grand name for the VIII Brigade of the RFC at Ochey, and Newall became Trenchard's second-in-command. Trenchard's position tells us much about his political clout and how military operations were being bent to fit military personalities as well as the politicians' ideas of what constituted sound military strategy. When a French general queried, 'An independent air force? Independent of whom? God?' he was doing no more than expressing legitimate bafflement at the purpose of Trenchard's command.[9] Trenchard enjoyed a double independence. He was not subordinate to Marshal Foch, who had been given supreme command of the allied forces in France at the crisis of the German offensives in March 1918. He also operated outside the normal military command structure for the RAF, bypassing his successor as CAS, the almost universally despised Sir Frederick Sykes, an undistinguished careerist. Trenchard reported directly to Lord Weir, the Glasgow industrialist who had become the new air minister. Weir was one of Trenchard's most powerful personal backers and a very early believer in the military value of bombing cities. The whole idea of the IAF neatly combined to promote Weir's twin enthusiasm for Trenchard and bombing the German heartland.

Trenchard threw himself into the work of building up the IAF with his accustomed dedication and efficiency. He was not, however, at that stage a full-blown convert to bombing German cities. He still saw the priority as being to defeat the German forces on the battlefield. What had changed was that he believed that the allies now had the resources to indulge in the luxury of strategic bombing: 'In my opinion, the British aviation is now strong enough both to beat the German aviation in France and to attack the industrial centres of Germany.'[10] Trenchard was also perfectly willing to put the Independent Air Force into action in direct support of the ground offensive by the recently arrived American Army at St. Mihiel. Not that Trenchard had any particular reason to fear the wrath of his theoretical superior Sykes, but he could shrug off the CAS's complaint that he was neglecting his primary task of strategic bombing by devoting his resources to such a tactical objective.

Trenchard might not have been totally committed to strategic bombing but he developed a rationale for it that lasted up to the Second World War. His point of departure was that air raids against Germany were not reprisals. Instead, 'the word reprisal should be removed from the military vocabulary'.[11] 'From the military point of view', these were operations against 'military objectives' and 'civilian morale', as important as 'those of the infantry'. Civilian morale became a legitimate target for military action. Trenchard rejected any restraint in bombing policy. He thought attempts to reach an agreement with Germany on the use of bombing or simply to threaten systematic reprisals, would be calamitous. Allied bombing power was rapidly becoming an important force for victory. To give it up made as much sense as for Germany to forego its advantage in submarine warfare.

The First World War had transformed Trenchard's career. He had risen to be the undisputed candidate to head an entirely new fighting service but his future was far from assured. He had happily fought Rothermere when sucked into political battle over the RAF, but the service was not part of a vaulting career plan. Nor was its outgrowth, the IAF, which had given his air force career a second wind. When the Armistice came in November 1918 Trenchard was as keen as any infantry private to see the end of wartime expedients and spontaneously moved to wind down the IAF and turn its forces over to Marshal Foch. He was perfectly happy to turn his back on the IAF. He could have ended up like the dozens of major-generals now no longer needed by the war effort. The possibility of a minor colonial governorship, traditional last professional home of service officers who had not quite made it to the top, flickered across the horizon.

In January 1919, coincidence gave Trenchard a chance to display to the politicians the strengths – force of character, resolution, focus and straightforwardness – that had made him such an indispensable leader. He was the man on the spot when a massive army camp at Southampton was wracked by a severe mutiny amongst soldiers aggrieved at the pace of demobilization. He did not hesitate when the Commander of Home Forces, Sir William Robertson, asked him to intervene. There was no thought in his mind that he was no longer formally an army officer. Displaying great physical courage, he marched into the camp. By a mixture of firmness, tact, patience and absolute minimal use of force Trenchard settled the affair. The risks had been big enough for the politicians to be grateful and the task just far enough removed from battlefield command to show another facet of Trenchard's abilities.

Once again it was a change in air minister that set Trenchard's fate. Trenchard's friend and patron Weir had returned happily to the world of industry, but his successor, Winston Churchill, also fully appreciated Trenchard's talents and was not a man to see them go unexploited. Churchill had been given simultaneously the air and the army ministries, quite possibly as a prelude to bringing the independent life of the RAF to an end and folding military aviation back into the army. If that had ever been the plan, Churchill decided otherwise and the first building block that he needed to establish the RAF firmly was a CAS in whom he had confidence. Sykes was not that man and Churchill set out to replace him with Trenchard. In the background Weir had been lobbying Churchill for the survival of the RAF and a change in its leadership. Churchill exploited the fact that the Air Ministry was also responsible for civil aviation and Sykes was packed off to become the Director General of that side of its activities with the medium grand distinction of a moderately prestigious knighthood (the GBE) to console him further. This time Trenchard accepted the job without even a show of reluctance. A new peacetime career opened up to him which was again to transform his life.

Chapter 2

The Prophet

Trenchard had lasted only 100 days in his first stint as Chief of the Air Staff but in his second stint which began on 31 March 1919, he was to stay in office over ten years, the longest tenure by far of the post, as well as an uncommonly long time in a job for the professional head of any of Britain's armed services in the modern era. Trenchard's second appointment as CAS marked a turning point in his own career and, in practice, a second birth for the RAF. Its first birth had been a perfunctorily thought-out expedient, combining two organizations that had developed by the urgent expedients of war. Neither Trenchard nor Sir Frederick Sykes, who had barely a year in office, half in wartime and half in peacetime, had any real chance to impose a personality on the new service. It was the RAF's rebirth in 1919 and its childhood years during Trenchard's second stint, which did far more to shape the service that was to enter the Second World War than its inception or its brief existence in wartime. The dominant influence was Trenchard's iron will, drive, vision and personality. These were the years in which he earned the title of 'father of the RAF'.

On the Western Front in the First World War Trenchard had had the backing of Haig, a supremely powerful commander with a clear military task. He was now in uncharted waters dependent on his own wits and resolution to achieve his goals. There was no question of his claim to lead the RAF into peace, but he had to establish his own standing in the wider world as well as that of his new service. Trenchard was no longer a fighting major-general and the RAF was still very much the junior of the fighting services. In the newly created hierarchy of the force, Trenchard ranked as an air vice-marshal, the same two-star grade that he carried through the war, whilst his navy and army counterparts could boast five-star rank. Against this, Trenchard began to receive some of the symbols of professional success. He was created a baronet later in 1919 and was amongst the men awarded healthy cash grants by parliament for their service during the war, although his grant of £10,000 placed him firmly in the second rank of recipients behind the top navy and army commanders. His personal life changed too and he forsook the stern world of the Edwardian bachelor military professional. Late in life, at the age of 47, came a family, when he persuaded Katharine Boyle, the widow of a friend, who had nursed him through a severe bout of the Spanish influenza that was ravaging the world, to marry him in 1920. She already had three sons and the couple went on to have two sons of their own. Only two of the five boys were to survive the Second World War.

After fighting the German army and air force over the trenches of the Western Front. Trenchard now had to fight for the interests of his service in the merciless battlefields of Whitehall and Westminster. The warrior morphed into a peacetime military bureaucrat and one with a huge mission ahead of him. Trenchard's steadfast conviction that the RAF was key to national military survival sustained him though an exceptionally taxing Whitehall career. He learned to manoeuvre in a three-dimensional bureaucratic battlefield, shrewdly shifting strength from one front to another one. It is hard to overstate the scale of the task with which he was confronted. British military aviation had grown to be a mighty force through a succession of expedients to meet urgent military challengers during the four years of the First World War. It was now being shrunk radically to meet the peacetime need of economy in common with the navy and the army. Like almost everything in the unsettled world of 1919 the fate of the RAF was anything but certain. With almost all the massive armed forces built to fight the war being demobilized and political instability rampant throughout Europe and the Middle East, challenges went far beyond simply setting peace terms with a defeated enemy. The RAF was a comparatively minor issue in Lloyd George's prime ministerial in-tray. His priorities were controlling the budget and imposing his own ideas on the post-war global settlement. Trenchard's first priority was simply the survival of the RAF as an independent service. Lloyd George seriously considered winding it up as a quick and easy way of saving money.

Simple survival as the sole repository of British military aviation was Trenchard's first goal for the RAF. The first, Gotha-driven flush of enthusiasm for forming a powerful, independent air service was a distant wartime memory. The RAF had to be given a new reason for existence in the utterly different bureaucratic landscape of peace, where economy rather than military efficiency dominated. Saving money by simply doing away with the RAF as a separate entity was a tempting and obvious option. The most dangerous advocates of abolishing the RAF were the traditional fighting services from which it had sprung. The high commands of the Royal Navy and the army turned jealous and nostalgic eyes towards the aviation assets which they had lost when the RNAS and the RFC had been snatched away from them in 1918. As the new kid on the block, it was up to the RAF to justify its existence. In 1918, the Royal Navy and the army had to contend with the mundane matter of fighting a global war and strong political support for an independent air force, but in the following years they could revert to the traditional territoriality of peacetime military organizations and recapturing the aviation patch came high on the agenda. Trenchard's friend and patron Sir Douglas Haig had left the scene and Sir Henry Wilson, the new Chief of the Imperial General Staff, was no fan of an independent RAF. More important, the First Sea Lord, Sir David Beatty, burned with a desire to bring naval aviation back under proper Royal Navy control. Trenchard needed to develop into a formidable Whitehall warrior to save the RAF from dismemberment. Unlike the older services it did not have centuries of traditions and accumulated knowledge to fall back on. The Royal Navy far outgunned the RAF in tradition and 'dining out' power but Trenchard managed to fend off its depredations for his entire time in office.

As well as dogma and theory, personalities played their part in the RAF's fight for survival and contributed to the venom of the atmosphere. The single most savage confrontation brought Trenchard up against the First Sea Lord. By some measure Beatty behaved the worse, simultaneously supremely arrogant and duplicitous, but Trenchard did not pull the punches he delivered in return. Beatty asserted that he and his fellow Sea Lords held ultimate responsibility for the success or failure of the Royal Navy and must therefore have direct and total control over any military assets engaged in naval combat. By implication Beatty was claiming that the Royal Navy would not be able to extend the glorious record of naval triumph and dominance that had been the sure shield of the mother country and the rock on which the Empire was founded, unless it commanded any aviation assets deployed in a naval fight. Behind this front of lofty rectitude and splendid tradition the Admiralty delivered every low blow available. One of Beatty's key allies, Admiral Geoffrey Keyes, the hero of the Zeebrugge raid in 1918 – who was married to the

The Prophet

sister of Trenchard's wife – launched a covert press campaign against the RAF, loaded with rank insinuations. None of this created an atmosphere propitious to calm or reasoned debate.

In the ensuing welter of fake principles and aggressive claims, an important military development was swamped in a way that weakened Britain militarily. The role of air forces in naval warfare had developed far more slowly than their contribution to land warfare; it was an entirely legitimate question as to who should shape this development. One barely developed but crucial aspect of naval aviation was key to the question, but rational consideration was swamped by infighting. Aircraft had been launched from naval vessels during the war but only in 1919 was HMS *Hermes*, the Royal Navy's first purpose-built aircraft carrier, commissioned, heralding a new era in naval conflict, in which carrier aircraft became the principal weapons in sea-to-sea conflict. This gave the Royal Navy a far stronger claim on shipboard aircraft, but Beatty made almost no distinction and insisted on control of land-based aircraft working with the navy as well. The other two great practitioners of this new form of warfare, the Imperial Japanese and US navies, kept firm control of their air arms and were able to develop aircraft and tactics that made them powerful forces. Trenchard responded to Beatty with a similarly maximalist position that the creation of a Royal Navy-controlled fleet air arm would be tantamount to the abolition of the RAF. In Britain the naval air arm was to be a bureaucratic football for the next two decades and suffered accordingly.

On the Western Front Trenchard had been a fighting soldier, largely untainted by the politico-military intrigues that marked the conflict. But he was not a complete innocent, as evidenced by the campaign against Lord Rothermere. How quickly Trenchard morphed from a straightforward battlefield commander into a seasoned, skilful and ruthless Whitehall warrior is an open question, but by the end of his time in office he was unquestionably adept in deploying all the tactics of bureaucratic combat and reading the minds of adversaries and undecided politicians alike. The lessons came quickly. Trenchard's arrival in Whitehall coincided with the unstable and chaotic world of Lloyd George's peacetime coalition government and its immediate aftermath as the great wartime leader distracted himself from the near-insoluble problems of peacetime with misguided forays into global statesmanship until he had run through almost every ounce of political credit and credibility that he had accumulated. The fight over the RAF was no different to any such bureaucratic/political battle even if the combatants sincerely believed that their point of view was genuinely in the nation's best interest. This moral conviction fed the ferocity of the battle and the willingness of both sides to use unscrupulous methods, but the ensuing orgy of mud-wrestling did almost no one credit. Nor did it produce much beyond insincere, fundamentally political compromises that trained Trenchard to be ever on his guard for the next round in the fight. Peacetime debates on military policy are doomed to remain firmly abstract and sheltered from the acid test of battle. Principles and theory, real and imaginary, slugged it out in a vacuum where practical tests of right and wrong were impossible. Not until 1940 were the outcomes to be subjected to the ultimate test of war. By that stage pragmatism on crucial questions had long been abandoned in favour of a shambles of expediency and a welter of opposing and unprovable ideas about a new, and still developing, form of warfare.

Pressure from the other services was remorseless. Trenchard had to defend the RAF's interests in four different top-level formal inquiries as well as a near-constant succession of Whitehall intrigues, Parliamentary attacks by a large group of pro-Royal Navy MPs and press campaigns, often led by Rothermere still smarting from his failure as air minister. Trenchard emerged the winner from almost all these fights but this was by no means inevitable. The most dangerous challenge came from Lloyd George's successor as prime minister, Andrew Bonar Law, acting under the malign influence of his son-in-law, Sir Frederick Sykes, determined to pay Trenchard back for displacing him as CAS. When Sykes had married Andrew Bonar Law's daughter, Trenchard had quipped, 'I suppose Megan [Lloyd George] wouldn't have him.'[1] But for Bonar Law's forced resignation because of terminal cancer after only a few months in office whilst the inquiry led by Lord Salisbury was still under way, the outcome would probably have been very different.

Trenchard faced not just the rivalry of the older services but a challenge and one faced by all three armed services once peace had returned to Europe. In the atmosphere of stringent economy that prevailed after the First World War as governments struggled to repair the gigantic financial deficits brought by the war, the armed services had to fight for every penny of budgetary funds, which added an extra dimension to the intra-military turf war to the conflict and sucked in political calculations utterly remote from the notions of military strategy that were in competition.

The RAF had to be given every aspect of a distinct fighting service and Trenchard's hand guided each step. Committees and formal inquiries do not feature in the records of the time much at all. The consensual approach held no appeal to a soldier like Trenchard, his own judgement was sufficient. Only on the question of the RAF's unique table of ranks does he seem to have been overruled, albeit by King George V himself. Trenchard's original proposal that the RAF's commanders should be various grades of 'Air Lord' had to be discarded, but the rank table adopted with five grades of 'air marshal' did serve to irk Chief of the Imperial General Staff Henry Wilson, as in the army only its topmost rank was a marshal of any kind. On the pattern of the Army Council, the RAF had an Air Council, dominated by serving officers as the service's controlling body. It had its own imposing headquarters building, albeit not as well located or historic as the other services'. Adastral House was baptized in honour of the RAF's motto 'Per ardua ad astra' (Through difficulties to the stars) but it was one of a pair of developer's speculations and undersized. It was at the bottom of Kingsway, then being redeveloped from near slums, even further from the centres of Whitehall and Westminster power than the Inland Revenue in Somerset House. The RAF was given a full complement of dedicated training establishments: from boy apprentice tradesmen at Halton, through the heart of the service, the military and technical training of pilots at Cranwell to a dedicated staff college at Andover for future senior commanders.

Chapter 3

Who Squeals First?

Chance placed a high card in the Whitehall deck in Trenchard's hands at an early stage in the game. The RAF found a mission quite different to any that its constituent parts had performed during the war. It was one that looked as though it would be a permanent feature of the military landscape.

For twenty years the British colonial rule of Somaliland in East Africa had been challenged by the Dervish leader Sayid Mohammed Abullah Hassan, almost invariably referred to by the British by the more memorable epithet, the 'Mad Mullah'. The new technology of air attack appeared to offer a far cheaper method of tackling him than a land campaign and so it proved when RAF bombing of his villages forced him to flee the territory in February 1920. Soon afterwards the inhabitants of Mesopotamia failed to recognize the benefits of being ruled by Britain which had been handed the region under a mandate awarded at the Versailles peace conference in 1919. They rose in revolt. Here again RAF aircraft provided a cheap and effective tool to suppress the insurgency by attacking the rebels' homes. Thus was born the system of 'air control' under which the RAF could claim to provide a lower cost alternative to the army as a colonial gendarmerie. Trenchard insisted that the RAF should control all of Britain's air forces, but he saw no reason why the army should have a matching monopoly on land forces. When the Chief of the Imperial General Staff, Henry Wilson, refused to provide the RAF with armoured cars for its campaign in Iraq, Trenchard simply had them manufactured by RAF workshops and manned by RAF personnel. The RAF's ground forces were even greater in its next colonial engagement, fending off Kurdish encroachment into northern Iraq inspired by Turkish ambitions in 1923. The local RAF assets included battalions of Assyrian Levy Infantry; presumably local people did not count as real soldiers on the scale of colonial military values. Moreover, the success of Sir John Salmond, the local RAF commander, in facing down the Kurds and Turks had little to do with the technical aspects of air warfare and everything to do with a classic piece of frontier tension brinkmanship. But these quibbles over definition did not count in the Whitehall ledger of how well an organization performed and all three campaigns supplied Trenchard with ammunition to support his claim that the RAF could displace the older services from some of their traditional tasks. In his pitch, increasing the RAF's allocation would still allow the total military budget to be cut. The RAF was soon deployed to bombard dissident villages in the permanently unsettled North-West Frontier of Britain's key imperial possession, India. In essence 'air control' was simply the deployment of aircraft to perform a specific mission; it did not require an autonomous air service. With far less fuss the French army, which still firmly controlled its air arm, was using aircraft to suppress revolts in its North African colonial territories.

Just as Trenchard had established a strong claim to be Britain's chief colonial policeman, fate placed into his hands the material to support an even broader claim for status in Britain's defence armoury. In March 1922, *The Times* ran a series of articles arguing that Britain was being left behind in the aviation arms race and that France's air force was far bigger than Britain's and growing, not shrinking. The background to the articles is obscure, but the author, Brigadier-General Percy Groves, who had just retired from service, had been regarded as being close to Trenchard's bête noire, Sir Frederick Sykes, when he was an RAF staff officer. *The Times* was also controlled by Lord Northcliffe, brother of Trenchard's enemy, Lord Rothermere. The articles were full of barely veiled criticism of Trenchard, notably practically stating that he was dictatorial in his control of the RAF. The articles' chief thesis was that Britain should spend more on civil aviation as this created assets that could rapidly be transformed into weapons, a common belief at the time. As director general of civil aviation, Sykes had not been lavishly financed. This was all water off a duck's back to Trenchard but he did latch on to one very valuable point, that he was able to turn back into a weapon against this new assault.

Today it seems preposterous that France should be treated as a potential enemy less than four years after the end of the First World War, but the gloss had come off their wartime alliance. There were deep tensions between the countries over the implementation of the Versailles settlement which were being fought out at the disastrous Genoa conference in the spring of 1922. France was distinctly more hawkish over extracting financial reparations from Germany, which was to boil over into the unilateral occupation of the Rhineland some months later. In 1920, France had declared a national day in commemoration of Joan of Arc who had just been canonized at French instigation. Supposedly she symbolized France driving any foreign invader out of the country, but there was little doubt that her triumph was over the English. Groves's articles were much more concerned that Germany might rearm via civil aviation. They did not even present a hypothetical scenario under which France might attack Britain from the air. There was, however, sufficient concern for the Committee of Imperial Defence, the highest controlling body in Britain's military apparatus, to form an 'air menace' sub-committee to investigate. In reality, the decision to rebuild the French air force was driven by the risk that Germany might once again become a dangerous enemy, but Britain's cautious military bureaucrats were taking no chances.

Concern over Britain's weakness in the air was strong enough for the government to ignore the infamous Ten Year Rule, the doctrine enunciated in 1919 under which all military planning was subjected to the assumption that Britain would not face a major war for ten years. In 1923 it sanctioned the expansion of the RAF in Britain to fifty-two squadrons. This policy was confirmed by Ramsay MacDonald's short-lived Labour government in 1924. In a budgetary environment still conditioned by retrenchment after the First World War this was still a major step. In the event the RAF was never to reach this size until war broke out again as the predictable force of economy held the pen back from the cheque book, but the principle had been established that the RAF was a major component in Britain's defences.

Trenchard had no special reason to treat France as an enemy and he was privately willing to label the threat as chimerical, but he was perfectly happy to make use of anything that stimulated debate on Britain's strength or weakness in the air relative to another power in the corridors of Whitehall. Once the principle of expanding the RAF had been accepted, the threat could be made to serve his ends. The following year he was defending the RAF in front of an inquiry into its future under Lord Salisbury and he gave evidence that the proposed expansion of the French air force would put it in a position to drop 325 tons of bombs on Britain in a single day compared to the 242 tons that the Germans had dropped in all of the First World War. By contrast the RAF could only drop 67 tons of bombs in a day. Unwittingly Trenchard was rehearsing the far more agonized debates of the 1930s in which a theoretically calculated weight of bombs that a foreign aggressor's air force might drop on Britain inspired paralyzing fears of military inferiority and vulnerability. Even though it soon dwindled to nothing, the turnip ghost of a French air attack on Britain lingered on into the 1930s. Years before radar became a practical possibility, the RAF experimented with the use of elaborate sound-detection systems to give advance warning of air attack. The surviving huge concrete 'sound mirrors' built to concentrate the noise of approaching aircraft can still be seen near Dungeness on the south coast. They point towards the French coast.

The invention of a bombing war with France as the next major conflict that Britain would face had an extra benefit to Trenchard's vision for the RAF. After the horrors of the Western Front the idea that Britain would again field major land armies in a continental conflict was almost unimaginable; by contrast air war seemed almost innocuous in comparison. Banishing any thought that the British army might be involved in large land battles meant that the RAF would never be called upon to fight that same battle that the RFC had fought. It would not have to struggle for control over a land battlefield to allow its aircraft to spy on and bomb the enemy's army. It could concentrate on a far more ambitious task.

As the RAF debated how to deal with the supposed French air menace, Trenchard set out his vision of the air war of the future to his senior commanders and it was a very simple one. Nations would bomb each other's cities and the nation with the greater powers of bombing and resilience would win:

> the French in a bombing duel would probably squeal before we did. That was really the final thing. The nation that would stand being bombed longest would win in the end … but the policy of hitting the French nation and making them squeal before we did was a vital one – more vital than anything else.[1]

Trenchard saw morale as the decisive factor in war and paid scant attention to material damage and casualties in achieving victory. He believed that air attack could hurt enemy morale sufficiently to achieve victory on its own. When faced with setting the balance between offensive and defensive aircraft – the ratio of bombers to fighters – his choice was unambiguous and featured an analogy that would recur over again in the debate between the wars. A football team that consisted entirely of defenders would never win a match. Only by devoting the maximum possible to offence could the match be won. At no point did anyone challenge him that war could not be won as though it were a football match. Down the centuries the navy and the army had argued over their relative importance, but neither ever claimed it could win a war by its sole efforts. This was precisely what Trenchard had come to believe. The attack on civilian morale was just another, albeit potentially decisive, part of warfare. He saw no reason to await the pretext of enemy air raids on Britain before launching his own:

> the remainder of our available resources [after providing the minimum number of fighters] should go into the forces for attack. You note I do not say counter attack for that implies that the other side will be attackers first; we must try to get the lead from the start.[2]

In time Trenchard's ruthless willingness to launch a bombing war would be diluted, but his vision of bombing as war winning strategy was never questioned. Trenchard's standing in the RAF was more than that of an inspirational leader. The longest serving interwar air minister, Sir Samuel Hoare (1922–9) publicly described him as a prophet.[3] Hoare revered Trenchard and wanted to appoint him to lead the RAF when he was very briefly air minister in 1940. As Hoare was a byword for cynicism and dishonesty, this adulation is all the more remarkable, but captures the quasi-religious aura that surrounded Trenchard. Hoare was popularly known as 'Slippery Sam' after a card game of the era. Trenchard's opinions acquired the force of holy writ. One of his disciples and, ultimately, successor as CAS, John Slessor, wrote, 'Our belief in the bomber, in fact, was intuitive – a matter of faith.'[4]

His second term as CAS had inculcated in Trenchard the new discipline of bureaucratic warfare; now the endless debates over the purpose of the RAF as an independent armed service, transformed him from a passionate proponent of the air force's mission to provide close support to the army to an equally passionate advocate of a mission that meshed more closely with his vision for an autonomous air force: directly attacking the enemy's homeland from the air. The debate over 'air control' had allowed Trenchard to establish attack from the air on rebellious colonial subjects as a task for the RAF; the phantom menace of France's air force allowed him to add the job of attacking an industrialized European nation to the RAF's potential objectives. At one level this did no more than revive one of the service's founding missions, but it also marked the moment when the Trenchardian doctrine of attack as the only means of defence truly acquired a life of its own. Trenchard had never had any faith in the notion of passive defence in the air and his view was not about to change on this. With a major threat from a traditional enemy as a working hypothesis, the RAF could become Britain's main means of defence, but a defence conducted through attack. The RAF's capacity to defend Britain was to be measured in its capacity to bomb the country's enemies.

The RAF's mission to attack the enemy homeland extended the doctrine of unremitting aggression that Trenchard had championed with the RFC on the Western Front. It was one of the traits that he shared with Haig and a source of the bond between the two men. Trenchard's determination that the RAF should be a service dedicated to the attack was something of an extension of this. The doctrine was Trenchard's own. In 1921, Guilio Douhet an Italian air general, published a book called the *Il Dominio dell'Aria* (*The Command of the Air*) which foretold the bombing of cities and it is often mentioned in accounts of the development of Britain's air strategy as though Britain were being carried on an international current of thought. This is pure hindsight. Of the many British documents consulted for this book, none even mentions Douhet and his book does not seem to have been translated into English until 1943.[5] Trenchard's assistant, disciple and eventual successor as Chief of the Air Staff, John Slessor, published a book entitled *Air Power and Armies* in 1936 which set out his view of air war in the future; Douhet is not mentioned once even though the book acknowledges that there was a vigorous debate between different schools of thought on the future of air warfare. Both Slessor and Bert Harris, famous for his command of the RAF's bombers in the Second World War, later claimed never to have heard of Douhet before the war.[6]

Long before the passionate arguments over the morality of bombing civilians triggered by the Second World War, Trenchard's doctrine faced moral challenges. The RAF's ruthless application of air control inevitably aroused a debate over the ethical rights and wrongs of bombing towns and villages. It was seized on by Trenchard's rival service bosses as another stick with which to beat their rival. At the inauguration of a memorial at Amiens in November 1922, CIGS Wilson publicly denounced the 'aeroplane movement' and bemoaned the degradation of warfare into 'killing women and children'. More predictably the Labour opposition in Parliament regularly complained about the 'brutality' of air control. Apart from instructing his underlings not to provide excessive information on the tonnage of bombs dropped, Trenchard's chief defence was the effectiveness of the policy. He made extensive use of a letter that he had solicited from John Salmond, his local commander in Iraq, which claimed that bombing achieved its effect through damage to morale and property not by casualties. Trenchard had long insisted that morale was the chief target of bombing and this doctrine endured well into the Second World War. Every now and again Trenchard went through the motions of regretting that the aeroplane should be such a horrific weapon of destruction but purely at the level of abstraction. It had been invented, developed into a powerful tool and there was no going back. As a soldier and servant of the country, Trenchard was going to see that Britain's resources were structured and employed as effectively as possible. Military glory has always been a specious concept; Trenchard was not going to waste effort to dream up a glorious narrative of air warfare.

***

As his time as CAS drew to a close Trenchard circulated two papers which set down his vision for the role of the RAF. The first was another round in his battles against the Royal Navy. The Imperial Defence College had been established in 1927, supposedly to bring the future senior leadership of the three services together as part of a programme to develop doctrines and modes of thought to deal with the wars of the future. It also provided another battleground for inter-service rivalries. Its first commandant was Admiral Sir Herbert Richmond who recommended that all three services describe the principles of warfare in identical terms in their manuals. Trenchard riposted in a paper entitled 'The War Object of an Air Force', which asserted that an air force could practically defeat an enemy nation without the need for an army or navy. He ascribed a unique ability to air forces:

> the object of all three Services is the same, to defeat the enemy nation, not merely its army, navy or air force: 'The aim of the Air Force is to break down the enemy's means of resistance by attacks on objectives selected as most likely to achieve this end.'
>
> For an army to do this, it is almost always necessary as a preliminary step to defeat the enemy's army ... It is not, however, necessary for an air force in order to defeat the enemy nation, ... to defeat its armed forces first. Air power can dispense with that intermediate step, can pass over the enemy navies and armies, and penetrate the air defences and attack the centres of production, transportation and communication from which the enemy war effort is maintained.[7]

Trenchard qualified this claim with the bald statement that he did not wish to imply that 'the Air by itself can finish the war', but he did not explain how exactly he saw the other services fitting in beyond a vague, general statement that victory would be achieved 'in conjunction with sea power and blockade and the defeat of his [the enemy's] armies'.

Trenchard's attempted strategical land-grab brought him up against Sir Maurice Hankey, the Cabinet Secretary and Secretary of Committee of Imperial Defence, arguably the most powerful single figure in Britain's military establishment, one of whose myriad tasks was to smooth over inter-service rivalries to produce a coherent military strategy. Hankey criticized Trenchard's draft for implying that air power by itself could win a war.[8] Trenchard took the rebuke with good grace and offered to 'correct the impression that I expect to win the war without the Army and Navy'. In the upshot one of Trenchard's staff officers suggested a more acceptable formula which sharply scaled back what the RAF considered that it could do on its own. It was to read that the air force could '*contribute* towards breaking down the enemy's means of resistance' [author's italics].[9] This was a forced tactical withdrawal, though not a change of heart. The RAF dropped an official claim to be the only service to hold a decisive key to victory, but the belief lived on in the hearts of Trenchard and his successors.

There was never any doubt in Trenchard's mind of what the RAF could achieve and he had vaulting ambitions for his service's place in Britain's armed forces to match. In the 'The War Object of an Air Force'[10] Trenchard made grandiose claims for air power in abstract theory; in the paper written shortly before he left office in 1929, which he came to call his swansong, he stuck firmly to practicalities but in a way calculated to enrage the other services with a gigantic exercise in military/bureaucratic land-grab. 'The Fuller Employment of Air Power in Imperial Defence' was circulated to the Cabinet and the other service chiefs over the signature of Trenchard's political master, Lord Thomson, the air minister, but there was no doubt as to its true author.[11] The paper proceeded from the assertion that the effectiveness of 'air control' had been established beyond question and featured a comprehensive shopping list of colonial territories where the job of imperial policing should be turned over to the RAF, displacing the army. Nor was the redundancy of the conventional navy ignored; the RAF should take over 'routine' duties in the Persian Gulf and the Red Sea. The RAF should also displace ships and fixed artillery for coastal defence. Trenchard skirted over the fact that the RAF had no success comparable to 'air control' in Somaliland and Iraq to demonstrate that it was better able to patrol seas and defend coasts.

Trenchard may have hoped that his swansong would commit his successors to the programme, but if so, he miscalculated. His messianic authority was unique and unrepeatable and it was inevitable that he would be followed by men more firmly in the routine mould of senior service officers. He was followed as CAS by his loyal lieutenant from the RFC, Sir John Salmond, himself a distinguished commander. Salmond's tenure coincided with the financial and industrial crises of the Great Slump which put brutal cost-saving far ahead of any structured thinking about Britain's defence needs. The Disarmament Conference that began in Geneva in 1932 brought further pressure on military spending. Salmond held the job for only three years before stepping down in favour of his elder brother Geoffrey who died of cancer within a month. The Salmonds were succeeded by Sir Edward Ellington, who was to go down in history as the least dynamic or inspiring occupant of the post.

Chapter 4

Rabbits

To call Trenchard the 'father of the RAF' masks a crucial aspect of the relationship: he was only ever an adoptive father. Whilst his service was being conceived in the corridors of power in London in the autumn of 1917, he was commanding the RFC in France. He was shaping and directing a weapon for Sir Douglas Haig, his patron, role model and friend. Haig had no reason whatever to want an autonomous air force and could stand above the debates that shaped it; his subordinate Trenchard simply followed suit. Trenchard inherited the independent RAF. He had not been involved in the debates that led to its formation and he had neither motive nor obligation to defend the political process involved. Trenchard could pick and choose whatever elements of the finished product appealed to him and reject those that did not. Much of the thinking ran counter to the principles by which he had run the RFC in France. He was happy to take over the institution but not its political justification. As the child of public concern at the German air raids on Britain, the RAF and its adoptive father Trenchard were fated to reject the service's biological parent. The Air Staff would devote much time and effort to this task.

One of the forces that brought the RAF into existence was popular political agitation which created a paradox. How could an armed service created by mere political process function properly? Military command and democracy are polar opposites. Military commanders owe their allegiance to the state, personified by the sovereign in Britain, but have an ambiguous relationship to political governments. It is a truism that service chiefs resist civilian involvement in how their services operate as a matter of principle. This is doubly so in wartime. Open debate in democratic assemblies has no admitted role in the management of armed forces. At the very bottom comes public opinion – the 'ignorant masses' as Trenchard labelled this force – however this might be expressed.[1] Thus, the public calls for aircraft to be brought back from France to protect British civilians from German bombers were deeply illegitimate, deserved to be fought to the utmost and were, anyway, utterly wrongheaded.

The chicken of the RFC as a fighting force in France clearly came long before the egg of a unified air service. The hypothetical head of an independent British air service in 1917 would have been duty bound to decide how his resources ought to be split between the Western Front and fighting the Gothas over London. No such person existed and there is no sign that Trenchard (or anyone else) mused over this imaginary historical choice. The reality for Trenchard was a deeply unpleasant and ill-conceived call to withdraw his fighter squadrons from their vital work over the Western Front. Trenchard saw it as one of the chores of an air commander to resist the 'popular clamour, to provide visible defence aircraft overhead'.[2] Worse, this might lead to a distortion in the composition of his forces, 'Moreover he may be forced into making fighter types instead of bomber types for his increase in squadrons.' It was a struggle against misguided ignorance:

> The question as to the provision of more fighters and less bombers is being put forward even now long before the war is in sight by those who do not know the facts and figures and apply conditions of [illegible] quite different problem on the ground to ours in the air without really thinking about it.

The call to bomb Germany in reprisal was similarly unwelcome. Vengeance is not part of the military vocabulary, so Trenchard came up with the notion of civilian morale as a legitimate target for bombs.

The actual experience of the First World War shaped Trenchard's thinking about the fighter defence against bombers and his conclusion was pessimistic. Neither side had been able entirely to prevent the other side from bombing, whatever resources they devoted to the task. From this Trenchard made the jump to believing that it was simply a waste of resources to fight bombers. Moreover, he had commanded the attack but only very briefly and theoretically, the defence. He reckoned that the British had deployed ten times as many fighters to protect London as the Germans deployed bombers to attack it, quite ignoring the fact that the Gotha bombers cost far more than fighters and took greater resources to maintain.³ He believed the British had made a greater error in committing resources to the defence and put the comparable ratio of attacking bombers to defending German fighters that his Independent Air Force had to confront at one to five. Either way, a force of attacking bombers could tie down – to little practical purpose – a multiple of its own size. He also believed that his (unescorted) bombers had been able to inflict significant losses on the defending fighters over Germany.⁴ He accepted that few German bombers had been shot down over Britain in the war but did allow himself a glimmer of prescience: 'It is hoped that in any future war the training and the methods of fighting both in the air and from the ground will prove many times more effective.'⁵ However, the possibility that passive defences might be improved to a point where they exercised a decisive influence remained entirely hypothetical to him and his successors in the Air Staff.

As commander of the RFC, Trenchard had never hesitated to build a fighter force to drive the Germans out of the skies above the Western Front. By contrast, his vision of the RAF as the sure shield for mainland Britain had little place for fighter aircraft. When asked by a then junior staff officer, Peter Portal, what the correct balance was between fighters and bombers in the RAF's arsenal, Trenchard told Portal sharply that what mattered was to have the maximum number of bombers.⁶ The analogy that kept recurring in the utterances of Trenchard and his disciples was that you cannot win a game of football by having all your players in goal.

Trenchard never took this preference for bombers to the extreme logical end point of removing fighters entirely from the RAF's arsenal but he (and his successors) believed that there should be as few fighters as possible. The air force under the 1923 scheme ultimately triggered by the French war scare had a two-to-one ratio in favour of bombers, but this was clearly a provisional and arbitrary figure: 'It is not suggested that it constitutes a sufficiency of fighters or of bombers either.' Trenchard had bitterly resented the fighter squadrons being recalled from his command in 1917 to meet the Gotha menace, but he was confronted by a political force too deep rooted in sentiment to respond to military realities, as he saw them. An RAF that did not offer some kind of passive defence to Britain was a political non-starter, but this did not translate to a military vision which inspired him with any enthusiasm. He gave his true feelings about the role of fighters in a speech to the Cambridge University

Aeronautical Society in April 1925: 'Nothing is more annoying than to be attacked by a weapon which you have no means of hitting back at; but although it is necessary to have some defence to keep up the morale of your own people, it is infinitely more necessary to lower the morale of the people against you by *attacking* them wherever they may be.'[7] Fighters served no concrete purpose but must be tolerated as the public would feel exposed without them.

On one point, Trenchard rejected not just the implicit rationale for an independent air force, but the actual experience of air warfare in the First World War as a model for what would happen in the next. The fortunes of the air war over the Western Front had swung back and forth as each side held the advantage for a few months. The dominant side had exploited this superiority to conduct reconnaissance over – and occasionally bomb – the enemy's armies. The development of fighter technology had usually been the decisive factor but it was only ever temporary. Trenchard did not expect this kind of battle to happen again. In the next war the only direct combat between aircraft that Trenchard foresaw was British fighters harrying French bombers.

> The conflict will not be initiated by any clash of the fighting aircraft of both sides in an endeavour to secure this aerial superiority on the lines of the last war in France. It will be achieved rather by the steady development of our bombing strength to a point at which it will sap the moral [sic] of the French people and by the efficiency of our defensive fighters who will gradually reduce the moral [sic] of the French bombing pilots.[8]

The only offensive mission that he assigned to air forces was the attack on the enemy's civilian morale. Trenchard's vision of future air war was a narrow one. He expected British aircraft to be able to bomb France into submission and to deter French bombers from doing the same to Britain. The combat of fighter against fighter never entered the equation. Trenchard was being simultaneously over-ambitious in asserting what British bombers might achieve and under-ambitious in his prediction of what British fighters might achieve. He held no pretension to the scale of dominance achieved by the Royal Navy over the world's oceans.

> In a war between two first-class powers, it is doubtful whether 'command', as the word is interpreted in relation to sea-power, will ever be achieved by either belligerent. The Air Staff prefer the term 'Aerial superiority', and it must be recognised that this is sometimes only local and sometimes only temporary.[9]

Trenchard was confident that Britain could win a war in which each side competed to bomb the other harder. Trenchard looked into the future but not far enough. The ebb and flow of air combat that he had seen in the RFC did not provide a model. He was wrong in both his ambitious though narrowly focused positive vision and in his cautious vision of the broad picture. No air bombing campaign destroyed an enemy's morale but 'command of the air' was precisely what the Americans and British attained over the Axis in 1944 and 1945. Without it the Allied victories would have been either impossible or vastly more costly. It is unfair to blame Trenchard for failing to foresee this; no other theorist of air power did. The First World War had taught national leaders that modern war was a clash of economies, but no one appreciated that this applied more than anything to air warfare. Tactical ability in command and the efficiency and courage of the fighting men weighed far less in the final equation between defeat and victory in air warfare than on the land or sea; the decisive big battalions were factories and oilfields; the definitive champions were scientists and designers.

Trenchard was fixated on the importance of morale and repeated incessantly that in air warfare morale was far more important than material. He knew that some attacking bombers would be shot down but he saw the benefit in terms of spectacle. Much as the burning Zeppelins had provided British people across large areas with the gratifying and heartening sight of their enemy suffering a horrible fate, he concentrated on how the success of fighters could affect the public mood. Having designated 'public morale' as a legitimate military target, this was simply an item in a ruthless military calculus:

> Further, the ignorant masses of the people have to be considered, as it is upon their morale that the necessary 'will to win' in the country as a whole will depend. Being generally unversed in the laws of strategy, they will be

prone to judge the fortunes of war rather by what they themselves suffer than by what they are told that the enemy is suffering.[10]

The public merited some protection, not because they had any political claim on such a thing, but because their productive output had a military value. Only a competent military strategist could decide the correct policy. The public would only know the effects of the bombs falling on them, and not the effect of bombs falling on the enemy.

The sense of fighter defence as public entertainment dictated Trenchard's thoughts on how to deploy his fighters. London was the most vulnerable and important target – and also the most populous – in Britain so the RAF's fighter defence would be concentrated on it. The inhabitants of other regions would also be allowed to have a share in the spectacle of attacking bombers being shot down. A few fighting squadrons could be deployed along the south coast to harry homebound and – occasionally – inbound bombers and also to 'support the morale of the inhabitants of coast town'.[11]

Trenchard never went as far as claiming that there was no reason to have fighters at all. It would have been unmilitary and poor policy to allow an enemy to conduct any kind of operation entirely unmolested. There was also again the civilian morale element to bear in mind:

> If the enemy's bombers are shot down in this country in appreciable numbers, the nation will be encouraged and will probably stand more bombing than they would if the enemy were allowed to come and go without interference.[12]

Fighters could also interfere with the enemy's attempts to bomb but again morale was prominent, if not dominant, in the equation he applied. Trenchard had great contempt for bomber pilots who would let anything as puny as fighter aircraft deter them, just as Bert Harris later despised 'fringe merchants' who did not press home their attacks.

> Of course, there must be fighters also to ensure that any aircraft coming over must face the risk of attack. This will cause the rabbits not to persevere to the target.[13]

Elsewhere he wrote off bomber pilots who let themselves be deterred by fighters as 'weak-spirited individuals ... ready to accept an excuse for turning back'.[14] At no point did he allow for the possibility that the air commander might decide that the losses incurred by bombers were too severe to continue the attack. At the RFC Trenchard had not been deterred by losses from ordering operations over the Western Front; this was part of his appeal to Haig. Trenchard's philosophy as he built the RAF was even more extreme. The only function of bombers was to attack enemy civilian morale, so it had to be accomplished regardless of the cost.

Inevitably the idea of an RAF consisting solely of fighters was anathema. Trenchard did not hold back from the most grotesque levels of imaginative overstatement of his case on this point. If the RAF had as many fighters as the enemy had bombers, they would shoot many bombers down, but those that survived and managed to drop their bombs would achieve calamitous results. The French people would be indifferent to 'that little amount' (casualties amongst French bombers) and could rejoice in 'pictures of the Houses of Parliament in flames'.[15] To complete the awful picture of what would happen if the RAF had invested only in fighters and did not have the means to bomb France, 'there is no doubt that the Minister responsible would be lynched'.

Lurking behind Trenchard's disdain for fighter defence was the prejudice that this was merely something that the politicians wanted, which was reason in itself to resist the call. The Air Staff insisted that one of its tasks was to establish the correct ratio between fighters and bombers but the choice was loaded in advance by the philosophy that attack was more important than defence.[16] Their starting point was that the pursuit of political objectives was dangerous and 'unlikely to lead to decisive results'.[17] The Air Staff accepted that public opinion would be right to demand a force of fighters be kept in Britain but set this against the military objectives that bombers could achieve.[18] From this arose the 'principle that the bombing squadrons should be as numerous as possible and the *fighters as few as popular opinion* and the necessity for defending vital objectives will permit'. (author's italics) Fighter numbers would be fixed by a Dutch auction between militarily illiterate voters and knowledgeable professionals. One of Trenchard's most damaging legacies to his successors was knee-jerk resistance to any attempt to increase the number of fighters. Sir Cyril Newall, who moved into Trenchard's job as CAS in 1937, remained faithful to the doctrine as the RAF planned the gigantic expansion necessary to meet the imminent possibility of war in 1938. It was a complex task to compute the number of fighters needed; the danger lay in the possibility that too much resource might be devoted to them:

> The number of fighter squadrons allotted to the Home Defence Force is considered to be the bare minimum necessary but at the same time the maximum that can be spared from the striking force which alone can obtain a decision in war.[19]

At no point was there any discussion of what might have happen if there were too few fighters. There was a single optimum figure for the number of fighters: the maximum and the minimum were the same. Only one outcome of faulty calculation of the correct ratio between fighters and bombers mattered: there might be too many fighters.

> One main principle governing the proportion of fighters to bombers is: 'The addition of bombers at the expense of fighters will inflict more damage on the enemy than the absence of the fighters inflict will permit the enemy to on us.'

There could never be too many bombers.

When Trenchard and the Air Staff set their principle for the number of fighters they put out a firm manifesto that embodied the RAF's ethos and raison d'être:

> It was agreed that in air warfare more than in any other active offensive is the best form of defence. However powerful the Air Force of a country may be, they cannot ensure complete immunity from hostile air attack, consequently although a proportion of the available air forces must be allocated to Home Defence this force must be the minimum.[20]

Behind these bold statements lay a series of arbitrary and debatable assumptions. The supposed uniqueness of air warfare was an unsupported assertion. It was the Air Staff who departed from unvarying military experience in failing to understand that absolute defence was an impossible ideal in any form of warfare and that partial success was still a legitimate goal. Trenchard's dictum hid an extreme and flawed judgement that, because defence against air attack could never be one hundred per cent successful, there was no point in trying to improve the level of success.

The objection to fighters was hard-wired into RAF thinking. When a high-level committee chaired by Air Marshal Sir Robert Brooke-Popham sat down to discuss the re-orientation of Britain's air defence system in late 1934, it took (apparently without debate) as one of its general principles that

> The defensive system must consist of a proportion of the available air forces and of A.A. defences. Both these should be limited to the lowest possible minimum.[21]

The committee were aware that the development of what was to become radar (coyly described as a 'new and much more efficient instrument' than sound locators) had begun but there was no hint that it might revolutionize the ability of fighters to defend Britain.

The requisite minimum numbers of fighters were distributed around Britain, concentrated in the London area so as to 'to afford protection against the heaviest scale of attack that can reasonably be foreseen'. It was anticipated that a handful of fighter squadrons would be based in Belgium to provide a first line of defence without worrying too much about the diplomatic aspects of how this was to be achieved. Fighters were to be distributed as a cordon because the bomber held the initiative in the choice of targets. As with so much of the Air Staff's thinking this involved flawed or questionable thinking. It embodied a notion that air power was firmly tied to fixed bases. This made little allowance for the mobility of aircraft units. It ignored the possibility that intelligence of enemy dispositions would allow the defence commander to shift fighters according to an informed judgement of where the bombers might strike. The Air Staff was implicitly subscribing to the doctrine that 'the bomber will always get through'; it was almost as though bombers had preternatural powers, against which it was futile to take precautions.

One of the Air Staff's most suspect claims was that the number of fighters required could be calculated precisely by reference to the size of the area defended and the scale of the attack to be expected.[22] In the fifty-two-squadron plan for the RAF of 1923 the ratio between bomber and fighter squadrons had been two to one. This was to remain in place until the great expansion of the mid-1930s. Air Staff pronouncements are littered with strident but unconvincing assertions that it was insignificant in itself. It is more likely that this was Trenchard's rule-of-thumb judgement of the smallest number of fighters that the politicians would swallow. If necessary the equation was bent to favour bombers. In 1935 came the recognition that the operational range of the Luftwaffe's new bombers extended as far as the north of England and the south of Scotland. This meant that the frontage to be covered by the fighter force was extended by 200 miles or so. This yielded a most unwelcome conclusion for the Air Staff as to the effect it would have on the composition of the RAF's force: fighters would account for almost 40 per cent of the RAF's strength in all types, 'This proportion of fighters would appear too high to give a desirable bomber strength.'[23] To deal with the risk that the ratio of fighter to bomber strength might swing too far to the defensive the Air Staff set to juggling the figures. The key part of the scheme was to abandon the idea of fighters in Belgium, which brought it back to only fractionally above one-third of total strength.

The bomber-versus-fighter debate had the flavour of an ugly religious controversy. In 1937, the air minister was Lord Swinton, ordinarily a resolute Trenchardian in his support for the strategy of the offensive, but in one of his internal papers, he fell short of the blind conviction expected of true adepts. Heresy was in the air: 'I scent the ever-recurring danger of being driven towards concentration on defence by fighters at the expense of offense by bombers.'[24] Newall, then the CAS, took Swinton to task for underestimating the 'vital importance of the strategically defensive role of our bomber force'.[25] Unless they were bombed, the Germans could be able to build aircraft fast enough to replace even the losses that an unlimited number of fighters could inflict on them: 'it is doubtful whether any number of fighters we could provide could impose a rate of wastage upon the enemy which he could not make good in the absence of effective counter-action against his air force and their source of supply.'[26] There was no limit to the number of bombers that the RAF might usefully deploy, but there was no possible benefit in exceeding the minimum number of fighters.

It was not just the air marshals who promoted the Trenchardian doctrine of favouring bombers. As the Czech crisis got fully under way in the summer of 1938, the senior civil servants of the air ministry feared that if even more fighters were ordered, on top of the 1,000 Spitfires from the new Nuffield shadow factory at Castle Bromwich earlier that year, the balance between fighters and bombers would be 'upset'.[27] This suggestion of further orders was criticized by one civil servant as it would lead to there being, 'too many fighter aircraft.'[28]

The final iteration of the Air Staff's case for bombers against fighters was given to Admiral Lord Chatfield who became Minister for the Coordination of Defence in January 1939.[29] It came up with a list of new problems with fighters: there would be times when they were outclassed by German bombers; they could do little to defend the Royal Navy or merchant shipping from German bombers; they would not impress potential European allies; they could do little to prevent German night-time terror air raids on the civil population. They would, of course, be unable entirely to prevent devastating and disruptive air raids on infrastructure. Britain admittedly needed as many fighters as 'can usefully be disposed' but this number depended on geography and not on the size of the attacking enemy force. There was no choice but biting the bullet and curtailing expenditure on the older services, in particular the army, and buying bombers..

Chapter 5

Evasion of Responsibility

The RAF's strategic doctrine remained frozen in the state it had reached at the time of the French war scare in 1923, but the nature of the aircraft that were to execute it, was changing out of all recognition. The early 1930s experienced a revolution in aircraft technology. By some measures it was even greater than the one that occurred between the Wright brothers' first powered flight in 1903 and the end of the First World War, which had transformed aircraft from artisan-made experimental machines into mass-produced cutting-edge weapons of war. In practice, though, the war largely froze fundamental design innovation because marginal and progressive enhancement of proven technology was a more rapid, reliable and effective way of improving weapons that would be needed immediately on the battlefield. Most visibly, the biplane structure offered the best package of lift and strength to go with the engine power then available and thus became the standard. Two sets of wings, one above the other, gave a large surface area and hence lift; they could be braced against each other using struts and wires which provided the strength.

The postwar evolution of aircraft design began with the engine. During the war, the rotary engine, where the whole engine block rotated turning the propeller with it, had been by far the dominant technology. In the dawn of aviation its favourable power-to-weight ratio was a vital advantage, but it had crucial flaws; above all, the potential to increase its power output was severely limited. By the mid-1920s it had been overtaken by radial and water-cooled engines where progressive improvement in design could increase output. Engine power rose steadily from 200 horsepower or so to about 1,000 in the mid- and late 1930s and went on to top 2,000 horsepower in the course of the Second World War when the advent of the jet engine rendered the piston engine obsolete. More powerful engines gave far better performance in every respect and dictated a switch to metal airframes so as to cope with the greater stresses involved. In turn the switch to metal structures began to offset the strength-to-weight appeal of the biplane and monoplanes began to take over. Greater power permitted the extra weight of retractable undercarriages and increased aerodynamic drag from enclosed cockpits. For military aircraft the extra load-carrying capacity meant more powerful armament.

By the late 1920s engine power had grown but not enough to change airframe design radically. The 650-odd horsepower Rolls-Royce Kestrel engine powered the standard RAF bomber, the Hawker Hart and its derivatives. The Hart had been designed and first flew in 1928, and its performance was good enough for a fighter version, the Demon, to be used in large numbers. Other derivatives served as carrier-borne and army cooperation aircraft. The same fundamental design was capable of fulfilling every significant military role. The Hart looked much the same as a First World War type: a biplane made of wood and fabric, with an open cockpit and fixed undercarriage. All mainstream RAF types were alike; most had a single engine, but a few had two. The Hart and its derivative, the Hind, were excellent in their day: reliable, cheap and widely exported, but it was the high point of its generation of technology. Thereafter the change was radical.

Like all air forces the RAF would have been compelled to switch to new planes using the new technologies whether it was expanding or not.[1] Like all air forces it had to face the conundrum of applying the potentialities of the new technologies without the empirical experience of combat to guide them. Such combat experience as could be gleaned from imperial policing operations was irrelevant to war against industrialized powers. No one knew what a future air war would be like. Would it require radically different capacities in the aircraft that fought it? In the RAF's case another factor came into play. The brief flurry of the 1923 war scare had established France as the potential enemy that it would have to fight but as the 1930s progressed it became increasingly obvious that Germany would be the enemy. This had huge implications for bombers. Specifications for the first generation of new technology bombers in 1933 demanded operating ranges appropriate for attacking France but nowhere further afield: 720 miles for day bombers and 920 miles for night bombers.[2] The new technologies created a far broader palette of design and performance options from which to choose. By contrast, the switch in enemies would be unproblematic for fighters whose mission remained the same: engaging attacking bombers over Britain.

The tools that the RAF brought to bear on the question were shaped by the personality and experience of Trenchard. Trenchard had had no training in engineering, still less in aeronautics, and as an infantry officer he had had little exposure to weapons technology. A naval officer would have been far more attuned to the implications for his entire service of the technical changes – big gun turrets, oil-fuelled engines, torpedoes – that had transformed navies in the decades before the First World War. As a front-line commander Trenchard's priority had been the immediate needs of his force. Flaws in aircraft designs had to remedied as quickly as possible but he did not need to influence the initial design process. Private-sector companies and the state-owned Royal Aircraft Factory offered a steady stream of new designs and the RFC just needed to pick the ones that seemed best. As has already been mentioned, neither he nor the RFC had had a hand in the conception of the purpose-built long-range Handley Page 0/400 bomber, the most powerful weapon in the IAF's arsenal. The independent RAF would have been powerfully placed to become the dominant force in aircraft design in the same way that the Admiralty controlled warship design, but it was not to be. The Royal Aircraft Factory at Farnborough did the job during the First World War. An RAF counterpart to the Department of Naval Construction would have cost money and the watchword was economy in the RAF's early years. Farnborough was cut down to a research and testing organization, the Royal Aircraft Establishment, after the war for just this reason. Aircraft design was not high on Trenchard's priority list. His only noteworthy intervention was to override nationalist prejudice and insist that the RAF bought an American design built by the British company Fairey under the name of Fox because he thought it was a superior machine and would encourage British manufacturers to up their game. This was the exception; aircraft specification and design evolved into a multi-layered and labyrinthine part of the bureaucracy of the Air Ministry at Adastral House.

There was no top-level aircraft design directorate and no single member of the Air Council was charged with the task. The closest there was to this, the Air Member for Supply and Research (AMSR), exercised only a vague oversight. Instead, there was a collegial and convoluted process involving meetings of sometimes very large committees on which quite junior officers might sit. Responsibility for initiating designs and actually getting them manufactured was split and this was still causing difficulties well into the rearmament programme.[3] The plane-makers often proposed designs to the RAF and they also had a greater or lesser input in the development of designs as they went on. It was time-consuming and as the 1930s began to impose a less leisurely regime, hopes rose that it might be possible to cut the time required by half.[4] An Operational Requirements Committee was established in 1934 to formulate the tasks for which new types were required instead of the ruling practice of merely replacing existing types in service with something better. Almost every aircraft type that found its way into production had followed a unique and often tortuous path. It is practically impossible to identify individuals as clearly responsible for any given type. Almost the only instance of a member of the RAF being widely credited with (or blamed for) a particular development touched on in this book is Squadron Leader Ralph Sorely and the eight-gun armament of the Hurricane and Spitfire. This is though debated. Otherwise, the influence and advice of individuals can be traced through the flow of paper and committee minutes but it is practically impossible to assess which contributions might have been decisive. Value-for-money if anything served as the chief watchword. In practice the mechanism served to build a consensus as to what the RAF needed. This largely prevented excessive risk-taking but it did invite the development of what we would now call group-think. Unspoken shared preconceptions became dangerously powerful.

The industrialist Lord Weir who was deeply involved in building up Britain's air forces, was a critic of the procedure for specifying and selecting new types of aircraft:

> The outstanding feature of the existing system is a sort of evasion of responsibility by a procedure which postpones decision until choice of type becomes almost automatic. It may result in a reliable decision, but the march of progress renders the ultimate selection obsolete.[5]

Weir cannot be exonerated of bias, but there can be little debate that the RAF entered the Second World War with some questionable and at least two disastrous aircraft.

The operational requirements committee did not invariably function well. A Fighter Command staff officer was shocked and appalled when he attended a session for the first time. It bore a distinct resemblance to the Mad Hatter's tea party.[6] There were too many people, a number of whom issued general statements; large attendance was an invariable feature of the committee. Changes were made without considering what they would do to the final design, leaving the author of the draft specification to mourn the wreckage. The chairman and a key delegate left before the end of the meeting, which might reflect the fact that the meeting was supposed to fix the specification for an aircraft to replace the Lysander army-cooperation type which did not rank high on the Air Staff's list of priorities. Everyone deferred to a civilian 'expert' from the Air Ministry and no one seemed to have the technical knowledge or confidence to challenge his assertions anyway. The meeting adopted a low-wing configuration which gave the crew a poor view of the ground even though operational crews who had to carry out battlefield observation preferred the high-wing layout of the Lysander.[7] The draft specification demanded that the aircraft would be able to operate from the high-altitude airfield at Razmak on the North-West Frontier, which the visiting officer questioned, presumably given that the requirements of a European war were rather more relevant, but there seemed no way to judge whether the original requirement was sound or not. He concluded: 'if Air Ministry specifications are normally developed in this way, it is a reasonable explanation for the trenchant criticism which always comes from the Contractors and designers who have to deal with the problem.' Perhaps mercifully, no aircraft was built to the specification.

By the end of the 1920s the RAF's aircraft were reliable and well able to perform the limited tasks expected of them. Another fighter type, the Fury, was also built by Hawkers and was broadly similar to the Hart. The Bristol Bulldog completed a trio of fighter types. The Hawker types and the Bulldogs were all successful and widely exported. By contrast the RAF's two larger bomber types, the Boulton Paul Sidestrand day bomber and the Vickers Virginia night bomber were not great successes and were built in only small numbers

The growing urgency of the rearmament programme added another feature to the history of the aircraft types acquired by the RAF. The lengthy selection, prototype and test pattern usual in 1920s had opened the prospect of being able to standardize purchases on a single type of aircraft, which offered the best package. This was not invariably put into practice, but it was a distinct option until the conflict between the need to bring new types into service undermined its appeal. With time ever more important, the RAF could not afford the risk that a single design might prove unsatisfactory months or even years into the procurement process, leaving the service having to begin all over again. The best insurance was to set things in motion for two (or even more) different designs.[8] The results were not perfect but the RAF did escape finding itself without a worthwhile type in a particular class at all as was to happen with the Luftwaffe in heavy bombers. The Spitfire was a fallback option in case Hawkers were unable to deliver enough Hurricanes; it proved the better design but actually suffered far worse initial production problems.

By some margin the most disastrous product of the RAF's conservative strategy of replacing existing types was the Fairey Battle. It arose from the search for a successor to the Hawker Hart, which had comparable performance to contemporary fighters, which was not that demanding in the era of open-cockpit, fixed-undercarriage biplanes. This was a far harder thing to achieve in the 1930s, even if allowance is made for the fact that it was not necessarily obvious how good the performance of modern single-seat monoplanes was to be. To begin with it was hoped that a new Rolls-Royce engine, the Griffon, derived from the R-Type engine which powered British Supermarine floatplanes to victory in the Schneider trophy races between 1927 and 1931, would provide sufficient power to make the Battle a truly fast bomber. In the event, Rolls-Royce had to concentrate its design efforts on the Merlin which gave the Battle far too little power so its top speed was only 257 mph. The specification process was further complicated by a vigorous squabble between advocates of single-engine and twin-engine aircraft. The process began later than the search for Sidestrand and Virginia replacements, but perhaps because the product was that much simpler, led to designs that were in service in quantity appreciably earlier. The Battle looked deceptively modern. At first glance it appeared as an enlarged edition of the modern fighter designs with clean simple lines. RAF publicity at the time made much of the aircraft as a modern bomber. Its armament, however, was pitiable: a single forward-firing fixed machine gun and a manually operated gun in the rear cockpit. The bomb-aiming position was impossibly cramped.

The RAF's other new small bomber was shaped by the belief that high speed was possible in a bomber. The Blenheim was a military adaptation of the Bristol 142 *Britain First* built to meet a challenge by the press magnate Lord Rothermere, who had become an enthusiastic campaigner for British air rearmament. When it first flew in 1935, it was faster than any contemporary fighter at 307 mph top speed. Rothermere presented it to the nation and the Air Staff rapidly saw potential for it as a bomber. Sadly, the speed advantage was severely eroded in the production bomber version and the bombload was little better than the Battle's. It, too, was designated as a medium bomber. However, the Blenheim was not as abject a failure as the Battle and it soldiered on into 1941, largely as a battlefield bomber because the RAF had nothing else suitable for this task which had been despised and ignored before the war.

From the point of view of the Air Staff's strategic focus on bombing Germany both of the smaller bombers had crippling disadvantages. The Battle did not have enough operating range to reach Germany from British bases, which begs the question of why they were ever brought into service, and the Blenheim could only reach the western edge of the country. Both were officially classified as medium bombers but this was merely a branding exercise to mark a distinction against the Hart light bomber, which was by then entirely obsolete. Their bombloads of 1,000lb or rather more in the case of the Blenheim were more than double the Hart's, but inadequate for strategic bombing purposes even if their performance had allowed the type to deliver it safely. In the event the Blenheim did give useful service as a short-range bomber, but only because the RAF faced battles that it had never anticipated. The best that can be said of both types was that they were relatively cheap and easy to build, but even this had its downside. When the imperative to produce aircraft in numbers outstripped the need to build quality aircraft, the Battle was a strong candidate for the job. The Battle features prominently in any account of stop-gap orders. One particular order lot of 189 aircraft absorbed a disproportionate amount of time at numerous Air Council meetings; it was first cancelled, then reinstated. It was recognized how poor a design the Battle was and that it was practically useless. As early as the start of 1937 the Chief of the Air Staff wanted no more to be delivered after March 1939 even if no adequate replacement were available.[9] Soon after war broke out, the Air Staff confessed that it was 'impossible to define the exact role of the Battle'.[10] It was tantamount to saying, 'we've got lots of them, so we have to use them for something'. When they were committed to combat in May 1940, half the force was shot down in two days. The type was withdrawn from combat service.

The first major step in the re-equipment of the RAF that was to shape the force that entered the Second World War had actually been taken before the process that led to the Battle and Blenheim. In 1932, specification B.9/32 was issued for an aircraft to replace the Boulton Paul Sidestrand day bomber. The Sidestrand was named after the home village of the long-serving air minister Sir Samuel Hoare, and thus pioneer of the RAF's practice of naming its bombers after British towns (as well as toadying to its political masters). Only twenty Sidestrands were made, equipping a single squadron, but its indirect legacy was to be considerably greater. Two aircraft were to be built and entered service under B.9/32: the Handley Page Hampden and the Vickers Wellington. The latter was the only truly successful bomber design with which the RAF was to enter the Second World War and remained in front-line service until well into the war. However, the outstanding strengths of its design were not fully obvious and to begin with similar numbers of the Handley Page Hampden were built. The Hampden was in practice only an insurance policy against potential problems with the most innovative feature of the Wellington: the novel geodetic construction method invented by Vickers's chief designer Barnes Wallis. It involved a lattice of diagonally arranged members in a pattern of diamonds onto which the skin was mounted. Natural, practically minded military unwillingness to bet heavily on radically new and untested techniques combined with what appears to have been hostility to the Vickers company as the over-mighty, largest military contractor in Britain.[11] As the re-equipment of the RAF gathered pace from 1938, the Wellington faced considerable hostility from the rest of the aircraft industry. The Hampden was an expensive and ultimately unnecessary piece of insurance, as it had numerous flaws but Frederick Handley Page was one of the most influential figures in his industry.

The story of the development of the Hampden and the Wellington amply illustrates in extreme form the time-lag factor in the equation. The relevant specification was issued to manufacturers in 1932, and only in August 1933 was it decided which of the competing designs were to be ordered in prototype form and this had been mainly by process of elimination.[12] They were designed to meet the requirements of a world before Hitler came to power, but were not available for Britain's first great confrontation with Nazi Germany over the Czechoslovakia crisis. Neither the Hampden nor the Wellington first flew until 1936 and it was only at the beginning of 1939 that there were significant numbers in service. Admittedly the design of the B.9/32 aircraft was held up by the disarmament conference at Geneva. At one stage it was proposed that aircraft be limited to three metric tonnes in weight. Whilst this rule was never adopted, the British were punctilious in not ignoring the possibility that it might be. This provided a handy excuse with which Sir Edward Ellington, the Chief of the Air Staff at the time, tried to fend off any accusation that the RAF had been slow to rearm, although it can be argued that the delay meant that the Hampden and Wellington were better aircraft than they would have been if specification B.9/32 had been followed through without pause.[13]

The last of what was to become the trio of middle-size bombers in the RAF's arsenal at the beginning of the Second World War arose, again, from the quest for a direct replacement of an existing aircraft, the Virginia night bomber. In the 1920s, the RAF believed that day and night bombing required distinct classes of aircraft. This was to become the Whitley, which fell roughly between the Wellington and the Hampden in military value. The story of the Whitley's genesis shows how the pace of change was being forced by the urgency of the diplomatic and military situation, which demanded far shorter lines of decision-making than the established ones of peacetime. In part it was necessary to speed things up because the first attempt to find a long-term replacement for the Virginia had not been going well and the RAF was caught between its preferred design, the biplane Hendon, and an interim monoplane, the Heyford. The B.9/32 specification had been pursued under the torpid peacetime procedures of competitive tendering, but Ellington and Sir Hugh Dowding, then the AMSR, recognized that something more urgent was now called for. Ellington proposed that 'a selected firm should be given a free hand to produce the best they can design to a very general and short specification'.[14] The specification was amended late on in the process to increase the range sought from 1,200 to 1,250 miles suggesting that the need to penetrate deep into Germany was beginning to loom large in the RAF's requirements. To begin with they proposed to limit the potential suppliers to the three companies with an established track record of making satisfactory heavy bombers – Fairey, Handley Page and Vickers, but Armstrong Whitworth forced their way in. The process did not get off to a happy start and Dowding reported that 'our original ideas, however, have emerged rather battered from the fray' after an initial meeting with the four contractors.[15] The contractors chiefly objected to assuming financial risk for design themselves and to compete on price to get there. Things were further complicated by the RAF's choice of defensive armament. Dowding had to lop 20 mph from the originally specified top speed of 225 mph to accommodate a powered tail gun turret. When the Air Ministry weakened on the question of price competition, the contractors demanded almost double the figure first sought. In the end Armstrong Whitworth agreed to come up with a prototype for not much more than the starting cost. The switch to a single supplier did not make for a better aircraft, but it did take less time to arrive. The specification was issued in 1934 and the Whitley was in squadron service by the autumn of 1938, well ahead of its B.9/32 cousins.

One aspect of the early design stage of the Virginia replacement shows how poorly focused the process was and the range of considerations that might influence designs. It was hoped that the new aircraft would be able to replicate the Virginia's capacity to carry armed troops, a regular feature of the RAF's imperial policing mission. In the event this was crowded out from the ultimate specification by the purely bombing requirements. By a twist of fate, the Whitley was pressed into service as the RAF's first combat paratrooper carrier in 1941 as its usefulness as a first-line bomber dwindled.

The differing destinies of the Hampden, the Whitley and the Wellington provide object lessons in a major aspect of the rearmament programme, but one that ran mainly in the background and, by its nature, escapes an easy narrative, still less a narrative that runs harmoniously alongside other threads to the story. As with any armed service in the midst of a major technologically driven reequipment programme, the RAF faced a permanent tension between the imperatives to bring on new equipment and to manufacture existing and relatively well-proven designs in volume. This equation is further complicated by the need to maintain the production capacity of factories making older designs intact until they can be switched to new designs. Neither factory owners nor skilled workers had any reason to keep plant idle. Thus, types that had outlived their appeal to the Air Staff were still ordered in volumes as 'stop-gaps' to preserve capacity. Another layer of complexity came from the fact that these decisions on production were often being taken before the new types had even flown and generally before they had entered squadron service. Guesswork, prejudice, hope and the choice of which aircraft factories it was deemed desirable to be kept going, all played their parts.

The three 'heavy mediums' had greater far greater bombloads and bombload than the 'light mediums' (4,000lb and 1,700 miles for the Hampden, 4,500lb and 2,500 miles for the Wellington and 7,000lb and 1,650 miles for the Whitley) but they still fell short of what the Air Staff truly wanted. No single, overarching verdict was handed down, but the Hampden and the Whitley were not the favoured of the three types although the order and production dynamic meant that they figured largely in the RAF's inventory from 1939 to 1942, before being withdrawn from service. The Wellington had a more ambiguous fate. It was recognized as the best of the three types and it ended up serving in practice as an interim type before the truly large bombers that the Air Staff favoured could come into service. Even a year after the Air Staff had taken the crucial strategic decision to move to a big-bomber force in early 1937, Chief of the Air Staff Sir Cyril Newall described the Wellington as the 'backbone' of the 31 March 1939 programme.[16]

In practice the RAF's first two generations of modern bombers served as interim types even though this was never explicitly planned; the RAF entered the Second World War with an arsenal of bombers that fell short of what it believed that it required. None of these five modern design bomber types was destined to stay the full course of the war. Apart from the Wellington which was still giving useful front-line service in 1943, they were practically obsolete by the end of 1941. The RAF's bomber inventory was further cluttered by even less useful types: the Whitley's two inadequate precursors, the Heyford and the Hendon, and a single-engine monoplane bomber or general-purpose aircraft from Vickers, the Wellesley, built to a 1931 specification thus earlier than the Hampden or Wellington, which provided a test-bed for geodetic construction but little else. By 1936 when the Hampden, Wellington and Whitley all made their first flights, the RAF was hard at work on specifying the types that were to replace them and which embodied rather more clear strategic thinking. These were not ready for service until well into the war.

Roughly the same pattern can be observed in the RAF's first generation of single-seat fighters using the new technologies, but this had a significantly happier outcome than the bombers. They too had their origins at the start of the decade and first flew at about the same time as the new bombers. There were many twists and turns before the Air Staff arrived at the final aircraft. It issued three distinct operational requirements for production aircraft, beginning with the F.7/30 in 1934, then the F.5/34 in 1934 and finally the F.10/35 in 1935, and another two requirements for experimental designs in 1934 aimed directly at Hawkers and Supermarine. Arguably, these designs were more heavily influenced by the initiative of talented individuals at the aircraft companies than the Air Ministry's internal processes. The very first of these requirements, F.7/30, led to the Gloster Gauntlet fighter and thence indirectly to its more powerful successor, the Gloster Gladiator, the last of the RAF's biplane fighters. Delays in volume production in monoplane fighters meant that the Gauntlet and Gladiator accounted for the bulk of the RAF's fighter strength until early 1939. The Gladiator performed useful first-line service in secondary theatres until 1941 even though it was outclassed by modern German fighters such as the Messerschmitt Bf 109 and Bf 110. Perhaps in tribute to the now legendary status of the Hurricane and the Spitfire, there are many versions as to the exact history of their development.[17] They are famous but not unique; the Spitfire and Hurricane embodied the same fighting concept as most day air superiority fighters of the Second World War – high performance interceptors with a fixed, forward-firing gun armament, and followed the same design of single seat, with low wings and a single tailplane. They were only revolutionary in comparison to what had gone before but this did not detract from their success. The fact that the Spitfire was the insurance policy against delays in the Hurricane has been obscured by the huge problems encountered in putting it into production. It proved the far more successful aircraft, but much of this is due to the unintended feature of its design that it was possible to make dramatic improvements during the course of the war. The engines of the final marks of the Spitfire had twice the power of the early ones.

The success of this basic design and concept should not, though, obscure the fact that, like so much else in aircraft design at the time, there was no certainty that this would prove to be by far the best package possible. The RAF had a long history of two-seat fighters, beginning with the highly successful Bristol Fighter of the First World War which was continued in the Hawker Demon. In parallel to its work on the Hurricane and Spitfire, the Air Staff was looking for a successor. Here the result, the Boulton Paul Defiant, was almost as catastrophic as the Battle, but the debacle was deeply influenced by a major technical choice in aircraft armament that also impacted bomber design.

Chapter 6

Protection from the Slipstream

The advances in aircraft technology brought huge changes in aircraft armament. More powerful engines allowed aircraft to carry heavier and more powerful weapons. Increased speeds imposed new demands on weapons both to shoot down enemy aircraft and to defend against other aircraft. Defensive armament would have to evolve somehow and the RAF opted for the most radical solution. The first phase of the RAF's move to new technologies for its aircraft saw it adopt an invention which was to shape greatly the design of its bombers right up to the end of the Second World War.

The very first way in which military aircraft had been armed for air combat was to provide the observer with a gun with which to shoot at enemy aircraft. In the very early days this was merely a rifle or shotgun, but very rapidly the machine gun took over. It became the norm for two-seat aircraft to carry a machine gun for the observer mounted on some form of flexible stand at his open cockpit which permitted him to train it towards his target. To allow the machine gun to move flexibly it required a fixed magazine which had to be changed to reload, not an ideal arrangement in combat. In one of the rare instances of a non-officer being responsible for a major development, Warrant Officer F. W. Scarff came up with an efficient flexible ring mounting which became a standard fitting in British service. In practice only a single machine gun could be usefully mounted; it was cumbersome to move and reload two guns which imposed a weight penalty anyway.

The early large bombers featured more than one of these open gun positions. As aircraft design remained static through the 1920s, these arrangements continued to dominate but as the performance of aircraft improved radically it became less and less tenable. The gunner, especially at the front of the aircraft, was exposed to an ever-faster slipstream which made it difficult for him to aim his weapon, as well as making him cold. To begin with the British simply provided some shelter from the slipstream but stuck to a single gun. This was the defensive armament of two of the RAF's Second World War bombers, the Battle and the Hampden, and it proved deeply inadequate.

Something more would be needed; the RAF began to look at enclosed and powered gun turrets.[1] The powered gun turret offered great advantages: it could be trained across a large area with only a small effort by the gunner. Installed at the rear point of a bomber's fuselage it covered almost the entire rear-facing hemisphere. It addressed a problem that was foreseen for night operations by allowing the gunner a completely free field of fire with no risk that he might damage the tailplane which would be invisible at night.[2] The turret's ability to move rapidly allowed it to engage the faster-moving fighters that were entering service. The movement was smooth and precise and could be mastered rapidly. A favourite stunt that the gun turret manufacturers used to impress visitors was to place a stick of chalk in the muzzle of one of the machine guns and to write the visitor's name using the training mechanism. King George VI was treated to this when he visited a factory.[3] Crucially, a powered turret could mount two or four machine guns with belt-fed ammunition, giving it both far heavier firepower and length of uninterrupted fire than a single, pivot-mounted drum-fed weapon. It was a compelling package and it was adopted as a standard feature of bomber design despite reservations at some senior levels.

This improvement in bomber's defensive firepower brought disadvantages. The turret added a significant amount of weight which came at the expense of speed, bombload or fuel and thus range. It spoiled the aerodynamic shape of aircraft. A tail turret meant that the fuselage could not taper to a smooth point and a protruding turret generated severe drag. When the specifications for one new bomber were being debated it was estimated that the desired speed would have to be reduced by 20 mph to allow for a tail turret. With bomber speeds around 200 mph this was a significant sacrifice. Fitting turrets made for inflexibility in design. It could be argued that the RAF's heavy and medium bombers were designed around their defensive armament as much as any other aspect of their missions.

Turrets were not accepted without debate.[4] The Deputy Chief of the Air Staff, Sir Edgar Ludlow-Hewitt, had been hesitant from the start because of the cost in speed but there was a powerful voice in favour of turrets at the heart of the Air Ministry.[5] Group Captain Arthur 'Bert'

Harris was junior in rank but he held great influence as the Director of Plans. Harris was one of a generation of young officers with distinguished combat records in the First World War and Britain's imperial wars who were to shape the RAF as it prepared for the Second World War. The RAF's most important operational commander, Sir Robert Brooke-Popham, began as a sceptic on tail turrets but was converted by Harris. 'As regards the heavy bomber. I think we must face the fact that this shall be an aeroplane of comparatively low performance, both as regards ceiling and as regards speed, and therefore I think will be used only by night or in very cloudy weather by day.'[6]

So, gun turrets became a standard feature of British bomber design.[7] The usual distribution was one (with four machine guns) in the tail and one with two in the nose, but the larger designs which started to dominate planning had a third turret on the back of the fuselage, known as a dorsal turret. All but two of the nine bomber designs with which the RAF entered the Second World War were equipped with turrets and these exceptions were regarded as obsolescent. Turret armament had become a keystone in the RAF's vision of its bombers as capable of operating alone and unescorted over enemy territory. One of the various projects that did the rounds in the 1930s for a high-speed bomber which had no defensive armament and was to rely solely on speed for protection – the concept of the highly successful de Havilland Mosquito – was referred to simply as a 'bomber without turrets'.

Ensuring the supply of turrets became a significant part of the re-equipment programme. With official encouragement and, later, financial support a famous racing motorist, Archibald Frazer-Nash, had established a company to manufacture turrets to his own design. Three airframe manufacturers also had their own designs: Vickers, Bristol and Handley Page, which adapted a French design. There were no fundamentally difficult technical challenges, although it took an immense amount of detailed development work to produce a reliable and efficient weapons system.

Designers elsewhere, notably France, had been working on powered gun turrets but the RAF of all the major air forces of the Second World War was by some measure the most enthusiastic user and made by far the heaviest bet on the system. Until well into the war none of the Luftwaffe's operational aircraft had them. The Luftwaffe was content to accept the sacrifice in hitting power and arc of fire imposed by mounting machine guns on flexible mounts firing through the plexi-glass of the main crew compartment or, on the He 111 heavy medium bomber, semi-exposed, open positions. Many RAF fighter pilots found that these arrangements provided dangerous levels of defensive firepower. Later in the war and notably on its He 177 heavy bomber, which failed for quite different reasons, the Luftwaffe fitted remotely operated turrets (or barbettes) which gave just as much protection as manned turrets with far less aerodynamic drag. The high command of the RAF was certainly alert to the question of how the Luftwaffe armed its bombers defensively. When the CAS, Sir Cyril Newall, was informed of the existence of a high-level source of intelligence on the Luftwaffe, he specifically asked if the source could provide information on whether the Germans were fitting gun turrets to their aircraft. In the event the source did not answer any of the follow-up questions so we cannot begin to answer the question as to whether Newall's interest was prompted by fear that Luftwaffe bombers would better be able to defend themselves or, less likely, the glimmer of doubt that the RAF might not have made the best choice. The prevalence of gun turrets on British bombers bred a degree of complacency. The provision of fighter escorts for bombers was anathema to the Air Staff and it was seen as proof of a flawed strategy that the German Condor Legion in Spain escorted its bombers; this was attributed to the bombers' supposedly poor defensive armament.[8] With his usual hyperbole, Bert Harris described German bombers as 'almost unarmed'.[9]

***

The Air Staff's enthusiasm for turrets influenced fighter design as well. The British air forces had a long tradition of two-seat fighter aircraft that had begun with the highly successful Bristol Fighter of the First World War and at the start of the 1930s the Hawker Demon two-seat fighter was a standard part of the inventory with many in service. It was a natural instinct to find a replacement that embodied the new technologies and just as turrets were replacing open, man-powered single machine guns on bombers, it was a short step to doing the same with two-seat fighters.[10] The RAF cannot be blamed for exploring alternatives but here it went down a disastrous blind alley. In studying the best way for fighters to attack bombers in the face of their growing defensive armament, the RAF latched onto the idea of engaging them from the beam or below, using the fighter's superior performance – even burdened with a turret – to put it in the best position. To deliver the attack the RAF saw the powered gun turret, which was also becoming a key part of its bomber design, as the right tool. It would allow the fighter's armament to be trained through a partial sphere above, either side, astern and, to some extent, beneath the aircraft. Even though it was acknowledged that turret fighters were slower than single-seat fighters and had less firepower, it was claimed that they were required for 'tactical diversity'.[11] The aircraft was to be of the same basic configuration as the Hurricane and Spitfire although there would be a second crew member to operate the gun turret. Chief of the Air Staff Sir Edward Ellington was especially favourable to this idea.[12] Enthusiasm for the concept was not restricted to RAF officers. Winston Churchill, then a back-bench MP but deeply interested in air matters, had an even more grandiose vision, foreseeing that the established pattern of fighter combat in which aircraft manoeuvred to get into a firing position straight behind the enemy would become obsolete.

The concept of what were labelled 'free-gun' fighters had another powerful advocate in Sir Cyril Newall who succeeded Ellington as CAS in 1937. He believed that it would always be an 'essential operational requirement' and even predicted that the single-seat fighter might disappear entirely but not the two-seater, when he hypothesized on the future.[13] When development problems held back the availability of two-seat fighters, Newall was only prepared to accept Hurricanes, a type which he viewed with deep disfavour, as a temporary but not a permanent substitute.[14] Top-level enthusiasm for turret-fighters spilled down the hierarchy. When the RAF was briefing the Canadian government on the ongoing development of fighters in early 1938, it gave the firm opinion that movable-gun fighters would eventually replace fixed-gun fighters.[15] The Air Staff came close to pure fiction in its propaganda for the turret fighter. In one high-profile paper, it claimed outright that all foreign air forces were 'turning their attention' to this class of aircraft, when in reality it was admitted in an internal paper, 'We know little of developments regarding turreted fighters but we must give potential enemies credit for initiative equal to our own.'[16] Just as the Air Staff could not believe that any air force would not hold a Trenchardian doctrine for its bombers, so it could not conceive of an air force unable to come up with as brilliant an idea as a turret fighter.

In the event, what was to emerge in 1939 as the Boulton Paul Defiant fighter proved an abject failure. It was designed to attack unescorted bombers and it might well have done so successfully. What no one foresaw and only the most extreme pessimist could have foreseen was that the German invasion of France in May 1940 brought all the Luftwaffe's fighters within range of Britain and thus able to escort the bombers for their whole mission. Here the inferior performance of the Defiant proved fatal. That said, the fact that the Defiant is now a mere footnote in the history of air combat should not distract attention from the fact that the turret fighter absorbed very significant RAF and economic resources during the crucial years of rearmament. Well after war broke out serious work was afoot to design and manufacture a successor to the Defiant, embodying the same ultimately flawed design concept. Fortunately, the RAF's opening bet on the concept was limited and under its formal plans Defiants would have made up only one-fifth of the fighter force, but nonetheless valuable time and money were absorbed and a number of visionaries believed that the class might play an even greater role.

The Air Staff's enthusiasm for gun turrets affected a number of designs. A turret-armed carrier-borne fighter, the Roc, was made for the Fleet Air Arm, whilst naval aviation was still controlled by the RAF, and proved no more useful in service than the Defiant. When Geoffrey de Havilland finally persuaded the RAF to try his design for a fast bomber that relied on speed and not weapons for its defence, which was to become the phenomenally successful Mosquito, he had to test-fly one fitted with a mock-up gun turret to assuage the Air Staff's addiction to the system.[17] It would have defeated the entire concept of the design had it been built in this form. Turret mania found its most extreme manifestation in the Air Staff's F.11/37 specification for a turret fighter that could also carry out ground attack with a turret mounting four 20mm cannon which got as far as a half-scale flying prototype before common sense prevailed.[18]

The concept of the turret-armed fighter in turn affected bomber design. On the basis of no real evidence whatever, the RAF persuaded itself that all other air forces were seriously considering turret fighters and that it was necessary to protect their bombers against this form of attack.[19] The Air Staff came up with the idea of a retractable gun turret underneath the aircraft, which became known as the dustbin turret. These were unpopular from an early stage: cumbersome, inefficient, cost weight and, above all, were entirely pointless.[20] No other air force came up with an equivalent of the Defiant; the RAF was in effect fighting itself. The dustbin turrets were soon discarded, as Bomber Command switched to night operations. By a cruel irony, later in the war the Germans did adopt the tactic of attacking bombers from beneath, albeit by the far simpler and lighter method of mounting fixed cannon on their night-fighters that fired upwards at an angle, called *Schrägemusik* (Jazz music). These were lethally effective, but the RAF's intelligence section, forgetting the prewar enthusiasm for this form of attack, failed to recognize that this was happening until too late and no efficient defence was devised.[21]

At the same time as it was developing the gun turret, the RAF was also developing a new armament for conventional fighters. This was to have a battery of eight machine guns mounted in the wings of fighters, a vast improvement on the two machine guns mounted on its fighters up to then. The American Browning machine gun proved sufficiently reliable to be put somewhere out of reach of the pilot, who would be unable to clear jams during combat as the pilots of the First World War had done. As the armament of the Hurricanes and Spitfires of the Battle of Britain, the eight-gun set-up shares the legendary status of these aircraft and a discreet competition has been waged to assign the credit for it.

In reality, both the eight-gun fighters and the gun turrets had a severe defect. They both used a standard .303-inch-calibre machine gun, the same as British aircraft of the First World War and infantry light weapons. By late 1938 the 'doubtful efficiency' of the .303 machine gun was more or less an accepted fact.[22] At one point it was suggested that each turret should mount a minimum of four and even six or eight to confront more heavily armed modern fighters. Even before the RAF faced the reality of air combat with Luftwaffe aircraft, already armed with efficient large-calibre cannon firing explosive shells when war broke out, it was widely albeit not universally recognized that even in batteries of four, rifle-calibre machine guns did not provide adequate firepower.

The RAF briefly considered using .50-inch-calibre machine guns firing a solid bullet of around four times the weight of a .303 but eventually opted for the 20mm (0.79-inch) calibre rapid-fire cannon, firing an explosive shell which delivered enormously greater hitting power for a small sacrifice in rate of fire and a smaller supply of ammunition. The first obstacle was to find a satisfactory design of cannon and the

French Hispano-Suiza model was selected. Despite its long existence, the British arms industry proved remarkably unsuccessful in developing modern automatic weapons. The Hispano-Suiza company created a British subsidiary, the British Manufacture and Research Company (BMARC) that built a factory at Grantham which entered production in 1939. BMARC was managed by a colourful former Citroën executive, Dennis Kendall, of decidedly right-wing sympathies who went on to become an outspoken wartime MP and attracted considerable interest from MI5.[23] The 20mm cannon did not win universal approval. Hugh Dowding of Fighter Command was sceptical that the increased punch of the 20mm cannon justified the loss of ammunition capacity compared to the .303 machine gun and decried it as a 'woolly imitation of woolly continental air forces'.[24] Only a weapon of, say, 37mm calibre which was nearly certain of destroying an aircraft with a single hit was worth the disadvantages of slower firing and fewer rounds.

Supplying the 20mm cannon was one thing, mounting it on aircraft was another. Initially the RAF expected that purpose-built new fighter designs would be necessary, making Hurricanes and Spitfires obsolete. CAS Newall was particularly taken by an elegant twin-engine design, the Whirlwind from Westland, which was ultimately betrayed by unreliable new Rolls-Royce Peregrine engines. He believed that the Whirlwind would offer a substantial improvement in performance over the Hurricane and Spitfire and wanted it to be ordered off the drawing board, with 600 to come from the Castle Bromwich shadow factory on top of the Spitfires that it was already struggling to make.[25] Air Marshal Sir Wilfrid Freeman had his work cut out to pour cold water on Newall's enthusiasm; it took him eight months to succeed in persuading his colleagues to abandon the Castle Bromwich scheme. Little more than 100 Whirlwinds were made. A fighter version of the twin-engine Bristol Beaufort torpedo bomber, the Beaufighter, proved more of a success, albeit not as an interceptor fighter. It also took some time to iron out initial snags with the cannon. One squadron of Spitfires did fit cannon experimentally in 1939 but they proved too unreliable. Ultimately wing-mounted cannon on the single-engine fighters proved to be the true solution and from 1941 was standard on RAF aircraft.

Upgrading the armament of the bombers proved to be far more difficult. It was clear that .303 machine guns were not going to provide adequate defence, but it was simply impossible to mount anything but

.303 machine guns in their turrets. Ludlow-Hewitt, then commanding the RAF's bombers, came up with the desperate suggestion that some .303 guns should be kept for morale-boosting purposes even though ineffective as a deterrent to fighters; their greater ammunition supply would allow them to fire for longer.[26] The Air Staff began to scrabble around for possible solutions. One suggestion was to graft one defensive arrangement that had been proposed for a blue-sky 'ideal bomber' project – two turrets each with two 20mm cannon, one at the top of the fuselage and one below with no tail turret – onto existing designs.[27] Newall was gently led away from this impractical scheme which would have called for a redesign of at least 30 per cent of the aircraft structure.[28] By 1939, when this debate got under way, the time it would have taken to develop 20mm cannon turrets would anyway have delayed further the RAF's already tardy re-equipment with modern aircraft, so the RAF's bombers went into action with inadequate .303 machine-gun turrets.

The Air Staff's vision of turret-armed bombers cruising serenely to attack targets in Germany was shattered in 1939 when its first raids suffered huge losses at the hands of German fighters. When they were subjected to the acid test of combat, the defensive armament of the British bombers was completely outclassed by the speed and manoeuvrability of modern fighters. It is an entirely moot point whether the early daylight raids by Bomber Command would have fared any better had the defensive armament been heavier; the US heavy bombers mounted even more of the heavy .50-calibre machine guns that RAF bombers had .303s, but suffered crippling losses until they were provided with long-range escort fighters. Bomber Command was forced to operate practically exclusively at night but as the Luftwaffe developed night interception techniques, the .303-inch gun turrets were no more effective against night fighters than they had been against its day fighters. As commander of Bomber Command, Bert Harris engaged in furious attempts to have his aircraft armed even with heavier-calibre .50-inch machine guns, cursing the Air Ministry for what he labelled in his inimitable style as incompetence and obstructionism, but in vain.[29]

Chapter 7

Incalculable Potential

It is practically impossible to understand the thinking and actions of Britain's leaders in the 1930s without taking into account the strength of anti-war feeling in the period. Only at the very end of the decade did the popular mindset begin to move away from near unconditional, visceral and powerful anti-war sentiment that had been caused by the First World War in which a large proportion of Britain's active manhood had been killed or maimed. Few families had escaped the loss of one or more of its members. There were constant reminders in the shape of war memorials in practically every locality and crippled, often hideously scarred survivors. Special blue-painted benches were provided in public parks for the severely disfigured to warn passers-by to brace themselves for horrible sights. It was simply inconceivable that Britain would ever send masses of men abroad to fight in another major war. There was a direct and automatic belief that war was the ultimate folly and evil and that another full-scale war was too horrific to contemplate. The tag applied to the First World War of 'the war to end all wars' was heartfelt and strong enough to offset its unrealistic optimism.

Fear and rejection of war did not just come from the memory of the Great War; it was also fed by the terror that another war would be even worse. The new technology of powered flight had long fed visions of its use against civilian populations. In part there was an instinctive dread of the possible evil consequences of a new, potent and mysterious extension of human abilities. It was a fruitful topic for commercial writing. The pioneer was H. G. Wells's *War in The Air* of 1907, a mere four years after the first powered flight, in which even the Atlantic proves no defence against the aeroplane and New York is devastated. The huge advances in aircraft technology during the First World War, combined with the reality of air raids on civilians, nurtured hideous predictions. The topic generated a huge amount of literature. Publishers and features editors sensed a large and voracious readership for writing both imaginative and speculative pieces that examined the damage that bombing could wreak on mankind. The other great technological horror weapon of the First World War inevitably featured. Poison gas had been extensively deployed by both sides in the war and the ravages it inflicted on the human body were present everywhere in the plight of the gas survivors who suffered for the rest of their lives. Fear of gas attack from the air was rooted in fact. The Italian air force was to use gas bombs against Ethiopians who resisted the invasion of their country in 1935 and every nation saw gas as a serious potential weapon. It is an open question as to whether the stockpiles of gas bombs were not used in the Second World War because they would have been an inefficient way of killing people or out of ethical considerations.

The fear of air attack was especially acute in Britain. The former British prime minister and MP in the 1930s, Harold Macmillan, described the terror inspired by the thought of air bombing amongst people then as being as strong as the fear of nuclear warfare during the Cold War. Aircraft had shown they had the ability to breach the nation's centuries-old protective rampart, its surrounding seas. The British population had been spared the horrors of war to any serious extent for centuries, unlike much of continental Europe, where foreign invasions and civil wars were a feature of life. The Kaiser's Zeppelins and Gothas had shattered the cosy feeling of smug inviolability that this had engendered. The level of British air raid casualties was trivial when set against, say, tens of thousands of civilians killed in the siege of Paris of 1870/1, still within living memory, but the psychological impact was still immensely powerful.

The effect was magnified because the attacks were focused on the single city of London and this added a specific and powerful dimension to British fears. As the capital of the mighty British Empire, London was a symbol of national power and self-confidence. Its population of eight million people made it one of the largest cities on earth. London's size, meshed with the growth and complexity of huge cities, had already created a sense of fragility. Many saw danger in huge, badly controlled urban populations. The better-off saw a threat to themselves and order generally from the 'submerged tenth': an urban under-class of the very poorest who had no stake in society or economic structure, who might vent their jealousy and fury at any point. Bombing was seen as a way in which a latent breakdown in the social, economic and technical networks of major cities could be triggered. The existence of people at both extremes of the social and economic spectrum was an obvious fact of life in London. London was unarguably the most tempting target for air attack, with its huge concentration of administrative and commercial activity. It was also one of Britain's biggest ports and a major manufacturing centre, including a huge weapons factory at Woolwich. The distinctive and unmistakeable form of the River Thames provided a uniquely easy path that bombers could follow to its heart day or night.

When Winston Churchill treated the House of Commons to a detailed vision of the horrors that bombing London would cause in late 1934, no one accused him of exaggeration. It is worth quoting at length:

> But without accepting these claims no one can doubt that a week or 10 days' intensive bombing attack upon London would be a very serious matter indeed. One could hardly expect that less than 30,000 or 40,000 people would be killed or maimed ...
>
> The most dangerous form of air attack is the attack by incendiary bombs. Such an attack was planned by the Germans for the summer of 1918 ... The argument in favour of such an attack was that if in any great city there are, we will say, 50 fire brigades, and you start simultaneously 100 fires or 80 fires and the wind is high, an almost incalculable conflagration may result. The reason why the Germans did not carry out that attack in 1918 must be stated. ... It was because the advance of the Allied Armies, with the British Army in the van, already confronted the heads of the German State, the Imperial Government of Germany, with the prospect of impending defeat, and they did not wish to incur the fury of retribution which would follow from such a dreadful act of power and terror as that which would have been involved in such a raid. Since those days the incendiary thermite bomb has become far more powerful than any that was used in the late War. It will in fact, I am assured by persons who are acquainted with the science, go through a series of floors in any building, igniting each one simultaneously.
>
> Not less formidable than these material effects are the reactions which will be produced upon the mind of the

civil population. We must expect that under the pressure of continuous air attack upon London at least 3,000,000 or 4,000,000 people would be driven out into the open country around the Metropolis. This vast mass of human beings, numerically far larger than any armies which have been fed and moved in war, without shelter and without food, without sanitation and without special provision for the maintenance of order, would confront the Government of the day with an administrative problem of the first magnitude, and would certainly absorb the energies of our small Army and of our Territorial Force. Problems of this kind have never been faced before, and although there is no need to exaggerate them, neither on the other hand is there any need to shrink from facing the immense, unprecedented difficulties which they involve.

Then there are the questions of the docks of London and the estuary of the Thames. Everyone knows the dependence of this immense community, the most prosperous in the whole world, upon the Eastern approaches by water. I need say no more about that.[1]

Fear of bombing was not restricted to politicians or the general public. In the deepest secrecy the British government had started to examine how the state might mitigate the damage of bombing. One of the outgrowths of the French air force scare of 1923 had been the establishment of a high-level Air Raid Precautions committee in Whitehall. They calculated a figure for the casualties that would be inflicted by a ton of bombs and arrived at a figure of fifty from the relatively narrow statistical base of experience during the First World War. This figure held good until the Second World War and was one of the first building blocks in a severe official exaggeration of the consequences of air raids.[2] The civil servants saw threat; the Air Staff saw both threat and opportunity:

It is no part of my intention to launch into a problematical account of the effect on London and other industrial centres – of fire, of starvation and of the wholesale exodus to the north, but I do feel we are justified in assuming with

Marshal Foch that: 'The potential of air attack on a large scale are almost incalculable, but it is clear that such attack, owing to its crushing moral effect on a nation, may impress public opinion to the point of disarming the government and thus become decisive.'[3]

In the Trenchardian vision mass air raids were horrific but they also held the prospect of winning (or losing) a war.

Churchill promoted his vision of the horrors of air war as a platform for his return to government, but it was one that was shared at the heart of government in circles bitterly opposed to him. Possibly Churchill's most formidable opponent was the civil servant, Sir Horace Wilson.[4] When Baldwin had stepped up to be prime minister again in 1935 Wilson had become his personal civil service adviser; he had no formal remit or job title but he had Baldwin's confidence and a strategically sited office next to the Cabinet room at 10 Downing Street. Soon after Wilson had moved into 10 Downing Street, he set out his concerns to a personal friend, the Lancashire cotton industry executive Raymond Streat, as they walked through the peaceful lanes of Sussex around Wilson's weekend cottage. The spine-chilling vision that Wilson set out to Streat was a mixture of inside information from the Whitehall Civil Service and intelligence machine, his own gloss on this and what was already common gossip. Britain was Hitler's first target and the likely victim for a surprise attack from the air:

> [the Germans] felt they could overwhelm France at their leisure, but England was still their stumbling block. They had already gone to enormous lengths in the air. Their air fleet was known to be enormous ... Production of aeroplanes was already organised on a constantly ascending scale. Indeed, so successful had Goebbels* been in organising production that he was now embarrassed to know where to store the machines that were being produced.

---

* Probably Göring was actually meant but even this unintentional muddling of the Nazi air force and propaganda chiefs hints at a significant dimension to German air rearmament as we will see.

Personnel had been trained by the thousand: gas and incendiary bombs had been perfected to a diabolic pitch: defence against aircraft was at best a most partial affair ...

He mentioned an actual plan for an air attack on London which should have taken place last November and dwelt on the panic from which the population of London must inevitably suffer if attacked from the air, since the evacuation of London was impossible.[5]

In November 1934 Germany had only recently slammed the door on the disarmament conference in Geneva and there is no evidence of an acute threat of war so Wilson's fears were well in advance of reality. The belief that Germany enjoyed great superiority in the air was hardly exceptional, but it is telling that someone so well informed and normally level headed as Wilson should have believed in the risk of an unheralded attack from the air. Wilson remained in the job when Neville Chamberlain replaced Baldwin as prime minister in 1937 and they formed an even closer partnership, which was cemented by Chamberlain's defining policy of appeasement as the way to avoid war. Wilson supported appeasement passionately, helped by his terror of air attack on Britain.

Chapter 8

The Air Defence of Great Britain

As it took shape under Trenchard, the RAF acquired a strongly regional flavour. In the wake of British air involvement in the campaign against the Turks in Egypt and Syria during the First World War, Middle East Command headquartered in Cairo was a major force. It oversaw the campaign against the Mad Mullah, which put it at the heart of the RAF's new imperial policing work. Middle East Command took the first responsibility for the suppression of the revolt in Iraq but as the RAF was given the prime responsibility for the control of Iraq and the border dispute with Turkey gathered momentum, Iraq Command came into being under an air vice-marshal in 1922. A separate command for India was set up in 1920 which was in charge of policing operations on the North-West Frontier. These commands had a permanent establishment of squadrons and were the ones where commanders and crews learned the different demands of combat operations, including cooperation with the other services. Being Air Officer Commanding of one of these units became established as a stepping stone to high command in the RAF. Lesser detachments were scattered around Britain's smaller and calmer imperial territories. However, the heart of the RAF was in the home country where it developed a distinctive flavour under the direct supervision of Trenchard.

By far the largest portion of the RAF's aircraft and units was in Britain. These came to be known as the metropolitan air force, which was the part of the service that was responsible for the key mission that Trenchard defined for the independent air force. After the reorganization of the RAF in the mid-1920s the relevant units were grouped together in a formation formally called the Air Defence of Great Britain (ADGB) which remained in existence for most of the RAF's formative years before being abolished in 1936. The name itself was a living demonstration of Trenchard's doctrine that the best, if not only, way to defend Great Britain from air attack was to bomb the enemy, at the time France. It comprised all the combat aircraft – both bombers and fighters – in Britain except for those designated for maritime patrol or army cooperation. ADGB commanded the 'striking force' of bombers, which Trenchard and his disciples on the Air Staff saw as the service's key asset. It would be a pardonable but grave error to suppose that ADGB was principally intended to shoot down attacking aircraft. Trenchard and his disciples would have vehemently rejected any suggestion that the name was an oxymoron. ADGB's operational units were divided into the 'Bombing Area' for bombers and the 'Fighting Area' for fighters each with its own AOC, but these formations were shadowy and insubstantial. Both were based at Uxbridge and neither had a distinct headquarters infrastructure of its own. The real chain of command ran directly from ADGB to the individual squadrons. There were so few of these that a single headquarters could exercise sufficient oversight.

The command of the ADGB was a plum appointment: of the six air marshals who held the job during its brief existence three of them (the Salmond brothers and Edward Ellington) went on to become Chiefs of the Air Staff. Another, Sir Robert Brooke-Popham, rose to the highest levels of military command, albeit in deeply unhappy circumstances. It seems to have served as a post for the heir apparent to the top job and another tool with which Trenchard aimed to secure his legacy in the RAF with a sequence of like-minded successors whose careers had flourished under his rule. Trenchard did later turn savagely against one of the AOCs of ADGB, Edward Ellington, but only after Ellington failed to prevent the government's decision to transfer carrier-borne aircraft to the Royal Navy in 1937. Ever afterwards Trenchard cursed Ellington for having lost a battle that he had fought passionately and successfully, but before then they had had a close and happy relationship.[1] Ellington was godfather to Trenchard's oldest son and it is inconceivable that Ellington would have been appointed as AOC-in-C of ADGB or the key overseas posts as AOC Middle East, Iraq and India had Trenchard not been confident in him.

As the plans were drawn up for the huge expansion of the RAF as it finally rearmed from 1934 onward, it was clear that the command structure of the RAF would have to be changed to cope with the greater number of units and aircraft. ADGB was done away with and replaced with a new structure as part of a wholesale reorganization of the RAF in Britain. ADGB was split into two 'commands', at the top of the organization, each responsible for all the aircraft carrying out a particular function: Bomber Command and Fighter Command. Beneath these came groups, a revival of the First World War practice of having a formation in between the top level of command and the individual squadrons. Confusingly enough, the army kept the label ADGB for its searchlight and anti-aircraft artillery forces until the war. The change marked the shift from a peacetime, administratively focused organization to one that was designed to command units in battle. Even in 1935 it was recognized that the RAF might soon face the test of combat. The new structure aimed 'To provide an organization that is suitable for war conditions. This seems vital and peace-time considerations should definitely take second place.'[2] This big decision proved its value when war came but in much else the new organization kept a distinctly peacetime flavour. The operational commands were clearly subordinate to the central bureaucracy. They were expected to obey detailed battle plans prepared by the Air Staff's plans department. Letters from the commands to the Air Ministry did not receive replies for weeks or even months.

In keeping with the collegial flavour of the Air Staff, the plan had been vigorously debated. By a supreme irony, the loudest voice against the split into Bomber and Fighter commands had been that of Hugh Dowding, then still Air Member for Supply and Research. He feared that in wartime the Air Staff might become bogged down in operational matters and that coordination between bombers and fighters would suffer.[3] As head of Fighter Command at the beginning of the Second World War Dowding found himself fighting serious battles to resist Air Staff interference and Bomber Command was too deeply sunk in slavish Trenchardianism to pay much attention to anything outside the world of bombers. Fighter Command did much better, taking shape of its own, but Bomber Command was beyond help.

Two more commands were set up at the same time. Coastal Command was in charge of all shore-based aircraft operating over the sea in cooperation with the Royal Navy, and Training Command was charged with the training needs of the RAF. There was no formal ranking of the combat commands, but Bomber Command was clearly the most important. There is no indication that it was seen as demotion for Air Marshal Steel that he went from being the last commander of ADGB to just that of Bomber Command alone. Fighter Command sat uneasily between it and Coastal Command. The RAF's army cooperation squadrons were not significant enough to rate a separate command. They were placed under Fighter Command, which gives an idea of how unimportant Fighter Command's principal task might have seemed. It is revealing that two functions despised in the Trenchardian world view should be lumped together. The existence of Coastal Command was part of the price the RAF paid for its monopoly of military aviation. Aircraft had a part to play in sea warfare, but these had to be kept out of the hands of the admirals who might become excessively greedy; 'until Germany possesses submarines, or sufficient surface craft to be a serious menace to our Fleet and overseas trade, it would appear essential to concentrate our small resources [on defence against air attack, in other words, on bombers]'.[4]

The new structure came into effect in July 1936 with little fanfare. Perhaps curiously the split has never attracted the debate or analysis that it deserves. No other country's air service applied a comparable organization. It lay at the root of the RAF's success in defeating the German assault on the country in 1940 and in its far less impressive performance in taking the offensive to the enemy in the early years of the war. The split seems to have been viewed as a simple progression from ADGB and did not imply any change of strategy for the metropolitan air force as a whole or its, now, constituent parts. There is, though, a clue as to the relative status and philosophy of the two commands in the mottoes that were chosen for them. Bomber Command's 'Strike hard, strike sure' rings out clearly and confidently. It embodies the heart of the Trenchardian vision for the task of an air force. The term 'striking force' was used almost interchangeably with bomber force through the 1930s. There was no doubt that Bomber Command lay at the centre of the RAF. By contrast the motto devised for Fighter Command was more than mildly ambiguous: 'Offence, defence' gives no clue as to what the Command's actual task might have been. It seems to be making a wholly spurious claim that the unit's primary mission was an offensive one, putting second its defensive task as though apologizing that any unit should be given anything so humiliating as its primary function. There is no sense of pride or intent.

Fighter Command might have come low in the pecking order of the refashioned metropolitan air force but it was still an advance on its predecessor. After the nebulous existence of Fighting Area, Fighter Command was a far more substantial entity. It had a headquarters and staff of its own: Bentley Priory, a vast, mainly nineteenth-century Victorian mansion, to the north-west of London, which had belonged to the RAF for ten years, serving as the headquarters for ADGB's training organization which had been upgraded to Training Command as part of the same reshuffle that created Fighter Command and moved to Shropshire. Bentley Priory was to be the home of Fighter Command for its entire existence – until it was folded into Strike Command in 1968 – but in 1936 everything had still to be done to transform it into the operational headquarters and the control centre of the most important part of Britain's air defences. The old Fighting Area at Uxbridge was downgraded to 11 Group of Fighter Command in something of a blow to the pride of the personnel at Uxbridge, but at least the RAF's department of heraldry came up with a more inspiring emblem than its parent formation's: a protecting crown around Big Ben and the motto 'Tutela cordis' (guardian of the heart).[5] When Fighter Command was established, 11 Group was the only group in the command although it was soon to be joined by 12 Group and, ultimately, two more fighter groups. The RAF's fighters had begun to develop an identity of their own, far beyond their status as the junior partners in ADGB.

The RAF's fighters had more than a new home and the beginnings of a new identity; they had a new leader. In keeping with the general upgrade of the service, the first AOC-in-C of Fighter Command was one rank above and was considerably more senior than the last AOC of Fighting Area, Philip Joubert de la Ferté who was only an air vice-marshal. Air Marshal Sir Hugh Dowding was one of the RAF's most senior officers and was promoted to four-star rank as air chief marshal soon after his appointment to Fighter Command, putting him on a par with his counterpart at Bomber Command, Sir John Steel. More important for the future of Fighter Command, Dowding had crucially relevant experience for his new task. He had been AOC Fighting Area from 1929 to 1930 then been an unusually long-serving Air Member for Research and Development until his move to Fighter Command, which had given him a detailed overview of all the changes in aircraft technology during this period of rapid advance. Most important of all, he had overseen the RAF's involvement in the first experiments with radar or RDF as it was then called.

In some ways it is remarkable that Dowding had risen so high. Trenchard had severe doubts as to whether to include him in the peacetime

RAF but seems to have warmed to him after Dowding's brief stint in Iraq in 1924.[6] He did not fit fully into the mould of the Trenchardian commanders. Iraq had been his only peacetime overseas posting and he had never been a bomber commander. By his own account he was intellectually a non-conformist:

> I have never accepted ideas because they were orthodox, and consequently found myself in opposition to generally accepted views.[7]

Non-conformity is rarely the avenue to high promotion in peacetime armed services, especially one like the interwar RAF which was held together by the faith in a dogma and reverence for Trenchard. Allied to his single-mindedness and strongly held opinions Dowding's willingness to swim against the current equipped him to forge Fighter Command into the vital arm it had become in 1940. To do so he had to demonstrate that one of the fundamental tenets of the independent RAF was not entirely true. Trenchard's doctrine of counter-offensive rested on the assertion that the bomber will always get through. Trenchard worked on the basis that if a single bomber could get through, counter-bombing was the only effective response, and that it was wasteful to devote resources to fighters. He and his disciples ducked the simple military and logical imperative that it was the duty of an air force commander to make the fighters' riposte to bombers as effective as it could be. Unspoken in the Trenchard doctrine was a conviction that fighters could never do more than irritate bombers and deter only cowardly bomber crews. Trenchard entirely ignored the possibility that defence against bombers might succeed to an extent that the enemy would be forced to change strategy. Dowding's job as head of Fighter Command was to turn this theoretical possibility into hard, military reality. Dowding never challenged the RAF's orthodox preference for a strategy of offence. His only sin on this score was to believe that the offence should be directed against the opposed air force, either on the ground or in the factories producing it. He never seems to have adopted the Trenchardian doctrine in its most radical form: that an air force should attack the enemy's nation full stop. Dowding never seems to have entered into any debate on whether civilian morale was a distinct military target or whether bombers were an efficient way of attacking it.

Dowding was diligent, hard working and entirely committed to the success of Fighter Command. His single-mindedness, clarity of thought and openness to innovation were the vital factors in forging the weapon that won the Battle of Britain, but there were flaws. There is no sign that he had much ability as a leader of men; he had none of Trenchard's almost mystic aura or the appealing personability of Sir John Salmond, Trenchard's immediate successor. But unlike Ellington, he was capable of clear expression. He was given to acid opinions of his fellow officers. He was reserved and dry at work, and might not have been ideally equipped to cope with one of the structural features of the RAF. There was an uneasy relationship between the bureaucracy of the Air Staff at Adastral House and the operational commands. The Air Staff had the double strength of proximity to the founts of power – the CAS and the Air Council – and it was far longer established than Fighter Command. Dowding was not the man to deploy the lobbying, diplomacy and office politics that would have been necessary to impose his will. He fought a long battle with the Works Directorate of the Air Ministry to try to obtain expensive concrete, all-weather runways for his aerodromes. Fighter Command could not do its job if it could operate only when the ground was dry enough to fly fighters off grass runways. Ultimately Dowding won but a more astute operator might have outflanked the Works Directorate and secured a decision in his favour far earlier with right so clearly on his side.

Dowding held hopes that he might move on from Fighter Command to the top job in the RAF when Ellington retired in 1937. He seems to have believed that Ellington told him that he would be his successor. However, Ellington's civil service secretary, Maurice Dean, believes that the CAS might have seen Dowding as the right candidate simply as the next most senior officer in the service.[8] But heads of British armed services do not appoint their own successors. Most famously when he was retiring as Chief of the Imperial General Staff in 1948, Field Marshal Bernard Montgomery protested to prime minister Clement Attlee that it would not be possible to give William Slim the job as he (Montgomery) had already told General Crocker that he was to be CIGS. 'Untell him,' replied Attlee. Dean points out that the choice of Ellington's successor was made in keeping with normal practice by Lord Swinton, the air minister, and his only candidates were air marshals Newall and Courtney. Later in life Dowding expressed resentment at having been passed over, but the RAF had given him much more to be resentful about by then.

Chapter 9

No Longer in a Position Inferior

According to your taste, one of the high points of human optimism or naivety came in 1932 when the League of Nations, itself an optimistic outgrowth of the First World War, launched the World Disarmament Conference in its home city Geneva, with the intention of securing lasting peace by the abolition or restriction of weaponry. It was the last, magnificent hurrrah of the dictum that the First World War was 'the war to end all wars'. The Disarmament Conference stands as something of watershed between the peaceful, comparatively hopeful years of the 1920s and the disturbed 1930s when the Second World War was the now seemingly inevitable outcome, but this should not diminish the power of the hope that nations were prepared to invest in it. In hindsight the conference now appears tragically doomed from the outset though it did enjoy widespread and sincere political and, naturally, almost universal public support. Little gives a better sense of how much revulsion at the idea of war dominated thinking than the fact that every member nation of the League paid at least lip service to the project which had been in planning since 1925. Just because the conference failed so totally should not lead to it being dismissed as a piece of historical marginalia. The detailed story of its deliberation gives clear insights into many of the international and intranational tensions that marked the age, none more so than air power policy in Britain.

Even before Hitler's accession to power the Germans had seen the conference as a lever to reverse the near-complete disarmament which had been imposed by the victor nations at the Versailles Conference in 1919. They had logic on their side: why should a disarmed nation be asked to cut its armaments along with nations which were fully armed? Germany demanded equal treatment, *Gleichberechtigung* (equality of entitlement), and naturally the French refused to grant it.

The opening of the conference coincided almost exactly with a conspicuous act of brutal aggression by Japan that put air power and the dread of bombing civilians to the forefront. With hindsight this has helped feed the sense that disarmament had missed its moment. In September 1931, Japan had begun the occupation of the Chinese territory of Manchuria and this sparked violent protests in Shanghai. Just as the conference was opening Japan responded savagely with full-scale military intervention, including the bombing of the residential district of Chapei with heavy but never properly quantified loss of life. This was not just the first (and unprovoked) intentional and large-scale bombing of civilians since the First World War but was a conspicuous challenge to the sensibilities of the European powers as Shanghai was then under international control; Britain had large commercial interests there with a substantial expatriate community.

The British had been amongst the most enthusiastic of the conference's sponsors. Britain had been well to the fore in disarming after the First World War, leaving it weak militarily and with a vested interest in seeing other nations disarm. The seeds of imperial overreach were beginning to ripen and Britain was having to juggle idealism with realpolitik calculations that came with the recognition that the mighty empire was largely a sham. The Foreign Office enthusiastically supported an outcome which would tackle this problem. To begin with the British saw an opportunity to address their particular fear of bombing. The prime mover seems to have been Stanley Baldwin who was horrified at the Shanghai bombing, a 'nightmare'.[1] Baldwin was officially Lord Privy Seal in the 'National' cross-party coalition government formed the previous year, but as leader of the Conservative Party which had emerged from the September 1931 general election with a commanding majority in Parliament, he was arguably the single most influential politician in Britain. Britain prepared to table formal proposals to ban air bombing as an instrument of international war.

Predictably this met ferocious opposition from the RAF. The Air Staff claimed that the proposal would limit the RAF's ability to exercise 'air control' over British-governed territories and, more important, cripple its ability to defend London from air attack.[2] 'Defend' meant of course defend by 'counter-bombing' as it was 'impossible to provide an effective defence of London by Fighter Squadrons only'. The French – still the first-choice enemy in 1932 before the advent of Hitler – would be able to drop 210 tons of bombs daily even without deploying the military aircraft from North Africa that they could sneak through the proposed ban. According to the estimates, even 100 tons of bombs in the first twenty-four hours of an attack, seventy-five in the next and fifty tons daily thereafter would kill over 6,000 people and injure twice that number in the first week. The government bowed to its advisers at first and the proposal withered on the vine, but the dream of air disarmament had not died. The proposal left a legacy of bitterness and downright paranoia; even three years later Ellington, the CAS, was still complaining at 'the Government's determination to regard the complete abolition of military aviation as their eventual goal'.[3]

As the conference ground on, Baldwin cherished the hope that a formula might be found. He was sustained by Sir Maurice Hankey, the Cabinet Secretary and master of Whitehall, who had decided that it lay in Britain's military interests for bombing to be banned. The Cabinet approved one more attempt at the project and as he prepared to go to Geneva for another session of the conference, Baldwin delivered a speech to Parliament, responding to a Labour motion demanding government commitment to disarmament. He had received a thorough briefing from Hankey but what he said bore a deep imprint of the Air Staff's view:

> I think it is well also for the man in the street to realise that there is no power on earth that can protect him from being bombed. Whatever people may tell him, the bomber will always get through, and it is very easy to understand that, if you realise the area of space. I said that any town within reach of an aerodrome could be bombed. Take any large town you like in this island or on the Continent within such reach. For the defence of that town and its suburbs, you have to split up the air into sectors for defence. Calculate that the bombing aeroplanes will be at least 20,000 feet high in the air, and perhaps higher, and it is a matter of simple mathematical calculation – or I will omit the word 'simple' – that you will have sectors of from 10 to hundreds of millions of cubic miles to defend. I beg pardon. I am not a mathematician, as the House will see. I mean tens or hundreds of cubic miles. Now imagine 100 cubic miles covered with cloud and fog, and you can calculate how many aeroplanes you would have to throw into that to have much chance of catching odd aeroplanes as they fly through it. It cannot be done, and

there is no expert in Europe who will say that it can. The only defence is in offence, which means that you have to kill more women and children more quickly than the enemy if you want to save yourselves.[4]

Baldwin's speech caught the mood of the House and the country. He scored a tactical triumph over Labour by endorsing vividly one aspect of disarmament, but unwittingly he cemented into the public and political consciousness a fearful notion of air attack. He did Hankey's work by promoting the abolition of bombing but he also promoted the Trenchardian doctrine: defence was futile, only counter-bombing offered protection. Baldwin's speech did more than anything to legitimize the Air Staff doctrine that the only means of defence is attack. In the years when Britain's fear of devastating air attack was at its greatest, the hope that it might be possible to find a defence was at its weakest. It was left to a tiny handful of senior figures in Westminster and Whitehall to try to resist the Air Staff argument that defence was futile.

Baldwin's plea for the abolition of bombing had missed the bus. He was already too late for his warning of the horrors of air bombardment to have any practical effect on international negotiations. Japan had already left the League of Nations and the conference in protest at the mildest of rebukes directed at it for aggression in China. Hitler came to power weeks after the speech and soon signalled the proceedings of Geneva held no appeal for his regime. He staged a referendum on League membership as one of his early steps to consolidate his power, which secured an overwhelming rejection. The Nazi regime was going to achieve its goals by its own efforts and not by multilateral discussion. The Disarmament Conference lingered on until 1934 but only because none of its sponsors had the heart to kill it off.

However reluctantly, Britain had to face up to the fact that the League's project to preserve peace was failing, and a return to the classical tools of diplomacy from a position of some kind of military strength was required. In the face of still overwhelming public revulsion at the idea of war, no politician was going to take responsibility for this sea change and the initiative had to come from the military. If the start of rearmament can be said to have an exact beginning it is the decision on 23 March 1932 by the Cabinet to accept the advice of the Chiefs of Staff Committee that the Ten Year Rule was no longer appropriate. The politicians accepted the principle but it was Hankey who was the driving force behind measures to push through the implications. He was prepared to run ahead of the politicians.[5] A Defence Requirements Committee (DRC) was created in the wake of the Chiefs of Staffs' advice, with a remit to define how the services might advance to a greater state of preparedness for war by repairing the 'worst deficiencies'. It comprised the Chiefs of Staffs themselves, Hankey, Sir Warren Fisher, the Head of the Civil Service, and Sir Robert Vansittart, the professional head of the Foreign Office and Whitehall's loudest voice of anxiety at the threat of a resurgent Germany. The DRC deliberated for six months; its discussions presented the unusual spectacle of the senior military figures being almost reluctant to seek extra resources but its civilian members urging them on. One of the military figures of the day has ascribed this to the legacy of a decade in which every penny had been grudged them, creating an atmosphere of desperate resentment. Hankey had his work cut out to chair the DRC; both Fisher and Vansittart were erratic if not unstable figures and there seems to have been as good as no constructive dialogue with or amongst the service leaders.

As war became once again a real, horrible possibility, pacifism began to develop as a distinct political force and not just an unspoken personal instinct. The League of Nations might have been a failing force internationally, but the League of Nations Union, a public advocacy group for transparent and harmonious international relations actually formed before the League itself, with a peak membership of 400,000 was a powerful voice in British politics. The British public was still overwhelmingly anti-war as the stunning victory of a pacifist campaign in the East Fulham by-election in October 1933 demonstrated. The Peace Pledge Union (PPU) was founded in 1934. The Labour Party had been led by the pacifist George Lansbury since 1931 and it was one of the many organizations that supported the PPU's Peace Ballot of 1934/5 in which the overwhelming majority of the 11.6 million people who responded voted for disarmament.

In the space of a few weeks in early 1934 the ground began to shift. After the catastrophe of East Fulham, the government could take comfort from winning a by-election at Portsmouth with no great loss of votes. Moreover, the Conservative candidate, Sir Roger Keyes, was a naval hero of the First World War, who campaigned on an openly pro-defence spending platform.[6] With the League of Nations dying on its feet, Britain found itself unwillingly with the task of preserving peace. France had always a taken a far more hawkish stance towards German rearmament than Britain's but now the massive Stavisky riots in Paris showed France in a situation of near-civil war and unlikely to be able to play a worthwhile part of any kind in diplomacy. Britain was left with the miserable task of bilateral diplomacy to keep some form of constructive dialogue open and was almost immediately confronted with the reality of dealing with Hitler. Hitler had cancelled a visit to Berlin by Sir John Simon, the British Foreign Secretary, feigning rage at a modest increase in Britain's defence budget that had been made in response to Germany's – far greater and then still illicit – rearmament. The actual British proposals for RAF spending were decidedly modest with the RAF putting forward only a tiny increase in spending: £130,000, less than £20 million in today's values. The DRC had just submitted its report, but it would take some time for its bolder recommendations to work their way through the system and neither the Air Staff nor Londonderry, the air minister, had caught the change in sentiment. This left the government exposed to a new and powerful voice to speak in favour of rearmament. Winston Churchill had fought a long and bitter campaign against the India Act, which was supposed to grant India a small measure of self-government, but the campaign was near to failure and Churchill needed a new platform. He had begun to harry the government on the menace posed by Germany even whilst the India campaign was still live, but he now made his first high-profile criticism of the government's defence spending: Churchill leapt on the modesty of the proposed increase in RAF spending in the House of Commons debate on the Air Estimates. The figure of £130,000 was perfect for Churchill's technique of bludgeoning repetition: small and otiosely precise. The reply that Baldwin made to this was to shape the political dimension of air rearmament for the next four years and more.

Baldwin spoke for little more than ten minutes but his words were fateful. He was still publicly pinning his hopes on Geneva, but now accepted that the country had to have a fall-back,

> In conclusion, I say that if all our efforts fail, and if it is not possible to obtain this equality in such matters as I have indicated, then any Government of this country – a National Government more than any, and this Government – will

see to it that in air strength and air power this country shall no longer be in a position inferior to any country within striking distance of our shores.[7]

Baldwin did not textually promise 'parity' although he had used the word in far less charged circumstances the year before. Churchill pinned him to a promise by using the word 'parity' repeatedly in his speech so he had set the agenda. Like most of Baldwin's best-remembered speeches, it is unclear how he came to decide on what he was going to say. There is no indication that he discussed it with his colleagues even though he was speaking for the government. Of course, there was no agreement as to precisely what parity meant, but the government was now firmly on the hook. Britain had just blundered into an arms race.

Chapter 10

A Pretty Bad Half Section – Scheme A

The Committee for Imperial Defence was Britain's topmost military planning body, which operated in an undefined parallel process to the Cabinet itself. It had no statutory authority but its status was never seriously questioned. Apart from the prime minister no one had a right to membership and even this was nowhere written down. Its members were an ad-hoc collection of politicians, military men, civil servants and, occasionally, figures from outside public service. Its vast network of sub-committees embraced practically every aspect of defence. The Chiefs of Staff committee which brought together the professional heads of the three armed services was one of them. The key figure in the whole structure was Colonel Sir Maurice Hankey, secretary to both the Committee of Imperial Defence and the Cabinet itself, as well as the head of the small secretariat that serviced both bodies. Hankey had held the first job for almost twenty-five years and was the mightiest figure in the whole Whitehall machine.

The man to whom it fallen to present the RAF's case at the DRC and who was to have the task of implementing the plan that arose from it was Sir Edward Ellington, who had been Chief of the Air Staff since May 1933. Ellington goes down as one of the least impressive service leaders Britain has ever produced. Like many of the early officers of the RFC and RAF, he had been taught to fly at his own expense but stayed in the Royal Artillery for the first years of the First World War when he saw his only combat service. He transferred to the RFC in 1917 where he served in a number of staff jobs. He never flew operationally or commanded units in combat. During the 1920s his career flourished with appointments as AOC Middle East, India and Iraq, culminating in the number two job in the service as chief of the Air Defence of Great Britain, the RAF's metropolitan air force of fighters and bombers. He had been a well-backed candidate to replace Trenchard in 1929. Clearly Trenchard held him in some esteem in this phase of his career. It was only after Ellington lost the battle to keep shipborne aviation out of the hands of the Royal Navy in 1937 which Trenchard had waged ferociously and successfully, that Trenchard came to despise him openly and vocally.[1]

It is practically impossible to find anyone who had anything positively complimentary to say about Ellington. Ellington's colleague, Air Marshal Sir Wilfrid Freeman, one of the most distinguished architects of the RAF in the Second World War, described him as 'the worst CAS we ever had. He never pulled a single unofficial string. He was not only a misanthrope but he never made the least attempt to do his job or get to know politicians. He pretended to despise them but was, in fact, frightened of them'.[2] John Slessor, then a rising star on the Air Staff, found Ellington utterly uncommunicative.[3] Ellington's performance on the DRC was unimpressive; the future Lieutenant-General Sir Henry Pownall, who served as its secretary, described him as 'extremely weak in discussion and his utterance most confused':[4]

> is very unconvincing and, from the point of view of Secretary, difficult to deal with. And he is a cheerless cove. In eleven meetings I have never once seen him smile nor heard make a cheerful remark to anyone.

Ellington performed no better in regular meetings of the Chiefs of Staff.[5] Edward Bridges, a rising star in the Treasury, felt he was incapable of holding his own against the other service chiefs and Sir Warren Fisher's later contempt for the leadership of the RAF was fed by his experiences on the DRC.[6] Ellington's civil service private secretary for most of his time in office, then plain Maurice Dean, passed the worrying judgement for the head of a service rooted in technology that was undergoing immense and rapid change, that Ellington, 'despite splendid qualities [as a staff officer] knew little about aviation as it existed in the mid-Thirties'.[7] Ellington had rather eccentric ideas about aircraft development and bemoaned the fact that speed was becoming a requirement. He associated speed with running away rather than fighting it out. He wanted the experimental fighters being built around the then new 1,000-horsepower Merlin engine – the origins of the Hurricane and Spitfire – to have movable front guns rather than the maximum performance possible.[8] Fortunately, the Air Staff's collegial approach to aircraft design meant this idea went no further. The best that can be said of Ellington is that he was not blindly conservative so did not positively obstruct some of the developments that strengthened the RAF in the Second World War.[9] He was also greatly taken with the American Boeing heavy bomber design which led to the B-17 Flying Fortress and this contributed to the RAF's own big bomber policy.

Freeman's judgement of Ellington was wide of the mark in one important detail. He might have been awed by politicians in general but he did entirely dominate the one politician with whom he worked most directly, the air minister Lord Londonderry. If Ellington was a candidate for the worst CAS, Londonderry was a candidate for being the worst service minister ever. He had been included in the 'National' government of 1931 because his wife, a great hostess, had assiduously cultivated the prime minister James Ramsay Macdonald, playing on his loneliness and growing infatuation with the grand aristocratic world. Londonderry himself had no political claim on office or particular capacity. He was an immensely rich hereditary peer with huge landholdings and coalmines, whose most notable act had been to complain when the Prince of Wales, later Edward VIII, spoke out against the appalling living conditions of coalminers. His presence in the Cabinet was a throwback to an earlier era of politics; Baldwin's confidant, J. C. C. Davison, marked him down as a 'soft Regency beau type'.[10] Admittedly Londonderry was a naive enthusiast for air matters and held a flying licence, but he was devoid of technical knowledge of modern military aviation. He accepted unquestioningly the judgement of his professional advisers, naturally including Ellington. This might not have mattered had he been able to represent the Air Ministry effectively in Cabinet and committee. Baldwin, the dominant figure in the government, seems to preferred to deal with the Air Ministry through talking to its chief civil servant rather than directly with Londonderry.[11] Neville Chamberlain, who as Chancellor of the Exchequer, had the opportunity to observe the duo's attempts to frame a defence budget, complained, 'The Air Ministry is hopeless. Poor Charlie Londonderry means well but he never does himself justice & Ellington makes us all despair.'[12] In the words of Pownall, who saw Ellington and Londonderry in operation over the DRC, they 'must be a pretty bad half section'.[13]

Chamberlain's verdict on the top leadership of the Air Ministry was echoed even more broadly and damningly by his private secretary: 'nobody who is acquainted with the Air Ministry has confidence in the present direction either civil or military' and it was 'lamentable that we should not have men of the highest calibre at the head of the Air Ministry and the Air Force'.[14] This blanket condemnation suggests that even the Air Ministry's civil servants, its high-profile Permanent Secretary Sir Christopher Bullock in particular, had a poor reputation in Whitehall.

The feebleness of the Air Ministry was unredeemed. As an English peer Londonderry could not defend the government's policy in the House of Commons and the task fell to his junior minister, Sir Philip Sassoon – the fabulously rich scion of the Sephardi banking family that produced the war poet Siegfried Sassoon – who was almost equally lightweight as a politician. Both he and Londonderry used their great wealth to become conspicuously active society hosts. To an even greater extent than Londonderry, Sassoon relished the company – and perhaps more – of glamorous junior RAF officers, who were frequent visitors to his lavish Kent mansion to the amazement of the MP, diarist and arch-snob 'Chips' Channon who was no stranger to sexual ambiguity himself.[15]

Ellington made a poor job of representing the RAF on the DRC. The strongest voice on the DRC in favour of increasing spending on the RAF was actually Sir Robert Vansittart's, the Foreign Office representative. He was fiercely anti-German and acutely aware of the need not to let the Luftwaffe outdistance the RAF. He was supported by Sir Warren Fisher, the Head of the Civil Service, who would later criticize bitterly the Air Ministry's handling of rearmament. By contrast, the navy made a more aggressive bid for resources and enjoyed the tacit support of Hankey, the committee's chairman. The First Sea Lord Chatfield was forceful and effective, the only service member of the committee to impress. Ellington went so far as to issue a muted protest at the committee's conclusions that fell short of a dissenting report.[16]

The discussion of the DRC report got under way in the first half of 1934 in an atmosphere of poorly focused confusion. Even the normally staid official record made by Hankey's secretariat occasionally drips with sarcasm at the obstacles in the way of serious decision-making.[17] The problem started with the absence of the two top men in the government, Macdonald and Baldwin, from the discussions; they were bogged down in the procedural minutiae of the Parliamentary Privileges affair, triggered by Churchill in his rearguard action against the India Act. But the most susprising aspect of the discussions is the manifest lack of enthusiasm on the part of the RAF to undertake large-scale expansion and its seemingly inexhaustible fund of reasons for not doing so. Londonderry had set out with no higher ambition than the completion of the fifty-two-squadron programme for the metropolitan RAF of 1923.[18]

Ellington was the chief foot-dragger. He even managed to shrug off the first serious intelligence pointing to the the Luftwaffe's aggressive plans for expansion. Looking back to the genesis of the 1923 programme, he saw 'no reason to suppose that a German Air Force in 5 years time [1939] will be more formidable, than the French were in 1923'.[19] Neither Ellington nor his deputy Edgar Ludlow-Hewitt saw any urgent need for action and singularly failed to see any menace in German rearmament. The Air Ministry's intelligence experts provided the DRC with a figure for a Luftwaffe at a current strength of 338 aircraft in early 1934 but held back from any projections of its future growth. Both the CAS and his deputy refused to accept that the Luftwaffe could be built up to a menacing size even by 1939, despite reputable evidence that that was what the Germans intended to do. In May 1934 a report from French intelligence triggered a step towards a reliable forecast of Luftwaffe growth. The French report pointed to a Luftwaffe with a total strength of some 500 aircraft in the autumn of 1935, already a significant increase on the Air Ministry's base figure. Even more alarmingly, the report pointed towards an ultimate figure three or four times this size. The British accepted the figure for the near future, but Ludlow-Hewitt argued successfully against a longer-range figure towards the top of the range. He even advanced a Luftwaffe bomber strength of merely 600 bombers in 1939. The British were applying their own mental image of how an air force should be built up from near scratch and attached a higher priority to quality than to mere numbers. Lurking behind this was the unstated conviction that in the fifteen years of its existence the RAF had created an organization of quite unrivalled professionalism which the Germans would naturally adopt as a model in the light of their national cult of efficiency. The French might be in the right ballpark as to eventual size of the Luftwaffe but in the Air Staff's eyes it would take them a long time to get there. In their official advice to the Cabinet, they did not quite follow Ludlow-Hewitt's extreme conservatism, but did forecast that only in 1942 would the Luftwaffe be able to field an 'efficient' force of 1,230. This was the striking force on which the Air Staff based its projection for the scale of a potential German attack on Britain. It was comfortingly remote but steered short of outright complacency.[20]

Ellington was wildly optimistic as to the pace at which the Luftwaffe would expand. His confidence was only tenuously rooted in intelligence and rested essentially on his prescriptive assesssment of the German national character. He could accept that Germany might reach the first stage set out in the French report and form an 'air division' (*Luftflotte*, the top-level formation in the Luftwaffe structure) by October 1935 and a further three or four subsequently, but

> *assuming they aim at a reasonable degree of efficiency* it is unlikely that they can form a second before 1939 and the others at intervals of three years ... This must be regarded as a maximum rate since it must be assumed that a nation so admittedly thorough as Germany will not be content with a mere window dressing collection of aircraft and pilots [author's italics].[21]

The Germans would have to recruit and train senior officers which would take at least five years. Only then could

> an air force can be properly organised into units ... and evolve tactical and strategical doctrines based upon war training and exercises without which no military service can be fitted for war. Bearing in mind the importance which Germany attaches to an adequate air force we can assume that they will go to great lengths to realize their plans at the earliest possible moment, but they cannot achieve the impossible. There is a limit to the emergency measures which can resorted to under peace conditions, even when account is taken of the incalclualable potential derived from the drive and enthusiasm of the Nazi movement.[22]

Ellington was quite frank about the importance of assumption in his analysis, but he was looking in the mirror of RAF experience through a haze of belief in 'Teutonic efficiency'; that the German's would do exactly what the RAF did through the 1920s to rebuild their air force, but even more slowly because that was the way they did things. He took it for granted that Germany would have to devote the same time and effort to creating an autonomous air force staff bureaucracy that it had taken to create the mechanisms of Adastral House. He overlooked the fact that Germany would simply apply the structures, methods and personnel of its legendary army general staff, and do the job far faster. He mistook the political ambition that Göring expressed though the Luftwaffe for something akin to Trenchard's ambition to build a free-standing military service. The inability to recognize that the Luftwaffe enjoyed a far closer relationship with the German army was a perennial weakness in RAF thinking.

Ellington was dangerously complacent towards the threat posed by Hitler's regime. He might have understood the force of Nazism, but he underestimated just how much it was capable of ignoring convention and revolutionizing economic and military practices and, more crucially, did not appreciate how firmly entrenched it had become. Worst of all, Ellington entertained – to modern eyes – preposterously optimistic hopes for Germany's political future. He saw no 'certainty that the present régime in Germany will still be in existence in twelve months' time' and believed it could fall and be replaced by a 'more democratic form of government'.[23] Ellington seemed to think that even if this happy scenario did not manifest itself there could be some 'effective moderation of the existing dictatorial control'. In the 1930s military men appeared to think that their opinions on political developments abroad were every bit as valid as anyone else's. It would have been interesting to see his reaction if a British diplomat in Berlin had advised a particular course of action based on his own, unsupported predictions for the development of military aviation.

Under the Ellington/Londonderry regime at Adastral House peacetime standards were not to be compromised in the expansion programme. Ellington aimed for the double goal of ensuring that quality was not diluted and preventing the onward march of technology from wasting resources. To add the twenty-five extra squadrons within five years to meet even the 1923 programme would have required expedients in terms of temporary accommodation and 'changes in the conditions of training and recruitment which the Air Ministry could only accept with reluctance'.[24] The Air Staff was anxious not to let the politicians force it into building up large inventories of obsolescent aircraft, which might have to be thrown on the scrapheap without ever having been used. This effect was magnified by what might otherwise have been a praiseworthy piece of military prudence in the Air Staff's policy. It insisted on backing the front-line strength of its combat squadrons ('initial equipment' in its jargon) with large reserves, so investing in extra aircraft would double down the bet on types of aircraft currently in production. For each aircraft deployed, the Air Staff wanted one or more held in reserve to meet attritition as and when war started. In another dimension to his conservatism Ellington feared the dilution of the RAF's ambiance by overhasty expansion, which might involve the recruitment of 'an indifferent class of man to officer the force'.[25]

The technology factor was especially strong in 1934 and Ellington was clearly aware of it. Aircraft development went largely unmentioned in the debate over the DRC recommendations, quite possibly because the debate was so vexed that the Air Staff had no clear idea how to manage the conflicting goals of achieving the greatest output and the most modern designs. Partly because of the uncertainty over what would be allowed in future aircraft created by the Geneva talks, there was a significant lag in the RAF's development programme. Even the 1932 generation of designs – the Battle, Hampden and Wellington – were some years away from being introduced into squadron service, which was still an active concern in 1937 when the Air Staff was planning the next expansion scheme.[26] The RAF did not even have designs for a new heavy bomber to hand and Ellington – whatever his civilian secretary Dean might have thought later – knew that other countries were already building more advanced aircraft. Ellington even wanted Britain to buy a specimen large, advanced American aircraft to learn from their experience.[27] He knew that the process of designing Britain's next heavy bomber would have to be done far faster than such things had been done in the past. He was warned that it would take until late 1937 to bring new designs into service.[28]

The Air Staff's reservations were doomed to be overridden. The sands of time were running out for Londonderry, Ellington's ally in his obstinately complacent conservatism. His patron, the prime minister Ramsay Macdonald, was riven by fears of an arms race coupled with futile hopes that Geneva might come back from the dead and rescue the situation, but Macdonald's two senior Conservative colleagues, Stanley Baldwin and Neville Chamberlain, were prepared to push for action. Macdonald was anyway a spent force politically. The National Government was ever more obviously a Conservative government with token Labour and Liberal support and a purely figurehead Labour prime minister. Macdonald was also fading mentally. Baldwin was acutely aware of public concern at the threat from Germany and had placed himself firmly on the hook with his pledge of parity.[29] He wanted the maximum deterrence even at the expense of the Air Staff's desire for reserves. Chamberlain was equally keen on deterrence and to him the RAF offered the best value method to achieve it. He sounded positively Trenchardian when he set out his vision:

> Our best defence would be the existence of a strong deterrent force so powerful as to render success in attack too doubtful to be worth while. I submit that this is most likely to be attained by the establishment of an Air Force based in this country of a size and efficiency calculated to inspire respect in the mind of a possible enemy.[30]

Chamberlain's favourable view of the RAF was a relative one, rooted in a sense of priorities. He was a conservative finance minister, determined to preserve Britain's financial strength which was only slowly recovering from the Great Slump; the real, ever-present concern was that a misstep would damage the economy and this was not a risk he wanted to take to ward off a military threat that might never become a real one. He slashed the total extra spending recommended by the DRC from £76.8 million to £50.3 million but kept the RAF's share intact at £20 million. The RAF would get its thirty-three extra squadrons for home defence.[31] On closer examination, though, the scheme shows the hand of a cautious finance minister as much as that of an enthusiast for deterrence. One-third of the spending was to fall in 1938, the last year of the programme. The plan to expand the RAF as it was approved by the Cabinet was chiefly Chamberlain's handiwork. In the words of Chamberlain's biographer, his strategy 'effectively established the defence agenda for the next five years'.[32] Chamberlain saw Germany as the greater threat than Japan and the RAF was the best defence. There was no serious thought of sending a large army to the Continent to challenge Germany's might on land, so the army came last. The Royal Navy's mission to protect the Empire, against Japan in the Far East above all, fell in the middle.

The plan was the first of a series of expansion schemes for the RAF that succeeded each other over the five remaining years of peace, designated by letters of the alphabet. This was Scheme A and one aspect of it shows just how the balance of power had swung to the politicians from the airmen. Of all the schemes advanced by the Air Staff, it was the only one to depart from the historic 2:1 ratio in favour of bombers. The number of bomber squadrons was to be increased by half but the number of fighter squadrons was more than doubled from thirteen to twenty-eight. Fighters would make up more than 40 per cent of the total for both classes of combat aircraft. Ellington had tried vainly to resist this and hold the number of fighter squadrons at seventeen.[33] The increased ranges of German bombers meant that the area that they could now attack included the Midlands and some of the North. The Air Staff had been caught out by its mantra that the number of fighters it required was fixed by the area that the RAF had to defend.

The Air Staff could console itself for the bias in favour of fighters with the thought that it would not have wanted to order many more of the type of bomber that featured in Scheme A. Twenty-two of the total home bomber squadrons under the scheme were to be light bombers: Harts and Hinds, biplanes with open cockpits and fixed undercarriages.[34] They did not remotely have sufficient range to reach Germany from bases in Britain. Their only merit was that they were cheap to manufacture and reliable. In practice they would serve as training aircraft to allow the RAF to expand its cadre of aircrew.

Such was Britain's first attempt at rearming to face down Nazi Germany in the air. Chamberlain had cast the RAF in the star role but Scheme A fell well short of what the Air Staff wanted. Bemoaning the lack of reserves, Hankey dismissed it as 'a politician's window-dressing scheme'.[35]

Chapter 11

A Malay Running Amok

Scheme A did its job as a short-term fix to a problem in the transient world of domestic politics. It acknowledged public concern at the threat from the air posed by Germany's air force and sent a signal that the government was going to re-equip the RAF. It also started the process that forced the RAF out of the inactive torpor of the Londonderry/Ellington regime in which the preservation of the 'best flying club in the world' in all its glory was the lodestar of military planning. The Air Staff's collective mind was set to considering what might actually be necessary to shape an air force fit for purpose in the modern world; the RAF of Scheme A was certainly no such thing and never came to have much more than a paper existence. It singularly failed to deter Hitler from pursuing his policy of rearming Germany and generally dismantling the obnoxious aspects of the Versailles settlement.

Churchill is supposed to have said, 'Alas, poor Baldwin. History will not be kind to him. And I shall make sure of that. For I shall write that history.' Churchill's remorseless enthusiasm for rearmament and hostility to Hitler today appears vastly more creditable than Baldwin's caution; Baldwin was never an inspiring leader. But Churchill was in practice an opposition politician and Baldwin bore the responsibilities and reality of government. Above all, Baldwin had to operate in a public political environment where hostility to war was the dominant force. He was fortunate that the opposition was weak and divided, which left the National Government room for manoeuvre. Britain in the 1930s stands in dramatic contrast to France, where weak and corrupt right-wing governments alternated with left-wing governments, whose unrealistic and idealistic plans were doomed to failure. Churchill deserves credit for recognizing that Hitler was a dangerous and implacable enemy to Britain, but his campaign against government air policy was barely constructive and, in one respect at least, downright harmful.

The announcement of Scheme A served to expose publicly the yawning cracks between the government's various opponents on the issue of rearmament generally and air rearmament in particular. The Labour Party put up a particularly weak showing. Sentiment within the party still reflected the more-or-less unconditional pacifism of its leader, George Lansbury, and this weighed heavily on the harder-headed Clement Attlee who was to succeed Lansbury the following year, 1935. Attlee took refuge from the substance of the rearmament debate in pure wishful thinking: there was no reason to rearm at all because Hitler's regime was fading away. The scheme was also attacked by the ever-less relevant opposition Liberals in a desperate, dying attempt to carve out a distinctive platform before they drowned in their own irrelevance. Their criticism of the government's policy barely registered and their leader, Sir Herbert Samuel, did Baldwin a great favour by a savage attack on Churchill's enthusiasm for greater air spending, which expressed sentiments shared by many mainstream Conservatives, but could not be endorsed by the party's leaders because Churchill was still playing the card of party loyalty:

> Utterly regardless of any question of what parity really means in terms of airplanes and other equipment, utterly regardless of any needs of the situation, he [Churchill] comes forward and tells the nation that we ought straightway to double and redouble our Air Force, that we ought to have an Air Force four times as big as we have now, without giving the smallest reasons why this colossal expenditure should immediately be undertaken. That is rather the language of a Malay running amok than of a responsible British statesman; it is rather the language of blind and causeless panic. The House of Commons ought surely in these matters to have some regard to the public finances.[1]

Samuel did Baldwin the double service of creating an opening for one of Baldwin's more successful pieces of rhetoric to market the National Government's conversion to moderate rearmament in vivid and comforting terms:

> Let us never forget this; since the day of the air, the old frontiers are gone. When you think of the defence of

England you no longer think of the chalk cliffs of Dover; you think of the Rhine. [HON. MEMBERS: 'Hear, Hear.'] That is where our frontier lies.[2]

Chamberlain's strong-arming of the Cabinet over the DRC's recommendations had put air rearmament at the top of the agenda for defence spending. In the world of practical politics, the combination of Baldwin's parity promise and the image of the Rhine as England's new frontier, set the tone for the public debate of the issue. The National Government's credibility on defence policy would stand or fall by its performance on the RAF.

Baldwin's attention to the German air menace played well with the public, but deep inside Whitehall he faced a serious potential challenge to the priority that the government was giving to the RAF. Hankey had been baulked in his attempt to push through a pro-Royal Navy scheme as an immediate response to the DRC advice, but he was keeping up the pressure on Baldwin and, in the process, sounding positively Ellingtonian in his optimism about the German air threat: 'The peril is there all right but it will take much more than 2 years to develop in the military and air sense.'[3]

If anyone had ever hoped that Scheme A would provide a long-term solution to the German air menace, this was exploded a few months later. The blow was delivered by the French intelligence service which ratcheted up its projection for Luftwaffe expansion plans. The Germans would not pause in the growth of the Luftwaffe and would add even more strength in their programme for the year ending October 1936 than in the programme for the year before. The French estimate for end October 1935 had been 500 first-line machines split across thirty bomber, six fighter and five reconnaissance squadrons.[4] A year later they now expected 1,300 aircraft in sixty bomber, eighteen fighter and twenty-one reconnaissance squadrons.[5] Just as their first estimate had complicated British thinking by arriving in the middle of the discussion of the DRC advice, the new figures arrived shortly before the government was due to face the House of Commons again on its air policy. The new data found its way into a Committee of Imperial Defence report that was presented to a Cabinet committee only a few days before the debate was scheduled.[6]

Unknown to the government inside information on its intelligence on the German air threat was being leaked to Churchill who was soon to step up his campaign on air rearmament and to start to criticize the government on the issue. He was being fed data by Major Desmond Morton, head of the Industrial Intelligence Centre and one of the hawks within the intelligence community.[7] Churchill had already given notice that he would be challenging the government's performance in the debate. Just over a week before it was due, he broadcast on the BBC warning in stark terms of the danger that Germany posed and the need to rearm the RAF to counter the threat:

> Now they [the Germans] are rearming with the utmost speed, and ready to their hands is the new lamentable weapon of the air, against which our navy is no defence, and before which women and children, the weak and frail, the pacifist and the jingo, the warrior and the civilian, the front line trenches and the cottage home, all lie in equal and impartial peril …
>
> First, we must without another day's delay begin to make ourselves at least the strongest air power in the European world. By this means we shall recover to a very large extent the safety which we formerly enjoyed through our navy, and through our being an island.[8]

Churchill was putting his own judgement ahead of both family and party. Privately Churchill was muttering about 'that half-wit Charlie Londonderry' who was his cousin so family loyalty counted equally little.

In the debate itself Churchill challenged Baldwin's parity pledge head on. Without giving any explanation for the source of his belief, he claimed Germany's air force would very soon be equal to Britain's, half as big again by the end of 1936 and almost double the size in 1937. He insinuated that British aircraft were slower than foreign – and so, German – ones. Baldwin met Churchill's challenge head on and chose to nail the government's colours very firmly to the mast, in practice claiming that its policies had brought safety. He went beyond dull Ellingtonian complacency and delivered detailed claims for the progress that was being made:

> Germany is actively engaged in the production of service aircraft, but her real strength is not 50 per cent. of our strength in Europe to-day. As for the position this time next

year, if she continues to execute her air programme without acceleration and if we continue to carry out at the present approved rate the expansion announced to Parliament in July ... so far from the German military air force being at least as strong as and probably stronger than our own, we estimate that we shall still have in Europe a margin – in Europe alone – of nearly 50 per cent.[9]

The exchange between the de facto head of the government and his leading, if not sole, internal critic pushed to the top of the political agenda the question of whether Britain's air force was sufficiently strong in the face of Germany's new and still formally illicit air force. The debate attracted favourable comment outside Parliament.

Public fears were intense. The ground was ready for what came to be called 'The Air Panic of 1935' and there was plenty of seed available to guarantee a healthy crop.[10] Even Churchill's pessimism was not as extreme as some figures for the Luftwaffe's strength that were being bandied around. Just as Churchill had moved on from his India campaign of the early 1930s to the air issue, Baldwin's enemies in the press took it up in the wake of their defeat over Empire Free Trade. Leading the pack was Lord Rothermere who believed firmly that Germany had 10,000 aircraft or more and repeated the claim in his newspapers, including the *Daily Mail*, Britain's biggest-selling newspaper at the start of the decade. There was a deeply personal edge to this battle. Rothermere and his ally Beaverbrook had been defeated by Baldwin when they attempted to hijack policy over Empire free trade. Baldwin's rebuke that the press barons aimed for 'power without responsibility ... the prerogative of the harlot' was chiefly aimed at Beaverbrook but applied also to Rothermere. Air strength provided Rothermere with a convenient, popular cause on which to assail Baldwin and he took the campaign beyond his newspapers by sponsoring the National League of Airmen to promote the cause politically. Further fuel was added by – amongst many others – the wealthy far-right eccentric Lucy, Lady Houston, who owned the *Saturday Review*, and General Groves, co-author of the French war scare of 1923, who pitched in with *Behind The Smokescreen*, an alarmist book about air warfare in 1934.

Behind the mounting public fears, faint hopes did remain of some kind of diplomatic solution to the impasse with Germany and in early

1935 the French proposed what came to be known as the Air Locarno, after the agreement between Britain, France, Belgium, Italy and Germany of 1926 which had settled the worst of the tensions left in the wake of Versailles Treaty. The signatories would use their air forces together to punish any other signatory who opened a bombing war. It was vaguely similar to a plan Chamberlain had floated under the name 'limited liability' and equally doomed. Hitler made non-committal supportive noises. It was agreed to send Sir John Simon, the Foreign Secretary, to Berlin to extend the discussions in response to a German invitation, but before he could make the journey, Hitler dropped two bombshells. The existence of the Luftwaffe was confirmed publicly and Germany introduced conscription in March 1935; Hitler had decided to abandon any pretence that the removal of demilitarization clauses of the Versailles Treaty were a matter for negotiation of any kind.

Undaunted by Hitler's moves, the British still hoped that bilateral conversations with Germany might yet bring about some settlement and sent their delegation off to Berlin after a gentle protest and a token postponement. By some measures this was the first step in the policy of attempting constructive dialogue with Hitler that came to bear, as a label of shame, the term 'appeasement'. Predictably enough, the visit by Simon and Anthony Eden, the then junior Foreign Office minister, achieved nothing whatever. Hitler followed up his demonstration of contempt for negotiating with democratic statesmen with a brutal claim for how far he had already got in unilaterally building Germany's military strength and how great his ambitions still were.[11] He then dropped a third and even more spectacular bombshell. After insisting that Germany should have an air force as large as the France's combined European and North African units, which he put at 2,000 aircraft, he stated bluntly that the German air force had already reached the same size as Britain's. When the British Air Attaché asked for clarification afterwards, he was told officially that Hitler had meant parity with an RAF first-line strength of 800–850 aircraft.[12] At a stroke Hitler had demonstrated the impotence of the democratic statesmen and made one of their leaders appear fatuously out of touch with reality. To support his drive to emphasize the threat that Germany posed, Sir Robert Vansittart, the Foreign Office's germanophobe chief, leaked Hitler's claim to the press which brought it firmly into public consciousness and left Baldwin wriggling on the hook of his parity pledge.

The RAF's intelligence department looked as though it had allowed itself to be caught on the hop by the Germans, leaving the politicians to face the public embarrassment of recycling their complacency. It was not a promising beginning for intelligence professionals and it got worse as a vigorous battle developed in the corridors of power as to what the correct figures were. Sir Robert Vansittart led the charge from the Foreign Office with his suspicious view of the pace of German rearmament. He accused the Air Staff of attempting to resurrect the Ten Year Rule with its insistence that the Luftwaffe would not be ready for war until 1942.[13] The opposed parties fought out what the pioneering historian of the intelligence dimension to relations with Nazi Germany described as '[a] vigorous battle of half-truths'.[14] The prime minister Ramsay Macdonald had to intervene to bring in a measure of harmony on an issue he described as 'far too serious for interdepartmental friction'.[15] This produced a classic fudged compromise: the Air Ministry's figures would be accepted as hard data but urged that the position be monitored closely. But having been hustled into the unfamiliar exercise of working out how fast and extensively the Germans were going to pursue their threatening expansion, the Air Staff would be in no hurry to go further in the near future.

Chapter 12

An Air Minister Bypassed – Scheme C

By the early months of 1935, Londonderry was, politically, a dead man walking. He was a political liability amongst his colleagues and the public. He was the minister responsible for the most important part of Britain's defence policy that had become immeasurably more urgent and crucial, but he was neither driving the rebuilding of the RAF in private nor calming public concern. The government was more than willing – unusually – to provide the finance for him to spend on improving the RAF, but all he did was to try to insist that he (and the Air Staff) had been correct in their assessment of the previous year: that nothing really needed to be done. His removal from office was only a question of when and, in an unusual twist, how.

Londonderry's only remaining political asset was valuable, but distinctly short-dated: his standing with the prime minister Ramsay Macdonald, but Macdonald too was near the end of his political life as he approached the age of 70. His mental faculties were weakening and he appeared increasingly confused. As well as the burden of office with no serious party organization to support him, he had been fending off determined financial blackmail by a former, casual mistress. His only real function was as figurehead for the ever-more hollow pretence that his government was really a national one, rather than a Conservative government, supported by one part of the split Liberal Party and a tiny rump of Labour MPs. The National Government had been in power since 1931 and a general election was imminent. The government would again present itself to the electorate as a truly national government but Macdonald was not the man to lead the campaign. He would step down before the election and once the government had been re-elected under a new prime minister, it would be possible to remove Londonderry as air minister in the ensuing Cabinet reshuffle without the risk of it seeming to be a measure of panic or delivering too obvious a snub to Macdonald.

That was the political timetable, but the need to improve Britain's air defence was too urgent to let it delay the measures that were needed. Stanley Baldwin as leader of the Conservative Party was de facto the deputy prime minister and the true head of the government and he knew that action was required. He knew that the mood of the British people was still profoundly anti-war as the Peace Ballot and a string of by-elections won by anti-rearmament candidates showed, but it is misleading to think that this determined a government policy of reluctance to rearm. Baldwin knew that Britain had to rearm; the public mood was a complication not a decisive factor. Baldwin's image as slothful and indecisive is false; his acute sense of the importance of political timing too often appeared to be prevarication. When he knew that there was a job that needed to be done and that the moment had arrived, Baldwin was swift and ruthless.

The man that Baldwin wanted to lead the rearmament of the RAF was Sir Philip Cunliffe-Lister, one of his long-term close political allies and, more important, equipped with the right mindset for the task. Marriage had made him independently wealthy and he had had a good war: decorated for bravery at the front and then at the heart of the wartime bureaucracy in the ministry for National Service where his work had earned him a knighthood. He was a minister in every Conservative government after the war, invariably in posts with a strong economic component. He had no direct experience of running a large company, but he had the flavour of a business leader rather than a politician. He was energetic, acerbic and unforgiving of incompetence, but he had been selected for his new task because he could execute it well and not to make friends either personally or politically. Baldwin backed him to the full.

Baldwin opened the campaign to put Cunliffe-Lister in Londonderry's place when the government took its first steps on the tortuous path to using new scientific developments to strengthen Britain's air power. The discussion of science and air warfare had crept on the agenda since the autumn of 1934 from two directions. The Air Ministry's Director of Scientific Research, Harry Wimperis, had been pushing for proper study to be made of a good number of potential applications for scientific development, which led to the creation of an internal Air Ministry committee under a distinguished outside scientist, rector of Imperial College, Professor Henry Tizard. One of its members was Professor Frederick Lindemann, an Oxford professor of no great scientific eminence who like Tizard had been a scientist and experimental pilot in the First

World War. Lindemann entertained enormous personal ambitions and had hitched his star to Churchill, who accepted uncritically his views on scientific questions. Lindemann wanted Tizard's committee to set policy and not just advise and, unsurprisingly, he wanted to dominate its conclusions. Churchill supported Lindemann vigorously. The outcome was to establish in parallel to Tizard's committee a political committee, announced in Parliament in March 1935. Cunliffe-Lister was the chairman of this committee. By coincidence, just as the government was putting in place this flawed and compromised machinery to direct science in air warfare that was to blossom into a battleground of intrigue and bad science, the first practical experiments were being made to test the theory of radar that were to lead to victory in the Battle of Britain.

Londonderry's only faint hope of survival lay in his response to Hitler's parity claim, but the Air Staff responded to Hitler's boast and the responses to subsequent British requests for clarification with a paper dripping with complacency and obfuscation.[1] It admitted that the Luftwaffe might indeed have attained a first-line numerical strength as great as the RAF's but proceeded to pour cold water on the military value of what the Germans might have achieved. In the Air Staff's judgement, it would be a 'serious over-statement' to claim that these aircraft were part of 'fully trained and equipped' squadrons. Moreover, this kind of first-line strength could only have been obtained at the expense of, in the Air Staff's eyes, vital reserves. This analysis lay at the heart of the paper's key assertion that, 'Whatever first-line strength Germany may claim we remain today substantially stronger *if all relevant factors are taken into account* [italics in original]'.

After proclaiming that the RAF was maintaining its qualitative superiority to the German air force, the Air Staff proceeded to rewrite the history of its quantitative strength so it would not appear that the RAF had been caught out by the speed of its expansion. In the revised version, the Air Staff had based the calculations for Scheme A on an ultimate German goal of at least 1,500 aircraft and perhaps 2,000, without reminding readers that these figures had been given both tentatively and as part of general background, not as the basis of planning. Against this background the revised estimates of November 1934 triggered by the second tranche of French intelligence were presented as fine-tuning of detail and not, as had been the case, a sharp increase. The revised projection featured a supposedly two-stage programme by the Germans giving a total front-line strength of about 1,300 aircraft in October 1936, eventually expanding to a total strength of 1,500–1,600. Hitler had not been telling Simon and Eden anything that the Air Staff couldn't have told them already. With a further few tweaks the German target was quantified at the suspiciously precise figure of 1,512 aircraft by April 1937. But of course, in the Air Staff's eyes, this would barely count as an air force:

> it will be virtually impossible for [Germany] to produce within that period an air force so fully organised, equipped and trained that it will be adequately prepared for war. [The Air Staff] consider that such a standard cannot be fully attained for a further two years after 1937, and that if our own preparations are designed to ensure parity with Germany by 1939, they will be likely to provide the measure of security which we require.[2]

Once again, the British judgement of what was possible and what was impossible in building an air force was trumping any thought that an aggressive totalitarian nation that had built an air force secretly from scratch in a couple of years, might have the will and ability to go far further. The Air Staff's table for projected German strength showed the 1,512 figure remaining constant from April 1937 to April 1940. As far as it was concerned the German air force had reached a firm limit to its growth.

After one quick sprint, the Germans would present a static target for the British to aim at and the RAF would not need to rush its own expansion programme. The Air Staff did propose an increase in Scheme A in the form of Scheme B, which would nearly double the additional squadrons for the RAF, but the boost to the expansion would occur in a comfortingly remote future. Only four of the extra squadrons would be formed in the year to March 1937, with fourteen then seventeen and a half in the two succeeding years. Clearly there was no urgency and by April 1940 the RAF would have reached comparable size to the Luftwaffe. Here the Air Staff slipped in an important piece of Trenchardian dogma: 'It is in regard to ... the bombing or offensive strength that parity with a possible enemy is essential.'[3] The political commitment to a nebulous measure, was being translated into a firm shopping list for military equipment procurement that reflected the service's doctrine. The parity promise became something of a cross for governments to bear, but it provided a constant raison d'être for the RAF that the dedicated Trenchardians of the Air Staff wanted. It became almost a goal in itself. The key target they set for themselves was to match the sixty-seven bomber squadrons with 804 aircraft that they expected the Germans to have when they reached the magic figure of 1,512 aircraft. The new expansion scheme thus reversed the heretical bias towards fighters of Scheme A and brought the ratio of bombers to fighters back to the 2:1 figure. Twenty of the additional thirty-five and a half squadrons foreseen would be bombers to bring the RAF up to sixty-seven bomber squadrons, exactly the same as Germany.

The Air Staff found another way to wriggle its thumb into the scale to support a lower target number of RAF planes. It argued that because the German army was bigger than Britain's, it would require more army cooperation aircraft. Supporting land armies was a mission that the Air Staff despised and treated as almost a worthless drain on RAF resources. If the Germans were sucked into wasting their resources in this direction, the number of planes involved could safely be excluded from any calculation of real parity.

Londonderry endorsed the handiwork of his professional advisers as evidence that there were 'no grounds whatsoever for anything in the nature of panic' as 'We are at present, and for the next three years, at least far ahead of the German Air Force in efficiency'.[4] He had signed his own political death warrant. When Scheme B and the supporting estimates of Luftwaffe strength and plans were presented to the Defence Requirements Committee, Londonderry and Ellington were given a chilly reception and put a woefully inadequate defence of the Air Staff's plans. Sir John Simon, possibly still smarting from his shock in Berlin, told them bluntly that Scheme B simply failed to offer parity. Ellington was consistently negative and pessimistic, always ready with explanations of why the RAF could not possibly expand rapidly. The meeting decided to appoint a sub-committee to look into how parity might actually be achieved. This was most emphatically not an instance of an issue being kicked down the road by setting up a new body; it was tantamount to taking responsibility for a crucial piece of RAF policy away from the air minister and the CAS. Neither was on the new three-member sub-committee which was chaired by one of the most aggressive and well-briefed critics of Scheme B, Sir Philip Cunliffe-Lister.

The RAF's destiny had been taken out of its hands. In the words of Cunliffe-Lister's biographer, 'It is difficullt [sic] to see what greater snub could have been offered to Londonderry as the Minister responsible for the Air Ministry and the RAF than that both these appointments should have gone to a Cabinet colleague whose departmental responsibilities were only marginally connected with air matters.'[5] (Swinton was then Colonial Secretary). Intentionally or otherwise, bypassing Londonderry as minister also bypassed the Air Ministry and the Air Staff. Air war, or the preparation for air war, was too important to leave to the air marshals. Not that Ellington had displayed any serious claim as a military leader.

Immediately the Air Parity Committee had been established Cunliffe-Lister set to work intensively and produced two papers for the Defence Requirements Committee setting out his view of what the RAF required, a full-scale alternative to Londonderry's Scheme B.[6] Cunliffe-Lister's plan, Scheme C, was debated briefly and approved by the Cabinet with little more conditionality than an admonition that the Air Ministry should get the best professional advice available on contracts and to avoid overpaying.[7] The future of the RAF had been decided by politicians with no direct formal responsibility for the service. This all took place in the astonishingly short space of time of under a fortnight in May 1935. The government was manifestly determined to respond to the German air menace as a matter of urgency and were prepared to back Cunliffe-Lister's programme to the full. Anyone who imagines that the Baldwin government was dragging its feet on rearmament need look no further.

Having stripped Londonderry of the substance of his job, Baldwin proceeded to line up the old regime at the Air Ministry to take the blame for having slept whilst Germany rearmed. After almost two months silence on the topic of Hitler's shattering parity claim, he treated the House to a spurious *mea culpa* in a major debate on defence in May 1935, the day after the Cabinet meeting which had set the seal on Londonderry's elimination from the future of the RAF:

> First of all, with regard to the figure I then gave of German aeroplanes, nothing has come to my knowledge since that makes me think that that figure was wrong. I believed at that time it was right. Where I was wrong was in my estimate of

the future. There I was completely wrong. I tell the House so frankly, because neither I nor any advisers from whom we could get accurate information had any idea of the exact rate at which production was being, could be, and actually was being speeded up in Germany in the six months between November and now. We were completely misled on that subject.[8]

As if to make completely sure that he would be sacked, Londonderry had praised 'air control' as a way to police the Empire with less bloodshed than traditional punitive expeditions in the course of a debate on air rearmament barely a week before the change in government. The critics of his feeble performance as air minister had been mainly his Conservative colleagues, but this ensured that the Labour opposition with its humanitarian pretensions would also be gunning for him.

When Baldwin replaced Macdonald as prime minister a couple of weeks later, he made the well-flagged propitiatory sacrifice. In his inaugural Cabinet reshuffle, he sacked Londonderry as air minister and replaced him with Cunliffe-Lister. Londonderry's feelings were soothed by being given a non-departmental Cabinet job as Lord Privy Seal. As a further sop the word was spread that Baldwin needed an air minister in the House of Commons to present the government's policy on so important a topic. Few people can have paid much attention to this as there was barely a ripple a few months later when Cunliffe-Lister ceased to be an MP on accepting a peerage as Viscount Swinton. He had never been a full-blooded House of Commons man. The move made no difference to the way he conducted the ministry's policy, but it left him vulnerable to Commons criticism, which was to prove fatal to him two and a half years later.

Chapter 13

The Man for Push and Go

Baldwin's scheme to inject vigour into the rearmament of the RAF featured another figure who stood outside the established structures of administration. The Glasgow industrialist Viscount ('Willie') Weir was a self-made man who had built a large company manufacturing pumps, originally for shipbuilding but reaching into most areas of the economy. It still exists as a powerful, independent company today. He was, though, no stranger to the corridors of power. He had been brought into the organization of Britain's first total war economy in the First World War as one of Lloyd George's 'men for push and go', businessmen ruthless and decisive enough to override the sleepy bureaucracies of the armed forces and the civil service. Long before Trenchard espoused them himself, Weir was a powerful advocate of two key features of the RAF's future doctrine: strategic bombing and an independent air force.[1] He succeeded Rothermere as air minister and became arguably Trenchard's most passionate and effective supporter, despite Trenchard's early reservations about an independent RAF. He had no taste for political life and had little patience with any form of directing industry other than autocratic management by the owners of companies or their direct representatives. A direct role for the state in industry was acceptable as a wartime expedient, but no more. He was also an advocate of tanks. Weir resigned his ministership as soon as decently possible and never sought office or even political influence. Nonetheless he became one of the great and good of the land. He gave freely of his time to a clutch of mixed government and industry bodies, covering topics such as air transport, shipping and electricity generation, but the thread of equipping the armed forces correctly and efficiently ran through his doings. At the end of 1933 he was one of three businessmen invited to join an advisory panel to the Principal Supply Officers' Committee, one of the myriad outgrowths of the Committee of Imperial Defence responsible for industrial planning for war.

Weir had a long-established happy working relationship with Cunliffe-Lister and was a natural partner in his campaign to ready the RAF for war. He brought energy, imagination and competence, and also name recognition. Baldwin and Chamberlain knew full well that bringing him into the air rearmament programme would be seen as evidence that the government was finally taking the question seriously. Weir knew this too and negotiated shrewdly over the terms under which he would accept the invitation to help the government. The government was so desperate to sign him up and publish the news that they had little room for manoeuvre. Weir drove a hard bargain but his terms were driven entirely by what he recognized he would need to work effectively; neither self-regard nor money played a part. He knew that his influence would not depend on either status or staff. His role was undefined and officially no more than advisory. He drew no pay, worked from his own flat and his brother was his only direct colleague. No one had any hold him and he was beholden to no man. The only condition he set on his agreement which did not relate to the way in which he operated was that the question of the RAF's relationship with the Royal Navy would not be raised again. Like Trenchard he believed passionately that the RAF should have a complete monopoly over all military aviation. In 1935 the question was peripheral, but this was a time bomb that would explode two years later.

Weir's appointment was welcomed in the informed circles of Westminster and Whitehall, but the wider world still had it reservations. Even the right-wing *Daily Express* saw him as a potentially divisive figure:

> Air-boss Lord WEIR might have been the prototype of one of Galsworthy's industrialists – the big capitalist in 'Strife' perhaps, or a Forsyte of the harder-headed sort ... A stern employer. Uncompromising in trade union matters.[2]

Weir was not just a Trenchardian *avant la lettre*, he was a ministerial special adviser in the same sense. His appointment was an implicit vote of no confidence in the Air Ministry and, to an extent, the Air Staff itself in the same way that Cunliffe-Lister's appointment to his two committees had been a vote of no confidence in Londonderry.

Sir Christopher Bullock, the head civil servant at the Air Ministry, had been a happy partner of Trenchard in his battles to establish the

RAF firmly and keep it independent in the 1920s. Bullock was one of the series of men who served Trenchard by translating his notoriously inarticulate views into effective documents. But after Trenchard retired he kept up the connection and intrigued with him against Hankey.[3] He was high-handed and developed a far-reaching view of his own standing with other departments. Bullock also lobbied back bench politicians directly to support his policies.[4] Londonderry blamed Baldwin for giving Bullock 'an entirely wrong idea of his own importance' because Baldwin had preferred to deal directly with Bullock rather than his Cabinet colleague.[5] Bullock was never a partner of Cunliffe-Lister in the same way that Weir was.

Cunliffe-Lister rapidly imposed his own stamp on the working methods of the Air Ministry with the institution of Expansion Progress Meetings (EPMs) that occurred weekly and sometimes more frequently to oversee the progress of his expansion measures. The meetings continued until the war, but the intensity of their work fell off noticeably when Cunliffe-Lister and Weir left the Air Ministry in 1938. In practice the EPMs were focused meetings of the Air Council, but after Cunliffe-Lister and Weir left, often reverted to being routine meetings. The group addressed the nitty gritty of firm orders for aircraft, whether the aircraft were being delivered and, if not, what was to be done to get them manufactured and delivered. The early EPM minutes read like those of a business organization, not a government department. Almost the first thing that Weir did in his new job was to meet the heads of all the aircraft companies and they were regularly summoned to attend the progress meetings.

Cunliffe-Lister's parity papers had gone much further than arguing that Britain needed a bigger air force sooner; he argued that this would have to be done by revolutionizing aircraft procurement procedures from the leisurely practices that had ruled before. One paper pointed to five separate stages in the process, in particular the need to build and test prototypes of new designs before production in quantity began. Weir believed that this stage was unnecessary, that modern design techniques gave a sufficient picture of an aircraft's performance to make a decision. The Cabinet nodded though one feature in Cunliffe-Lister's programme which gave concrete form to Weir's view and still stands as an emblem of urgent rearmament: the system of ordering aircraft 'off the drawing board'. Volume orders could be issued before a prototype had even flown. Cunliffe-Lister stopped short of a blanket recommendation that the process should be telescoped for all new aircraft, but did single out two designs in the most urgently needed categories where orders should be placed immediately, before the prototypes had been made or tested. The old guard at the Air Ministry was not convinced of the practice and Bullock incurred Weir's displeasure by opposing off-the-drawing-board as a standard practice.[6]

Less eye-catching was the sacrifice of one important element in the Air Ministry's negotiating strength against the industry. The Air Ministry was to move away from its established practice of letting the whole manufacturing process be driven by firm orders only. The Air Ministry would now state its annual programme in advance so that the plane-makers could start to buy in supplies in anticipation of orders or even begin assembling aircraft once they had completed making the planes firmly ordered for a given year.

In his analysis of comparative air strengths Cunliffe-Lister knew that quality was important, not just quantity. Here the Germans were also seen to be well ahead. In particular, he saw the Luftwaffe as far ahead in bombers. In the heavy bomber class, even the better of the RAF's designs, the Fairey Hendons, were slower than the German Junkers 52 and carried barely half the bombload. The RAF had nothing at all to match the Heinkel 70, a civil aircraft that the RAF imagined could be transformed easily into an effective medium bomber. In both cases RAF intelligence overestimated the German designs. The Junkers 52, too, had begun as a civil aircraft and operated only briefly in the bomber role to which it was ill-suited. It did its main service as a transport aircraft until the end of the Second World War. The Heinkel 70 was a badly flawed design which soon disappeared from service. Only in fighters did Cunliffe-Lister see the RAF as holding its own. The Gloster Gauntlet fighter was faster than the Luftwaffe's Heinkel 51 and with a new engine would be even faster. This was to become the Gladiator.

The political imperative to attain parity with Germany was too strong not to play a large part in Scheme C. Cunliffe-Lister explicitly rejected any thought of ducking the need to match German first-line strength on a simple, numerical plane-for-plane basis. He accepted that the yardstick would have to be whatever Hitler had claimed, however suspect this might be. He was entirely sympathetic to the Air Staff's devotion to Trenchardian dogma which placed bombers far above any other class of aircraft in calculating true military strength; this was not a case that could be argued in the political arena, public or parliamentary. The ultimate target first-line strength of the RAF under Scheme C was 1,512, exactly matching the Luftwaffe's projected strength, but other more important considerations were the true determinants. Scheme C aimed to boost the RAF's first-line combat strength by almost half in rather less than two years, adding thirty-six new squadrons to the eighty-seven existing or previously approved. The scheme was dominated by bombers: twenty-seven new squadrons compared to only seven new fighter squadrons. Bomber numbers rose more than 60 per cent to 840 but fighter numbers were set to rise by only a little more than one-third. The imbalance in the financial and industrial terms was even greater. Almost half the new bomber squadrons were to be heavy bombers, which would boost the total number to twenty heavy bomber squadrons from eight. The 2:1 ratio in favour of bombers was being maintained in crude numbers of aircraft in the RAF once the scheme was complete, but the commitment of resources was greater to bombers.

Scheme C aggressively turned its back on the 'window-dressing' of its predecessor. The RAF's new front-line strength was to be backed by full reserves on a peacetime scale. This meant that 3,800 new aircraft, 1,400 more than Scheme B would have to be manufactured in less than two years to achieve the increase in front-line strength that was targeted. This was militarily sound but it did set a high bar for the programme. It implied that the German strength which the British programme strove to match, was being attained on a similarly conservative basis. In reality, British intelligence on the Luftwaffe's expansion stopped well short of a serious appreciation of German reserve policy. Without consideration another piece of worst-case thinking was being hard-baked into British strategy. This added another layer of confusion to a numbers game that hovered between hard military reality and low-grade political grandstanding.

On one point, Cunliffe-Lister bowed to the residue of Scheme A's window-dressing and Air Staff conservativism. He knew that the biplane Hart and Hind light bombers were utterly outclassed and of negligible military value against Germany, but could not yet abandon them entirely. They were cheap and easy to make; the plane-makers were delighted at the profitable prospect of manufacturing more of them. They still had their place in the far-flung corners of the Empire, where they could help enforce air control. The simpler aircraft were more suitable to the needs of the part-time fliers of the Auxiliary Air Force squadrons which were a key component in providing the RAF with trained aircrew. Light bombers would be less important in the Scheme C RAF but there would still be five new squadrons of them – of which three would be Auxiliary – and they would still make up forty-three percent of total bomber numbers. Weir calculated that more than a quarter of the new planes to be made in order to meet the Scheme C target – 1,000 – would be light bombers.[7]

Cunliffe-Lister saw an urgent need to replace the light bombers with modern aircraft and the chosen design was one of the first to be ordered off the drawing board, the Fairey Battle. Cunliffe-Lister consoled himself with a small piece of verbal sleight of hand. Even though the Battle had been specified as a replacement for the Hinds and Harts, it would be classed as a 'medium' bomber. Trivial though this was, it was another small factor that fed the overvaluation of what proved to be one of the most catastrophically bad aircraft ever procured by the RAF. Cunliffe-Lister and Weir were driven by the urgency of their task and long-term considerations took second place. Air Marshal Sir Wilfrid Freeman who played a distinguished role in rearming the RAF accused them of putting quantity ahead of quality.[8] It was an urgent job to replace the Hinds and Harts; the Battles and, soon, the Bristol Blenheims were easily available in quantity so the first phase of re-equipping the RAF's bomber force featured modern aircraft, but ones that were inadequate for their task.

One of the key aspects of the industrial strategy that Weir promoted to prepare Britain for war was the 'shadow factory' scheme under which the government would fund weapons factories that would be operated by businesses, usually from unrelated industries. Shadow factories featured prominently in the re-equipment of the RAF and the choice of aircraft that they produced gives an idea of the priorities accorded to different classes and types. The first two, both operated by car manufacturers, produced bombers: Austin made Battles and Rootes made Blenheims. The Battle was picked for shadow production as it was the only type flying when the scheme was launched.[9] It was only the third shadow factory, which was not even decided on until 1938, that made fighters. The Castle Bromwich factory was to become famous as the chief centre of Spitfire production, but it took much effort and disappointment until then.

It was with a heavy heart that Cunliffe-Lister had ordered more Harts and he was similarly unhappy to include orders for existing designs of heavy bombers in the scheme. The RAF's inventory of this class of aircraft was not a spectacularly antique as in its light bombers, but was far from truly modern. Most of the extra aircraft were to be the ungainly fixed undercarriage Handley Page Heyford biplanes, which had entered service the year before, although the Air Staff hoped that marginally more modern Fairey Hendon monoplanes could be built instead. But even if the choice should fall on the Hendons, this was not the real future of the bomber force. Alongside the off-the-drawing-board order for Fairey Battles, Scheme C envisaged an order off-the-drawing-board for forty Whitleys, a truly modern aircraft. Just as the design order that led to the Whitley had short-circuited the Air Ministry procurement system in 1934, the Whitley itself would be one of the pioneers of the new order process. These aircraft would equip the new heavy night bomber squadrons, which were the key element in the RAF's striking force.

Contrary to later legend which Cunliffe-Lister himself promoted in his memoirs, the Spitfire and the Hurricane fighters were not ordered off the drawing board.[10] The Gauntlet might not have been fully up to modern standards but it was not as outclassed as the Hinds or the Virginias. Moreover, Cunliffe-Lister deferred to Air Ministry opinion that as low-wing monoplanes 'trouble may be expected' with the designs and they were be put through the full process of testing prototypes. Somehow the fact that the Battle was also a low-wing monoplane does not seem to have counted against it being ordered off the drawing board. The Air Staff's Trenchardian order of priorities was already present. Bombers were a more urgent requirement than fighters. The aircraft that were to prove vital in winning the Battle of Britain ranked behind designs that proved catastrophic or mediocre.

Scheme C was also designed to fit into the government's conservative economic instincts. The sacrifice in terms of impact on the national finances was bad enough already: it would boost Air Ministry spending by about half in the next financial year which would remain at that level for the following two years. Cunliffe-Lister knew that he would have to steer round the industrial conservatism of Baldwin and, more important, Neville Chamberlain, then the Chancellor of the Exchequer. Not doing anything that would interfere with normal trade was to become a shibboleth of the government's planning for rearmament across the board for the next two years. Cunliffe-Lister's papers insisted that making 3,800 new aircraft could be done without reorganizing the industry. The Air Ministry was even prepared to concede some latitude to plane-makers in meeting their specifications.

Chapter 14

A Striking Force of Such Power – Scheme F

Scheme C was a great advance on Scheme A but that was starting from an undemanding base. From the start it had an air of impermanence about it. Swinton, Weir and the Air Staff had grasped what was readily to hand to assemble something that was not obviously an exercise in window-dressing. It was centred on established aircraft designs and its production targets could be met by Britain's aircraft industry as it stood. Its most obvious weakness was that it was calculated to meet the most slavish, crudely numerical and arbitrary parity target; more than a quarter of the planes which would be made under it would be the militarily worthless light bombers. It was not a question of whether but when and how Scheme C would be replaced.

In the months that followed the adoption of Scheme C, rearmament became more urgent and more possible. Baldwin led the National Government into a comfortable win in a general election in November 1935. The majority was noticeably down on the huge figure reached in 1931 at the height of the world financial crisis but it was still more than adequate. The government's election platform had featured the promise of 'no great armaments' as a sop to anti-war voters, but this was unspecific rhetoric rather than any definable commitment. It stored up future perils for Baldwin's reputation but left the government plenty of room for manoeuvre. The most acute diplomatic problem came as Mussolini gave ample proof of his aggressive intentions. Italy had been stoking a crisis with Abyssinia through 1935. Britain and France attempted to mediate and to find a way to settle Italy's demands at the expense of Abyssinia, but this early draft of appeasement exploded when one set of proposals thrashed out between French prime minister Pierre Laval and British Foreign Secretary Sir Samuel Hoare was leaked publicly. The ensuing public outrage cost Hoare his job. The episode eliminated the possibility of a quiet diplomatic deal as a way out of the impasse. League of Nations sanctions had the cosy feel of the international community in action, but did raise the ugly prospect that they might have to be applied by force. Britain could not escape the need to look once again at the parlous state of its armed forces.

Just as he had done with the DRC in 1933, it was Sir Maurice Hankey who set the wheels of Whitehall in motion to examine Britain's options and to come up with a plan. The Defence Requirements Sub-Committee of the Committee of Imperial Defence including service and Civil Service chiefs under Hankey was tasked with drawing up a plan and it came up with a five-year programme that increased Britain's spending on its armed services by £417.5 million, a gigantic increase on the additional £97 million figure that the committee's 1934 predecessor had come up with. It marked a true turning point in Britain's plans for rearmament. For the first time it was accepted officially that rearmament would not just need more financial or budgetary means; it would require changes to Britain's industrial structure. The RAF was the biggest beneficiary of the new largesse. Spending in 1936 was set to more than double to £45 million and it would rise to more than a quarter of total spending for all three services from 17 per cent in 1935. The new plan for the RAF under this programme was designated Scheme F. Schemes D and E never progressed beyond the outline planning stage.

At first glance Scheme F might not have seemed to be that huge an advance on Scheme C. The headline outcome was only to reach the same figure of 1,512 first-line aircraft set down in the earlier scheme, which had been driven by the estimate of Luftwaffe strength of exactly the same number. The detail told a quite different story. To begin with there was scope to go beyond the 1,512 target figure for April 1937 if the Luftwaffe's strength rose to 2,000 aircraft; the Air Ministry rapidly managed to go further anyway. Almost the only mention of parity – or 'numerical parity' as Swinton insisted – was to create this extra headroom. But the real differences were qualitative. Scheme F would provide the RAF with modern aircraft and nothing but. The despised and useless light bombers and the ungainly, near obsolete Heyfords could finally be dropped entirely. Their place would be taken by modern types. The first-line air force that was to emerge from the scheme was to consist exclusively of modern types: monoplanes made mainly out of metal with retractable undercarriages and enclosed cockpits.

The total number of bombers was set to rise by more than a fifth, driven by the huge expansion in the number of medium bombers trebling to 750.[1] The bulk of the increase would come in the form of what were now described more precisely and accurately as 'smaller medium bombers'. The RAF was making a big bet on Battles and Blenheims. They would not just replace the Hinds but would drive the expansion of the whole bomber force. What were now classed as 'large medium bombers' – the Wellingtons had proved themselves well enough in prototype to feature in the line of battle – would equip eight squadrons with ninety-six aircraft.[2] All 240 of the heavy bombers would be Whitleys. Investing heavily in these new types came at a large financial cost. Reequipping Bomber Command would add an extra £12.5 million above the Scheme C figure for the aircraft themselves with an extra '£2m annually for the greater cost of maintenance and the like'.

Swinton promised great things for Scheme F in a separate paper to the Cabinet setting out his vision for the 'Air Striking Force'. The aim of the programme of upgrading the bombers was to 'improve the offensive power of this force and constitute the most effective deterrent against German aggression'.[3] He boasted inaccurately that even the Battles and Blenheims would be able to drop 1,000lb of bombs anywhere in the western half of Germany.[4] This would include the industrial districts of the Ruhr. Nowhere in Germany would be beyond the range of the largest mediums with their bomb load of one ton. Fighter protection was not entirely forgotten in the optimistic picture that Swinton set out for his colleagues. He thought they 'will wish to know' that a prototype of one high-performance design was flying already and another was soon so follow. These were the planes famous as the Hurricane and Spitfire but in 1936 these were no more than a sop thrown to amateur Cabinet ministers who could not be expected to understand that only bombers counted as a measure of the RAF's strength.

Somewhere between the 1935 DRC report and Swinton's – such was Cunliffe-Lister's title after he had been made viscount in 1935 – paper the Air Ministry had sneaked in a boost to the RAF's total target strength of another 182 aircraft.[5] The 15 per cent increase in the total size of the RAF to 1,694 was not earth-shattering in its own right, but it was far more important because of the classes of planes involved. All the extra aircraft were bombers which marked the end of the unofficial and unstated 2:1 ratio of bombers to fighters that had ruled for more than ten years. Fighter numbers were to remain unchanged at 420. For the first time the Air Staff was in a position to obey its long-held doctrine of devoting any resources over and above the minimum judged necessary for purely defensive aircraft into offensive power. An internal Air Staff document gave unambiguously the first objective of Scheme F as 'to increase the striking power of the Metropolitan Air Force'.[6]

The relatively greater importance attached to bombers was already clear in the picture of the RAF's front-line strength. It was even more pronounced in what lay behind these figures. The scheme was posited on the expansion of the war reserve of aircraft to sustain the fighting front-line strength and here again bombers did better than fighters. The reserves of bomber aircraft behind the front line were to be significantly higher than reserves of fighters. Bomber reserves were set at 167 per cent of front-line strength whilst fighter reserves were only 136 per cent.[7] This meant that the Air Ministry would need to order far more bombers than fighters to attain the total number of front-line and reserve aircraft target in each class.

The commitment to bombers was even greater when looked at in money terms. The whole programme demanded that 8,000 or so new planes of all types be made.[8] The need to build up reserves and provide for wastage meant that the manufacturing requirement was a multiple of the increase in first-line strength to be attained. Including their engines all the extra aircraft were set to cost £62 million.[9] Some 3,600 or almost half of the new planes were to be bombers and this would cost at least 60 per cent of the total. By contrast, fighters had even lower priority in the scheme's manufacturing plans than in its targets for first-line strength. Only 1,300 fighters were to be built at a cost of £5 million, less than a tenth of spending on all new planes and well under one-fifth of what was to be spent on new bombers.

The internal Air Ministry discussions of Scheme F showed the growing enthusiasm of the air marshals for ever-bigger bombers and a corresponding lack of enthusiasm for the lighter bombers on which the Swinton/Weir approach seemed to focus. When Weir floated the idea of finding new production sources for the Bristol Blenheim, Ellington disagreed:

> the essential thing to aim [for] was that the Striking Force should be able to deliver the heaviest possible broadside, and for this purpose we really wanted the heavier machines

in the MEDIUM BOMBER class, viz the Vickers and Handley Page B 9/32s [Wellingtons and Hampdens], which operationally were regarded as HEAVY MEDIUM BOMBERS rather than the BLENHEIM, BATTLE ... which were only regarded as LIGHT MEDIUM BOMBERS.[10]

Scheme F was the last of the RAF prewar expansion schemes to be approved in its entirety and the RAF that entered the Munich crisis and the Second World War was to a large extent the force set down in the scheme.[11] It certainly marked a dramatic extension of the plans by the RAF's political and military leadership to boost bomber numbers at the expense of fighters which were largely carried out as planned. Admittedly it was dominated by the Battle and the Blenheim which were modern but fell short of the Air Staff's ideals. The Trenchardians were soon to roll out far more ambitious plans for the commitment to the striking force which were to prove even more influential. Scheme F did not close the book of Air Staff revelations.[12]

The discussions of the huge rearmament programme marked the peak of Weir's influence in the British machinery of government. His dual role as an all-purpose adviser on broad industrial policy and as an expert on the vital question of rearming the RAF made him a key figure in the process. What was far less clear was his implicit claim to be competent as an arbiter of defence strategy overall. His expertise in organizing industry was beyond challenge but on the broader question he was unqualified. His passionate commitment to Trenchardian doctrine was no substitute for the kind of bureaucratic standing that counts in Whitehall. He was running the risk of acting as a mouthpiece of the Air Staff and found himself coming up against Sir Maurice Hankey whose natural battleground was the competing claims of the individual services and their various allies. During the preliminary discussions on the report by Hankey's committee, Weir had already locked horns with Hankey. Predictably Weir championed greater allocations for the RAF at the expense of the army. However much he might have disagreed, Hankey was too astute a Whitehall warrior to opt for a direct confrontation and followed his usual strategy of neutralization by involvement. Rather than try to eliminate or overrule Weir, he was to be brought into the heart of the debate.

In line with the normal pattern the next stage for the DRC report, which was the product of military and professional advisers, was to refer it to a body with political power. Once again this was another offshoot of Hankey's Committee of Imperial Defence empire. The Ministerial Committee on Defence Policy and Requirements featured the most senior Cabinet ministers and the service ministers; de facto, it was an inner Cabinet whose decisions would almost certainly be approved by the full Cabinet. Weir was invited to join the committee. As a peer and Privy Counsellor there could be no argument over his standing for the task, but it is still a register of Weir's position that someone with no formal responsibility for policy should be given a voice in the process. Weir had attained an almost unprecedentedly powerful status in the heart of government. To begin with a tentative attempt was made to restrict Weir's involvement to the purely industrial aspects of rearmament but he brushed these aside almost effortlessly.[13] Weir was determined to influence defence policy across the board. He was soon boasting to Lord Rothermere that he had already stymied an army plan to reequip its artillery and was about to go on to a role of immense power:

> As far as I can learn he [Weir] has the final word .... [he] gave me to understand that he is to coordinate the three defence departments ... It looks as though Weir is going to be the big figure of the Government.[14]

Weir made no pretence of bringing any new balance to match what he saw as his new, wider responsibilities. His comments on the DRC report were Trenchardian red in tooth and claw. He passionately advocated a proactive commitment to air offensive.[15] He set the bar high by arguing that the RAF could enjoy the same global status as the Royal Navy, a force so powerful that it would deter any rival power from fighting Britain. The correct policy for Britain was 'a powerful Air Offensive'. He decried the lack of emphasis in official papers on 'Striking Air Strength'. He was scathing about the irrelevance of the army, in particular the infantry, to any future conflict. Weir argued for 'a striking and offensive ... air weapon ... so powerful as to compel the most wholesome respect from both friend and foe'. Anything else that the RAF did – defensive fighter cover, army and fleet cooperation together with its imperial role – were lumped together as very secondary destinations for available resources.

Weir found a powerful ally in the person of Neville Chamberlain, then Chancellor of the Exchequer, and easily the second most powerful man in the government. When the need to face up to German strength had been forced upon the government two years before, he had identified the Luftwaffe as the element of German power that it was most vital to confront and had successfully pushed for the RAF to have priority. By early 1936 he had travelled even further down the strategic bombing route and blossomed into a quasi-Trenchardian:

> if we can keep out of war for a few years we shall have an air force of such striking power that no one will care to run risks with it. I cannot believe that the next war, if it ever comes, will be like the last one and I believe our resources will be more profitably employed in the air & on the sea than in building up great armies.[16]

The Cabinet accepted the DRC plan with no serious modification in February 1936. The one prominent qualification that it gave made plain that the rearmament of the RAF might have even further to go. The programmes were 'liable to modification in the light of new considerations such as the developments in range and offensive power of aircraft'.[17]

The approval of Scheme F with its bold vision of the RAF as a vector of new power based on offensive air strength marked the high-water mark of uncritical acceptance of Trenchardian doctrine in government. Closely linked with this, it was also the high point of Weir's influence on policy. The same Cabinet meeting that signed off on the programme also set in motion a process that spelt the end of Weir's dream of becoming a permanent fixture in setting defence policy. The wheels were being set in motion to bring a new figure onto the scene who was to prove considerably less amenable to the project.

Chapter 15

An Ideal Scheme of Defence

The same forces that drove the second DRC report also drove a call to move rearmament higher up the political agenda in some tangible fashion. The task was too big, too urgent and too complex for government to leave to the individual service ministers and the nebulous coordinating machinery of a labyrinth of committees. What was wanted was a single individual with the political power needed to do the work. The possibility of having a minister with a broad responsibility for rearmament had been in the air for some while. With political pressure in favour of rearmament building steadily, the move would give credibility to the government's claim to be taking the matter seriously.

The man who would most dearly have loved the task was the man who was never going to get it. Churchill aspired to drive forward every aspect of Britain's rearmament, applying his forcefulness, dynamism and fascination with military matters to the problem. His hopes were kept alive in the time-honoured fashion of dangling a distant reward for good behaviour in front of a dissident to restrain his criticism of the government, but he had no real prospect. His reputation amongst mainstream Conservatives had not quite hit rock-bottom, but it did not have far to go. Baldwin's political raison d'être was his rejection of the Lloyd George coalitionist government of glamorous and unscrupulous high-livers, of whom Churchill was the last survivor. His opposition to the India Bill in the early 1930s had been futile and damaging; even the natural opponents of the Bill amongst the party's extreme imperialists were suspicious that his support would damage their cause. At a time when there were still hopes of conciliating Germany, Churchill's trenchant criticism of the Hitler regime would have been a liability. Giving him a major defence job would have been tantamount to telling Berlin that war was on the horizon.

The most obvious conventional candidate from the ranks of politicians with sufficient standing was Sir Samuel Hoare, who had been ejected from the Cabinet as a scapegoat for the plan for Britain and France to acquiesce in an Italian carve-up of Abyssinia. His return to the Cabinet was only a matter of time but he delivered a speech promoting his claim to the defence job that was so nakedly ambitious that he almost ruled himself out. The job was important enough for it to be offered to Chamberlain, the second ranked minister in the government, but this was just a matter of form. Chamberlain needed only to bide his time to succeed Baldwin as prime minister and had no natural instinct to drive a programme of rearmament.

There is no indication that the appointment was intended to curb Weir's powers but nowhere is there any indication that he was considered for the job. He stood at the apogee of his power in early 1936. He was the government's anointed expert on the industrial side of rearmament, with a special focus on reequipping the RAF, and a powerful advocate of Trenchardian strategy within Britain's overall military planning. He might not have held any official position at all, but he was arguably the best-placed individual with a remit that spanned all three services after the prime minister. Weir certainly entertained ambitions to become Britain's defence supremo, but he had the instincts of a businessman and administrator. He does not seem to have lobbied, intrigued or haggled for his powers either to be extended or to be transformed into something permanent and official. Weir had no taste for the world of politics where this kind of process rules, both in terms of securing and retaining power and exercising power effectively. Britain did need an individual to take oversight of rearmament, but it was practically inevitable that this would have to be a politician by vocation.

Placing a single defence minister above all three individual service ministers would have strayed into a political minefield. By long tradition the First Lord of the Admiralty and the Secretary for War had held a distinctive status as the political representatives of their services with all their national standing and traditions; the creation of an air force counterpart had been part and parcel of the creation of an independent RAF. All the services nurtured their own squads of MPs and peers as claques in parliament to resist any encroachment on their position. Another piece of the jigsaw puzzle lay deep in the Whitehall jungle where Sir Maurice Hankey was lobbying hard against the appointment of a single defence minister to oversee the three individual service ministries.[1] It is hard not to suspect that he feared that this would erode his uniquely influential status at the centre of a web of connections and knowledge spanning the entire defence establishment. Whatever political solution was adopted, it would inevitably involve the Committee of Imperial Defence, the centrepiece of this web, where Hankey made full use of the power that fell on his shoulders as secretary because the prime minister's status as its official chairman meant that he was no more than part-time or even absentee. Hankey's advice to Baldwin came up against a fierce lobbying campaign aimed at his overmighty status as a military bureaucrat.[2] This attack was being promoted by a clique of individuals connected to the RAF, notably Trenchard himself, who had just ceased to be Commissioner of the Metropolitan Police and thus freed from the restraints of government service. Hankey was identified with the navy side of the long battle with the RAF which was just flaring up again.

Stanley Baldwin's choice of Sir Thomas Inskip for the newly created post of Minister for the Coordination of Defence caused widespread astonishment. Inskip was a government lawyer – attorney general in 1936 – whose only noteworthy political act had been to lead successfully the Evangelical opposition to revising the Church of England Prayer Book in 1927 and 1928. Curiously enough, given his low political profile, he had briefly been promoted by the Whips' Office as a successor to Baldwin, which was never realistic but hints at a more substantial standing in the government than would otherwise be apparent. During the First World War he had served in naval intelligence and the Admiralty's legal department, but otherwise he had no military experience, but in the poisonous atmosphere of inter-service rivalry, the freedom from notable affiliation to any particular service was a positive advantage. Bitterly disappointed at being bypassed, Churchill made the hackneyed criticism of the appointment as 'the most extraordinary since Caligula made his horse a Consul'. Inskip was provided with only minimal resources – two professional secretaries – and a nebulous brief, in a curious parallel to Weir himself. His office was in the Committee of Imperial Defence's building and he was based firmly in Hankey's empire.

The job was going to be what Inskip made of it. It was a delicate question to define his task without 'interfering with the responsibilities of the Service Ministers'.[3] The new minister would be the Deputy Chairman of the Committee of Imperial Defence and he would act as its chairman in the absence of the prime minister – implicitly the normal state of affairs – but the prime minister would remain as its formal chairman.⁴ He would not normally chair the Chiefs of Staff committee but 'supplement [its] present activities and initiative ... by guidance and initiatives of his own'. He had no authority over anyone. Inskip was, however, an excellent chairman and he made a very significant contribution to the inner workings of rearmament programme, but he was too much an adherent of prewar financial conservatism to be truly the man of the hour. Contemporary advocates of extensive rearmament like Churchill would have preferred a similar enthusiast, who drove the process forward, but such enthusiasts were few and far between. Inskip appears as a failure in the eyes of history, but he was as good as the contemporary political dynamic allowed. His greatest flaw is that he appears to have been more of an ally of the Chancellor of the Exchequer in trying to restrain defence spending, than an ally of the defence ministers in arguing for more money. He was like a nanny who approves of the mother's niggardly approach to distributing treats, makes sure that what treats there are should be shared fairly but seems unaware that her charges might deserve some more. His image as a creature of centralized bureaucracy was rather reinforced by his close and harmonious collaboration with Hankey, whose choices he tended to share. He was a tall, imposing figure who ran to fat. It is perhaps a symptom of the tendency to write off the entire prewar rearmament effort that no one has yet written his biography.

Inskip's most conspicuous action as Minister for the Coordination of Defence was finally to terminate the long-festering conflict between the Royal Navy and the RAF over the control of naval aviation. The decision fell against the RAF and the shipborne aircraft of the Fleet Air Arm (FAA) were turned over to the Royal Navy. The upshot was regarded as a judgement of Solomon as the land-based maritime aircraft remained as part of the RAF in Coastal Command. The Air Staff and Trenchard himself were still fighting the elemental battle for the survival of the RAF that had raged through the 1920s, when the next step would have been oblivion, and considered this to be still a calamity. They were on the wrong side of history; the RAF's control of the FAA made the Royal Navy a laggard in the crucial development of air–sea warfare compared to the two other major maritime powers: Japan and the US. The decision came too late to improve the Royal Navy's air effort. Unlike the US Navy no senior Royal Navy admiral had an aviation background and the service's bias in favour of big-gun battleships was a notable weakness. The late development of an organic air arm was evident in the poor quality of British-designed aircraft that served in the FAA during the Second World War; aircraft designed for the US Navy were far more effective and were usually preferred to British types. It must be admitted that the Admiralty handicapped the design of naval aircraft by insisting on features such as two-man aircraft even as fighters.

The FAA decision came as a body blow to Weir who attempted to resign in protest at the government's reneging on the pledge it had given him not to re-open the question when he was being convinced to take on his work. He was only just persuaded to stay. The inquiry that led to the decision and its final choice also poisoned the final months in office of Ellington as CAS. It also brought upon his head the contempt of Trenchard, who had so often beaten off previous attempts to break the RAF's monopoly.

The FAA dispute fell into the area of relationships between the services which was almost undeniably Inskip's remit to handle, but his next initiative launched a fundamental challenge to the orthodox view that individual services had a sovereign right to decide on their internal affairs. He set out to subject the Air Staff's judgement of how many fighters were needed to defend Britain to external scrutiny. This was a fundamental assault on the Trenchardian orthodoxy that the number of fighters was to be kept to a strict minimum, a minimum that only the Air Staff was qualified to calculate. Inskip clearly believed that the current number was too low and wanted to force the Air Staff to increase it.

Inskip was operating from a far weaker position than the one from which he had been able to work on the FAA question. He had no brief to address what the Air Staff would have regarded as purely an internal RAF question; he did not have one of the other services as his ally; he did not have the executive authority to force any measures through even if they could be shown to be necessary. Inskip had to work with the material to hand and the Committee of Imperial Defence network of committees gave him a point from which to start his campaign. He seized on the fact that one of Sir Maurice Hankey's progenies, the Home Defence Committee, held a remit to look at Britain's air defences as a whole. Because this involved anti-aircraft guns which were the army's responsibility as well as the RAF's fighters, more than one service was involved so this was not a topic for the Air Staff alone. Inskip went through the motions of examining the army's part in defence but his true target was the number of fighters. The brief on which he set the committee to work in October 1936 was loaded from the start:

> The question of the total strength of fighter aircraft for home defence and of the anti-aircraft artillery and searchlight defences, as at present contemplated requires reconsideration. There is room for doubt as to whether the provision already approved for the defence of particular localities is on an adequate scale.[5]

The choice of committee and nature of the brief elegantly sidestepped two potential complaints, one from the Air Staff and the other from the Treasury. The brief formally endorsed Trenchardian orthodoxy and acknowledged that offensive air action was the most important function of aircraft, but because offensive operations were outside the committee's terms of reference, it could pronounce on the question of fighter strength as a stand-alone topic. Inskip asked for an 'ideal' scheme, the question of what it might cost could be ignored.

The sub-committee went to its work on defining the best response to a massive threat. It was working on the basis that the Luftwaffe could send far more planes to attack Britain than they had previously been able to: 1,700 bombers compared to the 900 that had been assumed in 1934, so the challenge was correspondingly greater. The increased ranges of German aircraft also brought more of Britain within their reach. The scheme they finally decided to recommend would allow Fighter Command to concentrate nine squadrons in the air at 10,000 feet at any part of a line 250 miles long stretching from Catterick in North Yorkshire to Biggin Hill due south of London within ten minutes of a raid being reported. This would require forty-five squadrons totalling 630 aircraft compared to only twenty-one squadrons in the existing plan.

But this was definitely the 'ideal' scheme only and the airmen displayed no very great enthusiasm to take up the implicit invitation to write a wish-list for extra fighter resources. Dowding sat on the committee as the head of Fighter Command and he was particularly unwilling to come up with anything as a recommendation that did not fall into the realm of 'practical politics'.[6] He wanted only something that had a chance of seeing the light of day. At first glance what he came up with was ambitious enough with an increase in the number of home defence fighter squadrons to thirty, a 43 per cent rise compared to more than doubling in the 'ideal'. On closer examination it was much less so. Five of the additional squadrons would be ones earmarked to be sent to bases in Belgium as an advanced defence screen and simply re-allocated to mainland bases. The other four extra squadrons would be Auxiliary Air Force light-bomber squadrons, in practice slated for re-equipment anyway, which would convert to fighters. Moreover, it was recommended that four new regular bomber squadrons should be formed to replace them.

Dowding did not succumb to the temptation to ask for more fighters, and he accepted the responsibility of defending Britain with a Fighter Command strength of thirty squadrons. He did, though, insist on a number of things if he was to take on this responsibility and these show the clarity of his vision. None was particularly ambitious but they included an insistence that all the fighter defence aerodromes would be provided with sector operations rooms and the relevant staff. Dowding fully understood that the command and control element in his plans for Fighter Command were vital. As to the larger goals, the committee accepted in principle, but no more, that the 'ultimate aim' should be to complete the 'ideal scheme' but this should be balanced by an increase in the RAF's bomber force. As the target bomber strength had been calculated on the basis of what was necessary to counter 900 German bombers, it was implied that the RAF's bomber force would need to almost double in size. If Inskip had hoped to get approval for a massive reallocation of resources to fighters, he was disappointed. The best that Inskip could wring out of his military colleagues was the acceptance that the 'Ideal' defence scheme was 'by no means an over-insurance', a military–bureaucratic double negative that meant that they did not think it went too far.[7]

Inskip had a major ally in Hankey. During the First World War as he was building his Whitehall power base, Hankey had played a major role in overcoming service conservatism to force a crucial change in policy in 1917. Almost to a man, the senior admirals of the Royal Navy were violently opposed to the adoption of convoys as a means of defeating the German U-boats, which were on the point of cutting Britain's trade routes. Hankey understood that convoy was the only effective system and risked multiple breaches of military practice and protocol to alert the government to the cynical and dishonest manipulation of statistics practised by the Admiralty to support its case.[8] The prime minister Lloyd George swung in favour of convoys and faced down the Admiralty. Convoys were adopted and the U-boat menace was defeated. Hankey had grasped a vital point that negated the admirals' distaste for something that seemed to be a defensive strategy. As he set out in a justly celebrated paper, the convoy would serve as a trap for the U-boats, creating a battleground where the navy could deploy all the means at its disposal, 'compelling the enemy to risk an action if he is to inflict injury – in fact this a form of offensive on our part'.[9] Hankey saw a similar dynamic at work for the Luftwaffe's bombers: London would act as a '"wasp trap" to which German aircraft would inevitably be attracted'.[10] By some standards the battle over convoys was Hankey's finest hour but he was destined not to repeat it by overturning the Air Staff's doctrinaire addiction to the bomber twenty years later.

With at best minimal support from within the RAF, Inskip's campaign never built up a sufficient head of steam to mount a serious challenge to the low priority given to fighters in Trenchardian doctrine. He and Hankey were condemned to wage a guerrilla war only. Hankey took up the 'over-insurance' comment as an endorsement of the 'Ideal' defence scheme and he was still quoting it months afterwards when he gently attempted to win Dowding away from Trenchardian orthodoxy.[11] Dowding resisted the implicit invitation and stuck to his insistence on practical schemes only. Hankey was a significant ally for Inskip in his campaign to persuade the Air Staff to look more kindly on fighters, but his assistance was far from decisive. When the 'Ideal' defence scheme came up before the Committee of Imperial Defence itself in July 1937 the matter was deferred pending a general review of defence needs.[12]

The 'Ideal' defence scheme flickered back into life in the autumn of 1937 when the newly installed prime minister, Neville Chamberlain, interested himself in Britain's air defences with the encouragement of Weir.[13] Weir had put the strength of fighter squadrons at the top of list of questions, so Inskip was in a strong position to chivvy Swinton. He wondered whether it might be right to revisit the ratio of fighters to bombers but Swinton rebuffed the suggestion very firmly.[14] When Inskip prepared his answer to the prime minister's question the best he could manage was a chronology of the campaign and concluded with admission that he had been able to achieve nothing despite the support of the Committee of Imperial Defence.[15]

Dislike of Inskip's 'Ideal' defence scheme lingered on amongst the Trenchardian faithful months after it had been laid to rest. When the Air Staff was building up support for another bomber-rich expansion scheme, Swinton, a firm Trenchardian doctrinaire, delivered a side swipe at what he referred to as the 'unfortunate title' of Inskip's project.[16]

Chapter 16

Horrors in the Most Intense Form

The ink was barely dry on Scheme F and the other proposals enshrined in the second DRC report when Hitler tested the resolve and military preparedness of Britain and France. In March 1936, the German army marched back into the Rhineland which had been demilitarized under the Versailles Treaty. Just as he had repudiated the Versailles limits on Germany's military resources, Hitler was unilaterally repudiating one of its territorial provisions. On a purely military level, Hitler was taking a major risk. He had only a few battalions available, which could have put up little resistance to the forces that the French could have deployed, but he was reading his opponents' political will shrewdly. The story that a taxi driver influenced the British foreign minister Anthony Eden by telling him that Hitler was merely taking back his back garden may be apocryphal but it accurately captures the public mood; the voters of neither Britain nor France were yet willing to challenge Germany for reversing a suspect part of Versailles; that he was doing so by force alone counted for little. Moreover, the British were well on the way to sinking into a psychosis of fear provoked by Germany's growing strength in the air and a near-paranoid expectation that Germany would attack Britain first. According to the Joint Planning Committee of the British military chiefs of staff, 'the most dangerous threat' the Germans could produce would be a 'mad dog' attack from the air.[1] Even though it would be France that took any practical action against Germany in the Rhineland, Britain was more vulnerable to air attack than anything in France. The planners noted that the Luftwaffe's forty-two squadrons of heavy bombers could reach London from bases in Germany. Moreover, the Germans had recently produced heavy bombers that could outrun British or French fighters, although the planners did not specify whether these were actually in service or not; it was an early symptom of an inferiority complex which was going to get far worse. Any reaction to the reoccupation would thus have to take as a major consideration the 'extreme weakness of air defence' of Britain. At that stage Scheme F existed only on paper. The verdict on whether the RAF were ready for war immediately from the Chiefs of Staff themselves was categoric and emphatic: 'the Royal Air Force could produce no offensive or defensive effort whatever.'[2] The British government barely needed the advice of their military to hold back and it joined the French in going through the motions of objecting but no more.

Evidence mounted of Germany's determination to build its air strength, fuelling the fear that Britain's inferiority was getting worse. In early 1936, the Foreign Office passed on to the Air Staff the first of a series of intelligence reports from a high-grade freelance operative, retired Group Captain Malcolm Christie, who had built a successful business career and extensive contacts in German political and military circles.[3] He gave details of German plans to reach 2,034 front-line aircraft by the end of 1938, far greater than the 1,512 figure on which scheme F had been based. Admittedly, the second DRC report had held open the possibility of an eventual German move towards this figure, but Christie's sources were unsettlingly precise. Except, that is, to Sir Edward Ellington who appeared to be wedded to languid forecasts of German rearmament governed by his own analysis of what was possible that had marked his response to the first evidence of German rearmament. The change in the Air Ministry's political direction meant that the Christie report was not entirely discounted. Unlike his predecessor Londonderry, Swinton was not minded to swallow the CAS's myopic complacency and scrawled 'No' in his habitual red ink across Ellington's minute, poring scorn on the report and summoned him to see him immediately.[4] Whatever Swinton might have said to Ellington, it was not enough to prevent an Air Staff rearguard action against information that was not home grown. The intelligence section showed its dedication to Ellingtonian's *a fortiori* and non-empirical reasoning: 'We do not believe that Germany with her ability and love of good organization would adopt the methods which X [Christie's label for his source] would adopt.'[5]

1936 was a watershed year both in terms of international events and, with something of a lag, the British response to the them. It was the year when it finally became clear that the western democracies were confronted by a truly terrifying force in the shape of the Fascist dictatorships and were singularly ill-equipped – both politically and militarily – to meet the challenge. After the Rhineland crisis the international situation worsened as spring turned to summer. Domestic politics undermined any hope that France might be able to take resolute action. Leon Blum's Front Populaire leftist government that had come into office in May 1936 was instinctively in favour of this kind of move but faced an array of domestic problems. Its policies, notably nationalization, had triggered severe internal tension almost comparable to the near-civil war conditions of February 1934. The Front Populaire polarized opinion so severely that an openly anti-Fascist diplomatic policy would have been a direct challenge to an increasingly militant right wing. The nationalization of the aircraft industry also dislocated France's already shaky plans to reequip its air force. In July the Spanish Civil War began with a revolt by reactionary generals against a leftist democratic government. Britain and France abstained rigorously from intervening but made only perfunctory moves to block active and sustained intervention by Italy and Germany. The League of Nations diligently pursued its deliberations and rhetoric in Geneva, but only with the most convinced eye of faith did it appear to be in a position to exercise any real influence to the good. The future lay with armed conflict; the only question was how soon and how fully.

The second DRC, together with the possibility, however faint, that the Rhineland crisis might have brought war between Britain and Germany, had rather begged the question of what this war might actually be like. The Joint Planning Committee was set to extend the work it had done over the Rhineland crisis with a comprehensive survey. The three officers on the committee were comparatively junior but all were forceful individuals, destined to reach high rank in their services, none more so than the RAF's Director of Plans Group Captain Arthur 'Bert' Harris, future commander of Bomber Command. The others were Captain Tom Phillips, who was to die as an admiral in command of Force Z, dispatched to the Far East in a desperate attempt to stem the Japanese offensive in 1942, and Colonel Sir Ronald Adam Bt. adjutant general throughout the Second World War. The composition of a paper under the title 'Appreciation of the Situation in the Event of War Against Germany in 1939' might have yielded no more than a dry and routine staff exercise in contingency planning based on available evidence, but the trio had quite different ideas. The predictions they reported in the autumn were far more alarming that the ones in April. Perhaps Harris had become aware of the Christie/X intelligence on the Luftwaffe's expansion plans. The paper issued as paper JP155 by the

Joint Planning Sub-committee of 26 October 1936 was little short of a polemical manifesto in favour of massive and urgent rearmament of all the services, in particular the RAF's bombers, to prevent a crushing defeat by Germany's massively superior armed forces.

The most compelling and simple feature of the scenario that the planners outlined was based on the same politico-strategical basis that had fed their Rhineland analysis: Germany's economic resources were restricted and that the country would not be able to sustain a prolonged war, which ultimately proved to be correct. This had been a constant of planning scenarios for at least a year.[6] The planners assumed that this constraint would impose a strictly rational strategy on Germany's leaders, which would involve achieving a decisive victory over its enemies as rapidly as possible. As few countries set out to fight prolonged wars this was hardly original, but their next prediction took them deep into the realms of speculation. Germany could only attain the goal of a rapid victory by delivering a 'knock-out blow'. They went through the motions of creating a scenario for a knock-out blow against France, but clearly the paper was centred around the threat of a knock-out blow against Britain, repeating their analysis at the time of the Rhineland occupation. They were following a well-establish tradition. The fear of sudden, unheralded attack by an aggressor had long haunted politicians and military planners in Britain. The Fascist dictators were thought to be especially prone to this kind of behaviour.[7] The risk of a knock-out blow had featured in the second DRC report, quoting no less an authority than the prime minister Herbert Asquith before the First World War, albeit listed as something that 'would fulfil the Teutonic conception of a short, sharp war', but the planners took this far further. In practice a knock-out blow was presented as by far the most likely German strategy and it would have horrific consequences.

The German navy was by far inferior to Britain's so an invasion on the pattern of the phantom attacks across the North Sea that had haunted Britain's imagination in the days before the First World War did not merit consideration. That left air attack and the planners, with Harris presumably to the fore, set out to paint a picture of the devastation that the Luftwaffe would wreak. The projection featured as an appendix to the paper but its sensational character made it by far the most potent element. The planners proceeded from a calculation that the Luftwaffe would be able to rain 400 tons of bombs per day for forty days, so a total of 16,000 tons. They admitted that these figures were vastly more pessimistic than those used in Home Office planning to deal with air attack, which foresaw the Luftwaffe delivering 100 tons on the first day and falling off sharply thereafter. The highest total figure that the Home Office produced was 1,575 tons over thirty days, but this was still enough for the Home Office's planners to estimate 20,000 casualties in London during the first twenty-four hours of an attack. The planners put this agreeably frightening figure in the body of their report but were far more reticent about the wide difference in projections of the scale of the attack which was not spelt out and was only clear to a reader who got through to the Annex B of the appendix.

Just as they had gone through the ritual of discussing a knock-out blow against France, the planners explored different scenarios but whatever targets the Germans selected, the 'attacks will be quite ruthless ... without regard for humanity'. They began with assessing a Luftwaffe attack on food supplies, but the heart of their argument lay in the section 'Attack aimed at demoralizing the people' where all the stops were pulled out. It listed the advantages of such an attack:

> In a democratic country, particularly, the ability of the Government to wage war depends on the will of the majority of the people. Germany's bombing aircraft could expose the people of this country to death, wounds and terror on a large scale. Our civilian population has never been exposed to the horrors of war and the Germans may believe that if our people, and particularly our women and children, were subjected to these horrors in the most intense forms that can be achieved through air attack, the majority would insist that surrender was preferable to the continuation of the attacks. If this belief proved correct this form of attack would probably achieve a decision more quickly than any other.

The planners gave a tepid qualification that history and experience suggested that the British could not so be cowed, but then ploughed on with the detail of their nightmare vision of the country brought to its knees in terms not very much less apocalyptical as the ones used by Churchill to Parliament in 1934:

Within a week attacks of this sort could have forced the partial evacuation of half a dozen of the centres of most dense population in England, forcing many millions of people to abandon their homes, caused casualties of the order of 150,000, completely disorganised telephone and telegraph communications throughout the country and to varying degrees dislocated railway, postal and electrical services and the distribution of food.

At no point in the report did Britain's fighter defences merit a word beyond the blanket assertion that the Germans had such a wide range of potential targets that 'A.A. defences could not possibly cover them all'. The true core message of the report was almost at the very end: 'Without adequate bomber strength we cannot hope to reduce German attacks.' Terror at the prospect of being bombed by the Germans was part of the RAF's pitch for more bombers of its own.

The document was issued as a 'Provisional' report but it was given a wide circulation which suggests that it was intended to make an impact. The man immediately responsible for the distribution was Marine Major 'Jo' Hollis, newly arrived on the Committee of Imperial Defence staff, who later explained this by his 'enthusiasm' and implicit unfamiliarity with normal procedure.[8] But the authors clearly anticipated a powerful reaction and they were not wrong. Their work reached the desk of the prime minister, Stanley Baldwin, who was 'extremely cross' and sought an explanation from the Cabinet Secretary, Sir Maurice Hankey. Baldwin's reaction is barely surprising: the report came as an unwelcome addition to his workload. The government was facing a major challenge to its comparatively gentle rearmament programme from a coalition across the political spectrum. Under the banner 'Arms and the Covenant' Churchill had pulled together League of Nations enthusiasts, trade unionists and both left-wing and right-wing Conservatives. Baldwin tried to protect his record with the singularly inept claim that electoral considerations had held the government back from 'great armaments'. The speech in which he made the admission with 'appalling frankness' has gone down in history as a marker of his government's political failure when confronted by an unforgiving diplomatic scene. Pure coincidence rescued Baldwin when the long-simmering abdication crisis burst publicly and tempted Churchill into supporting Edward VIII, badly hurting what was left of his reputation with probably fatal collateral damage to his Arms and the Covenant campaign.

Hankey set to the work of back-pedalling on the planners' efforts with gusto. Good military and bureaucratic form meant that he did not deal with the planners directly, but with their bosses. He used three successive meetings of the Deputy Chiefs of Staff Committee – the body to which the joint planners reported – to subject the two-star-rank representatives of the three services to a remorseless cross-questioning on a document in whose composition they had had no hand. Hankey had his sights not just on the planners' report but on the pessimism of the service chiefs. He challenged the belief that the dictatorships had immensely greater scope to organize their countries for war than the democracies and argued that Germany, too, faced difficulties. He was particularly critical of the image of German air superiority, pointing out that Britain and France together had a few more bombers than Germany and many more fighters. What, he asked by implication, had changed since 1927 when 'the French, as a nation, had been credited [in an Air Staff paper] with great efficiency'? In those days France was the enemy of choice. Attempting to gain a quick result in war was a gamble and Hankey did not think that a case had been made out that 'Germany would have the superiority which would justify such a gamble'.[9]

The defence that the RAF put up was committed but intellectually weak. Its representative on the deputy chiefs of staff, member Air Vice-Marshal Christopher Courtney, did try to give Harris cover for the key assumption of the report: that the Germans' preferred choice would be a sudden assault, 'in his opinion Germany would use unrestricted air attack from the outset, so as to get a quick decision'. Courtney trotted out the threat of a knock-out blow which appeared to have become an article of faith to the Air Staff. Courtney did not deign to explain coherently why the inferiority of the Luftwaffe in fighter aircraft set out in the planners' report would not allow British or French bombers an easier job of bombing Germany which would compensate for their inferior numbers. He admitted that the British knew little of German air defences but muttered darkly that 'it was quite likely that they had devised certain means of defence regarding which we were unaware'. The RAF would still need very large numbers of bombers. Courtney took a rather different approach when Hankey claimed that British defences including 'other measures' (a clear reference to RDF) would 'constitute a very strong deterrent to attack'. Courtney dismissed RDF as 'still in the experimental stage'.

Even while Hankey was grilling the second rank of the Air Staff on their forecasts, the top level had added its voice to the chorus of fear. In his own formal analysis of what a knock-out blow might mean if Germany launched her entire air force against London, the CAS Ellington had calculated that 2,000 tons of bombs could be dropped on the first day of a war.[10]

After much discussion the planners report was heavily revised and reissued in February 1937 as a full Chiefs of Staff paper under the more seemly title of 'Planning for War with Germany', shorn of its lurid visions of what a German knock-out blow would do to Britain.[11] Much of what the RAF held dear, though, did survive. Above all, a German knock-out blow stood as a potent threat:

> If Germany decides to direct her initial attack against this country with the object of trying to knock her out of the war as rapidly as possible these attacks are likely to be quite ruthless. She will select the objectives and the projectiles which she considers most likely to achieve her object without regard to ethical considerations ...
>
> Her first attacks would be designed as Knock-Out Blows.

On one point the Chiefs of Staff went even further than the planners in their assessment of German frightfulness. Gas would 'doubtless' be used whilst the planners had merely advised that they could not 'count on the observance of the Geneva Protocol' which banned gas warfare.

The dominant strategic message of the COS report was pure Trenchardian doctrine. The planners' view that bombing was 'the only other measure which could affect the issue during the first few weeks of the war' was quoted without qualification together with their assertion that 'local defence cannot provide the full measure of security we require'. The report backed away from an outright recommendation that German terror bombing would have to be matched directly and 'sum[med] up' in favour of attacking German bombers in the air or on the ground, but proceeded to quote the planners' view that attacking bombers on the ground was an unpromising military option. The strategic vision was blighted by a collision between Trenchardian doctrine and a properly

British commitment to the norms of civilization. Unless the Germans made the first move in terms of bombing civilians, the British would have to hold back from the (by implication) sounder military policy of attacking 'vulnerable points'. Much prominence was given to the planners' view that bombing the Ruhr, Rhineland and the Saar could yield military and psychological dividends quickly, but the catch was that the RAF would never launch a knock-out blow of its own.

Hankey had diluted the extreme pessimism of the planners' report but the Chiefs' of Staff retreat from the planners' hyperbole was only shared with a very select few on the instructions of the prime minister.[12] In the wake of the furore caused by the planners' original paper, the final COS report was treated as extraordinarily secret and copies were subjected to the most draconian handling precautions. The belief that war with Germany would open with a knock-out blow against London and the doctrine that counter-bombing was the only response, which was common to both papers anyway, were firmly set in the minds of Britain's decision-makers until war broke out. Hopeless pessimism was hard-wired into the system.

The fear of a knock-out blow remained firmly entrenched in the British national psyche until the Second World War broke out. A detailed analysis of German strategic options issued by the Air Staff in April 1939 featured attacks on civilian morale conducted with 'utmost ruthlessness and indifference to human suffering' as Germany's probable strategy.[13] On the very first day of the war the air raid sirens sounded out over London. To many this seemed to herald the long-dreaded arrival of an armada of Luftwaffe bombers set to wreck the capital, the hideous reality of modern war. It was a mistake; there were no German planes, only the French air attaché who had forgotten to file a flight plan for a return trip from Paris. Nor did the Luftwaffe bombers come until almost a year later when the fall of France had transformed the war. Until the spring of 1940 German bombs killed no one in Britain although hundreds of people were killed in traffic accidents caused by a rigorously enforced blackout intended to frustrate the Luftwaffe.

The hysterical fear of a knock-out blow and the reality of the German air attacks on British airfields and on London during the Battle of Britain have blurred together in historical consciousness, but they were quite distinct. The real events of the summer of 1940 were intended as the first step in an invasion of Britain but were only possible because France had

Above: Fairey Battle. Long before war came, it was recognized how poor the aircraft was, but it stayed in production to make up bomber numbers.

Left: H. G. Wells's novel was but one in a myriad of imaginative and pessimistic visions of the coming war.

The Bristol Blenheim was better than the Battle but short range undermined its value as a strategic bomber. (© Adrian Phillips)

Horrors in the Most Intense Form

been overrun. The Germans never intended to launch the knock-out blow which lay behind all the planning of the RAF. Nor would they have been capable of one. During the Czechoslovakia crisis a special Luftwaffe planning group examined the possibility and concluded that the best that could be achieved was pin-pricks and that a destructive attack was out of the question.[14] In May 1939, the Luftwaffe general responsible was only fractionally more optimistic. The Air Staff exaggerated German capacity and plucked a strategy out of their own dogma. The Air Staff believed the Germans shared their analysis of air war, but they did not.[15] Just as Ellington's assessment of how quickly the Germans could build their air force had been determined solely by what he believed was possible for any air force and just as the RAF's bombers had been armed to defend themselves against imaginary German versions of the Defiant, hard intelligence played little part in the RAF's calculations.

Many years later Sir John Slessor, Harris's successor as Director of Plans and éminence grise to the last peacetime CAS, Sir Cyril Newall, was writing from his commanding position as a former Chief of the Air Staff and Marshal of the RAF and he included a justification for the Air Staff's fixation on the knock-out blow.[16] He trotted out the same statistics that had fed the panic intelligence estimates at the time with no allowance for what had subsequently been learned of the truth of the Luftwaffe's strength in the late 1930s. He entirely ducked the fact that the Air Staff had presented a worst-case scenario as in practice its base case.

Chapter 17

A Striking Bomber Force Not Inferior – Scheme H

At the same time time as the joint planners were chilling the blood of Whitehall with images of the havoc a knock-out blow would wreak, it looked as though the Luftwaffe was going to be ever more able to deliver one. Over the course of 1936 the Air Staff began to revisit their estimates of Luftwaffe strength and progressively the figure which Scheme F had been designed to match began to ratchet upwards. Parity was being pushed further into the future. The most important single factor was the progressive acceptance of the Christie/X reports which the Air Staff had originally met with scepticism. These helped confirm the picture emanating from another corner of the intelligence bureaucracy, Major Desmond Morton's Industrial Intelligence Centre, which continued to report on the efficiency and strength of the German aircraft industry which made the Christie/X predictions for the growth in German air power all the more credible.

The positive evidence was matched by a shift in the way that the Air Staff approached the question that was just as effective in changing perceptions, if not more. Two of the arbitary assumptions that had limited RAF estimates fell by the wayside. Sir Edward Ellington's conviction that the Luftwaffe would manage its expansion in a rigorously restrained fashion with long pauses between each step to reach full efficiency as conceived by the RAF had been by far the most dangerous of the two. It was also tragic proof of the Air Staff's addiction to *a fortiori* reasoning and immunity to pragmatic or empirical methods. Similarly the naive belief that Hitler's casually stated goal of reaching parity with the French air force at around 2,000 aircraft offered any kind of worthwhile indication of where German rearmament might come to a halt deservedly faded from the scene.

The Air Staff's intelligence section recovered its nerve after the lambasting that it had suffered for supposdly having been caught out

Adastral House was undersized, badly located but mildly imposing and home to centralizing culture. (© Adrian Phillips)

Above left: The mission of Bomber Command was unmistakeable from its motto.

Above middle: The ambiguity of Fighter Command's motto betrays the RAF's distrust of fighter defence …

Above right: … but that of 11 Group Fighter Command redeems this.

been overrun. The Germans never intended to launch the knock-out blow which lay behind all the planning of the RAF. Nor would they have been capable of one. During the Czechoslovakia crisis a special Luftwaffe planning group examined the possibility and concluded that the best that could be achieved was pin-pricks and that a destructive attack was out of the question.[14] In May 1939, the Luftwaffe general responsible was only fractionally more optimistic. The Air Staff exaggerated German capacity and plucked a strategy out of their own dogma. The Air Staff believed the Germans shared their analysis of air war, but they did not.[15] Just as Ellington's assessment of how quickly the Germans could build their air force had been determined solely by what he believed was possible for any air force and just as the RAF's bombers had been armed to defend themselves against imaginary German versions of the Defiant, hard intelligence played little part in the RAF's calculations.

Many years later Sir John Slessor, Harris's successor as Director of Plans and éminence grise to the last peacetime CAS, Sir Cyril Newall, was writing from his commanding position as a former Chief of the Air Staff and Marshal of the RAF and he included a justification for the Air Staff's fixation on the knock-out blow.[16] He trotted out the same statistics that had fed the panic intelligence estimates at the time with no allowance for what had subsequently been learned of the truth of the Luftwaffe's strength in the late 1930s. He entirely ducked the fact that the Air Staff had presented a worst-case scenario as in practice its base case.

Chapter 17

A Striking Bomber Force Not Inferior – Scheme H

At the same time time as the joint planners were chilling the blood of Whitehall with images of the havoc a knock-out blow would wreak, it looked as though the Luftwaffe was going to be ever more able to deliver one. Over the course of 1936 the Air Staff began to revisit their estimates of Luftwaffe strength and progressively the figure which Scheme F had been designed to match began to ratchet upwards. Parity was being pushed further into the future. The most important single factor was the progressive acceptance of the Christie/X reports which the Air Staff had originally met with scepticism. These helped confirm the picture emanating from another corner of the intelligence bureaucracy, Major Desmond Morton's Industrial Intelligence Centre, which continued to report on the efficiency and strength of the German aircraft industry which made the Christie/X predictions for the growth in German air power all the more credible.

The positive evidence was matched by a shift in the way that the Air Staff approached the question that was just as effective in changing perceptions, if not more. Two of the arbitary assumptions that had limited RAF estimates fell by the wayside. Sir Edward Ellington's conviction that the Luftwaffe would manage its expansion in a rigorously restrained fashion with long pauses between each step to reach full efficiency as conceived by the RAF had been by far the most dangerous of the two. It was also tragic proof of the Air Staff's addiction to *a fortiori* reasoning and immunity to pragmatic or empirical methods. Similarly the naive belief that Hitler's casually stated goal of reaching parity with the French air force at around 2,000 aircraft offered any kind of worthwhile indication of where German rearmament might come to a halt deservedly faded from the scene.

The Air Staff's intelligence section recovered its nerve after the lambasting that it had suffered for supposdly having been caught out

Adastral House was undersized, badly located but mildly imposing and home to a centralizing culture. (© Adrian Phillips)

Above left: The mission of Bomber Command was unmistakeable from its motto.

Above middle: The ambiguity of Fighter Command's motto betrays the RAF's distrust of fighter defence …

Above right:… but that of 11 Group Fighter Command redeems this.

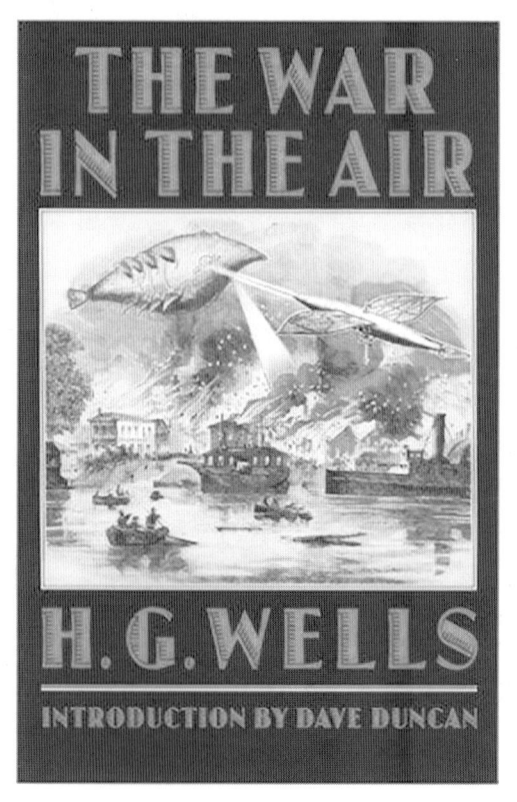

Above: Fairey Battle. Long before war came, it was recognized how poor the aircraft was, but it stayed in production to make up bomber numbers.

Left: H. G. Wells's novel was but one in a myriad of imaginative and pessimistic visions of the coming war.

The Bristol Blenheim was better than the Battle but short range undermined its value as a strategic bomber. (© Adrian Phillips)

Vickers Wellington, the best of the three second-generation modern bombers. The innovative geodetic structure can be seen through the side window.

Handley Page Hampden, cramped and under-armed.

Armstrong Whitworth Whitley, the last purpose-built night bomber and testbed for new procurement procedures. The powered gun turret on which the RAF pinned such hopes further marred the lines of an already ungainly design.

Short Stirling was Newall's vision of bombing perfection but a severe disappointment in service.

The big bombers were complex designs. A half-scale flying Stirling was built to test the aerodynamics.

Above left: Bird of ill omen, the Rolls-Royce Vulture. The RAF gambled and lost on the only available engine design powerful enough for the 1936 generation of big/medium bombers in twin-engine configuration.

Above right: Handley Page Halifax, the first twin-engine big/medium bomber design to ditch the Vulture in favour of four proven engines.

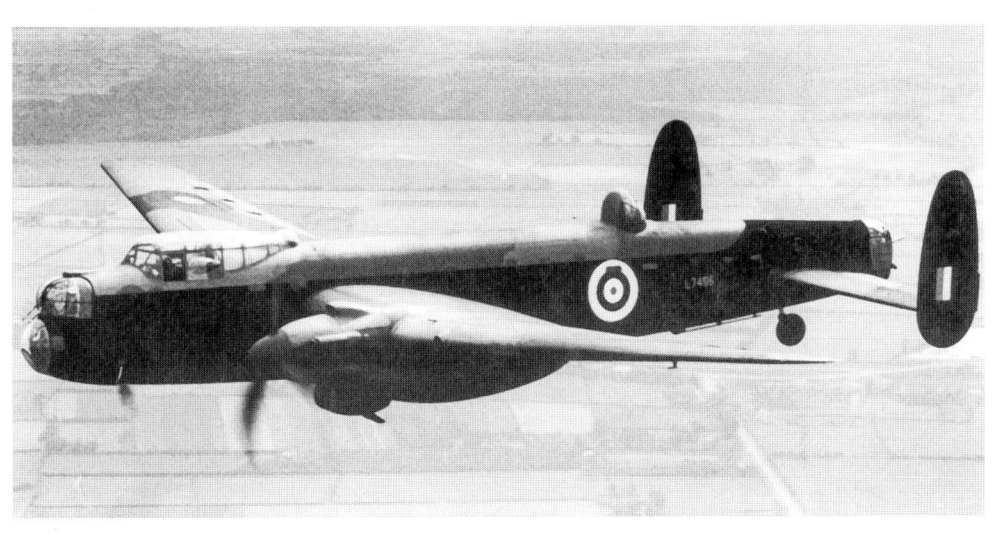

Avro Manchester, an excellent airframe compromised by the Vulture engine. Re-engined with four Rolls-Royce Merlins, it became the Lancaster, Britain's best bomber of the war.

Above left: Boulton Paul Defiant, a unique British misconception. Mercifully production was delayed otherwise it could have made up one-third of Britain's fighter force.

Above right: Blenheim fighter, a political stopgap for the Defiant and almost as useless.

Hawker Hurricane (top) and Gloster Gladiator (bottom). Newall thought the Hurricane was already obsolete in 1937. Even the Gladiator was still giving useful service in 1941. The switch to camouflage paint from plain silver in 1938 was another step on the path to war-readiness. (© Adrian Phillips)

Vickers Supermarine Spitfire. Working up full-scale production was painfully slow. (© Adrian Phillips)

Westland Whirlwind. The RAF thought wrongly that purpose-built fighters were needed to carry 20mm cannon. Newall promoted the Whirlwind but unreliable engines let it down.

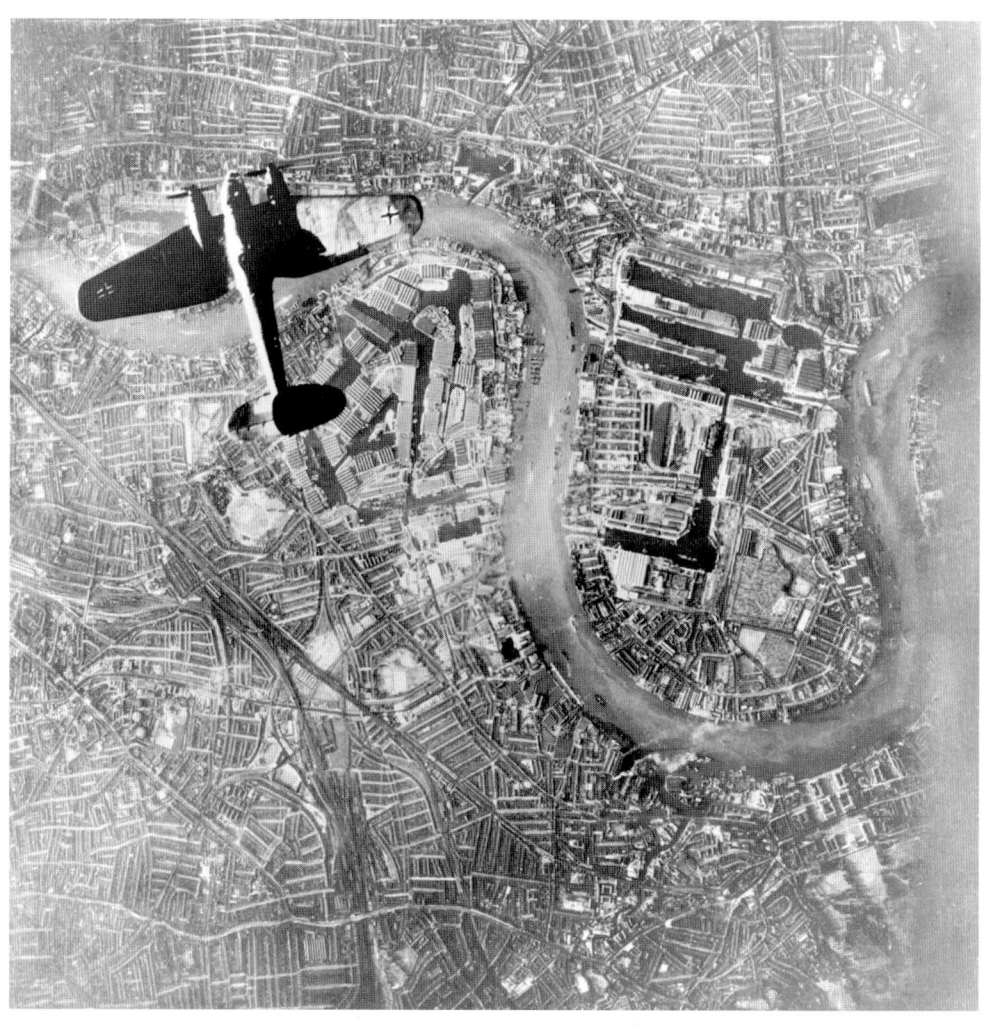

Neville Chamberlain's nightmare vision during the Munich crisis of German bombers following the Thames into the heart of London appeared to become a reality in 1940, although in 1938 the Luftwaffe would not have had bases in France and the bombload that a Heinkel 111 could carry from Germany would have been much lower as RAF intelligence rather belatedly recognized.

Right: The 'dust-bin' retractable turrets were supposed to defend RAF bombers from imaginary German turret-armed fighters.

Below: The 20mm cannon round delivered a far greater punch than the .303-inch bullet and it also exploded. Displayed at the Shuttleworth Collection. (© Adrian Phillips)

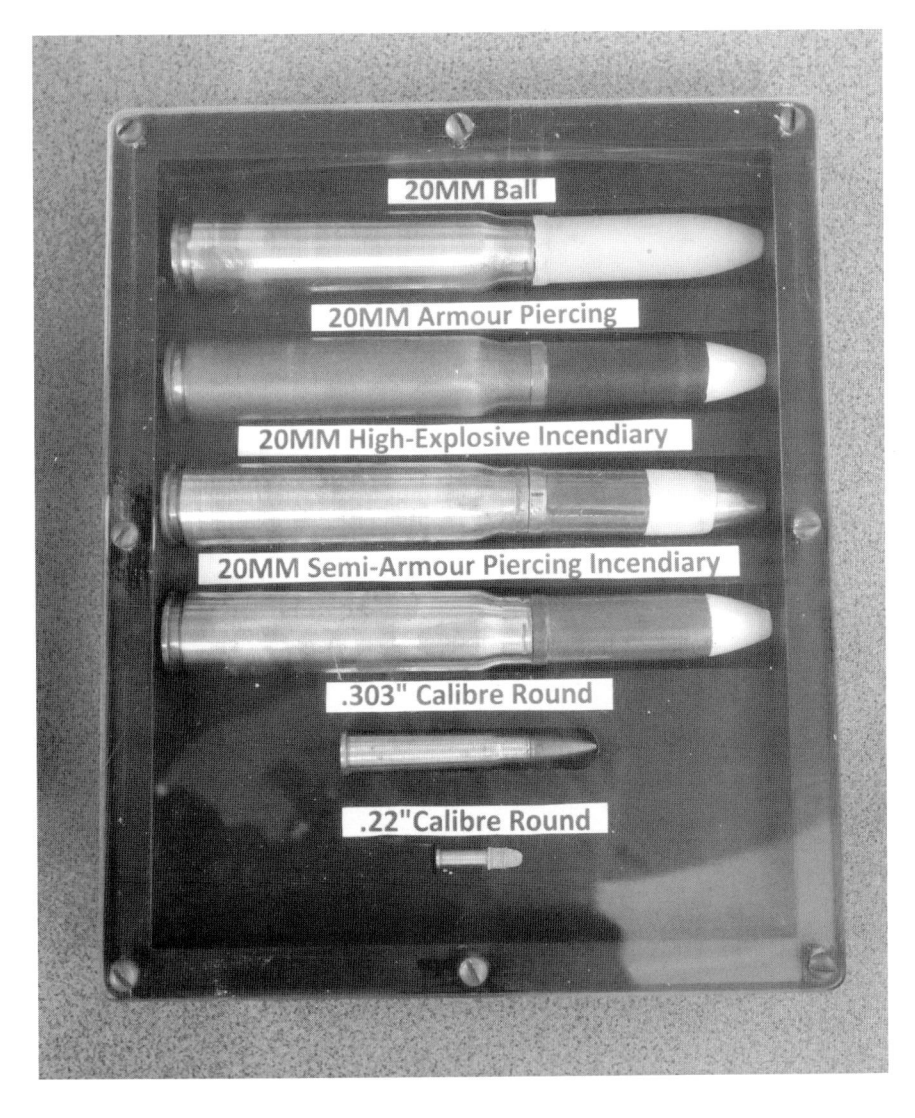

Fighter control rooms had been existence since the First World War but they now combined three new technologies: RDF, direction finding to locate friendly aircraft and VHF radar to exercise control. They also put women into the front line.

Sound mirrors were supposed to warn of approaching hostile aircraft but once the potential of RDF was proved, they served no purpose. (© Adrian Phillips)

Chain Home Low Radar masts. The final and decisive piece in Fighter Command's command and control structure. RDF was treated as extremely secret but no one came up with a cover story to explain the conspicuous infrastructure.

The gas-tight doors at the Bawdsey experimental radar station were appropriate for a priority Luftwaffe target. The female operators were on the front line of combat. (© Bawdsey Radar Trust)

The prophet, the priest and the prince, Sir Hugh Trenchard (second from right) imbued the infant RAF with the bomber dogma. Cyril Newall (left), his loyal lieutenant at the Independent Air Force, strove faithfully to apply this dogma as the RAF prepared for war. The future George VI (second from left) graces this 1919 dinner to celebrate the IAF. Christopher Courtney (right) succeeded Trenchard in command.

Above left: Lord Londonderry, the soft regency beau, appointed as air minister to sustain the social ambitions of Ramsay Macdonald.

Above middle: Sir Edward Ellington was blind to the Nazi menace and held back RAF expansion.

Above right: Philip Cunliffe-Lister, Lord Swinton, injected dynamism into the RAF's rearmament.

Above left: Lord Weir was more Trenchardian than Trenchard and father of the shadow factories.

Above right: Arthur Harris baked fear of a German knock-out blow into British thinking in a pitch for more bombers.

The Castle Bromwich shadow factory saw brutal infighting before it produced any meaningful number of Spitfires. The workers' canteen was decorated with murals by artist James Holland. (Estate of James Holland)

Above: Sir Cyril Newall (centre), passionate and increasingly wayward advocate of the bomber doctrine. Sir Kingsley Wood (left), a slicker politician than Swinton but equally committed to bombers. They are taking leave of Joseph Vuillemin (right), Newall's French opposite number, at Adastral House.

Left: John Slessor, low in rank but Newall's *éminence grise*.

Above left: Sir Hugh Dowding, an isolated military pragmatist amongst the RAF's bombing dogmatists.

Above right: Sir Wilfrid Freeman overrode Newall's fear that the Hurricane was obsolete and drove through the crucial expansion in production capacity at the time of Munich.

Above left: Sir Maurice Hankey, the hidden power in the defence establishment, could not defeat the RAF's bomber dogma as he had defeated the Admiralty's anti-convoy dogma in the First World War.

Above middle: Sir Thomas Inskip carried Hankey's scepticism on bombing into the Cabinet.

Above right: Sir Edgar Ludlow-Hewitt, AOC-in-C of Bomber Command, knew just how weak his force remained despite huge expenditure.

1. Jahrgang Nr. 7   **Luftpost-Ausgabe**

WOLKIGER BEOBACHTER

Im Dritten Reich

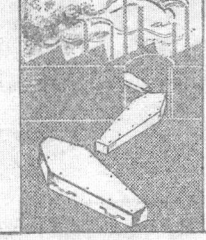

| Das Gefängnis | Die Fabrik | Die Küche |

Die Freiheit wird siegen!

„England ist entschlossen: Die Freiheit muß siegen. England ist in den Krieg gezogen, weil Tyrannei und Gewaltandrohungen die Freiheit zu knechten versuchten."

„England wird weiterkämpfen mit seiner ganzen Kraft und mit der seines gesamten Weltreiches, bis die Freiheit gesichert ist."

Mit diesen Worten schloß Mr. Chamberlain, der englische Premierminister, seine Rede in Birmingham am 24. Februar.

„England," so sagte er, „begehrt nicht die Länder anderer.... England kämpft, um den militaristischen Geist zu zerstören und die Anhäufung von Rüstung zu beseitigen, die ganz Europa und nicht zuletzt Deutschland verarmen. Nur so kann Europa die Sicherheit wiedergegeben werden; nur so können die Nationen Europas vor Bankrott und Ruin bewahrt werden."

Das andere Deutschland

„Unter der gegenwärtigen deutschen Regierung kann es für die Zukunft keine Sicherheit geben."

„Die Schichten Deutschlands, die bereit sind, am Neubau Europas mitzuarbeiten, sind in Acht und Bann getan. Das Volk ist selbst von neutralen Stimmen abgeschnitten, und seine Machthaber haben wiederholt gezeigt, daß auf das Wort, das sie anderen Regierungen oder dem eigenen Volk gegeben haben, kein Verlaß ist."

„Es ist an Deutschland, den nächsten Schritt zu tun und zu zeigen, daß es die Idee „Macht geht vor Recht!" ein für allemal aufgibt."

„Sobald Deutschland bereit ist, zuverlässige Beweise für seinen guten Willen zu geben, wird es in anderen die Hilfsbereitschaft finden, die wirtschaftlichen Schwierigkeiten nach dem Kriege zu überwinden."

„England," so sagte Mr. Chamberlain, „hat keine Ursache den Ausgang des Kampfes zu fürchten, wie lange er auch dauern mag."

Kurze Nachrichten

Truppenteile aus Australien und Neuseeland sind in Ägypten und Palästina eingetroffen und bilden einen Teil der unter General Weygand stehenden alliierten Streitkräfte.

England hat 150 Flugzeuge und grosse Mengen von Kriegsmaterial nach Finnland geliefert.

Englische Flugzeuge führten in der Nacht vom 22./23. Februar Erkundungsflüge über Österreich und in der Nacht vom 23./24. Februar über Böhmen aus.

Von 9 000 alliierten und neutralen Schiffen, die in Konvois gefahren sind, wurden nur 0,02 Prozent versenkt.

Auf Verlangen der deutschen Regierung ist in Holland ein Prozessverfahren gegen Baron Felix von Papen, den Vetter des deutschen Gesandten in Ankara, wegen seines Buches über deutsche Konzentrationslager eingeleitet worden.

The '*Wolkiger Beobachter*' was the British propagandists' clunky word-play on the Nazi *Völkischer Beobachter* newspaper. Goebbels held British airdropped propaganda leaflets in contempt.

by Hitler's claim. After months sticking to the increasingly indefensible figure of 1,512 for Luftwaffe strength right up to 1940, the Air Staff produced a paper which was circulated in Whitehall. It put Luftwaffe strength at 2,500 planes in March 1939 of which 1,700 would be bombers. The Foreign Office recognized that a crucial watershed in the understanding of German intentions had been reached: 'the cat seems to be out of the bag – the Germans are going to have the biggest air force they can.'[1] Just as he had done with Hitler's parity claim of two years before, Vansittart, the Foreign Office's resident obsessive on the German menace, had the story circulated in the press to cement the German danger in the public mind.

Once again it was the air minister Swinton who drove Britain's response to the new situation. He drew up a new expansion scheme for the RAF, Scheme H, which was presented in January 1937. This was amongst the least substantial and the shortest lived of all the schemes, but it still gave a clear indication of the strategy that Swinton and the Air Staff wanted to pursue. It brought an element of outright farce into proceedings. Swinton was moving far faster than Ellington who only formally accepted the new estimates for Luftwaffe strength after the proposed Scheme H had been circulated, without ever suggesting that his earlier forecasts had been in error.

At least outwardly the goal of Scheme H was to reach parity with Germany. The government as a whole was still firmly stuck on the hook of Baldwin's commitment. The theme of parity dominates the Scheme H memoranda although Swinton moved to fit the target into a clearly Trenchardian mould. In practice he discarded a purely numerical target and brought in a new yardstick. It would be unreasonable to aim slavishly to match Germany in pure numbers of aircraft. The key measure of parity was to be bomber strength: 'A striking bomber force not inferior to that of Germany.'[2] With a debate on defence looming the very afternoon of the Cabinet meeting that considered Swinton's proposal for Scheme H, it was inevitable that the purely political aspect of the question dominated.[3] Only Swinton strayed very far onto anything that seemed like a purely military aspect of the question and that was going into the detail of the Trenchardian definition of parity which excluded army cooperation aircraft. He threw a sop to his colleagues' doctrinally unsound predilection for fighters with a throwaway remark that Britain needed more of them than Germany, but this was strictly political; nothing in Scheme H suggests that Swinton or the Air Staff took this seriously.

The Air Ministry civil servants were alert to the risk of ill-informed public comment that was to be feared at any scheme that did not prioritize raw numbers:

> the general public – especially the section who thought what the Daily Mail told them to think – who had been accustomed to reckon parity in terms of numbers of first-line aircraft would find that there was a striking force of fewer aircraft (though admittedly with a bigger bomb broadside) in 1941 than in 1939. Would there not be an outcry when it was realised that as the programme advanced the first line strength of the Striking Force was decreasing even though the bomb load which the force could carry was going up?[4]

Weir shrugged off the risk with a 'full and complete answer – the bombload was the thing that really mattered whatever the Daily Mail might say'. He was speaking the language of the Air Staff.

Scheme C had aimed for 1,736 aircraft in April 1939, Swinton now wanted 2,422 at that date with another seventy as soon as practicable thereafter, a total increase of almost two-thirds. Almost all the extra aircraft under Scheme H were to be bombers: 1,631 bombers on 1 April 1939 compared to 1,022 under the existing scheme for that date. A final spurt of expansion after that date would take the RAF's bomber force to 1,701, precisely equal to the expected strength of the Luftwaffe's bomber force as the ultimate goal. All these top-up aircraft were to be bombers. Of all the RAF's various expansion schemes, Scheme H was the most purely Trenchardian in the numerical priority it gave bombers. Fighter numbers were to rise from 420 to 476 in the first phase to April 1939 but that was all. Bombers would ultimately outnumber fighters by three and half times in the RAF of Scheme H, a ratio of 3.5:1.

The British aircraft industry was working at full capacity on Scheme C already and Swinton knew that unless the government contravened the shibboleth of no interference in normal trade, it would be impossible to ramp output further over his time horizon. Here the Air Staff's prudence in insisting on large reserves under

Scheme C proved its worth. By juggling the reserves and holding back new squadrons which had been slated for deployment in remote regions of the Empire, he was able to structure the expansion needed to achieve the Scheme H numbers without placing any fresh orders for aircraft.

The extra funding for Scheme F had been approved as part of the implementation of the second DRC set of recommendations for all the services. Scheme H was a solo effort by the RAF alone so it would have to face the budgetary music from an exposed position. The memorandum setting out Scheme H was already the bearer of bad news about the cost of its predecessor, which does not appear to have been disclosed before. The expected cost of Scheme F had crept up from £350 million to £375 million as the higher cost of modern (and larger) planes was factored in. Even though Swinton had juggled his figures to avoid the need to increase the absolute numbers of aircraft ordered, the cost of Scheme H was higher than F: an extra £50 million, taking it to £425 million over the four-year period. The split of the extra cost was not detailed, but it certainly featured extra aircrew, aerodromes and the like. It is a fair guess that the migration to new, larger bomber types contributed even more. It would cost an extra £15 million per year to keep the Scheme H RAF operating once the expansion was complete.

Here the Germans themselves took a hand in the proceedings. They were fully aware that the size of the Luftwaffe was a topic of acute concern for the British. In July 1936 Swinton had met Erhard Milch, the man charged with the day-to-day task of building the Luftwaffe, and had pressed him for information on its size.[5] Milch bided his time and trickled out some historical information and then invited the RAF to send a senior delegation to Germany. The Germans were aware of the furore provoked by Hitler's parity claim, notably the huge publicity given to it and the even more far-fetched figures for the size of the Luftwaffe in Rothermere newspapers. This was clear and unwelcome to Milch.[6] It was all very well for the Führer to overawe foreign politicians with exaggerated statements of German strength, but another thing entirely if this led to them increasing their own forces to match his own. The moment had come to dampen British estimates of the size of the German air force with a carefully stage-managed show of ostensible openness.

Two air marshals, DCAS Christopher Courtney and Douglas Evill, the senior staff officer of Bomber Command, went over to Germany in January 1937 and were treated to a comprehensive tour of German air force and air industry sites. Throughout, the visit was conducted in conditions of ludicrous secrecy.* Milch gave his visitors figures for the performance of German aircraft but only on condition that they did not make notes of what he was saying. A constant theme of Milch's comment was that nothing he said should go beyond the Air Ministry, certainly not to the Foreign Office, on the pretext that it would be bound to leak onwards to the French. Milch's performance peaked when Courtney asked for data on the size of the Luftwaffe. On condition that he came alone, unaccompanied by any British diplomats or other officers, he was permitted to visit Milch's office, where he was treated to a melodramatic charade of Milch opening his safe and taking out confidential books with the relevant statistics. These purported to show that the Luftwaffe programme would yield a first-line strength of 1,755 aircraft by the autumn of 1938, far below the 2,038 figure in the Christie/X intelligence.[7] This included only 810 heavy and medium bombers compared to the figure of 1,700 in 1939 that Ellington had so recently circulated. Courtney seems to have swallowed this pantomime hook, line and sinker and Swinton played up even further when he reported Courtney's findings to the Cabinet in February only shortly after he had presented his Scheme H proposals posited on a far larger Luftwaffe. Swinton emphasized that even the historical figures had been obtained under near-confessional circumstances and under the conditions that they not be disclosed to Parliament or any foreign country.[8] With remarkable naivety for someone normally wise to the ways of the world, Swinton told the Cabinet that Germans would be unlikely to try to mislead them as British intelligence was so good. He also passed on Milch's promise to inform the British if the Luftwaffe programme changed with apparent seriousness.

Faced with the, in retrospect, curious willingness to take Milch's words at face value, Swinton led the Cabinet in retreating from most of his plans. All that remained of Scheme H was the purchase and

---

* The story of the Courtney/Evill visit to Germany was uncannily familiar to the author from his time as an investment analyst researching German companies. He came to recognize as a warning sign of a flagrant untruth that it was passed onto him under the guise of especially confidential information

clearing of the land for the thirteen new aerodromes of the scheme and, crucially, the recruitment and training of the pilots and skilled airmen anticipated. All told, the extra expenditure would have been around £5 million. Swinton left down a marker that the Germans would be fully able to move towards the strength on which Scheme H had been posited at short notice with the clear implication that his proposals would need to be revisited if signs emerged that they were. The relics of Scheme H accepted by the Cabinet were small but they were the only truly long-lead items. If the Cabinet came to revisit its decision no vital time would have been lost.

Chapter 18

Maximum Offensive Potential

In early 1936, the government had adopted Scheme F, which set the seal on plans to expand the RAF in size both in terms of first-line strength and in reserves. Britain was committed to a large air force equipped on a scale that its commanders believed was necessary. At every level the Trenchardian doctrine was baked into the scheme, but there remained a final part of the jigsaw to fall in place before the RAF attained the form in which the Air Staff wanted to fight the next war. The 'light medium' Battle and Blenheim bombers fell well short of this ideal and even the 'heavy medium' Hampdens and Wellingtons (plus the Whitley, which was only nominally a heavy bomber) still left much to be desired in terms of delivering the 'bomber broadside' to which the Air Staff aspired. The final step was to move on from the expedients of the early expansion schemes to truly big bombers. The modern types wanted under Scheme F were light years ahead of the biplane era but they were only the first practical uses of the latest steps in aircraft technology. There was still plenty of scope to design more powerful and effective aircraft. In the course of 1936, the RAF set out to define how it wanted to use this potential and what it wanted its next generation of aircraft to look like. This was to have a decisive influence on the shape of the air force that fought the Second World War. The bombers that dominated the RAF's inventory and strategy until the end of the war were conceived in 1936.

There was no argument in 1936 that bombers and not fighters were the crucial class of aircraft, so it went without saying that the RAF was going to concentrate on developing the next generation of bombers. The process allowed the strategists to reach for two objectives. The first and broader one was to wring the maximum extra potential from aircraft technology in the state that it had reached. The second and slightly narrower one was to shape the next generation of bombers to accomplish a task that was new since the planes of Scheme F had been conceived. The primary mission of the RAF was to attack Germany from Britain.

In the eye of faith, the Scheme F planes were – just – capable of the task but they were far from perfect. In a truth that was to become painfully obvious in 1940, they ranged from grotesquely inadequate to mediocre. Swinton might sell the Cabinet a confident vision of the new RAF's capabilities in the sure knowledge that ministers would not spot just how optimistic it was, but the Air Staff knew how much more could be done. The first step in the RAFs response to the new and mighty Luftwaffe had been Scheme F but the full application of new technology would fulfil the Trenchardian vision.

Scheme F had already pointed the way towards the next generation of bombers. It featured a new class of large bomber, which went a step beyond the types just coming into service. It was designed to a specification B.1/35 written in early 1935 just before rearmament got fully under way. The specification featured a total range of 1,500 miles, which was only just adequate to attack Germany, and a still modest bombload of 2,000lb. Something with far better performance would be needed to make a real impression. More as a backstop than anything, work continued on the specification and the Vickers Warwick, which had been designed in parallel to the Wellington, was the result but it was never produced in any number. It was likely that something bigger would be wanted and in 1935 the Air Staff had already been taken with the Boeing four-engine bomber design that was to become the B-17 Flying Fortress.[1] The idea of a 'giant bomber' had been around for some time but the belief that its performance was likely to be poor had served as a deterrent.

A number of separate factors coalesced to take the RAF to its definitive bomber designs. As early as November 1934, before the new generation of medium bombers had even flown, the Air Staff were beginning to have doubts as to their value. They even went as far as seeing them as obsolescent, although they backed away from this extreme view.[2] Even so, it was recognized that the upcoming generation of bombers had been specified before recent advances in speed were so apparent and that an up-to-date specification ought not to be delayed.[3] The Whitley was felt to be short of what might be desirable.[4] Doubts, though remained – 'the medium bomber specifications having been made out before recent advances in speed were quite so apparent as they are now' – early provision should be made for an up-to-date medium bomber.[5] In October 1935, plans for a new medium bomber were included in the Experimental Aircraft Programme for 1936 which took shape as the P. 13/36 specification, the specification to which the Halifax and – indirectly – the Lancaster were built. One strident and powerful voice in favour of the new generation of bombers was that of the Deputy Director of Plans, Group Captain Arthur 'Bert' Harris.[6] He saw a stark choice as to

> Whether we are to fritter away our air resources in defensive ancillary types [general reconnaissance] or whether we are to have as the primary requirement, the maximum offensive potential. This is what Germany intends to have and, in spite of extra commitments peculiar to our situation, it is Germany that we have got to meet when it comes to the show down.
>
> As for performance anything less than 1,000 miles effective radius at 250 m.p.h. will not compete with our requirements and will be hopelessly out of date by the time we get it.

Harris was also calling for another change which would be fulfilled by the new aircraft. He had long been dubious that night-flying called for any special skill – he had no time for what he labelled as the 'black magic' – of dedicated night flyers.[7] The distinction between day and night bombers would disappear with the new generation aircraft.

The main features of a bomber's performance package were bombload, speed, operating range and defensive armament. The mission to attack Germany set the bar higher for all, except bombload, which was a constant for any bomber design; Harris seems to have taken this for granted. The increase in the operating range needed was a simple geographic fact, but in turn this created what planners saw as the need for extra speed. The greater the distance the bomber had to travel, the more important it was that it could cruise at a higher speed and minimize the time it spent exposed to German defences. A long flight across Germany increased the risk of interception by fighters and the need for armament with which to fight it off. The only part of the design philosophy equation which would strike a modern observer as curious was a throwback to the biplane era: the conviction that it was necessary to increase aircraft weight to obtain greater speed. This assumed that the more powerful an engine was, the more it would weigh. The engine accounted for a far greater proportion of the total weight of an aircraft than the airframe in the early days of aviation. Coupled with the imperative to increase the bombload, this made for an inexorable increase in the size of bombers. The most vital part of the aircraft was a structure capable of transporting a heavy bomb-load so they were going to be much larger airframes than existing designs.

The RAF needed a step change in bomber performance and not just a small progression. A new technique appeared to put this within reach. When the Air Staff set to the work of writing specifications for the next generation of bombers in 1936, they seemed to have found a way to counter the problem of rising aircraft weight. The use of assisted take-off through some form of catapult would get bombers into the air with a greater load of fuel so as to travel further with heavier bombloads. For a short-period catapults appeared to be way of the future. The system never seems to have got any further than theoretical development; there is no evidence that even pilot practical tests were attempted, but the hopes that surrounded the idea still had an important influence on aircraft design. It served to push out the envelope for what was considered a practical operating weight. Perhaps fortunately, catapult launch was never put to serious test as more conventional approaches to dealing with the problem proved to be adequate. As budget became less of a constraint on the expansion of the RAF, aerodrome runways could increase in length, permitting longer take-off runs. The power-to-weight ratio of engine designs also improved. Catapults faded away but their legacy remained in the form of heavier bombers.

The 1936 designs led to the Halifax and the legendary Lancaster heavy bombers that were the main weapons in Bomber Command's offensive against Germany from 1942 onwards, but the path that led there was not entirely direct. The Halifax and the Manchester, progenitor of the Lancaster, started life designated as mediums. At that time the Air Staff still saw a need for two distinct classes of bombers: heavy and medium. Separate specifications were prepared for both classes which featured huge increases in maximum bombload compared to the previous generation and significantly greater ranges. The heavies were to be capable of carrying 14,000lb for 1,800 miles or 8,000lb for 3,000 miles. The mediums were to be able to carry 8,000lb for 1,800 miles with 3,000 miles range as a minimum more lightly loaded. These ranges brought any part of Germany within reach of serious attack.

Catapult assistance was assumed in setting the higher end of the performance specification for both classes.

Perhaps curiously, the path to the heavy bomber proved to be smoother than the path to the mediums despite the apparently more ambitious performance targets. The draft specification for the heavy bomber was signed off by Air Staff's Operational Requirements Committee with little change, but it took two meetings and far more debate to finalize the specification for the mediums. The process of specifying the mediums was complicated by hopes that it would be possible to produce an aircraft capable of four different missions: medium bombing, torpedo bombing, general purpose (in practice, troop transport) and reconnaissance. The heavy was purely a bomber from the start. This attempt to economize by reducing the number of types of aircraft in service fell at the usual hurdle of imposing multi-functionality as a starting point for the design. Many aircraft have proved highly successfully in multiple roles, but almost invariably they were designed for a single role and it was only after they had been built that it proved they could be used for other tasks as well. Compromise is the enemy of excellence. One relic of the multi-role requirement had a quite unforeseen benefit in the medium designs that did emerge which was quite unrelated to its original purpose. The wide weapons bay needed to hold two large-diameter torpedoes proved to be a vital advantage during the war as Bomber Command adopted ever-larger weapons, in particular the 4,000lb 'cookie' thin-case blast bomb. This gave the Lancaster and Halifax yet another advantage over the Stirling heavy bomber where the aircraft's structure imposed longditudinal divisions to the bomb-bay which restricted it to the inefficient prewar designs of bombs.

From the outset the heavy was designed as a four-engine aircraft, which could use proven power plants, but the mediums were to be twin engine and they needed a new power plant. Just as there had been an active debate between proponents of single-engine and twin-engine bombers in the early 1930s, there was now a debate between the advocates of four-engine bombers and advocates of twin-engine designs. The decision to draw up specifications for four-engine and twin-engine bombers is arguably more important than the fact that these were labelled as heavy and medium bombers respectively. These designations meant little in themselves; both heavies and mediums were to perform the same mission, operating together. The Air Staff was not applying any standard designation to aircraft weights. The Avro Manchester that emerged from the medium specification weighed considerably more at 14.2 tons than the Whitley at 8.5 tons which was classed as a heavy bomber.

Wartime experience proved that with the technology of the era, four engines was the best formula for heavy aircraft, but this lay in the future. It was the failure of one key engine design that led to Bomber Command becoming an all four-motor force. In 1936 there was only one sufficiently powerful motor design available for the heavier designs and their greater bombloads. In general, the Air Staff tried to avoid imposing a specific engine on airframe makers, but here it had no way to avoid a de facto single choice.[8] They were also taking the risk of combining new airframes with a new engine. The engine concerned was the Rolls-Royce Vulture, designed to produce 1,750 horsepower, which turned out to be a dismal failure despite extensive effort invested by all concerned. It was based on an untried arrangement of four banks each of six cylinders arranged in an X shape, which proved to be fatally impractical from the start. When the RAF committed to the big twins, Wilfrid Freeman, in charge of development and production, was confident that the Vulture would be ready in time.[9] Within weeks, though, doubts started to grow and the RAF was confronted by the fact it had chosen aircraft designs for which there was no alternative engine.[10] As an emergency measure, the Halifax was redesigned to take four engines, whether the Handley Page company liked it or not.[11] The Air Ministry persevered with the Manchester, which did see service, but the Vulture proved catastrophically unreliable. The Manchester was then also redesigned as a four-engine aircraft, earning glory under the new name, the Lancaster. The conception of the Lancaster as a four-Merlin bomber features in one of the stock tales of imaginative British boffinry that pepper the legend of the RAF. Freeman's assistant, Tedder, describes Avro's designer Roy Dobson removing the wingtip of a model Manchester that happened to be sitting on his desk and adding an extra engine and wingspan.[12] There is no reason to doubt the tale, but the fact that the Air Staff had ordered Handley Page to do the same with the Halifax some months previously rather takes the gloss off it.

The failure of the Vulture was not foreseen but it gives an indication of the scale of the technical challenge to which the Air Staff had exposed the RAF. Its chief strategy rested on ambitious designs for a completely new class of aircraft. The risk of delay from any number of factors was inescapable, but there was no serious discussion of the danger.

It was understood that the introduction of four-engine bombers was so complex that there was only an (implicitly weak) possibility that some squadrons might be equipped before 1943.[13] It was going to take at least five years for the RAF to be able to put in line the class of aircraft that the Air Staff believed that it needed to meet the German challenge. In the event, this was overly conservative and four-engine bombers did enter squadron service in 1941, albeit well short of their full potential as weapons of war.

At the outset the Air Staff attached far more importance to the four-motor bomber. Ellington went so far as to say that the RAF might live without the two-motor types as the four-motor bomber would be able to do all the jobs expected of them, but not vice versa.[14] It was well understood that the huge scale of the manufacturing challenge of the four-motor bomber meant that it 'would ... almost certainly demand for its fulfilment the highest priorities over *all* [author italics] other aspects of the Defence Programme in personnel, labour, materials, etc.'.[15] Britain's military future was to be tied to a single class of aircraft.

The Operational Requirements Committee's discussion of the specifications for the new large bombers provides a fascinating insight into the RAF's decision-making process, in particular how considerations far removed from the problems of fighting Germany still featured. There was extensive discussion of the effects on performance of the hot, high-altitude airfields of India. The 3,000-mile-range requirement was partly included so the new aircraft would be better able to reinforce the distant corners of the Empire. The head of Bomber Command queried whether this might be an overreaction to the display of Italian aggression in Abyssinia. He was briefly supported by the chairman of the meeting, the Deputy Chief of the Air Staff, Christopher Courtney, until he realized that a total range of 3,000 miles translated to a practical operating radius a little more than 1,000 miles. It took a mere wing commander to remind him that this was the minimum needed to attack Germany.[16] Courtney was an undisputed star of the higher ranks of the RAF and a serious candidate for the top job; he passed as one of the service's best minds. It took the brutal Trenchardian focus of Bert Harris, then still a mere group captain, to figuratively bang the table with the insistence that maximum offensive power for European war was the thing that mattered. Harris did, though, envisage that that the new bombers might be used against Russia. The committee did not confine its attentions to such grandiose questions. It found time to substitute the word 'latrine' for 'lavatory' in the specification, but it was unclear whether this was prompted by considerations of linguistic decorum or literal accuracy.[17]

By the end of 1936 the truly big bomber had become established in Air Staff thinking as the aircraft of the future. Just as the beginning of the year had marked the turn to a large air force in numbers, so the autumn marked the watershed between obsolete or intermediate designs of aircraft and equipment which the Air Staff was confident would be able to fulfil the service's Trenchardian destiny in the form of an effective striking force against Germany. The head of the Operational Requirements section, Group Captain Robert Oxland, went on to have no more than a moderately successful career but his role in 'a plan that committed the RAF irrevocably to the policy of long-range bombing' gave him a lasting reputation amongst his colleagues.[18]

The specifications were duly issued to the plane-makers. The heavy bomber was considered to be of 'vital importance'. Two companies tendered for the heavy bomber, Supermarine and Shorts. The Air Staff had a distinct preference for the Supermarine design but it was a small firm, which depended heavily on its highly regarded chief designer R. J. Mitchell. Mitchell's state of health was a constant worry for the Air Staff and his death from cancer in June 1937 led them to abandon his design.[19] The Air Staff took comfort from being left with a single design for this crucial class of aircraft with the fact that Shorts had a well-established reputation as a maker of large aircraft; its speciality was flying boats, the largest and most complex class of aircraft in general use. The order for a prototype was driven through because of the 'vital importance' of the heavy bomber.[20]

Of the eight companies who expressed an interest in the medium bomber, two were invited to tender, A. V. Roe and Handley Page. The most optimistic of these companies was A. V. Roe which promised a prototype would be flying in 1938 but this was met with well-founded scepticism.[21] Sometime in 1939 was far more realistic for this stage of the programmes. Given the time needed for test and development, the very earliest that the RAF would be getting its new large bombers was 1940 which soon crept out to 1941, but this did not diminish the vision of new power that they brought. Any urgency in the need to prepare for war was taking second place to an Ellingtonian imperative to prepare correctly.

Long before it played a part in fighting Germany, the large bomber was called on to fight the RAF's battles in Whitehall. A couple of months after the specifications were issued, Ellington found himself on the defensive at a meeting of the Chiefs of Staff.[22] The Air Staff had just been forced to revise sharply upwards its estimate of the scale of attack that the Luftwaffe could bring to bear on Britain. The new figures for the bombload that the Germans might deliver if war broke out that year showed a fivefold increase compared to the estimate published in 1934 and a thirteenfold rise on the bomb tonnage they could deliver two years into the future. The Royal Navy member of the Chiefs of Staff committee, Admiral Chatfield, openly threatened to disassociate himself from the new estimate, which he found impossible to reconcile with the 'substantial increases which had been made and were in contemplation ... in our own air force'. Sir Maurice Hankey joined in with the observation that the new estimates meant that planning across a range of topics, including precautions against biological warfare would have to be revised. Ellington's best defence against the implicit accusation that the Air Staff had been asleep on the job was to pull the heavy bomber design out of his hat. Even though it was only at the design stage, a bomber capable of carrying the then unheard-of bombload of 14,000lb was, in Ellington's mind, a response to the more substantial threat of Luftwaffe bombers.

The prospect of the new medium on its own was enough to bring a radical change in the Air Staff's planning. The concept exactly matched what was needed to execute a Trenchardian strategy. In the eyes of the Air Member for Supply and Organization, Cyril Newall, who was soon to succeed Ellington as CAS, 'the P.13/36 undoubtedly offered precisely those qualities which we were most anxious to obtain for the Medium Bombers comprising the Striking Force, and, broadly speaking, it was the equivalent of 3 Battles as regards, range, speed, and bomb carrying capacity.'[23] The planned shift in design policy in favour of far larger bombers had been sufficiently important to be referred in advance directly to the Chancellor of the Exchequer.[24] The new planes were going to cost appreciably more than the ones for which they would be substitutes: £52,000 for the Stirling compared to £22,000 for the Wellington.[25] The improved performance might allow the numbers to be reduced, but the Air Staff was not promising this to the Treasury as a quid pro quo. The Air Staff's aim was to end up with the same number of planes but more powerful ones. The Chancellor was to be held to 'general blessing to the idea of a more powerful Striking Force being achieved by a turnover to more modern types early in 1939'.[26]

The switch to large bombers involved a change to the RAF's rearmament plan as important as any of the letter-designated schemes although it was only informally referred to as the 'Substitution Scheme'. The Air Staff was willing to wait for its new larger bombers, but not for ever and in March 1937 it set the date of 1 April 1939 as the watershed for the switch. Orders for any Battles or Whitleys that had not been delivered by that date were to be cancelled. This meant that orders for no fewer than 681 of the older generation of aircraft would be cancelled. The Whitley might have been formally classed as a heavy bomber, but in the Air Staff's new scheme of things the future belonged to the new 'medium'. Two hundred and ten of the new mediums were to equip fifteen of the seventy bomber squadrons programmed in Scheme F. Neville Chamberlain held true to the vision of a dauntingly powerful bomber force that had shaped his approval for Scheme F and duly gave his approval to the 'Substitution Scheme'. It never featured in the list of lettered schemes, but perhaps this might have attracted too much attention. By the back door the Air Staff had secured a significant increase in the budget for its expansion programme.

The RAF's adoption of the big-bomber strategy involved jumping two generations of aircraft. The 1936 generation of bombers were intended to be the RAF's only bombers. They would certainly displace the Battles and Blenheims, but they also pushed the Whitleys, Hampdens and Wellingtons into a state of limbo. Given the time it would take to bring the 1936 bombers into service, the RAF was not going to be able to dispense with the Whitleys, Hampdens and Wellingtons quite as peremptorily but they would carry the stigma of obsolescence even before they entered service. The strategy was also comparatively long term; in February 1938, even a year after the decision was taken, the RAF was not looking at the prospect of deploying substantial numbers of the 1936 generation aircraft until 1943. With no political discussion about the implications, the RAF had committed itself to a strategy that would not ripen for years.

Chapter 19

Swinton's Hobby

Bomber Command and Fighter Command developed as very different organizations. In part this reflected a universal factor of aviation at the time and for decades afterwards: that the operational mission and technology of fighter aircraft was different to that of bombers; it also reflected the very different positions in the RAF's mental universe of the two branches. The development of the equipment and operations of Bomber Command was driven by aircraft technology in the narrow sense. The RAF's bombers were radically different to the bombers of the First World War, but they did their job in much the same way, operating essentially as autonomous units. By contrast Fighter Command operated under centralized control, which gave it a quite different set of infrastructure requirements. Just as aircraft technology made enormous strides, beginning in the late 1920s, so did radio technology. Fighter Command applied these advances to its equipment and procedures, but they barely touched Bomber Command.

When they were trying to fight the Gothas of *Türkenkreuz* in 1917 and 1918, Britain's home defence fighters had been subject to a centralized command and control organization which had been set up to perform a complex task. The organization had to detect the approach of German bombers by sound or by sight, estimate a position at which they could be attacked and communicate this data to the fighter aerodromes as an order to deploy the defence aircraft to attack them at these positions. Central to this system was a network of control rooms which received the reports of hostile aircraft and alerted the defenders. These control rooms were kept in being under the independent RAF and were part of the 'Fighting Area' branch of Air Defence of Great Britain through the service's early years of peacetime existence. They became increasingly dilapidated as the 1920s wore on into the 1930s.

That is not to say that the RAF did not invest in its air defence infrastructure during its early years of independence. In fact, the service devoted considerable resources to finding a solution to the greatest problem with which it had been confronted in the First World War: locating the airships and bombers attacking Britain. Other than under clear skies in daylight, the only method available was to track the sound made by their engines. Early in 1915, work had begun to refine the process of listening for the sound of engines, focusing sound waves so they could be detected at far greater ranges and analysed to give information on their sources, in practice on the size and nature of the attacking force.[1] The experiments continued into the 1930s with considerable resources being devoted to them. The vast concrete 'sound mirrors' that resulted can still be seen at Dungeness on the Kent coast pointing across the English Channel towards the French coast from which the bombers were expected. Some progress was made, but sound detection never achieved decisive results.

The true breakthrough in aircraft detection technology came in 1934 with the recognition that aircraft – especially the then novel all-metal designs – disrupted radio waves. Radio itself was also a comparatively new technology. The British defence establishment soon recognized the potential to transform this phenomenon into a practical system of aircraft detection. The development of what is now universally known as radar was arguably the first instance of scientists actually taking the lead in transforming warfare. The first proposal for the technology arose from a committee comprised exclusively of scientists, the Air Ministry Committee for the Scientific Survey of Air Defence. Air Marshal Philip Joubert de la Ferté who was later appointed as deputy CAS with special responsibility for the application of radar, complained that the matter was something of a closed shop for scientists.

From the start Air Marshal Dowding played a key role in the process. As Air Member for Research and Development, the project fell into his remit and it was he who insisted on a practical live demonstration which took shape as the famous Daventry experiment of 1935 in which an RAF bomber was flown across the path of radio waves from the BBC's transmitter with a receiver on the ground to monitor the reflected radio waves. This provided the vital proof of concept that underpinned the development needed to transform the system into a viable one. The bland cover name radio direction finding (RDF) was devised.

Sadly, at this point scientific development fell victim to political manoeuvres. Churchill's involvement in air defence planning became positively damaging as he promoted the position of Professor Frederick Lindemann, his personal adviser on scientific matters. Lindemann and Churchill lobbied for air defence research to be conducted by a powerful Committee of Imperial Defence sub-committee, which they would be well placed to dominate. Lindemann's influence was almost entirely malign. It crystallized in a vendetta he conducted against the Air Ministry's scientist, Professor Sir Henry Tizard. The feud combined personal antipathy, Lindemann's vaulting ambitions for his own position and disagreement over practical points of science. Amongst the latter was Lindemann's erroneous conviction that infrared offered a practical method for detecting aircraft. Lindemann also promoted his patron's pet scheme for aerial minefields as a defence against bombers. The venomous relationship between Lindemann and Churchill on one side and Tizard and his professional colleagues on the other brought nothing at all of any value and merely served as a severe distraction. Churchill failed to recognize his protégé's deleterious effects and regarded the opposition he faced on both personal and professional questions as evidence that the government was neglecting science in preparing Britain's defences.

One of the early backers of RDF in Whitehall was Sir Maurice Hankey, who had helped handle Lindemann's attempt to create his own mini-empire within Hankey's Committee of Imperial Defence network. Hankey fought a somewhat lonely battle to take RDF from its origin as a scientists' project into the mainstream narrative of Britain's defence planning. When he was trying to push back against the Joint Planners' wildly pessimistic assessment of the threat posed by Germany – and lightly disguised prospectus for the RAF's counter-bombing mission as Britain's best if not only defence – at the end of 1936, he tried to persuade the Deputy Chiefs of Staff that 'new and potent defence measures devised by scientists will have been brought into use [between now and 1939]' to underline the fact that Britain's defences would take 'a considerable toll of attacking Aircraft'.[2] The RAF representative acknowledged that the Joint Planners had been presenting a worst-case picture and had discounted RDF because it was 'in the experimental stage', but neither the revised version of the 1936 analysis nor any of its successors did more than note the existence of RDF; there was no hint that it had the potential to revolutionize air defence.

Philip Cunliffe-Lister, who had been given de facto the job of re-equipping the RAF by Stanley Baldwin, was an early convert to the possiblities and in July 1935 his committee recommended the installation of a chain of stations to provide the country with defence against air attack.[3] Even at that stage the possiblity of radar control of anti-aircraft guns and the detection of ships at sea was obvious. The committee recognized that the RAF would control the air interception system, but did expect all the services to use the technology. By October the scientist Robert Watson-Watt had been appointed by the Air Ministry to supervise the development of the system and detailed planning was in hand as to how it would operate.[4] By November 1935, it was envisaged that a chain of stations would ultimately provide coverage of the whole coastline from Southwold in East Anglia to Dover across which German bombers would most likely fly by August 1936.[5] At the end of the year, the first five stations were approved at a projected cost of £62,500.[6]

Dowding oversaw the next crucial step in the creation of Britain's air defence system that was to defeat the Luftwaffe in 1940. Shortly after he had taken command of the newly created Fighter Command in June 1936, there took place a series of trials of new methods based at the Biggin Hill fighter aerodrome, later famous in the Battle of Britain. Dowding was deeply involved in planning them and analysing their results. RDF lay at the heart of the experiments but they also brought together two other new technologies, which were also of immense importance. VHF radio gave aircraft the possiblity of continuous communication with the ground (and each other), which moved the command and control system into real time. Direction Finding allowed friendly aircraft to be tracked from the ground. In the space of a few months the intelligence, command and control environment for air defence was being transformed. Telephone and teleprinter links between the different ground elements – aerodromes, operation rooms, Direction Finding and RDF centres – were an integral part of the process from the start. The then substantial sum of £2,000 per year was authorized to provide Fighting Area with new telephone lines.[7]

The Biggin Hill experiment served as proof-of-concept of how the new technologies could be integated into a working system. Not only could RDF detect hostile aircraft, it could also be integrated into a robust air defence system that could use the intelligence for fighters to achieve interceptions. A powerful head of enthusiasm developed for the potential of RDF. Watson-Watt, who had been given direct responsbility for the system became a vehement advocate. The commander of 11 Group, the key unit of Fighter Command, was carried away by the new possibilities that were being opened by technology.[8] He foresaw that it might sharply reduce, if not remove, the need to have wasteful standing patrols and to move the defence line much further forward than it had been. In practice, he saw the possiblity to revolutionize air defence by fighters. His commander, Dowding, also saw the potential although he focused on mundane practical issues, in particular the need to be able to distinguish between plots of hostile and friendly aircraft, the system now known as IFF (identification friend or foe).[9] He also spotted that the early versions of the system were good at establishing the height of aircraft but less effective in finding their bearings. Nonetheless Dowding endorsed the idea that the first stations should provide preliminary cover over as great a length of coastline as possible, pending the completion of the chain.[10]

Further experiments in April 1937 confirmed that RDF was set to bring a step change in the RAF's defence capacity. On behalf of the Air Staff, Christopher Courtney, the Deputy CAS, recommended the creation of a chain of twenty stations covering the east and south coasts of England in line with the scheme mapped out by the scientists. It was the prospectus for RDF as part of air defence:

> In the view of the Air Staff the trials have established that RDF can give to Air Defence Headquarters very important information as to the approach of enemy aircraft which cannot be obtained by any other means, and which is essential to the successful operation of fighters.[11]

He was confident that limitations revealed by the trials could be overcome. More important, RDF had a backer at the top of its political leadership, Swinton, now the air minister. He won the Chancellor of the Exchequer, Sir John Simon, over to the value of RDF and put the Air Staff's proposals to the top-level defence decision-making body, the Defence Plans (Policy) sub-committee.[12] Swinton and Simon emphasized the unanimous support for the system from the members of the Air Defence Research Committee. Swinton also pointed to the comparatively small cost of RDF. With this level of support it was a mere formality for the Treasury to sign off officially the £1.2-million budget for the chain of stations. Even including the £68,000 authorized for the first four stations, the sum was almost trivial in the context of the

RAF's bomber-heavy Scheme H which was set to cost £425 million over four years.

A further large-scale fighter control exercise was conducted in July 1938. The defences were severely handicapped by poor weather, but the the level of interceptions achieved by the fighters impressed Dowding. He could see that the strategic advantage had swung to the defender:

> Thus as we always maintain our fighter equipment superior to that of the enemy bomber, in flying performance and htting power, we shall be able to inflict such casualties on him that he will lose his morale.[13]

The apparent general agreement about the potential of RDF masked a rather less harmonious reality. In a newspaper extract from his memoirs that appeared in 1947, Swinton stated that Ellington had opposed building the full-scale chain and that the matter had been referred to a personal discussion between Swinton, Ellington and the prime minister, Stanley Baldwin, who had supported Swinton.[14] Ellington wrote to Swinton, complaining that his account was not accurate, although he did not dispute the key assertion that he had been against extending the RDF chain. Ellington claimed to have forgotten whether the question of RDF had been discussed with the prime minister, but scored an effective point by noting that at the time that the Cabinet was asked to approve the expenditure, Chamberlain had already replaced Baldwin as prime minister. Ellington did admit to a degree of scepticism over RDF, writing that he might have questioned whether the 'Government would feel justified in spending the money' on the stations. He also confessed to doubts as to whether RDF would give information that was timely enough to be useful. He challenged Swinton's admittedly somewhat garbled account of how RDF had revolutionized fighter tactics with the dubious claim that the only 'fundamental advance' made before he ceased to be CAS in September 1937 was the introduction of VHF radio. Perhaps conscious that his error over who was the relevant prime minister left him exposed, Swinton removed the entire passage from the published book. This retreat did not deter Swinton from saying long afterwards that Ellington did not support RDF and that he frequently referred to it as 'Swinton's hobby'.[15]

Given the unarguable success of RDF, or radar as it is now universally known, Ellington is unusual in owning up to even a degree of scepticism in the 1930s. The British disclosed its existence in 1941 and since then almost all involved were falling over themselves to claim credit for its invention and introduction. There are scattered indications that Ellington's hostility was widely spread. Bullock, the then head civil servant of the Air Ministry, criticized the heavy focus on developing RDF.[16] This might help explain why Swinton did not try to save his official when he was dismissed for a breach of ethics. Joubert de la Ferté, the Air Staff's RDF specialist, acknowledged later that there were many doubters of RDF in the Air Staff.[17]

Even when the RDF chain was well on the way to being complete in early 1939, Air Staff was still taking a guarded view of its potential. When the government's air raid precautions supremo, Sir John Anderson, was briefed about the likely scale of German bombing, he was warned that the system would face 'teething troubles' and that RDF could not be expected generally to produce accurate data for some time.[18] RDF did not even feature specifically in a detailed assessment drawn up by the Air Staff, released in April 1939, as to the likely shape of an air war with Germany, which claimed that 'In active ground defence against air attack and in passive defence measures, Germany's preparations are superior to our own ... and may remain so during 1940'.[19] The efforts of Fighter Command to build up an efficient command and control system since 1935 based on modern technology passed almost unnoticed.

It was not just doubts about the effectiveness of RDF that prevented it from influencing British military thinking to the extent that it should have. Swinton knew its value, but he was also playing the Whitehall budgetary game and was reluctant to risk it being used by other players as a pretext for depriving the RAF of resources. In the midst of the ferocious battle over the funding of one of the expansion schemes, he told Inskip, 'we have also made a quicker advance in our RDF experiments than we had ventured to hope but a vast amount remains to be done here both in development and application.'[20] An effective RDF system was too closely tied to fighter-based defence for a dedicated Trenchardian to undermine the case for bombers as the best means of defence by talking up its value in the wrong quarters.

Another factor that worked against any wider appreciation of how RDF was strengthening the power of air defence was the extreme security which surrounded its development. Knowledge of RDF was deliberately restricted even at the highest decision-making levels; the decision on the twenty-station chain was referred directly to the DP(P) committee rather than first passing a more junior level.[21] The files abound in mentions of the extreme importance of maintaining confidentiality. At one point it was felt that the cover name RDF was becoming too revealing, and it was proposed to substitute ARDAP (Air Raid Description And Plotting).[22] The proposal was turned down and RDF kept its name until the American term radar displaced it. When the RAF undertook staff conversations with their French counterparts in May 1938, the delegation was specifically instructed not to discuss RDF.[23] The existence of RDF was not publicly disclosed until 1941 when it was beyond dispute that the Germans too had their own.

Early hopes that the invention might be a British monopoly had always been, though, wide of the mark; other countries including Germany had lit on the principle separately and were developing their own versions at the same time as Britain. The RAF was even given a good hint that Germany was fully aware when the Luftwaffe chief Erhard Milch asked about British progress in the field during a lunch at Fighter Command headquarters in the course of one of his visits to Britain in late 1937.[24] There is no sign that the British side ever followed up this disclosure, but Hitler somehow got wind of the conversation and later accused Milch of having betrayed a German secret. The Germans understood the principle and produced better quality radar sets than the early British versions, but, fortunately for Britain, the Luftwaffe intelligence section entirely failed to grasp the working of Fighter Command's command and control system, which was one of the key German weaknesses in the Battle of Britain.

***

It would be wrong to suppose that the Air Staff failed to grasp the potential of RDF because the naturally conservative leadership of the armed services of the day were automatically sceptical of such things. The Royal Navy's attitude to technological developments presents a mirror image of the Air Staff's towards RDF. ASDIC (also a misleading cover term) was a method of locating submarines by sound waves that had been developed at the end of the First World War albeit not used operationally. In the 1930s, navy destroyers were widely fitted with ASDIC. The Admiralty became excessively confident that ASDIC would master any threat from U-boats and did not seem to expect that it would ever have to fight the battles that it fought in 1917 to protect Britain's shipping lifelines.[25] A cynic might be tempted to say that this confidence meshed happily with the Admiralty's instinctive belief that true naval warfare was the clash of big-gun surface ships just as the RAF saw air warfare as duel between opposed bombing fleets.

***

The adoption of RDF was revolutionary. It applied cutting-edge technology to air defence and it also brought with it an unheralded but huge shift in the contribution that women were to make to the war effort. Once again it was Dowding and Tizard who led the way in recruiting and training women to operate RDF.[26] For the first time women were being given a front-line combat task in Britain's armed forces. They might not have been handling weapons, but they were locating the enemy and, soon, handling crucial work in processing intelligence. The image of female plotters with their long croupiers' rakes moving the counters representing friendly and hostile squadrons across the battle maps in Fighter Command control rooms is one of the enduring icons of the Battle of Britain. It was well understood that the women were at risk. The massive gasproof door that can still be seen at the Bawdsey Manor radar museum is eloquent testimony that the RAF fully expected RDF sites to come under ruthless attack.

Chapter 20

Striking a Careful Balance – Scheme J

On 1 September 1937, Ellington reached the end of his normal tenure in office and was formally replaced as CAS by Sir Cyril Newall. The appointment had been decided well before. Ellington had never exercised serious positive influence over policy and under the Swinton/Weir regime he had – deservedly – been pushed to the side-lines. Ellington's last few months in office had been poisoned by the fight for the control of the FAA, which he had lost, earning him the deep contempt of Trenchard. Ellington had been a negligible factor for two years, but now Swinton had the opportunity to put his own man in place. In keeping with normal practice the choice of Newall was really Swinton's in his capacity as the responsible minister.[1] According to one reasonably well-placed source, Swinton had boiled his options down to two: Newall and Christopher Courtney, both relatively young men, so he was in practice skipping a generation of air marshals.[2] Courtney would have been the more radical candidate with a reputation as an intellectual but he was a former RNAS officer, which might not have chimed with the service's ex-army atmosphere. Newall was the lower-risk choice. The historian Montgomery Hyde, who had followed air matters closely since his time as Lord Londonderry's private secretary, surmised, that Swinton had consulted Trenchard, which if true suggests that Trenchard played a major part in choosing the two candidates, as both had been his trusted subordinates at the Independent Air Force (IAF).[3]

Swinton had already encountered Newall in 1934 when, as Colonial Secretary, he made a journey through the Middle East and East Africa. Newall was then AOC Middle East and favourably impressed the visiting minister personally as well as being a manifestly popular and efficient commander. Newall was one of the RAF's pioneers of strategic bombing. He had commanded the first British dedicated strategic bombing unit: VIII Brigade of the RFC at Ochey, formed in October 1917 which was to be the core of the IAF the following year. He had earned the gratitude of Trenchard for launching the British bombing offensive against Germany when the politicians in Westminster were clamouring for reprisals against the Gotha raids on London. There is no indication that he resented the fact that he was only second-in-command of the IAF when it was established with Trenchard in command. Newall had only been promoted to brigadier-general in December 1917 at the very early age of 32 and the IAF would have expanded much further had the war continued, so being deputy commander of the IAF was hardly a demotion. The two stayed on good terms and Trenchard sounded out Newall as an ally in one of his habitual backstairs schemes. When Newall was being groomed for the job of CAS. Trenchard felt it was worth putting the aggressively unsubtle idea to him that it would require someone with ministerial authority to prevent the expansion of the RAF from falling behind schedule.[4] There is no sign that Newall considered this invitation to intrigue against his own minister, but he remained loyally Trenchardian in his strategic outlook.

Newall's blind faith in Trenchardian doctrine might have owed something to a limited intellectual background; he went into the army straight from school and did not attend any staff college either as a pupil or an instructor. As Chief of the Air Staff he was driven by ever-grander visions of the RAF's bomber force which he pursued with occasionally wayward enthusiasm. Even making allowances for the speed and uncertainty of aircraft development at the time, some of his judgements on aircraft design were severely flawed: he strongly advocated turret fighters like the disastrous Defiant; from 1938 he saw the Hurricane as obsolescent and resisted further orders for the type; he would have sacrificed Spitfire production in favour of the Westland Whirlwind, which was to prove a severe disappointment.[5] From an early stage, he was convinced that the Stirling heavy bomber was a winner.[6] In the event, the Stirling's excessive weight meant that both its speed and operational ceiling fell well short of early expectations. Newall tended to exaggerate how rapidly aircraft became obsolete and did not appreciate that often it might be necessary to have older types in volume and quickly rather than waiting for new types. Newall had a blind spot in understanding how politics worked and kept asking for things that were politically impossible: lump-sum funding for an expansion scheme that would allow him to choose between bombers and fighters as he wished; a sudden switch from rapid expansion of the RAF to a long pause to consolidate; the ability to hold bombers back from combat to create de facto reserves. He could not distinguish between pro-fighter eye-wash that one of his air ministers used to bamboozle Cabinet and Parliament and a genuine switch in strategy. He does not seem to have impressed the Committee of Imperial Defence Secretariat.[7] Newall did not stand up to the strains of wartime well. His colleague on the Air Staff, Sholto Douglas, described him as an 'absolute bag of nerves' living an almost subterranean existence [8] He fell foul of Lord Beaverbrook, Churchill's crony and a key figure in the political control of the RAF, and became a victim of Churchill's first purge of senior commanders in October 1940 who were 'sound, but old and slow'.[9]

Newall's appointment came as a very welcome relief to John Slessor, who had moved back to Adastral House earlier in 1937 to replace Bert Harris in the crucial job of Director of Plans. The post was not high up in the organization chart and its holders did not hold elevated rank – both Harris and Slessor were only group captains when they were appointed – but because the Deputy CAS had a heavy workload as Director of Operations and Intelligence, the Director of Plans served as the CAS's representative both internally and externally. In practice, he was the CAS's personal staff officer. Slessor had found Ellington challengingly uncommunicative and reserved, and Newall came as a refreshing contrast who 'took his staff fully into his confidence'.[10] Newall and Slessor became very close both professionally and personally. Slessor wrote of their 'treasured friendship'. They had a strong working partnership and Slessor seems to have had little hesitation about speaking for his master. Slessor became Newall's right-hand man and even far more senior officers treated him with deference. Years later, when the official historians of the bomber offensive showed unexpected independence of mind and threatened to expose the leadership of the RAF to serious criticism, Newall was willing to defer entirely to Slessor's judgement in commenting on the draft of the historians' work as he would have known what he would have thought.[11]

Slessor too was a loyal Trenchardian. He had served Trenchard happily whilst he was still CAS from a lowlier position in the plans section.[12] To Slessor Trenchard was unequivocally a great man. Slessor had been one of Trenchard's 'English merchants' who hammered his thoughts into effective written communications. These included Trenchard's controversially and bitterly divisive swansong as CAS which Slessor drafted for him. Slessor saw nothing to complain about in the paper's thesis that the RAF should replace the older services in a number of roles. His only reservation was that it might have been unsound bureaucratic tactics to alert the RAF's enemies that the attack was being launched.[13] Slessor was also the intellectual voice of Trenchardianism. In 1936 he published *Air Power and Armies* under the distinguished imprint of the Oxford University Press in which he set out a vision for the mission of the air force on the battlefield of the future. It pretended to steer a middle course between 'extremists' on either side of the debate but in truth was a manifesto for the value of bombing industry and civilians.[14]

The European dictators might have been relatively quiescent through 1937, but German rearmament was steaming ahead. The Air Staff got clear warning of this in what proved to be the final report from the Christie/X source which arrived in May 1937. After the shambles over the Milch figures, the Air Staff could draw on a trustworthy homegrown and comprehensive source of intelligence. Times and the mood had also changed at Adastral House. In place of the carping criticism that had met the first Christie/X reports in 1936, the latest iteration was warmly welcomed. Not merely did the Air Staff intelligence section endorse it as authentic and probably true but clamoured for more.[15] Little captures better the change in regime at Adastral House than the curt response that Ellington sent to Hankey when he supplied the report in June 1937 and the complimentary, delicately phrased letter that Newall sent in November to chase answers to a list of supplementary questions produced by Ellington which had gone unanswered for more than four months.[16]

The latest Christie/X report was the final nail in the coffin for any dream that the expansion of the Luftwaffe was going to end any time soon. Even before the contents were digested, it was 'now a foregone conclusion ... that the original Milch programme will be concluded in 1937 and that a further expansion programme is making headway'.[17] Hankey had warned Ellington that the new report 'would seem to confirm your worst anticipations' and the picture that it gave of the Luftwaffe in the future pushed any hope of parity far into the distance. The expansion plan that Christie/X had first reported had been replaced by a new, far more ambitious one even before the scheduled completion date for the first one had gone past. The new plan featured 5,400 frontline aircraft grouped in 360 squadrons. This was 80 per cent up on the previous plan. Britain was now having to aim at a very fast-moving target indeed if it wanted to avoid abject inferiority to Germany. There was no hard and fast completion date in view of the scale of the uncertainties, but the target was given as the end of 1939. The absurd complacency of Ellington's forecast that the Luftwaffe would remain unchanged in size at 1,512 aircraft between 1936 and 1940 had long faded into the past.

Newall's feet were barely under his new desk when he launched a campaign to inject extreme urgency into the Air Ministry's rearmament efforts. Newall did not hold back and the most alarming part of the picture that the Air Staff painted for his RAF and civilian colleagues was that 'at a conservative estimate, Germany will on the 1st October 1937 [three weeks in the future], have at least SIX TIMES the mobilizable strength of Great Britain in long-range bombers, of which a considerable proportion will be of the latest types'.[18] Things were not going to improve at all rapidly: 'we are – and at the present rate of progress will be, though in decreasing degree, throughout the next two years – in a position of shocking weakness in the air relative to our two most powerful potential enemies.' Even worse, the RAF was in the middle of switching to modern, complex types of aircraft and still on a steep learning curve. His final conclusion was frightening: 'as far as the Air Force is concerned, we are in no condition to go to war, and shall not be, at the present rate of progress, for at least two years.' The Trenchardian doctrine was apparent throughout: Newall was concerned about long-range bombers; other classes of aircraft did not figure at all. He also placed his thumb firmly in the scales on the German side of the balance. He could write from knowledge that the new units and aircraft entering British service were not fully equipped, but when it came to the new modern German designs, he 'assumed' that Luftwaffe squadrons would be fully equipped with the new types and offered no estimate of their technical fitness for service. Similarly, 'it must be assumed that whatever German bomber force is mobilizable at April 1938, will have adequate reserves behind it'. Ellington had erred massively on the side of complacency in estimating how quickly the Germans could expand, Newall went in entirely the other direction and became a passionate advocate of achieving (if not, exceeding) parity with the Germans. Newall did not restrict himself to purely air force matters. In common with other senior military men, he saw no objection to venturing into the realms of forecasting foreign political developments in raising the spectre of more violent aggression by the dictators as another reason for driving forward the rearmament of the RAF.

The Air Staff was determined to counteract any hint of complacency in political circles. Richard Peirse, the Deputy CAS, took particular exception to a public speech by Inskip which claimed that all but one of the new squadrons formed since rearmament began would be up to full strength by the end of July.[19] Peirse accused Inskip of lulling the government into the false idea that the RAF had reached a first-line strength comparable to Germany's. The time had come to do exactly what the Air Staff had just done and set out clearly the RAF's woeful unreadiness for war.

The manifesto for urgent action was speedily followed by a specific plan for what was needed. Inskip had asked for a review of rearmament proposals by all the services and Newall was not slow in producing a shopping list for the RAF. Inskip might have been biased in favour of fighters, but he was a valuable ally as a prophet of doom on the threat from the air and helped the fear of a knock-out blow to become hard-wired into British military planning:

> the greatest danger against which we have to provide protection is attack from the air on the United Kingdom designed to inflict a knock-out blow at the initial stage of the war, and that our first endeavour must be to provide adequate defence against this threat.[20]

The plan that the Air Staff submitted for consideration was Scheme J and it featured a large expansion beyond the 1,736 aircraft due under Scheme F, then the current programme, to 2,331 aircraft. At first glance this appeared to be less aggressive than the abortive Scheme H, which had called for 2,422 aircraft, but on closer examination it involved a dramatic increase in the commitment of resources. It would be far more expensive: £820 million over five years compared to £640 million.[21] By far the most important element in Scheme J was that it more than tripled the number of heavy bombers to 896 compared to 240 in Scheme F and 280 in Scheme H. Heavy bombers were much more expensive than medium bombers, costing at least half as much again. Moreover, there was no repeat of the exercise in juggling reserves that had been used to keep down the price of Scheme H. The RAF's front-line aircraft were to be backed by reserves at the full scale of 225 per cent. Over five years it would cost almost 50 per cent more to implement Scheme J compared to Scheme F.

Scheme J was resolutely Trenchardian in its priorities. What mattered was to increase the 'striking force'. Because the total number of bombers had fallen in Scheme J compared to Scheme H, the bomber/fighter ratio actually declined to 2.7:1, but it was still well above the old figure of 2:1 that had ruled when rearmament got under way. Newall treated the fighter/bomber ratio of Scheme J as an ideal and described it having struck a 'careful balance'.[22] The new scheme asked for a seventeen percent increase in the number of fighters compared to Scheme F, but the average unit cost of the fighters was the same across both schemes. When the Air Staff came to present their proposals to Neville Chamberlain, the recently arrived prime minister, they began by thinking that it would be a good idea to flag up the purely numerical shift back towards fighters in Scheme J compared to Scheme H, but then had second thoughts and dropped any discussion of the ratio of fighters to bombers.[23] It might have seemed to endorse the heresy that it was a good thing to move the ratio in favour of fighters.

In framing the proposals for Scheme J, the Air Staff wanted to defeat the dangerous pro-fighter heresy of Inskip's 'Ideal' defence scheme. This was going to involve some adroit manipulation of the intelligence data behind the opposed schemes and the Air Staff began to seem more like three-card trick artists that professional servicemen. Their sights were firmly fixed on the claim that the 'Ideal' scheme's forty-five fighter squadrons were 'by no means an over-insurance'. The first step was to assert that the ideal scheme had been designed to match a German bomber strength of 1,700 whilst the Scheme J only posited 1,458 German bombers, so it was no longer possible to maintain that the forty-five squadrons 'could be claimed to represent the minimum requirement for close defence'.[24] The Air Staff had managed to reach the lower figure for German bombers by eliminating short-range dive-bombers from the total and insinuating that the 'Ideal' scheme had assumed that all 1,700 German bombers were long range. In reality, it had been ambiguous on this point. Moreover, the addition of 462*

---

* The author has been unable to understand how this figure was calculated

aircraft to the RAF striking force would somehow neutralize the extra German bombers.

The Air Staff's approach was reminiscent of the perhaps apocryphal story that the statistical landmass of certain Mediterranean countries fluctuates, with a greater mass when EU agricultural subsidies are being computed and a lower one when domestic land taxes are assessed. When it was a question of assessing the RAF's needs in bombers, the Luftwaffe was menacingly large and growing; when it was a question of assessing its needs in fighters, the Air Staff's estimates of the size of the Luftwaffe were falling. The Air Staff cheerfully rubbished the 'ideal' scheme's figure for the number of fighters needed to respond to the supposedly lower number of German bombers, but seemed to have forgotten this when it advanced the fact that as anti-aircraft and searchlight defences would be less than half the total of the 'ideal' scheme, this justified boosting the RAF's bomber force. The latest Christie/X forecasts featured prominently and in his covering note to the proposals, Swinton darkly endorsed the suggestion that Göring might actually be planning to double the Luftwaffe in size.

Chapter 21

The Interpreter

The verdict on Neville Chamberlain's premiership is dominated by the verdict on his diplomacy, appeasement to his critics. He was convinced that the way to avoid war was constructive dialogue with the dictators but he did not oppose rearmament as is sometimes supposed. He referred constantly to his 'double policy of rearmament and better relations with Germany & Italy'.[1] Chamberlain never used the word appeasement in today's sense. Chamberlain can fairly be accused of wanting to be his own foreign minister, but he could never be accused of wanting to be his own defence minister. This was an area of policy that he was usually happy to leave to his underlings. Chamberlain's approach to rearmament was shaped by domestic politics. He was constantly being reminded of Britain's weakness in the air by Churchill, an old political bugbear, who had made the cause his own since the early 1930s. Churchill assailed the deficiencies in the RAF's re-equipment on a broad front. A network of disaffected middle-ranking officers kept him well briefed on the many difficulties inside the service. Churchill's relish for the fine detail of military organizations coupled with a personal interest in flying – he had begun to learn to fly before the First World War until forbidden by his wife – made him a powerful and effective critic. It was a policy area on which Chamberlain sensed that he was vulnerable. The differing approaches of Chamberlain and Churchill to the question well illustrate their priorities. Unlike Churchill, Chamberlain had no interest in the intricacies of re-equipping the RAF or the other armed services. It was his diplomatic efforts that inspired a passionate personal commitment and behind this passion lay an undefeatable optimism that his efforts would ultimately succeed and that Britain's military preparations would never be put to the test of war. Chamberlain only dealt with service matters when disputes could not be settled at more junior level and escalated to Downing Street.

In the late autumn of 1937, the Air Staff's drive towards the big-bomber policy got fully under way and the political fight that broke out over its financial consequences was in full swing. It also saw another dispute that had simmered beneath the surface for months, break out into the open in a way that brought new and powerful forces to play on the RAF's rearmament and shifted the balance of strength between established players. The concerns were severe enough to attract the interest of Neville Chamberlain, now prime minister, who not been directly involved until then.

Whilst the Air Staff was striving to gain approval for the grandiose expansion plans of Scheme J, it was struggling to execute its predecessor. Deliveries of the new aircraft ordered under Scheme F had already fallen badly behind schedule in 1936; fewer than half of the modern types had been delivered on schedule at the middle of the year.[2] Weir might have paid careful attention to the industrial dimension of expansion from the outset, but the programme still had to overcome serious difficulties. The scheme of shadow factories was an inspired method of adding extra raw manufacturing capacity, but this could only come as an addition to existing plant which was still rooted in the past. Even the products of the shadow factories were falling behind: of 220 Battles expected in 1937, only 80 arrived: of 330 Blenheims, only 117.[3] Neither side of the process was fully prepared to cope with a dramatic expansion of a whole industry. The British aircraft industry had to be transformed from an agglomeration of a dozen or so small producers that had survived through the 1920s and early 1930s on a drip-feed of orders for a few tens of aircraft which used well-established technologies. These companies now had to make modern aircraft in their hundreds. They had to learn the new techniques of producing far more complex machines embodying the new technologies of stressed metal construction with cantilever wings and retractable undercarriages. The relationship between planemakers and their de facto monopsony client, the Air Ministry, had not changed much since the lean years. The Air Staff paid little attention to how easy or otherwise it would be to manufacture aircraft to a new design. They failed to appreciate that a pricing mechanism that left all the power in the customer's hands did not work in favour of a realistic approach by the supplier as to what it would cost to meet an order. The plane-makers were loath to invest in new capacity or technology because they saw a risk that the flow of new orders might be turned off overnight, leaving them with expensive redundant capacity. The nub lay in their confidence, or lack of it, that the Air Ministry would not leave them high and dry if the political wind changed. Investment in high-grade costly tools only broke even for the manufacturers at production volumes of several hundred aircraft.[4] Unless the manufacturers could be confident that the Air Ministry would order such quantities, they would invest only reluctantly. By contrast, the German aircraft industry was in the hands of a small number of airframe makers, who were starting almost from scratch and geared up for an expansion to which they could see no end.

By the autumn of 1937, disquiet at production shortfalls was becoming vocal in the Air Staff. A few days after Newall took up the post of CAS, Slessor drafted his long paper setting out the RAF's 'shocking weakness' for the next two years, which was clearly a manifesto for a new, more aggressive approach to claiming that more resources be allocated to the RAF and, more generally, strengthening its voice in the corridors of power. Slessor put the blame for production shortfalls squarely on the plane-makers without offering any constructive proposals as to how this could be remedied. The Air Staff was desperate for the latest generation of aircraft, but completely abdicated responsibility for the industrial implications of the switch:

> The Air Staff believe the most vital factor in the whole problem to be the production of up-to-date aircraft. They are neither qualified nor entitled to criticise our production methods, nor are they responsible for offering suggestions for their improvement. It has, however, become increasingly apparent during the last few months that the supply of new aircraft is falling badly behind that which the Air Staff were led to expect; and that the aircraft industry is not facing up to the task on lines in any way comparable to those, for instance, in Germany.[5]

Richard Peirse, the DCAS, echoed Slessor's warnings in almost identical terms with the added admonition that public comments by Inskip might even create a false impression that Scheme F had brought the RAF up to a strength comparable to Germany's.[6]

The true problem of the shortfall in aircraft deliveries was magnified in the eyes of the military illiterates of Downing Street by the increasing size of the RAF's aircraft. Measured in crude numbers, deliveries rose only 12 per cent; however, this disguised a far more impressive performance in total structure weight where deliveries were 74 per cent higher.[7] Britain might have seemed to lag behind Germany in the production game, but in terms of providing the RAF with modern, more potent aircraft that it wanted, prodigious results were being achieved.

The first steps taken by the Air Ministry to gear itself up for greater production volumes actually worsened relations with the plane-makers. The shadow factory scheme was seen as a form of creeping nationalization.[8] A plan advanced by the ministry's recently appointed director of production, Major Disney, to group a number of firms together to manufacture a competitor's product – the Wellington – was even less well received.[9] Emblematic of the poor relationship between Air Ministry and plane-makers was one practice that irked the plane-makers beyond measure as well as delaying production. Comparatively junior Air Ministry inspectors who visited factories had the authority to interfere with designs at the manufacturing stage. It is an open question as to how much changes to aircraft on the production line repaid the delay with operating improvements, but all the manufacturers could see was a hold-up to their delivering planes and being paid. It was the sharp end of a confrontational approach to getting the aircraft produced in which the balance of power hugely favoured the customer.

The plane-makers were represented by their trade association, the Society of British Aircraft Constructors (SBAC). The two most powerful individuals in the SBAC were Frederick Handley Page and Richard Fairey, the founders and bosses of the eponymous companies. Neither these individuals nor their companies enjoyed good relations with the Air Ministry. The files abound in slighting references to the suppliers: Handley Page was 'running true to form' in failing to come up with a programme of deliveries; an Air Ministry delegation encountered the 'usual unpleasant Fairey atmosphere'.[10] Weir was unsettled when Handley Page told him that he was taking on the presidency of the SBAC and hoped for 'cordial' relations between society and Air Ministry, with a strong insinuation that relations were anything but cordial.[11] Further alarm bells rang in October 1937 when Handley Page was getting up a delegation to discuss contract terms with the Air Ministry and proposed including Fairey.[12] Relations with Fairey were suffering from one outgrowth of the substitution scheme in which part of the order for Battles – 189 aircraft – was being cancelled.

Tensions between industry and Air Ministry were reaching boiling point in the autumn of 1937 despite a series of meetings between the two sides.[13] The plane-makers composed a lengthy memorandum setting out their complaints at excessive state interference which they blamed for the delays.[14] It was written for publication in the press and to Parliament but it does not appear to have been circulated. The threat of public complaint by the plane-makers hovered in the background over the next few months as a potentially lethal pistol held at the head of the government.

Toward the end of 1937, the question was heading for a crisis as a combination of real political and apparent military vulnerability gnawed at Chamberlain and his chief Civil Service adviser, Sir Horace Wilson. It was a deeply frustrating situation and there seemed to be no easy way out. Chamberlain had begun his campaign to develop better relations with the dictators with overtures to Mussolini, but he knew full well that Hitler counted for far more than the Italian. Few rated Fascist Italy as a military power but Germany was quite different. Chamberlain wanted to negotiate with Hitler but he knew that he would be doing so from a position of military weakness. He did not want to confront Hitler but to talk to him without appearing to do so because weakness forced him to. Perhaps more worrying was the domestic political pressure. Churchill showed no inclination to relent in his attacks on the government and Chamberlain had no obvious weapon with which to fight back. The first problem to tackle was the slow pace of delivery of new planes to the RAF.

What followed bore all the hallmarks of Chamberlain's premiership; above all decisions taken with minimal discussion. Chamberlain was immensely proud of his grasp of detail, but this came from reading the huge mass of papers at his disposal as Chancellor then as prime minister. His method did not include talking to people to discover what lay beyond the paper. Open debate was not part of his decision-making process. To Chamberlain it was a matter of objective analysis of data, which was to lead to a correct conclusion. Once that conclusion had been identified, it was simply a matter of implementing the solution as effectively as possible. Chamberlain did not trust discussion generally or – more narrowly – any political process to do the job. In short, he did not trust the judgement or motivation of anyone else to give him advice with a single, immense exception. Sir Horace Wilson was untainted by personal or departmental self-interest and he shared Chamberlain's overarching priorities. Chamberlain was a largely friendless man but he and Wilson had become friends as well as operating a close professional partnership. Between them they would find the answer.

The issue seemed to be playing to Wilson's strengths. Producing aeroplanes could be regarded as an ordinary industrial matter and this was exactly the area in which Wilson was specialized. He had cut his teeth and established his reputation in the nascent Ministry of Labour as a conciliator in the brutal world of industrial relations that moved from the murderous world of pre-First World War coal strikes to the near revolution of the General Strike in 1926. He moved on to a lead role in the desperate and fruitless fight against Britain's massive unemployment before and after the Great Slump. Under the umbrella title Chief Industrial Adviser, he dealt with an array of problems of detail that fell between the stools of the established ministries. Along the way he came to know the lead figures on both sides of industry as well as finance. He formed a close bond with Montagu Norman, the Governor of the Bank of England. Norman dominated the world of British finance between the wars and, unusually for a British central banker, was a strong and active advocate of central intervention in private industry. Norman built a network of industrial managers who shuttled between the City and the companies themselves, spanning almost every segment of the economy. The Bank of England was then still a privately owned organization, but Norman was not after a quick profit. He knew that a healthy economy depended on healthy banks serving healthy industrial companies and strove to create and maintain this virtuous circle. Norman has been widely denounced for his ultra-conservative views on finance and the correct response to the Great Slump, but it is practically impossible to fault his motivation.

It was Wilson's natural response to the conundrum of weak aircraft production to hear what the plane-makers had to say about the problem. Unsurprisingly, they tended to see the fault as lying with their customer, the Air Ministry. In an atmosphere of distrust between a supplier industry and its near-monopsony customer, difficulties were inevitable. The solution was to break the logjam of distrust. This was to be done by inserting someone into the dialogue between the plane-makers and the Air Ministry, who could act as a spokesman for the industry but whom Downing Street trusted. The relationship between plane-makers and the Air Ministry was to be reshaped. Between them Wilson and

Norman found their man: Charles Bruce-Gardner who had been a senior executive in various iron and steel companies since before the First World War. He was a close ally of Montagu Norman and had headed two of the investment companies that had been established under the auspices of the Bank of England to drive through industrial restructuring by means of direct ownership of businesses. Bruce-Gardner was the chairman of the Armstrong Whitworth company and he had already helped Wilson to resolve an especially venomous dispute between the government and Vickers, the arms conglomerate which was thought by many to be an overmighty state within a state, over the management of a major weapons factory. Bruce-Gardner offered Armstrong Whitworth's services to take over the management of the works and Wilson had been so pleased by Bruce-Gardner's intervention that he praised him directly to the prime minister. Bruce-Gardner was clearly the ideal man for the job of liaising between the plane-makers and the Air Ministry.

With the backing of the prime minister and his most powerful adviser, the rest of the task posed no problems. Bruce-Gardner was favoured with an interview with Chamberlain in which Downing Street's vision for his task was set out. Explicitly or otherwise, Bruce-Gardner knew that he was Downing Street's anointed supremo for the air rearmament programme with a personal remit from the prime minister. Norman willingly released Bruce-Gardner from his Bank of England-related work. The heads of the three most important plane-makers were called into Downing Street and prevailed upon to elect Bruce-Gardner as the executive chairman of the SBAC. They had little to complain of; Bruce-Gardner gave them a powerful voice at the top level of political power at no cost to themselves. When Bruce-Gardner was appointed as chairman, he understood that his mission was 'to interpret the views and wishes of the industry to the Government and the views and wishes of the Government to the Industry'.[15] The SBAC had been no more than a representative or lobbying body which had no authority over its members. It had done useful work in minor matters like harmonizing aircraft designations, but it faced the usual problem of a trade association of rising above the individual interests of its members. Some companies were better represented than others. But now, thanks to Downing Street, the SBAC was now a force in the land. To set a very public seal on Bruce-Gardner's new status he was knighted at the start of 1938.

Chapter 22

Morally Sure – Scheme K

Scheme J was not just intended to expand the RAF; intentionally or otherwise, it would have the effect of making the RAF by far the most important of the three armed services. The RAF demand for resources now outstripped that of the Royal Navy, hitherto the unchallenged premier service for financial spending. It was asking for 38 per cent of all defence spending compared to 32 per cent under the previous allocation. Moreover, this was to be channelled overwhelmingly into a single branch of the service: the RAF's bombers would receive the lion's share. The question of allocation of resources for defence fell squarely in Inskip's remit and he rose to the challenge immediately. Inskip warned Swinton that it might not be possible to accommodate the new scheme. More important, he rebutted the intellectual argument that lay behind it. For the first time Trenchardian doctrine was to be put to a full-blown political test. The scene was set for a major confrontation.

Swinton and Newall had made a bold claim in asking for more than the senior service. Inskip pointed out that if the Royal Navy were defeated, Britain could not long survive. If the Kriegsmarine overcame the Royal Navy, it could cut off Britain's sea communications and inflict a decisive defeat, whilst if the Luftwaffe's bombers were superior to the RAF's, the effect would be relative and not absolute. British cities might suffer greater damage than Germany's but there was no reason to suppose that such a disparity would be critical. Inskip was denying that a knock-out blow was possible. Moreover, Britain would have means other than a counter-bombing offensive with which to respond to a German bombing attack on Britain.[1] Inskip advanced two severe heresies: that German bombers could better be destroyed over Britain by RAF fighters and that the goal of parity, which had served the Air Staff so well in justifying ever-larger numbers of bombers, was an unproven doctrine and not received truth: 'I cannot persuade myself therefore that the dictum of the CAS that we must give the enemy as much as he gives us is a sound principle ... My idea is rather that in order to meet our real requirements we need not possess anything like the same number of long-range bombers as the Germans.'[2] Inskip called for the proportion of expensive heavy bombers to lighter bombers to be reduced, but he also suggested that bombers themselves might be used to assist the fighter in air defence.

Inskip had a powerful political ally in his campaign against Scheme J. Sir John Simon, the Chancellor of the Exchequer, was no financial expert, but he had been an RFC staff officer at Trenchard's headquarters which gave him at least a grounding in military aviation; whatever he had seen of Trenchard at close quarters did not inspire the same adulation that he inspired in Simon's Cabinet colleague, Sir Samuel Hoare. Simon also had the barrister's ability to become an instant expert on even complex topics, by latching on to basic fundamental concepts. When Chamberlain had been Chancellor, he had been content to accept the Air Staff's view of air war, but Simon probed far deeper. He spotted how the cost of modern weapons had risen dramatically, noting that the cost of aircraft had risen threefold over the previous ten years. He pointed out that the continuing rate of technical development would make for a very rapid rate of obsolescence. This meant that the Air Staff policy of re-equipping with full reserves multiplied the risks of planes going out of date; if technology overtook a type in service, the RAF would find itself with more than three times the number of redundant former first-line aircraft types

Scheme J also provoked a typically extreme outburst from Sir Warren Fisher, the head of the Civil Service, whose view of the Air Staff had never recovered from the dire impression that Ellington had made on him in the days of the DRC. He questioned outright the pretensions of the air marshals to be the only source of wisdom on air warfare:

> Because individuals may wear a uniform and are called e.g. the Air Staff, it does not follow that they are infallible guides. In regard to major principles experienced laymen have a role to play. And the Air Staff have enslaved themselves to the parrot cry of 'parity' without taking into account the differences in conditions of Germany and England. ... Our policy, in my opinion, should be to concentrate in the first days or weeks on smashing the morale of the German pilots

on their way to and over England, bringing down say 20% of each attack instead of the 3% thought of by the Air Staff. We should at the same time be dropping a certain amount of bombs on Germany to keep her interested. But let us attack and down the attackers.[3]

Fisher's views went far further than Inskip's restrained attempts to reshape air policy and Simon's cost-saving. He was arguing for a complete reversal of strategy, advancing the exact opposite of Trenchardian doctrine in both its main tenets: fighters were the key element of defence and bombers the minor one. In all its tactless splendour, Fisher's rant stands as practically the only criticism of the Air Staff's utter inability to contemplate any approach to air warfare other than the unproven mantra handed down by their founding prophet.

The Air Staff would not budge and openly accused Inskip of being 'subject to a fundamental misconception of a vitally important point in air strategy' because he suggested that there might be a finite number of bombers that could usefully be procured.[4] The Air Staff were also hostile to Inskip's idea of a switch to light bombers in terms which give a good idea of the direction in which their thinking as to their ideal for the RAF. They argued that the Halifax/Manchester class of heavy medium bomber was a far more cost-effective tool to bomb Germany, claiming that these types were superior to light and light/medium bombers in practically every respect: bombload, speed, range and tactical defensibility. The venom of the Air Staff's abuse of Inskip was matched by the intellectual weakness of their own case. They accepted that it was 'difficult to establish a reasoned strategic basis for bomber strength'.[5] They stopped short of an outright assertion that an air force can win a war but implied that one could by decrying the claims of the other services on the grounds that it was 'not enough to avoid losing a war'. According to the RAF the navy couldn't win a war in less than a number of years and the army was too small. The Air Staff rounded off their case by quoting Nazi leader Terboven who asserted that Göring's Luftwaffe had practically defeated Britain by putting an end to 'her splendid isolation'.

Inskip came out formally opposing scheme J but his counter-proposals fell considerably short of the radical revisions that he had seemed to favour in the opening rounds of the confrontation with the Air Staff.[6] He accepted that first-line bomber numbers might be increased without committing himself to a number. Only the scale of bomber reserves was to be cut back. No increase was to be made in overseas units. Predictably, though, the entire increase in fighter numbers in Scheme J was to be implemented including reserves at the full scale.

Scheme J came before the Cabinet just before Christmas 1937 as part of a discussion as to how the total defence spending programme could be limited to £1,500 million. Anyone who had been expecting the ferocity of the argument between Inskip and the Air Ministry to be carried over into the larger forum would have been disappointed. Once Inskip had acknowledged that there had been controversy between himself and the Air Staff and Swinton had unburdened himself of a long diatribe to the effect that accepting Inskip's proposals meant a 'complete reversal of policy', the affair was concluded with a minimum of fuss. The top men in the government had no inclination to back Swinton. Simon, the Chancellor of the Exchequer, too endorsed Inskip's plan, focusing on the risk of obsolescence in the scale of reserves demanded by the Air Staff. It is easy to suspect that the Inskip proposals had been agreed in advance between the two ministers.

Most important, Chamberlain, the prime minister, appeared to have foresworn the enthusiasm for Trenchardian strategy he had shown two years before when he had been so keen to beef up the RAF's striking power. He even went to far as to bury his predecessor's parity commitment on the grounds that, 'no pledge could last for ever'. Why was Chamberlain willing to ignore the advice of the key service minister on the vital question of air rearmament and why did he seem to be back-pedalling on rearmament? The answer is clear from the topic onto which the Cabinet discussion segued without even a formal change in agenda item: Chamberlain's project to appease Hitler with the return of colonies in Africa awarded to Britain and France at Versailles. In December 1937, Chamberlain's hopes were at their highest that he could remove the risk of war through the policy of constructive dialogue with the dictators, which he had pursued since becoming prime minister in May. He was making good progress on his scheme to buy Mussolini off with the recognition of the Italian empire in Africa, which had been created by the conquest of Ethiopia; now he was turning his attentions to Hitler. Here, Chamberlain had latched onto a stray remark that Göring had made to Lord Halifax who had visited Berlin as the prime minister's personal envoy that autumn.[7] Göring had said that Germany would be satisfied with two insignificant territories, Togo and the Cameroons, and Chamberlain had seen this as the prelude to a wider settlement. Moreover, Hitler had also staged one of his periodic bouts of saying how nice it would be if bombers could be limited and Chamberlain was happy to see what might be done from the British end.

The Cabinet's rejection of Scheme J is often presented as a major defeat for the Air Staff, but they had secured much of what they wanted, above all the principle that first-line bomber numbers could be increased. Inskip's 'Ideal' defence scheme with its heretical call for a sharp increase in the number of fighter squadrons had passed into oblivion as far as the RAF was concerned, although the army still dutifully tried to meet figures for extra anti-aircraft artillery. How many more bombers would be allowed had been left open and the goal of parity had not been killed by Chamberlain; it remained a powerful force with the unspoken acceptance that the RAF's striking force should be the equal of the Luftwaffe's. It began to work to the Air Staff's advantage that the whole question had been left ill-defined. Swinton had stated to the Cabinet that the German bomber force was being increased by 50 per cent without giving any absolute figures, neither of which had been challenged. This set a usefully nebulous starting point for the Air Staff's new round of planning. When Inskip had squashed the Air Staff's first bomber-heavy plans and given priority to fighters, he had left open a chink through which the Air Staff spotted the possibility of driving a further increase in the RAF's commitment to bombers. Inskip had accepted that the RAF could meet the increase in the Luftwaffe's bomber strength with bombers of its own under the vague formulation, 'some increase in our bomber strength'.[8] The Air Staff calculated that parity with the 50 per cent increase referred to in the Cabinet meeting would translate to a bomber force of 1,215 aircraft, but this definite figure was not one that had been mentioned outside the Air Ministry.[9]

The figure for a 50 per cent increase in the Luftwaffe had come from Erhard Milch when he paid his reciprocal visit to London as part of the delegation of Luftwaffe figures in October 1937 and met all the leading players on the British side. This time, though, his contribution was quite unintentional and was used to support the Air Staff's case for more bombers. It had taken some months for the Air Ministry to work out that the British had been lulled into a false sense of security by the pantomime in Berlin Milch had performed for the visiting air marshals, which had torpedoed Scheme H with a falsely low figure for German intentions and it was now open to a more pessimistic stance.[10] Milch's next contribution to the debate came at a propitious moment as it coincided with a gap in hard intelligence on the Luftwaffe, and the Air Staff was hungry for data. Milch stated, more or less definitely, that the Luftwaffe plan was for a 50 per cent increase, which had fed through to Swinton's prediction to the Cabinet, but one of his other comments left open the possibility that the goal was for a 100 per cent increase.

As the Air Staff worked on ways to frame a response to the Cabinet's initial rebuff to Scheme J at the end of 1937, Newall's assistant, Slessor, had another look at the record of what Milch had said in London and was presented with useful ammunition. Amongst Milch's comments was found the supposed statement that 'Germany might increase the strength of squadrons from 12 to 15 or 18 aircraft during the coming year or 18 months'. RAF intelligence had firm data on the designation, number, location and plane types of Luftwaffe units, but no firm data as to their strength. Despite the imprecision and uncertainty of this evidence – even Slessor admitted there was no 'tangible evidence' – Slessor still managed to claim that 'there was 'no other reasonable explanation' of Milch's words than a Luftwaffe bomber force that had to be matched by an RAF force of '<u>1,350</u> first-line aircraft' (double underlined in original). This involved an arbitrary assumption that the size of Luftwaffe squadrons would in fact rise to fifteen aircraft. When Newall used Slessor's reasoning to inform Swinton of the new target figure for how many bombers the RAF needed a couple of days later, it had become sufficiently strong to permit him to be 'morally sure'.[11] Swinton fell in with Newall's reasoning as far as the reference figure of 1,350 for target strength went although he recognized the political difficulties it would involve to secure this level for the RAF.[12] The Air Staff had a new target number for its bomber force, which was not drastically less than the 1,442 envisaged in Scheme J.

Scheme K was also something of a compromise in terms of the aircraft types that it involved. To keep factories going, labour intact and to avoid 'critical' shortage of aircraft in March 1941, stop-gap orders would have to be given. Of the 2,033 bombers to be ordered, 1,253 would be Wellingtons. It would be possible to make 2,000 of the newer bombers by March 1943 but only at the expense of large cutbacks in orders for older types. Full-bore production of both older and newer types would mean that 1,380 more aircraft would be produced in total than the 2,655 actually needed.[13] The solution would be to hold orders for the large bombers to only 932.[14]

The scale of the industrial and technological challenges involved focused the RAF's attention well into the future; the question of immediate war readiness played little part in their considerations. Perhaps this would have been one too many balls to keep in the air. The orders for Scheme K were being discussed in February 1938 only weeks before Germany's seizure of Austria cut the likely time available to prepare to war down to months and not years.

The Air Staff was happy to play the parity game, when it supported their claim for extra bombers. When it came to setting how they would decide the RAF's strategy and organization, other considerations came into play. As they revised Scheme J, the question arose as to whether it would be better to increase the number of bomber squadrons or increase the size of squadrons. The latter was a cheaper option but the decisive argument in its favour was that it would allow the RAF to operate a de facto reserve behind a façade of first-line strength. The Air Staff feared that public opinion or political pressure would prevent them withholding entire squadrons from action, but it would be possible to sneak through a lower intensity of operations by only committing a portion of each squadron to battle.[15]

The Air Staff's revised proposals were labelled as Scheme K. As it was presented to Inskip this cut the planned five-year spending on the RAF to £567.5 million from the £650 million of Scheme J.[16] The key difference to its predecessor was that reserves of bombers were reduced to an estimated nine weeks of wartime attrition from sixteen weeks before. The number of first-line bombers was also brought down to 1,350 – precisely the same as the Luftwaffe's expected strength when the 25 per cent increase in individual squadron strength of which the Air Staff was 'morally sure' was applied. The Air Staff's swing to heavier (and more expensive) large bombers remained intact. By March 1940 heavy bombers would account for 56 per cent of RAF bomber numbers and a year later they would reach 69 per cent. The numerical ratio of bombers to fighters fell back further from the dizzying Trenchardian heights of 3.5:1 in scheme H to 2.6:1 (compared to 2.7:1 in Scheme J). Newall later complained that Scheme K 'upset' the balance both in terms of first-line strength and, because of the cut in reserves, 'effective bomber strength'.[17] 'Balance' between fighters and bombers was becoming a code for having as few fighters as possible.

Two of the lesser economies that were made in Scheme K show that the desires of Sir Hugh Dowding's Fighter Command came well down the list of priorities. The new scheme eliminated extra spending on new RDF stations that had not already been authorized: Scheme J had included fifteen extra stations which would have cost £1.24 million to build and £150,00 a year to operate.[18] Dowding was well aware that for his fighter squadrons to operate year-round and in all weathers, it would need hard runways, which would cost several million pounds, but this too was omitted. Another defence scheme which fell victim to the savings was the short-lived idea of 'silhouette lighting' which would have made attacking bombers visible at night against large illuminated areas on the ground. This would have cost even more than the extra RDF stations at £2 million.

Scheme K along with the other services was turned over to Inskip and it became the starting point for a purely budgetary exercise. All told, the individual service ministries wanted a total of £1,769 million or £1,811 million (depending on which of two Admiralty programmes was chosen). Inskip had ratcheted up his target for spending on military expansion by 10 per cent to £1,650 million from the figure that had been the Cabinet's baseline in December, when Scheme J had been rejected, but this was still not enough to cover the services' programmes. The ministers fought shy of imposing any solution and sent the whole question back to the services to try to find a way of fitting their plans to the Procrustean bed of the arbitrary total spending figure.

Chapter 23

No Reflection on Swinton's Administration – Scheme L

Bruce-Gardner's appointment was in effect the plane-makers' own direct line to Downing Street, bypassing the irksome minor functionaries of the Air Ministry, and, if need be, the Cabinet minister responsible for the RAF. Downing Street, in the person of Sir Horace Wilson, had delivered a vote of no confidence in Swinton's stewardship of the air rearmament programme at the end of 1937. This was entirely in keeping with Wilson's modus operandi; Chamberlain had merely rubber-stamped his adviser's selection. Wilson's tenure at Downing Street was littered with episodes when he helped Chamberlain to short-circuit ministers with whom he disagreed but did not feel able to sack, most famously Anthony Eden, who did not show sufficient enthusiasm as Foreign Secretary for Chamberlain's programme of appeasing Mussolini.

The 1930s were a high point in the power of permanent Whitehall officials compared to ministers'. Sir Maurice Hankey dominated the world of defence. Wilson's mentor and patron, Sir Warren Fisher, the Head of the Civil Service, who had been instrumental in putting him into Downing Street, openly denounced 'megalomaniac' ministers. Wilson was not shy in expressing contempt for Chamberlain's Cabinet colleagues; only Chamberlain himself was immune. It is hard to escape the conclusion that he despised the trade of politics. Wilson's influence on the appointment of ministers was widely recognized as he preferred to appoint men from outside politics, even if they were not technical experts in the work of their ministries. The standing and influence of all ministers – naturally including Lord Swinton as air minister – were expendable if Wilson judged someone else could do their work better, either formally as the minister or as some form of surrogate. Informed contemporaries were practically unanimous in their praise of Swinton's abilities (even if they did not appreciate his abrasiveness) but Wilson disagreed. Swinton was aware that Bruce-Gardner was being appointed but there is no indication that he was given any opportunity to affect it or to influence his terms of reference.

In the early months of 1938, Swinton and Bruce-Gardner competed for top-level support via Wilson in an uneasy and uneven three-cornered dialogue. Bruce-Gardner did deal directly with Swinton, but in reality, it was his conversation with Wilson that mattered. It was only from Wilson that the prime minister knew what was going on. Both Wilson and Bruce-Gardner briefed each other on their contacts with Swinton, but the full extent of their relationship remained hidden from the air minister. Wilson was far more sympathetic towards Bruce-Gardner than to Swinton and between them they decided the 'correct' line that the Air Ministry should be taking. At one point Wilson expressed 'the hope that the line which you and I discussed the other day will prove acceptable to him [Swinton].'[1] A civil servant and the head of a trade body for major suppliers to the government were combining to make government policy behind the back of the minister responsible. They enjoyed a huge tactical advantage in the battle for the prime minister's approval in that they both aimed for the same thing: a crude target of increasing the number of aircraft produced, with quality taking only second place. Behind their complaints of inefficiency at the Air Ministry, lay the plane-makers' self-interested pitch: if only the government would give them the certainty of large, firm orders, they would be able to step up production. The wishes of the Air Staff and their notions of a structured expansion of the RAF counted for nothing. Chamberlain and Wilson knew that big delivery numbers would keep the political pressure off the government. They were staking everything on appeasement and were confident that it would succeed, so it would never matter if the RAF were actually ready for battle or not.

Swinton too knew that aircraft deliveries had to be increased, but he made the political error of playing the long game and treating this as an issue of management and not of politics. He put in hand a series of reforms which in time would go far to help break the logjam in aircraft production and contribute far more to the acceleration in output than Bruce-Gardner's appeasement of the aircraft-makers, but, at the level of the crude political imperatives that were being played for, they hardly set the pulses racing. Their effect would only be felt over a period of months; what Chamberlain wanted was political ammunition in the short term. Swinton's key innovation was a small committee, the Air Council

Committee on Supply, that grouped representatives of the Air Ministry and Bruce-Gardner for the industry, but its most significant member was a highly regarded representative of the Treasury, Edward Bridges, soon to become Cabinet Secretary. Bridge's presence was the keystone of the committee's unprecedented power to authorize spending. The logjam of time-consuming paper-shuffling between the Air Ministry as the spending body and its paymaster, the Treasury, was broken. Firm orders could be placed with minimal bureaucratic process. There were also two key appointments at the Air Ministry. One of the RAF's forgotten heroes, Air Marshal Sir Wilfrid Freeman, was promoted, combining responsibility for aircraft design and aircraft production. This dual function allowed Freeman to drive through the introduction and full-scale manufacture of the RAF's most famous and effective aircraft types of the Second World War. Freeman worked in close partnership with Ernest Lemon whom the Air Ministry had taken on for the new job of Director General of Production with a remit to bring a much-needed understanding of industrial manufacturing into the organization, which had previously viewed industry with Olympian superiority. Lemon had been in charge of production for the London, Midland and Scottish Railway (the railway companies were acknowledged to be highly efficient manufacturing businesses). The Air Ministry also appointed resident progress officers – 'overseers' – to a number of important factories to replace the deeply unpopular and disruptive practice of sporadic visits by civil service inspectors.[2]

As well as being cut out of the loop in top-level decision-making, Swinton was also losing ground within the government on how rearmament should be presented politically. Persuading Parliament and the public that the government was doing a good job of re-equipping the RAF was at the top of the political agenda and how it was handled could decide the fate of Chamberlain's government, which was facing a severe challenge in Parliament in a debate which was shaping up to become a potentially decisive battleground. The government faced attack from both the official opposition and Churchill, the one-man internal opposition party. In both cases it was Wilson who was Chamberlain's key adviser on how to approach the matter and not Swinton. The new Labour Party leader, Clement Attlee, did his best to emulate Churchill's efforts and presented the government with his own catalogue of flaws in the Royal Air Force. 'Not very formidable' in the views of Downing

Street but it had to be answered.[3] Attlee was seeking an independent inquiry into the state of the RAF. Chamberlain and Wilson discussed how to reply and decided that Attlee would have to be seen personally. Only afterwards was this decision passed onto Swinton as air minister.[4] In a remarkable extension of his duties as a civil servant, it was actually Wilson who ended up meeting Attlee himself but he failed to persuade him to abandon raising the question in the House of Commons; a civil servant was deputizing for the prime minister in an unambiguously political discussion.[5] Attlee did not demur, which suggests that he recognized Wilson's standing in government, in practice that he ranked above Swinton. The Labour Party plan to call for an inquiry remained on the table, but handling Churchill was the real issue and here again Wilson was part of a tiny group planning the political response. Swinton was not present when Chamberlain, Wilson and Captain David Margesson, the Chief Whip, decided how to deal with Churchill.[6] They expected that Churchill too would call for an inquiry, but Chamberlain showed his customary inclination to confront opposition head-on and was adamant that 'an inquiry should be refused and should be refused flatly and firmly, the decision to be adhered to notwithstanding any criticism that may be raised during the debate'.[7]

Another prop was knocked from under Swinton's political position by a development unrelated to the RAF. The Air Ministry was also responsible for civil aviation and, indirectly, for Britain's national flag-carrier airline, Imperial Airways. Imperial was performing poorly and a government inquiry under Lord Cadman had been appointed the previous autumn following a raucous Commons debate.[8] Cadman's report was published in March 1938 and it was fiercely critical of both the Air Ministry and the airline.

As the debate came closer, Chamberlain made another and, as it proved, catastrophic political move, which also served further to undermine Swinton. Swinton's move to the House of Lords had weakened the government's debating fire-power in the House of Commons. Anthony Muirhead, who had succeeded the glamorous and wealthy Sir Philip Sassoon as junior air minister when the government changed in 1937, had neither of these qualities and made no impact whatever, so Chamberlain had good reason to seek a more powerful voice. Why he should have picked Lord Winterton to do this, though, is rather mysterious. Chamberlain had a distinct penchant for wealthy aristocrats as ministers and as sources of weekend invitations to grand houses. The Chief Whip Margesson was also a powerful factor in the choice of junior members of the government and leant towards the socially distinguished. Winterton had long service as an MP having been elected whilst he was still an Oxford undergraduate for what was practically a rotten borough in the midst of his family's immense landholdings. His was an Irish peerage so he could still sit in the Commons. Socially he was highly qualified, but lacked both ministerial experience or knowledge of air matters. He had been a junior India Office minister during a quiet period, but had been left out of the National Government. Winterton was brought into the Cabinet with the task of speaking on air matters. The promotion gave an uncanny echo of Swinton's appointment to chair the Air Parity Committee, whilst Lord Londonderry was still air minister, which had given the first public sign that Baldwin was losing confidence in Londonderry. Chamberlain and Wilson were now losing confidence in Swinton. Journalists were briefed that Winterton was being brought in to share a heavy workload with 'no reflection on Swinton's administration', the kind of comment that usually indicates that the skids are under a minister.[9]

Chamberlain had doubled up the domestic political stakes by refusing an inquiry into air rearmament, but just as Winterton was brought onto the scene, Hitler doubled up the diplomatic stakes. He seized Austria, in the so-called *Anschluß*, on 16 March 1938, putting Chamberlain's foreign policy to its first serious test. Chamberlain was blind-sided by the *Anschluß*. His early moves to appease Mussolini and Hitler had left him with the comforting feeling that his policy was on the right track and his pet scheme to buy Hitler off with Africa colonies was just about to be tested in Berlin, but now he had to face the reality of Nazi Germany's aggressive expansion. As nothing else could, this rammed home the fact that until Britain closed the air gap with Germany, the government would just have to swallow what Hitler threw at them. The emergency Cabinet meeting called to discuss the *Anschluß* decided to look at accelerating defence spending and called on Swinton to prepare a plan to speed up and increase the expansion of the RAF. The Cabinet also dropped the previously sacrosanct policy of not 'interfering with normal trade' to pursue rearmament but did not ditch the absolute spending limit of £1,650 million.

10 Downing Street was being sucked ever-more deeply into the air rearmament programme and Wilson found himself playing to his

strengths. Even if it was decided to spend the money, it had to be possible to manufacture the aircraft. Government thinking was dominated by a fear that shortage of labour would impede aircraft production and that the trade unions might prove obstructive. The Labour Party was still opposed to rearmament even though it clamoured for diplomatic firmness towards the dictators. Wilson was dispatched to meet the union leaders to set out the urgent need to build aircraft for the RAF. The supposedly unique vulnerability of London to bombing made up a major plank in his pitch.

> We can neither defend ourselves nor help others if we are not fully armed. Disarmament efforts left us weak: it inevitably takes time to recover ...
> Only too pleased if forces at our disposal enable us effectively to threaten. There is, however, the central weakness in the air. Cannot take the risk. (London, etc.)[10]

The stark picture was driven by the fear shared by Chamberlain and Wilson that the Luftwaffe had the power to bomb London flat with impunity. The Germans were doing their bit to stoke fears of air bombardment with a campaign to persuade the world of the Luftwaffe's power to obliterate cities.[11] Neither British politicians nor the air marshals appreciated the propaganda purpose of these claims and they built Nazi boasts into defeatist assessment of relative military strengths.

In parallel to Wilson's efforts, the Air Staff set to work to plan how the extra money could be spent. Over the weekend that followed the *Anschluß* they came up with Scheme L. The aircraft numbers were the same as in Scheme K but were to be completed a year earlier. This would be achieved by measures to release sufficient labour to allow factories to work double shifts. The new scheme featured the same shift towards larger bombers as its immediate predecessors and the detailed planning shows how the Air Staff's thinking was going as to which types of aircraft were worth having. It involved the procurement of 1,531 large bombers over two years.[12] Vickers Wellingtons accounted for almost two-thirds of this. The Wellington had clearly established itself as the type of choice; the Handley Page Hampden which had been built to the same specification did not feature at all. The pilot orders for the new four-engine bomber was mentioned, but the Air Staff was hedging its bets on the next generation of two-engine bomber. It left open the choice between the Wellington successor or the more ambitious large twin, B.1/35. There were still a lot of the lighter bombers becoming available but they were going out of first-line service: Blenheims to overseas units and Battles to target-towing duties.

The *Anschluß* made the government more willing to spend money but it had not completely abandoned budgetary procedure. Swinton skated over the question of what Scheme L was to cost, but implied that as his plan was intact, it would cost the same as Scheme K or even more. The other services would have to cut their spending to accommodate this. When the scheme came before Cabinet, this was the nub of an outright and irreconcilable clash with the Chancellor and Inskip. Sir John Simon, the Chancellor of the Exchequer, was working from an image of British financial security as something uniquely valuable and opposed the scheme as it would 'knock our finances to pieces prematurely'. Inskip endorsed the Chancellor's hostility as Scheme L would 'wreck the armament programmes recently adopted by the Cabinet'. Swinton was not to be moved and he upped the ante by telling his colleagues – entirely truthfully – that the Air Staff did not even think that Scheme K gave 'the minimum insurance'. Faced with a complete deadlock, the Cabinet took refuge in deciding that the question of labour supply was the thing that actually mattered.

The CAS, Sir Cyril Newall, and his sidekick Slessor, the Head of Plans, showed themselves in no mood to take the tergiversations of the politicians lying down. They rejected emphatically Inskip's statement that Scheme L would 'provide a safe air defence against Germany'. [13] They stuck firmly to their own version of the principle of parity. Only a striking force at least equal to Germany's '<u>at any given time</u>' (emphasis in original) could parry a knock-out blow and allow an even fight. Fighters had a part to play but only once the RAF's bombers had reduced the scale of the German attack through the alchemy of Trenchardism. Searchlights would be needed for the fighters to operate at night, but radar did not merit the slightest mention.

When the Cabinet wobbled even over as feeble a proposition as Scheme L, the airmen's fury boiled over. Newall berated his political masters:

> I feel strongly that the time for mincing words is past, and that the Air Staff must state their view of

the situation plainly. Their view is that unless the Cabinet are prepared to incur at the very least the full expenditure required for Scheme L and possibly more, we must accept a position of permanent inferiority to Germany in the air. In that event we must be prepared to accede to any German demand without a struggle, since in the event of war our financial and economic strength which the present financial limitations are designed to secure will be of no use because we shall not survive the knock-out blow.

The threat of a knock-out blow was taken for granted but Newall did, finally, admit that he was talking theory only and that there was no hard evidence. He could take refuge, though, in a doctrine of risk aversion. You had to be prepared for the worst and if Newall could find no other explanation for German and Italian rearmament, it had to be because they wanted to eliminate Britain at a stroke:

> No one can say with absolute certainty that a nation can be knocked out from the air, because no one has yet attempted it. There can be no doubt, however, that Germany and Italy believe it is possible as there can be no other explanation for their piling up armaments to a level which they could not hope to maintain in a long war. When, as I firmly believe, the issue is that of the survival of British civilization we cannot afford to take so great a chance for the sake of £60 or £100 millions.[14]

Britain was doomed unless the RAF had its big bombers. Newall's admission that there was no empirical proof that bombing could be decisive, was precursor to the famous remark 'Bomber' Harris made in the wake of the first 1,000-bomber raid on Cologne in May 1942, which marked the true start of the RAF's bomber offensive against Germany. Newall was playing on the fear of uncertainty; Harris was playing on the fact that Britain had no other way to attack Germany at that point so there was nothing to be lost by trying: 'a lot of people … say that bombing can never win a war … It has never been tried yet and we shall see.'

Chapter 24

A Wave of Uneasiness

Chamberlain set out to cut the Gordian knot of the budgetary impasse between Treasury and Air Ministry. He called an informal meeting of the most senior ministers involved and put to them a simple, burning question: 'what is the maximum the [aircraft] industry could produce in the next two years?'[1] Cost and military organization were to take a distant second place to raw numbers, which were all that mattered to Chamberlain. Unconsciouslessly, the prime minister was echoing Hitler's approach to his air force as he expressed it to Göring: 'The Führer does not ask me how big my bombers are, but how many there are.'[2]

Chamberlain's civil service adviser, Sir Horace Wilson, referred the simple question of the numbers of planes that could be manufactured to Bruce-Gardner, his man in the aircraft industry, and not to the Air Ministry; the plane-makers had become the arbiters of public policy and not the government itself. Just as Chamberlain had concluded that diplomacy was too important to be left to the Foreign Office, he and Wilson had decided that rearming the RAF was too important to be left to the Air Staff. The moment had come for Bruce-Gardner to strike. He began by anointing himself as a purveyor of intelligence on the Luftwaffe to Wilson, claiming that the Germans were currently producing half as many planes again as the British plane-makers and, given their head start, would make more than double the number of planes than the British in the course of 1938. He used this as the basis for a direct attack on the quality (and even democratic legitimacy) of the Air Ministry's decision-making; these were 'very disturbing figures and, for that reason any decision arrived at "by the few" should be made with the best information available and this, so far as I am concerned, I have endeavoured to provide'.[3] Bruce-Gardner parroted to Wilson and, by extension, to Chamberlain the Trenchardian claim that, alone of the armed forces, the RAF could 'get into the vitals of Germany'.

A Wave of Uneasiness

The underlying dispute between Lord Swinton and Bruce-Gardner was over how many planes the Air Ministry would buy, but the inevitable explosion was triggered by a fatally ill-timed move by the Air Ministry. It was announced that a mission was being sent to the United States to examine the possibility of buying aeroplanes from American makers. The Air Ministry was taking the long view quite correctly; the British aircraft industry alone was never going to have the resources to equip a full-scale air force for a European war, but it was not a politically astute move considering that the British industry was clamouring for orders and their man Bruce-Gardner had a privileged position at 10 Downing Street. The news provoked SBAC members to rage. Bruce-Gardner only just headed off a public protest by reading out the letter he was going to send to Swinton, 'complaining in the strongest terms with regard to the proposal to buy American war planes'.[4] As well as hurting their export business, it would signal that the British industry was fully loaded, which they believed was not true. The mission provided ammunition for a Conservative MP Oliver Simmonds who also owned an aircraft company to complain of, 'the inefficiency of the Air Ministry' at a time when many companies in the aircraft industry were dismissing their workpeople through lack of orders.[5]

Bruce-Gardner put Chamberlain's question to his members and came back with a long memorandum containing detailed answers, and answers that must have come as music to the ears of the prime minister and Wilson.[6] On the basis of their existing or immediately planned capacity, the plane-makers could produce more than twice the number of aircraft that they would be producing to meet Air Ministry orders: almost 8,000 aircraft in 1939 compared to 3,775 under the existing programme. Bruce-Gardner's paper was ostensibly addressed to Swinton, but it was designed to be read by the prime minister; each type of plane mentioned was described in outline, which would have been quite unnecessary for the professionals of the Air Ministry. The catch was that the extra aircraft were types that SBAC members were willing and able to produce and not necessarily the ones that the Air Ministry or the Royal Air Force wanted. Prominent in Bruce-Gardner's list of planes that could be produced quickly in large numbers, were aircraft of dubious value in the balance of power: the near-obsolete Gladiator biplane fighter; the Anson utility aircraft, dependable but hardly first-line combat material; and three bombers which barely featured in the Air

Staff's Scheme L plans. These were the catastrophic Fairey Battle, the small Blenheim and the Hampden bomber and its derivatives, which had been ordered as a fall-back if the Wellington had disappointed. Bruce-Gardner's list might as well have been drawn up as a mirror image of what the Air Staff wanted. He emphasized that switching production to the hated Wellington would cost output of other types in the short term and called for 'serious reconsideration' of the whole project. The only modern fighter for which Bruce-Gardner could claim there was extra output potential was the turret-armed Boulton Paul Defiant, which was to prove a severe disappointment. There was no scope to increase output of Hurricanes or Spitfires beyond existing plans.

Bruce-Gardner had the wind in his sails and took the opportunity to include a prospectus for types – from favoured suppliers – which did not even exist as prototypes, notably a twin-engine version of the Fairey Battle which was never to see the light of day. He also promoted the AW41, a similarly project-stage twin-engine bomber, from his old alma mater, Armstrong Whitworth, which offered the added attraction of undermining production of the despised Wellington. Armstrong Whitworth claimed it could produce the AW41 at twice the rate of Wellingtons, but this was not only incorrect but misleading to the point of dishonesty. The AW41's true raison d'être was that it was made of steel and wood and thus served as an insurance policy against aluminium supply becoming problematic. But this cost weight and thus performance and when it entered service as the Albermarle, no one wanted it.

Wilson forwarded Bruce-Gardner's paper and covering letter to Chamberlain with a full endorsement. He noted that the paper 'suggests that the industry is not being fully utilized'.[7] Wilson fed in a panic factor of his own aimed at Chamberlain's fear of public complaint: 'uneasiness is widespread and may come to a head quite soon.'[8] He reported conversations with other industrialists and claimed 'a wave of dissatisfaction with the Air Ministry is developing fast'. For good measure he forwarded to the prime minister samples of open complaint at the pace of air rearmament together with something that rammed home the political stakes involved: a reminder from Churchill that he was still waiting for a reply to a memorandum sent weeks before.

Swinton fought back at meeting in the Air Ministry on 25 April 1938 where Bruce-Gardner had to face the massed ranks of politicians and civil servants on his own.⁹ The air minister delivered a blunt message to the industry to warn it away from the vision of easy and lucrative orders for obsolescent aircraft types:

> he wished to secure the cooperation of Sir Charles Bruce-Gardner in making it clear to contractors that they would not be doing their duty merely by accelerating output of existing types. It was of the utmost necessity that the new types should be brought in at the earliest possible date and he would be very disappointed if, as the outcome of the discussions, acceleration of new types was not achieved.[10]

Swinton dominated the meeting, but the ground had been cut from under his feet at the highest level of politics. With the support of the prime minister's mighty adviser, Bruce-Gardner had little to fear and insiders could tell that the writing was on the wall for Swinton.[11] Two days after the meeting at the Air Ministry, the Cabinet discussed the programme to increase the RAF.[12] Chamberlain told the ministers that Bruce-Gardner and his colleagues at the plane-makers would be able to deliver 12,000 planes over the next two years compared to 7,500 previously estimated. The plans were in place to achieve this. The main issue was one of politics. The government was having to fight off accusations that the aircraft industry was being under-used and would face another onslaught from Churchill. Chamberlain's prescription was simple: ignore any specific programme and produce as many planes as possible. Bruce-Gardner was the man to get this done; the Cabinet formally agreed to authorize the Air Ministry to take delivery of 12,000 aircraft. There was no connection to any thought-out or structured rearmament scheme. The Air Staff's Scheme L was entirely ignored. In practice the government was outsourcing the rebuilding of the RAF to private sector manufacturers. Bruce-Gardner's vision as hammered out with Wilson and sold to Chamberlain of quantity first with no discussion of quality had triumphed. The only crumb of comfort left for Swinton came unintentionally from the Foreign Secretary, Lord Halifax, who unwisely asked the heretical question as to whether the government might get better value building fighters than bombers. Swinton could squash him with the Air Staff's stock formula that the number of fighters needed depended on the scale of the threat.

In Downing Street's eyes, the necessary had been done to settle the air rearmament issue. Within days the press was being told that it would soon be possible for the aircraft industry to double output. There only remained the Commons debate a fortnight later but it was going to be intense. Days before the *Anschluß* in March 1938, Churchill had sprung a devastatingly well-briefed memorandum on Chamberlain setting out the deficiencies in the Royal Air Force.[13] According to Churchill's figures half of its squadrons were equipped with obsolete types. Deliveries of modern aircraft were running slowly; only a dozen or two of the latest Hurricane fighters had arrived even though it had been ordered in 1936. Overall shipments were running at only 200 machines per month, which Churchill put at one-third of the German pace. Training accidents were inflicting severe attrition on those aircraft that were reaching squadrons. In the crisis over Austria, Churchill's memorandum had been left to one side but a month later as a Parliamentary debate on air rearmament loomed, Churchill reminded Chamberlain none too gently that Downing Street had yet to respond.[14] Wilson was prepared to be far more conciliatory than the prime minister had been a month earlier and advised that Churchill should be briefed 'in the course of the next 48 hours' about the reforms that were already being put in hand at the Air Ministry. Chamberlain contented himself with a perfunctory assurance to Churchill that he had 'been giving the matter my very close personal attention' and alluded vaguely to '[a] number of decisions ... most, if not all of which you would, I feel sure, approve'.[15] Churchill did not even rate a detailed briefing on Swinton's measures. Just as he had done over Churchill's demand for an inquiry, Chamberlain was spoiling for a fight.

Lord Winterton, recently appointed to represent the government on air matters in the Commons, had told the Cabinet that he was confident of defending the government but he was sadly in error. Criticism was stinging and well informed. The onslaught was led by Sir Hugh Seely, a Liberal MP and reserve RAF officer, inevitably supported by Churchill. The nub of their argument was simple: the Luftwaffe had a massive superiority in numbers over the RAF and the government appeared to be doing precious little to correct this. Winterton's response was catastrophically poor. He attacked 'the cloud of accusations, suspicions, and innuendoes' but failed to address any of the points of substance which he attempted to gloss over. Even the most loyal government MPs were unable to respond positively. Of course, they did not vote against the government which enjoyed the advantages of its huge majority but it was a major setback.

Even Chamberlain had to confess that he 'never expected him [Winterton] to be as bad as he was'.[16] The lobby correspondents were told that he had made a mess of an excellent brief.[17] It was inevitable that Winterton would be sacked from responsibility for air (although he was allowed to remain in the Cabinet), but there was widespread astonishment when Swinton was sacked from the Air Ministry as well. The pretext was the same as that given for Londonderry's elimination three years before: the government needed a heavyweight defender in the lower house, but the truth was that Swinton had dared to challenge Wilson's anointed supremo for air rearmament and his policy of quantity and not quality. The command and control system of the Chamberlain government demanded obedience to the policies of Downing Street, whether they cut across the prerogatives of ministries or not. Swinton had to be replaced by someone who grasped this fact; it did not matter what the civil servants of the Air Ministry or the commanders of the RAF thought about the matter. Swinton's abrasiveness did not make for a quiet life and he had become a lightning rod for the discontent of the aircraft industry. Wilson had backed the industry against the ministry. Weir resigned in disgusted sympathy almost immediately.

In his memoirs Swinton bemoaned the forces that had led to his removal:

> There were not wanting manufacturers who would like to have built a lot of the old Hinds and Harts, death-traps which could have been turned out in any quantity and would have produced a nice fraudulent balance sheet. All this influenced critics to think it all ought to be much easier. Chamberlain made up his mind he must sacrifice me in order to get an easier time in Parliament. This was not unnatural for a Prime Minister who was not much interested, at the time, in rearmament and was convinced that war could be avoided.[18]

He was exaggerating by suggesting that Bruce-Gardner and Wilson wanted to produce such true antiques but was accurate in recognizing that the political imperative of quantity had trumped the need for quality.

Chamberlain appointed his long-standing associate, Sir Kingsley Wood, to replace Swinton. Wood was far more of a professional politician. He had a gift for promoting schemes which attracted favourable publicity. As Postmaster General he had been credited with a successful drive to market telephones to the public. He had moved on to the Ministry of Health where he had pursued slum clearance, a topic close to Chamberlain's heart from his own time at the ministry. Superficially the change was seen as an improvement: 'Kingsley has lots of energy and business sense and creates public confidence without antagonizing people as Philip [Swinton] does.'[19] Wood might have been more emollient, but he became as enthusiastic a Trenchardian as Swinton and resolutely backed the Air Staff's bomber strategy.

For good measure Muirhead, the nonentity junior minister, was also replaced but his successor was a distinct improvement and a quite different proposition to Wood. Harold Balfour was rather a political counterpart to Air Marshal Sir Wilfrid Freeman as a forgotten hero of building the RAF in the Second World War. A highly decorated RFC officer and still skilled enough as a pilot to be entrusted to take one of the RAF's only two Spitfires for a flight, he had moved from journalism to running the aviation business of the Pearson Group. 'Chips' Channon relished him socially and as a fellow MP; he was 'desperately charming with the face of a hard boy'.[20] He remained in office until 1944, one of the rare junior ministers who contributed far more than his seniors. Amongst his many achievements was the Empire Air Training Scheme, which proved vital in in meeting the RAF's needs in manpower during the Second World War.

Chapter 25

From Telephones to Warplanes

Almost Sir Kingsley Wood's first move in office was designed to kill three birds with one stone. Above all, it would provide spectacular evidence that the government was addressing the question of aircraft manufacture on which it had taken such a severe beating in Parliament. The Labour opposition had latched on to the shortage of modern fighters as a stick with which to beat the government.[1] It would also elegantly bury two embarrassing parts of his legacy from Swinton in the same grave. Soon after Swinton had been appointed his abrasive personality had contributed to an embarrassing and venomous public squabble with Lord Nuffield, Britain's leading car manufacturer, over a small aircraft engine company that Nuffield owned personally.[2] Wood saw major dividends from conciliating Nuffield whose industrial empire might be used to good advantage in the rearmament effort. In particular, it could be used to make good the problem of producing Spitfires, one of the vital new generation of high-speed fighters that the RAF needed in force and it would have to be produced in volume. It was an excellent design but actually manufacturing it had become a nightmare. Supermarine, the company who designed the Spitfire, had only one small factory in Southampton, vulnerable to German air attack. Much of the work had to be sub-contracted which added another layer of difficulty.

Wood and Nuffield agreed that Nuffield would build and operate a massive factory at Castle Bromwich near Birmingham under the shadow factory scheme to make 1,000 Spitfires.[3] Wood ensured that every ounce of possible favourable publicity was wrung from the project. Publicly the deal was touted as the largest aircraft order ever placed, although the agreement fell well short of a legal contract. The Treasury was appropriately sniffy about the whole procedure especially as it had not been consulted. The cost of the factory was put at the then gigantic sum of £3.5 million and it was to be equipped with the most modern machine tools available. It had all the flavour of an essentially political deal.

The agreement compromised plans for Fairey's large factory at Stockport, which was making the already obsolescent Battle, to be turned over to Spitfires.[4] The Air Ministry sniffed that Nuffield had been given a free hand in planning the factory and the estimated cost was soon £4.5 million, far in excess of original projection.[5] In its early years Castle Bromwich proved a severe embarrassment. It was even proposed to turn it over to the Westland Whirlwind twin-engine fighter, a pet project of Newall's but ultimately a failure.[6] Production of Spitfires was agonizingly slow, in part because Nuffields were accustomed to the much lower tolerances and higher volumes of car production. Additionally, labour relations were atrocious. When Lord Beaverbrook became Minister of Aircraft Production in May 1940, he stripped Nuffield of control of Castle Bromwich and handed it over to Vickers.

The combination of Wood as minister and Bruce-Gardner as Downing Street's link-man to the plane-makers appears to have satisfied Downing Street that all was back on track. There is no sign that any attempt was made from the top to chase progress on making good the lag in production. Relations between government and plane-makers calmed down. Wood could work undisturbed and he in turn made no changes to the new men and structures that he had inherited from Swinton. In Freeman's words, 'We spent the money and Kingsley Wood left us alone.'[7]

Once Swinton had been eliminated and the eye-catching Castle Bromwich project launched to prove that the government was taking air rearmament seriously, things could go back to normal. With perfect political cynicism the SBAC's self-serving complaint at the possibility of buying in the United States could be ignored once it had played its part in undermining Swinton. The mission led to orders for two American aircraft types that played an important part in the Royal Air Force's wartime arsenal: the Harvard advanced trainer and the Hudson light bomber and maritime patrol aircraft. These were the first of many US aircraft without which Britain would have been severely handicapped. Swinton and Weir had recognized that the British domestic aircraft industry did not have sufficient capacity to meet the needs of a full-scale air war.

***

The outcome to the various practically unrelated initiatives of the early part of 1938 had produced little more than a political fudge, whose centrepiece was Chamberlain's 12,000-plane scheme, which barely rose above a short-term exercise in presentational figures. The Air Staff's influence on this approach was minimal and it sat in uneasy juxtaposition to Scheme L which had neither been formally rejected nor approved. In theory Scheme F remained the approved expansion scheme with Scheme K hovering in even deeper budgetary limbo than Scheme L. The overriding goal of making service estimates fit onto the Procrustean bed of an aggregate £1,650 million held good and the Cabinet was not committed to keeping spending at the level needed for the 12,000-plane plan once it had been completed. Serious decisions on long-term spending and strategy had been postponed indefinitely. The immediate requirements of the Air Staff were well provided for by the Committee on Supply; within limits the RAF had a blank cheque book at its disposal.

Predictably the relationship with the Treasury suffered. The premier branch of the Civil Service did not remotely relish the loss of its hallowed right to scrutinize and control proposed expenditure to the penny. Tensions were bought to boiling point by a scheme dreamed up by the Air Staff and Wood to develop Canada's infant aircraft industry as a source of aircraft for the RAF. A delegation had been despatched across the Atlantic to open discussions with the Canadian government and local aircraft companies. The key goal of the plan was to set up production of 1936-generation bombers in Canada.[8] As well as boosting capacity available to the RAF, the scheme had the added attraction that Wood thought it could be funded outside the normal budget for the Air Ministry and thus not restricted by the tight controls on his spending that the Treasury, with the support of Inskip, had been imposing. Canada offered the prospect of equipping Bomber Command with the heavy bombers on which the Air Staff had set its heart, bypassing domestic British constraints. Given the small and fractured state of the industry in Canada, the plan would have called for huge support from the British government and produced aircraft at a cost 25 per cent to 33.3 per cent higher than it would have cost to make the planes in the UK. Wood brazenly claimed that 'it has always been recognized that it would be particularly valuable to produce [the large bombers] in Canada'. As the Air Staff had been extremely circumspect in revealing the scale of its large bomber plans and this was the first real mention on the Canada scheme, this was provocative to say the least.

The Chancellor of the Exchequer, Sir John Simon, furiously tried to pull Wood back into line in unusually forthright language:

> a real effort should be made to bring Treasury financial control and responsibility and the numerous and growing activities of the Air Ministry into greater harmony and on to more normal and customary lines ... He wished to make a special appeal to the Secretary of State [for Air] to assist in restoring the relations between his Department and the Treasury in regard to Treasury control to the levels which obtained in other spending departments.[9]

Part of Wood's programme was to arrange 'marriages' between British and Canadian firms. Simon inquired acidly whether the 'the Treasury would be called upon to give wedding presents?' Despite the prime minister's support, Wood had overreached himself. He had not properly taken into account the fact that Canadian industry did not have the capacity to manufacture the engines that the big bombers needed so they would have to be made in Britain and shipped west across the Atlantic.[10] This undermined one of the scheme's selling points: that the finished bombers could simply be flown eastward to bases in Britain. Wood had to accept that he would look again at the kind of aircraft that should be made in Canada. It was not until well into the war that the British government paid for a factory to make Lancaster bombers, rather than the Halifaxes that Wood had planned in 1938, although smaller types, most famously the Hawker Hurricane fighter, were made there from an early stage.

The wrangle over the Canada project and Wood's blatant attempt to outflank normal budgetary control, gave Simon the opportunity to put the Air Ministry on the spot and come up with hard figures for what it would actually be spending under the 12,000-plane scheme. The Air Ministry set to work to reconcile the figures for Scheme L with what the Cabinet had decided and, of course, what it had conspicuously not decided.[11] It firstly had to stretch a point and work on the assumption that the Cabinet had approved by 'implication the expansion the RAF to a Scheme L basis'. The result was not comforting and the civil servants at Adastral House began to reflect on how to break the bad news to their financial masters. Scheme L was supposed to have reduced spending from the level proposed under Scheme K but bit by bit new costs had crept in. The five-year budget had jumped by 9 per cent to £620.75 million. In the unlikely event that Inskip's cherished £1,650 million total figure for all three services was going to hold good, the navy and army were going to have to tighten their belts. The Air Ministry recognized that even the 1939 figure was going to be 'new and unpleasantly large' for the Treasury and mused whether it should withhold the figures for 1940 and 1941.

***

Wood's instinct for publicity had one accidental result. He insisted on conducting his tours of inspection by air as the only fitting means of transport for an air minister.[12] On one flight his aircraft crashed, severely injuring Air Marshal Courtney, who was unable to take up his planned appointment of AOC-in-C of Fighter Command in succession to Dowding, who was coming up for retirement. But for this, Dowding's great achievement in preparing Fighter Command for war would be far less well known and Courtney would have had the task of defeating the Luftwaffe's assault on Britain in the summer of 1940.

Chapter 26

The Doubts of Sir Edgar Ludlow-Hewitt

The impassioned call that Sir Cyril Newall issued in the wake of the *Anschluß* to forget mere money in order to save British civilization delivered the most ringing plea imaginable for the government to implement the Trenchardian doctrine with ever vaster fleets of large bombers, but it was hollow. Behind the faith that it proclaimed in bombing lay the Air Staff's growing recognition that the RAF was incapable of delivering the offensive that Trenchardian doctrine demanded. The budgetary debate over Scheme L was raging across Whitehall, but in the quieter corridors of Adastral House and the headquarters of Bomber Command at Hillingdon a rather different mood was gaining the upper hand. After the months of breakneck expansion driven by Swinton and Weir, air force officers were seeing an urgent need to consolidate, which was brought into sharp focus by the *Anschluß*. However predictable it might have been, the move came as a severe shock to the Air Staff, to none more so than Slessor. The same day that Germany marched in he drafted a frantic memo to Newall whose advice and recommendations the CAS wholeheartedly sent on, equally promptly, to his political master, Swinton.[1] War was no longer distant and one of a number of hypotheses; it was an imminent possibility:

> 3. We are now proceeding on the basis that we must be prepared for war at some convenient time within the next three years and I would suggest that this basis should be altered and we should work on the assumption that we may be forced to into war this summer.
>
> 4. This suggestion means in fact that instead of occupying our time and energies in preparation for further expansion, we should devote them, with all the resources at our disposal to bring our <u>existing</u> forces up to as high a degree of readiness for war in as short a time as possible.[2]

Unspoken was the recognition that the RAF no longer had time on its side – if it ever had – to develop an air arm that matched its ideals for a fighting force. The Air Staff might have to fight with what it had at hand and, like military commanders down the ages, make the best of it that they could. The situation was so grave that Newall even deigned to address the question of the RAF's despised fighter squadrons. Deliveries of modern monoplane fighters were lagging and Newall suggested rearming squadrons equipped with antique Demon biplanes with more modern but still obsolescent Gladiator biplanes by withholding aircraft being manufactured for foreign orders.

Even worse was Newall's brutal admission: 'Under the present circumstances the RAF will be in no fit condition to fight at any rate in 1938.' Newall was confessing that the best part of three years' work and a privileged position amongst the armed services in terms of access to finance had failed to create a force that was ready for combat. As Ellington had darkly foretold when he argued against a breakneck expansion of the RAF, the process was taking a long time to digest.

The situation was dire enough, and Slessor's influence over Newall's was strong enough, for the head of the RAF to advise his minister to take a truly extraordinary step in the light of what had been happening since Lord Swinton had taken office: first-line expansion was to be brought to a sudden stop and work concentrated on bringing the air force up to a high degree of readiness. Only once this had been achieved should the Air Ministry return to the charge and try to get authorization for the further expansion set out in Scheme J. The CAS and his assistant – Swinton seems to have understood who was pulling the strings – were summoned to see the minister the following Sunday morning. They were in for a disappointment: Swinton told his uniformed subordinates in no uncertain terms of the political reality of the situation. Once they had asked for more there was no going back. The kind of complete about-face that Newall and Slessor were recommending was simply impossible. Slessor deferred to his minister's political judgement, as though this were some dark art rather than elementary understanding of how human beings interact. The Air Staff was caught between its outward demand for ever greater resources and its inward recognition that it could not even make use of the resources that it had already been granted. Even when the panic over the *Anschluß* had subsided and made way for the next stage of the budgetary battle over Scheme L, Slessor stuck to his guns and argued against any further first-line expansion.[3]

***

One of the most powerful voices for consolidation was that of Air Chief Marshal Sir Edgar Ludlow-Hewitt who had been commanding Bomber Command since September 1937. Ludlow-Hewitt was one of the most appealing figures amongst the air marshals although far from perfect. He was well liked by his juniors, notably because he insisted on flying himself around on tours of inspection; he was an excellent pilot.[4] Even the usually acerbic Bert Harris, his junior at Bomber Command, held him in enormous respect.[5] He was humane enough to have qualms about the Trenchardian mission to attack civilian morale. These showed through in a floundering performance at a Chiefs of Staff meeting where he deputized for Ellington when the navy representative put him on the rack over the Air Staff's enthusiasm for attacking 'morale'.[6] Ludlow-Hewitt feebly claimed that the useful result of air raids was the disruption that they caused. The penalty for these traits was that he lacked the steely resolution required to win in bureaucratic battles. In the words of another senior air marshal: 'Most knowledgeable; very sound on paper; probably more detailed knowledge of service matters than anyone in the RAF. As a commander a hopeless bungler and fuddler; unable to make up his mind and will change it five times in as many minutes; easily flustered.'[7] He was over-immersed in detail. The officer who succeeded him in one post was

> amazed at the assemblage of filing cabinets in his office. 'My dear Ludlow – have you read all these files?' 'Oh, yes, I make time to keep myself up to date.' 'But there must be millions of words in all those papers.'[8]

Ludlow-Hewitt was acutely aware of how much needed to be done. His command was by far the largest and most important component of the RAF, the striking force that would accomplish the service's Trenchardian destiny. Ludlow-Hewitt had been recalled from commanding the RAF in India where he had been since 1935, to take over Bomber Command so had missed the first phase of the big expansion. He was appalled at what he found. He bombarded the Air Ministry with specific defects which he summarized in his annual report on the command's efficiency for 1937 which he released in March 1938 and which stated:

> The Command as a whole is not only far from attaining a condition which could fairly be described as 'ready for war', but at the rate of present progress it is not even possible to make any reasoned forecast of the date by which it may be expected to reach a state of relative war efficiency.[9]

Even making allowance for the natural tendency of someone new in a job to magnify the challenges inherited from their predecessor, Ludlow-Hewitt's litany of difficulties made depressing reading for the Air Staff. The nub of Ludlow-Hewitt's analysis was that Bomber Command had simply expanded too fast and too much, leading to 'the attenuation of efficiency in every department'.[10] Almost nothing was truly ready. He opposed any further expansion and called for at least twelve months' consolidation if there was to be any hope of bringing Bomber Command up to war readiness. The most important deficiency Ludlow-Hewitt identified was in personnel, touching on one of glaring weaknesses in the RAF's expansion. He opened his report:

> An efficient force of bombers is today a highly technical and specialised organization. It requires in particular a very high standard of navigation and bad weather flying and this combined with the need for efficient defence of the aircraft against hostile aircraft demands a highly skilled and experienced crew.[11]

The key failing was that the Air Staff's decision in 1936 to move to an all big-bomber striking force had been limited almost exclusively to the hardware; other considerations had barely featured. Bomber Command was the arm of service most exposed to technological change. The large bombers with crews of four or more with separate but interlocking tasks posed a formidable challenge in personnel management and training. Today it is highly unlikely that non-service experts in human factors such as ergonomics and psychology would not be consulted on important, expensive and complex new weapon systems when training and operating procedures were established. They would probably advise at the design stage as well. The RAF's adoption of big bombers doubled up on its commitment to large aircraft in a very major strategic choice that defined the way it intended to carry out what was seen as its primary mission, but it had given minimal attention to the vital question of how their crews were to be organized. It was broadly understood that something far more serious and professional was needed than the RAF's previous practice of drafting stray ground crew as flight personnel and paying them a little extra, but there was no agreement as to how this should done. When the Air Staff replied to Ludlow-Hewitt's complaints with the claim that, 'Revision of aircraft crew policy, which will materially relieve existing difficulties in respect of aircraft crews, has recently been effected', Ludlow-Hewitt wrote 'NO' against the passage.[12]

Later experience showed just how great was the task that had merely been taken for granted. A completely new specialization of flight engineer came into being to handle the management of four-engine bombers but this was still only being discussed a few weeks before war broke out.[13] The only aircraft designed *ab initio* as a four-engine bomber, the Short Stirling, had two pilots who could share the load, but the RAF's other four-engine types had begun as twin-engine aircraft with only a single pilot. In practice, each crew evolved its own command hierarchy.[14] It became relatively common for bomber captains to be junior in rank to members of their crew and some exercised full command authority in this position. Sergeant pilots with commissioned aircrew were by no means unknown. Unless the crew functioned as a team it was doomed. The only phase of an operation where the pilot was in unarguable control was take-off and landing. On the bomb run the bomb-aimer directed the aircraft and under attack from German fighters it was the air-gunner with sight of the attacker who told the pilot what to do. At other times the captain would follow a competent and experienced navigator.

The weakest point that Ludlow-Hewitt pointed to was the poor state of training.[15] Here his commanders had had to contend with the fact that 'new drafts of inexperienced personnel' had to be given elementary training. The pace of modernization also meant that his squadrons had to 'master ... the maintenance and elementary operation of new equipment'. A vicious circle had been created in which experienced crews were so absorbed by training the inexperienced that they had not been able to perfect their own operational efficiency. In wartime this would mean that Bomber Command would rapidly face a crisis of manpower. Ludlow-Hewitt calculated that his medium bomber crews would be practically eliminated in three and a half weeks and his heavy bomber crews in seven and a half weeks, creating a need for 'literally hundreds of fresh crews'.[16] Responsibility for finding a solution lay squarely with the Air Ministry and he warned Adastral House to 'bear ... in mind that reinforcement crews are relatively useless until trained, and that our present experience is that it takes many months to train them'.

As well as Bomber Command's acute growing pains, Ludlow-Hewitt recognized that the rapid progress in aircraft technology meant that operational methods and equipment would have to advance as well in a process far more structured and professional than the haphazard methods of the past. He knew that the new types of aircraft being brought into service would require a rethink – or perhaps simply thought – about operating methods. The type of bombs used and the height from which they were to be dropped on each kind of target also needed to be studied. What he wanted was a Bomber Command version of the Air Fighting Development Establishment which had been doing similar work for Fighter Command since 1936. He argued for the creation of a Bomber Development Unit (BDU) as a permanent organization to undertake empirical, practical tests of new procedures and hardware with a cadre of experienced crews. He spent a long and frustrating time trying to persuade the Air Staff to authorize one. The idea was not turned down but months went by with no action.[17] Not only would it cost money, but there was a string of objections from bodies such as the National Trust to the thought of turning over country areas for use as a bombing range. Only in late 1940 did one come into operation.

It is barely surprising that the 'The Readiness of War' report that Ludlow-Hewitt submitted in the immediate aftermath of the September 1938 Munich crisis took a bleak view of the state of Bomber Command.[18] Ludlow-Hewitt's near-obsessive focus on every aspect of the detail of his organization emerges from the diverse litany of problems, high and low, that he highlighted.[19] None of the difficulties deserved to be dismissed out of hand but the overall impression is that of a commander lost in the minutiae of problems and unable to prioritize the big issues. Ludlow-Hewitt identified weaknesses in: the availability of target maps; the planning organization; the plans to move Blenheim squadrons to

France in the opening days of a war; the status of station intelligence officers; and the reproduction of target photographs. In the midst of all this he complained of slow delivery of modern aircraft – a near universal problem but far less acute at Bomber Command than Fighter Command – and the shortage of trained crews. It was this final point that was the crucial deficiency of his command and one that had been manifest well before the Munich crisis.

Ludlow-Hewitt had already detected many flaws in the early days of his command. There were hangovers from a decidedly unhurried peacetime, regular army approach to things. Squadron commanders had a clutch of unimportant jobs unrelated to combat efficiency: responsibility for the sergeants' mess, presidency of the Station Fire Safety Committee, organization of station physical training, recreation and sport. The formal sign-off by two officers was needed to accept any new premises.

The Munich crisis threw this into a stark light and triggered a stand-off between the two most powerful individuals in the RAF: the CAS and Ludlow-Hewitt as commander of the most important and the largest component of the service and the one on which the most money had been lavished – the one on which the Air Staff was relying to fulfil its Trenchardian destiny. What is more remarkable is that months afterwards, up to the eve of the Second World War, Ludlow-Hewitt was still signalling grave deficiencies in Bomber Command. The Munich crisis had brought problems well into the open, but not the means to solve them. This would have taken much time whatever but the process of identifying solutions was agonizingly prolonged.

One of the few major topics on which Ludlow-Hewitt saw eye to eye with the Air Staff was what his command was eventually supposed to bomb in Germany. Remarkably enough, it was only in late 1937 that serious thought was given to the targets that the RAF should attack if war broke out. It was a tortuous process, involving a minor turf fight with Desmond Morton's Industrial Intelligence Centre over whether the Air Staff should have a monopoly over the choice. Eventually the list of possible targets was boiled down to three, for each of which a plan was drawn up under the designation W.A. (Western Air). W.A.1. was an attack on the Luftwaffe on its bases; W.A.4. on the German army and its supporting network of communications; W.A.5. on German war industry, above all the Ruhr. Ludlow-Hewitt had little faith in the idea of attacking the Luftwaffe on the ground, but did see the Ruhr as an exceptionally promising target. He saw it as so vulnerable that it was in a 'category apart ... the only decisive objective which can be set off against London, the Black Country, and Manchester'.[20] He selected twenty-six coking plants and nineteen electricity-generating stations as key objectives and believed that he could reduce their output 'below the critical minimum in a month by 300 aircraft working at "sustained effort"'. In turn, this could bring 'virtual paralysis of the industrial activities of the RUHR [with] decisive effect on the war potential of Germany'. Later experience was to show that this was so optimistic as to lie firmly in the realms of fantasy, although Ludlow-Hewitt did recognize that attacking coke ovens and power stations would raise 'important questions' of a kind that a Bombing Development Unit could study 'rapidly and efficiently'.[21] According to his estimates, the 3,000 sorties that it would take to paralyse the Ruhr would cost Bomber Command 176 bombers, a rate of wastage that was implicitly low enough not to detract from the 'promising' nature of the Ruhr as a target.

The thought of Bomber Command wrecking German industry was too appealing to be subjected to critical analysis. On the last day of the Czechoslovakia crisis the Air Ministry received a letter from Bomber Command with news that was 'cheering as far as this country is concerned but scarcely helpful to Plan W.5'.[22] A bomber pilot had conducted a reconnaissance over power stations and steel works in the Midlands and reported difficulties in finding and identifying potential targets of a kind that would become depressingly familiar to Bomber Command from the autumn of 1940.[23] The correspondence was filed away and forgotten.

The vision of the RAF inflicting some equivalent of a knock-out blow on London by attacking the Ruhr was to have a long life. It marked a significant change in the Air Staff view of the world. As recently as the autumn of 1937 it had been given as a firm fact that the vulnerability of London had 'no parallels in Germany'.[24] The new availability of a comparable target in Germany created the possibility, theoretical at least, to unleash the full potential of Bomber Command.

Chapter 27

An Ideal of Bombing

In early 1938, whilst battle raged over the funding of the next leg in the RAF's expansion and political control of the process under the ever-growing shadow of the Nazi menace, the conference rooms at Adastral House hosted a series of discussions comfortably remote from day-to-day exigencies. The Air Staff launched an exercise that was part long-range equipment planning and part manifesto for its strategic dogma, together with an incidental boost for a peculiar approach to fighter design and the refutation of a minor heresy.

The decision to reequip Bomber Command entirely with 1936-design large bombers did not mark the end of the Air Staff's thinking on aircraft of the future. In fact, the next step in examining the RAF's requirements got under way before the first 1936 bomber had even flown for the first time, still less entered squadron service. The exercise was openly labelled as the search for an 'Ideal' bomber and as such represents pure blue-sky thinking. It was not brought into life by any technological or strategical development. Intelligence on developments in potentially enemy air forces played some, indeterminate role, but the quest for the 'Ideal' bomber was more important in what it reveals of Air Staff thinking. It is tempting to suppose that the label 'ideal' was picked as a direct rebuke to the fighter-heavy 'Ideal' defence scheme that Inskip had tried to foist on the RAF. There are a number of curious features to the process that set off the quest for the Ideal Bomber; it was unlike other procurement exercises. It did not begin as was usual with the Operational Requirements Committee defining a specific military need that it was to fulfil. The overarching goal was to identify a single type of bomber that could equip all of the RAF's bomber squadrons, abolishing the distinction between different classes of bombers that had ruled for the interwar period. It was the logical extension of the doctrine that the RAF had one single significant mission: bombing the enemy homeland. Even the 1936 large bombers had appeared as both medium and heavy bombers in their initial specifications; it was only later and largely by chance that all three designs came to be classed as heavy bombers. If the Rolls-Royce Vulture engine had proved a success, the Halifax and the Manchester would have remained twin-engine mediums.

The Ideal Bomber paper was unlike any other document in the RAF's aircraft procurement process. It featured a list of five entirely hypothetical specifications for bombers to perform the same role: dropping bombs anywhere in Germany. The paper delivered a nod towards the longer term by claiming to cover the potential that another country might be the 'most probable enemy'; intriguingly, Russia was put first on the list of these ahead of Japan and Italy. However, little or no attention was devoted to the need for global strategic mobility that would have been required to confront these first two secondary enemies. The figures given for the cost of the various types were precise but nowhere in the paper was any explanation given as to how they had been calculated. The Ideal Bomber was to do the same job as the 1936 designs, only better. How the Ideal Bomber was to achieve the higher speed and greater bombload required was unclear.

Whatever its origins, the language and methodology of Ideal Bomber paper chimed with the bigger picture. The most important part of the defence planning context that initiated the search for the Ideal Bomber was Sir Thomas Inskip's defence review of October 1937, which put all the service chiefs under the cosh to demonstrate that they were not only delivering programmes that would defend Britain effectively but also that they were doing so in a way that gave the taxpayer value for money. Long before the term was even coined, this was an exercise in cost/benefit analysis. The Ideal Bomber paper that emerged was a sustained argument in favour of a particular specification of bomber on the basis that it provided the heaviest cargo of bombs that could be dropped deep in Germany for the lowest cost. The favoured specification was selected from the list of five. This in itself was an unusual procedure and baked a degree of artificiality into the exercise from the start. The choices ranged from a 9,000lb lightweight costing £14,500 to a monster of 91,500lb which would have cost the phenomenal sum of £120,500. The dice were loaded in favour of the second smallest type B from the start. There was also a bias against existing designs: one list showed ideal bombers as noticeably cheaper than comparable designs: £29,250 for the B compared to £32,000 for the Manchester and £40,800 for the C compared to Stirlings at £55,000.[1]

The Ideal Bomber paper was as much a policy declaration as an exercise in practical aircraft design. It assumed that the RAF had one dominant if not sole job: bombing Germany. Otherwise there was not, as the paper, stated unequivocally, 'overwhelming advantages in having our whole Metropolitan bomber force (and Commands abroad if possible) armed with one type'.[2] When the air minister, Sir Kingsley Wood, was being briefed to argue the Air Staff's case in the political arena in the fractious debate over the RAF's Scheme L, he was pointed towards the Ideal Bomber paper as an explanation for why the Air Staff had adopted a heavy bomber policy, even though Scheme L was set to use the previous generation of aircraft and the Ideal Bomber barely deserved the label of a paper project. Even more strikingly Newall was using it to support his case almost two years later after the Ideal Bomber project had died. He was responding to his old enemy Hankey, by then a peer and member of the War Cabinet, and better placed to challenge the Air Staff's doctrine than he had been as a mere Cabinet Secretary.[3] Newall acknowledged that the paper was eighteen months old but 'this does not, of course, mean that its arguments do not apply today'.

True to the brief provided by his professional advisers Wood attempted to introduce the Ideal Bomber into ministerial discussions of the large bomber policy. Amongst the bodies to which the question was referred was the Defence Programmes and Acceleration Sub-committee.[4] To support his case Wood had presented the members with both his Scheme L paper which made a firm proposal to re-equip the bomber force with 1936 large bombers and the Ideal Bomber paper. There was no apparent attempt to explain the distinction between the firm designs of the former and the wholly theoretical nature of the latter. It is easy to suspect that Wood hoped that the committee's members would believe that the 1936 designs had emerged from the pseudo-rigorous process of selection from a series of options set out in the Ideal Bomber paper and that they could be considered Ideal Bombers themselves. In fact, he faced a rather more aggressive challenge than he might have hoped. The attack was launched from one of the traditional homes of suspicions of Air Staff doctrine, the Admiralty. Lord Stanhope, the First Lord, began by challenging the whole imperative to match Germany in bomber strength and moved on to the glaring weakness in Wood's case. 'He did not recognize the "ideal bomber aircraft" in the future types mentioned' in the Scheme L paper. Like any good politician Wood had a fall-back position available, which still kept the flavour of his original pitch. He admitted that the Ideal Bomber had yet to be evolved, but claimed '[t]he Stirling, Manchester and Halifax types were nearer to it than the present bombers'. They were steps on the road to perfection in performing the RAF's unarguable task, not the best available machines to carry out a debatable strategy. Blurring the processes of development and production for concrete and ideal projects also served to take the eye off the question as to how long it would take to bring the 1936 large bombers into service.

Whether the conflation of the 1936 large bombers with the Ideal Bomber was intentional or not, it permeated even the higher ranks of the RAF itself. Air Marshal Sir Philip Joubert de la Ferté, one of the RAF's most senior commanders, was so far misled by the fact that his colleague Sholto Douglas, then ACAS, had chaired the meetings dealing with the Ideal Bomber, that he thought that Douglas was responsible for the entire RAF heavy bomber project and called its products his 'brainchildren'.[5] Sholto Douglas advances no such grandiose claim in his autobiography, which takes a decidedly non-committal stance on the bomber offensive. Sholto Douglas even displayed clear reservations about how realistic the Ideal Bomber project was at all when he forwarded it to the relevant departments of the Air Ministry for technical evaluation. He asked the technical staff 'what items could reasonably be omitted or modified', a clear invitation to pare the Ideal Bomber down to a more practical project.[6]

In the event the Ideal Bomber project worked its way through the system with the various powers that be chipping in their opinions.[7] A rather less ambitious specification than the one in the Ideal Bomber paper was actually issued to aircraft firms but none of the resulting tenders was convincing. The most obvious flaw in the whole scheme was that no engines existed that would yield the added performance over the 1936 large bombers. There was, anyway, a strong argument for waiting until practical experience with the 1936 aircraft, which were still barely at the prototype stage, before seeking to improve on them.

The Ideal Bomber paper was not merely a positive manifesto for a large bomber, it also denounced one particular heresy that advanced an alternative vision of what the RAF's bomber force needed. The idea of a bomber that relied purely on speed for protection had been doing the rounds for some while. A number of projects had been submitted to the Air Ministry by outside designers and aircraft manufacturers.

The concept had even got as far as evaluation by the Royal Aircraft Establishment at Farnborough. None had got any further. The Ideal Bomber paper set out what seems to have been the Air Staff's dominant reason for rejecting the idea, which on closer examination proved to be no more than a truism of arms development: that the enemy would develop some means to counter it effectively. One of the arguments advanced against an earlier speed bomber project was that it would have to be developed in secrecy, which would be impossible in peacetime, to stop the Germans pre-emptively developing a fighter fast enough to catch it. The paper also claimed that a speed bomber would also need poor weather or night to operate effectively.

Like so much of the Air Staff's reasoning, the case against the speed bomber showed how flawed was its intellectual tool-kit. If the Germans could devise a means of attacking a fast bomber, why should they not devise a means of attacking a slower, but heavily armed one as well? In the event they did not need to, as ordinary interceptor fighters were perfectly adequate for the job in daytime and when they forced the large bombers to operate at night, conversions of a heavy fighter (Bf 110) and a medium bomber (Ju 88) had a sufficient margin of armament and performance even when burdened with primitive radar aerials to be decisively superior in combat. Thus, the Air Staff's predilection for heavy bombloads and multiple gun turrets served to delay the adoption of the de Havilland Mosquito, a private venture speed bomber project which proved a winner.

It would be unfair to accuse the Air Staff of lacking perfect foresight because only the advent of the Luftwaffe's Me 262 jet fighter gave the Germans a fighter significantly faster than the Mosquito. But the point does lead to a more subtle criticism of the Air Staff's approach. It is a key aspect of air power that confronting the enemy with a range of novel weapons compels him to devote resources. Finding a plane capable of intercepting the Mosquito had become something of a holy grail for German developers.

To complete the Ideal Bomber paper's mission as a statement of Air Staff orthodox thinking, it supported the enthusiasm for turret-fighters with the specious claim that this was shared by foreign air forces.

Chapter 28

As Much Damage as Possible on the Attackers

Dowding had a double mission as head of Fighter Command. First, he had the simple professional duty to make his command as efficient as possible as a tool to defeat air attack on Britain. Second, and more subtly, he faced the task of persuading the military establishment that Fighter Command was capable of more than it had been given credit for. This was not a question of self-advertisement. The country could not plan for war if it did not have an accurate understanding of what the different arms of the defence forces could achieve. The Air Staff's ruling doctrine was that fighters could achieve little. Dowding knew he had to improve both the effectiveness of fighters and to make it understood in the wider world that this was not merely possible but was being achieved. The battlefield was the committee rooms of Whitehall and the rules of engagement were the protocols of bureaucratic discussion.

Under the Trenchardian regime it had been accepted that fighters could – weather permitting – scare the 'rabbits' amongst German aircrew and help persuade the 'ignorant masses' to continue working under the German bombs, whilst the bombers did the true work of the RAF. Dowding had identified how fighters could go far beyond these trivial goals and developed an effective, well-thought-out organization. To achieve this Fighter Command made use of the latest technology in communication and aircraft location. Only by communicating this success would it be possible to overcome the undervaluation of fighters. The RAF had dedicated minimum resources to fighters so it seemed that they could not be very important or valuable. This was a vital plank in the doctrine that only offensive operations by bombers could protect the country. Dowding had to win the Air Staff away from a doctrine that had ruled since the service became established. Trenchard and his disciples were one-club golfers and proud of it. It was almost a matter of shame that they had to carry a full bag around the course. Dowding's task was not just to perfect a despised weapon in the RAF's arsenal but to persuade his colleagues that it served a useful purpose.

Dowding had shown impeccable loyalty to Air Staff Trenchardian doctrine when he had been offered the opportunity to challenge it head on at the time when Inskip was promoting the 'Ideal' defence scheme in the summer of 1937, but the growing threat of the Luftwaffe and the path of his own career began to stoke the fires of revolt. Dowding was responding to the simple instinct of any professional who sees value in his or her task in its own right, but the value of the work was also becoming ever greater. As the Luftwaffe expanded, magnifying the threat of its ability to attack Britain, so too did the true importance of Fighter Command. The relatively modest increases in the number of fighters in the first rearmament schemes compared to the accelerating increases in the number of bombers speak volumes. By implication and in the eyes of the Air Staff, Fighter Command was junior to Bomber Command; just how junior it was to be in practice depended, first, on whether its commander acquiesced in this position and, if he did not, how effectively he could lift Fighter Command's status. A cautious time-server with a long career ahead of him might have opted for a quiet life and ducked the risk of antagonizing the Air Staff by claiming resources for and trumpeting achievements of the part of the service that they held in little regard. Dowding did not. In early 1937, the bitter news that he was to be passed over as CAS by Newall meant that leading Fighter Command would be his last serious job in the RAF. He had nothing to lose and there was still much to gain. Britain and his professional pride would both be the winners if he succeeded.

The spark for Dowding's campaign came soon after his disappointment when Ellington finally bit the bullet and lifted the RAF's formal estimate of Luftwaffe strength from the complacent belief that it would reach 1,512 aircraft and remain there until 1940. The new, higher estimates driven by the Christie/X intelligence had already inspired Swinton's ambitious but bomber-dominated Scheme H. It was a fair question as to what the new assessment of the threat meant for Britain's fighter requirements, and Dowding took the initiative in telling Ellington that the moment had come for him 'to reconsider my views as to the adequacy of our defensive measures'.[1] There is no sign that Ellington had seen any need to discuss with the head of Fighter Command whether the new picture of German strength made it necessary to examine the plans for defensive measures. From the outset Dowding's approach was deeply heretical. He was sufficiently Trenchardian to put counter-attack first, but he reminded

Ellington that he believed that the most effective strategy was to bomb German aircraft on their bases. This was a direct contradiction of the Air Staff doctrine that it was bombing cities that would force the enemy to switch his attack. Dowding did not fall into the trap of naive confidence in the prospects for attacking the Luftwaffe on the ground as he knew the German practices of camouflage and dispersed aerodromes, but he drew a conclusion that was even deeper anathema. The best prospects for the RAF lay in a battle in the air between the aircraft of the opposed sides: 'it seems to me that we shall have to rely largely on shooting down their first-line aircraft as and when opportunity offers.' Dowding concluded with a barely veiled reminder that the Air Staff was not the sole decision-maker on the question of defending Britain and drew out the one sharp sword that fate had placed in his hands to wield in the wider Whitehall battle over air policy. He asked for Ellington's response to his comments before the CAS's paper with the higher formal estimate of Luftwaffe size came up for discussion before the Committee of Imperial Defence Home Defence Committee a few days later.

The Home Defence Committee was one of the Committee of Imperial Defence's myriad sub-committees and Dowding chaired it in his capacity as commander of Fighter Command. In itself the Home Defence Committee was not especially powerful and could not force a change in Air Staff policy. It did, though, provide Dowding with an official platform to make his opinions heard outside the RAF without breaching service rules. It opened the prospect of discreet collaboration with Sir Maurice Hankey, master puppeteer of the Committee of Imperial Defence and its world, a long-standing sceptic of Trenchardian doctrine. The Committee of Imperial Defence was also the realm of Sir Thomas Inskip who had shown himself far more open to alternative defence strategies. It was an uncomfortable prospect for the true believers of Adastral House that one of their own should seem to be aligning himself with such heretics.

Dowding's defection could not go unchallenged. Richard Peirse, the Deputy CAS, with the support of Ellington, tried to recall Dowding to his duty as an RAF officer and to help frame a counter-argument when another Committee of Imperial Defence outgrowth, the ADGB committee showed dangerously anti-Trenchardian tendencies.[2] The ADGB committee had not merely challenged the Air Staff's estimate for the tonnage of bombs the Luftwaffe could drop on Britain, but had also raised the unwelcome topic of how effective fighters might prove in reducing this tonnage and what a given level of casualties inflicted on the attackers might lead to. Peirse knew that he was fighting a crucial battle over the vision of a future air war in which the Air Staff was defending Trenchard's doctrine that fighting between the aircraft of the opposed sides was practically irrelevant and certainly infinitely less important than the bombing contest. To Peirse anything that gave prominence to the level of casualties that might be inflicted in air combat played into the hands of the Air Staff's enemies. He verged on paranoia on this point and believed that the older services were already spreading the story that the air forces of Britain and Germany would soon fight each other into a state of mutual exhaustion, bringing the air war to an end: 'This of course is the view generally advanced by the Admiralty and War Office.'[3]

Dowding ducked Peirse's attempt to make him disassociate himself from the views of the committee he chaired and left it to the Air Staff to challenge the committee's analysis head on if it wanted a fight.[4] The best that Peirse got out of Dowding was to make him distance himself from the excessively high figure of 10 per cent that had emerged from the committee as the attrition that Fighter Command might inflict on German bombers. Dowding held fast to the key principle that it should be considered what a given level of losses would do to the Luftwaffe's effort. As Dowding pointed out to Peirse, the RAF itself already accepted that its own bombing efforts would dwindle under the stress of combat so the Luftwaffe's could not be immune. Moreover, if the Germans concentrated their attack on London, they would be confronted by the strongest defences and suffer accordingly. The knock-out blow strategy was not a one-way street to German victory.

The top level of the Air Staff was not able to control Dowding's doings in the alien world of the Committee of Imperial Defence and its sub-committees, but they were kept informed of his misbehaviour by the only other RAF member of the Home Defence Committee as Dowding guided it into another and even more fundamental assault on Trenchardian orthodoxy.[5] This time the starting point was the Air Staff's formal estimate of the bomb tonnage that the Germans could drop. This was the key measure that the Air Staff used to established the scale of the striking force that the RAF would need to respond and the Air Staff had long set the figure high. The committee did not challenge the figure outright but firstly, they pointed out that it was 'conjectural' and of little practical value. The actual damage done by these bombs would depend on where and when they might fall. Their next point was even more insidious. So as to support its claim on ever more bombing resources, the Air Staff's strategy had been to come up with a high figure for the scale of German attack. To the sceptics the Air Staff had painted themselves into a corner by exaggeration and they turned this round as a weapon against the Air Staff view:

> It is obvious that the weight of attack as a whole which must be anticipated is so great that, even if unlimited and resources were available, it would be impossible to prevent heavy casualties and destruction of property. All that can be done is to *take whatever steps financial and other considerations may permit, on the one hand, to inflict as much damage as possible on the attackers* [author's italics] and on the other hand to minimize the effects of air attack upon the morale of the people and the working of essential services.[6]

The committee was seeking to turn on its head the Trenchardian doctrine that as fighters could not entirely prevent bombing, so the resources devoted to them should be kept to a strict minimum. Confronted by such a massive tonnage of bombs, it argued that the best course was to give priority to fighters and anti-aircraft guns, reversing the Air Staff's strategy of spending the minimum on fighters. This was not just a strategy of despair, and once again the sceptics exploited a figure that the Air Staff itself had produced to support their case. The Air Staff had put a limit to the daily casualties that an air force could stand at an average of 3 per cent. Without saying so explicitly, the sceptics clearly thought that the RAF could inflict this level of attrition on the Luftwaffe and force it to switch its attacks to less heavily defended targets: 'there is good hope that we should be able before many weeks have passed to get the measure of the enemy air attack.' This was a direct challenge to the Air Staff doctrine that only counter-bombing offered a defence.

Amazingly these views stayed intact as they worked their way up the defence bureaucracy. The pinnacle of the machine, the Chiefs of Staff Committee, repeated them almost verbatim in a report on the possible scale of German attack that forwarded without qualification the optimistic assessment of what fighters might achieve.[7]

The moment had come for Hankey to revive Inskip's 'Ideal' defence scheme with its 50 per cent increase in the number of fighter squadrons.[8] There were limits to Dowding's willingness to strike out on a quite different path to the Air Staff and he backed away from throwing himself fully behind the scheme and covered his back by keeping his boss, Newall, in the loop.[9] But he was far from apostasizing his heretical views. If anything, his case in favour of defensive fighters was set even higher, albeit on the basis of the new Hurricanes and Spitfires. Fighter Command on its own could stop Luftwaffe attacks:

> When we get our new equipment monoplane fighters, I confidently believe that we should inflict on an enemy equipped with contemporary bombing types such casualties that he would be compelled to discontinue his attacks.

Just as he had felt when Inskip first floated the 'Ideal' defence scheme, Dowding knew that Hankey's forty-five fighter squadrons could only be realized at the expense of the striking force. He was not prepared to go the final mile and come out in favour of reallocating resources to fighters, but he had it in him to issue a significant qualification to the doctrine that fighter numbers should be only the bare minimum. 'I feel it is essential to limit the defensive forces to the strength adequate, and amply adequate, but not extravagantly adequate, for defence.' He made no attempt to quantify ample adequacy, but it was clear that he believed that Fighter Command could soon defend Britain on its own provided that it was not kept too small. It was only a verbal departure but as a departure from Trenchardian doctrine, there was a yawning gulf between ample adequacy and a (strict) minimum.

Newall knew that the sceptics' movement had to be stopped and summoned Dowding to speak to him before he next had the chance to lead another committee astray.[10] He told his subordinate bluntly that he could not 'possibly agree' with Dowding's confidence in what he could achieve with Hurricanes and Spitfires. This might be acceptable as Dowding's personal opinion, but dangerous that anyone should imagine that they 'would seem to bear the hallmark of Air Staff policy'. Urgent action was necessary otherwise 'we may get into rather deep water over this question'.

At stake was the possibility that the Chiefs of Staff might be moved even deeper into error than endorsing the possibility that fighters could reduce the scale of bombing attacks. The next hurdle that the Trenchardians would have to jump was the revision of JP155, the explosive paper that the joint planners had sprung on the defence establishment in late 1936 with the terrifying vision of a German knock-out blow and the lightly disguised prospectus for a massive increase in the RAF's bomber force to meet this threat. It would mark a major change in defence theory if this were abandoned and a positive revolution if the Air Staff itself had changed its thinking. The Committee of Imperial Defence secretariat could read acutely the straws blowing in the wind. They latched firmly on to the significance of the new views having been endorsed by the Chiefs of Staff, even if Dowding's hand was plain as the author of the words. They recognized that Dowding's committee was in reality challenging the Air Staff's high estimate for the scale of German attack and were paying lip service only to the doctrine of counter-offensive.[11] The implication of the key paragraphs for Air Staff doctrine were immense: 'their general effect is to write off the effect of the offensive and boost the value of the defence.' It would follow that

> There has been a change over in the official Air Staff view regarding the most effective means of defence against air attack, and that considerably more value is now attached to the effectiveness of fighters and A.A. guns, while an air striking force is no longer considered to have the same value as heretofore.[12]

This was precisely what Newall feared. The Air Staff was being accused of throwing Trenchard onto the scrapheap and there was a distinct possibility that the update of Harris's JP155 would make this the formal view. Slessor knew from the start that the representative of the other services on the Joint Planners were not going to be as cooperative as Adam and Phillips had been in 1936.[13] He complained that 'we are constantly being attacked on the question of the proportion of fighters to bombers … [W]e are constantly having to meet the argument that we could get better protection by having more fighters and fewer bombers'.[14] Slessor knew that the 1936 paper was a prospectus for extra bombers as much as anything else and that Harris's navy and army colleagues had been willing to endorse this. In 1938, the RAF was going to have to argue its case for more bombers unassisted by the other services.

Slessor knew that he had a major job on his hands to protect orthodoxy and, rather late in the day, set out to find out what modern fighter defence might actually be capable of against bombers. He drew up a comprehensive questionnaire on the topic, which gives a fair idea of how little attention he had paid to the questions involved, including RDF. It seems that the Air Staff had better things with which to occupy themselves. Slessor's starting point was his feeling that 'with modern developments ... the value of the fighter in home defence is if anything declining'. He was prepared to admit that the fighter had 'great value, and probably rather more than the Air Staff are commonly inclined to think'. Clearly Trenchardian prejudice against fighters still ran deep. If Slessor had hoped for evidence or opinion that bombers were gaining the upper hand he was doomed to disappointment. Sholto Douglas, the ACAS, and admittedly the only ex-fighter pilot in the higher reaches of Adastral House, who seemed to have devoted rather more attention to the matter, disagreed with him outright:

> I think that within the last few months, what with the advent of the 8-gun fighter, RDF and the Biggin Hill interception scheme, the pendulum has swung the other way and that at the moment – or at any rate as soon as all our Fighter Squadrons are equipped with Hurricanes and Spitfires – the fighter is on top of contemporary enemy bombers.[15]

Slessor got even less joy from Dowding who was also shown the questionnaire. 'NO. The 8 gun fighter is very much on top of the unarmoured bomber.'[16] He was also told that all the techniques of modern fighter defence that Dowding was driving at Fighter Command – RDF, Direction Finding location and radio control of fighters – together with their greater flying performance, improved the chances of intercepting bombers.[17]

Slessor's faith in Trenchardian doctrine was not shaken by this expert evidence that fighters were poised to present a far greater threat to attacking bombers than they ever had done before and he set to work refuting the sceptics. He soon spotted the weak point in their case. Their focus on the 3 per cent casualty threshold was dangerously specific and, like any argument based on a single figure, it could be undermined by attacking that figure. Slessor began his counter-argument by asserting that the sceptics were claiming that the defences would be able to inflict 3 per cent attrition on the entire Luftwaffe every day.[18] This would have implied an unfeasibly large percentage of the bombers that actually reached British shores in the course of a single raid. In reality the statement was ambiguous and could have applied to the bombers mounting an individual raid. Next, he proceeded to undermine the validity of the 3 per cent calculation even though it was the Air Staff that had first come up with it. His evidence came from the First World War, beginning with the valid point that the IAF had suffered average losses on its raids of 3.9 per cent (he anachronistically rebaptized the IAF as the Independent Air Striking Force to ram home the parallel with its contemporary descendant) but then moved on to second-hand semi-mysticism, quoting a biographer of Herman Göring, who claimed that under his command the old Richthofen flying circus had displayed 'real contempt for death' after suffering drastic losses.

When the new appreciation was finally circulated in July 1938, it showed Slessor's handiwork even it fell short of the shock achieved by the draft of JP155.[19] It firmly discounted the possibility that 3 per cent attrition could be inflicted on the Luftwaffe. Moreover, as there was no reason to suppose that German pilots were any less brave than British ones, the whole notion that defence might be at all effective could be consigned to the dustbin: 'we should be unwise to rely upon an early deterrent effect of casualties for our security.' In keeping with Trenchard's division of pilots into rabbits and the rest, the only aspect considered was pilot morale; the thought that an air commander might order a stop to attacks if casualties became too high, did not feature at all. The existence of five RDF stations at the reference date was mentioned without comment. There was certainly no suggestion that they might increase the effectiveness of the defending British fighter force. The paper concluded with a vigorous restatement of Trenchardian doctrine: 'Our air striking force, however, provides us with a means of conducting an immediate tactical offensive which, if successful, may appreciably reduce the initial threat to our security.' Thus, the last regular assessment of Britain's prospects before its leaders faced the threat that the Czech crisis might lead to war with Germany, ignored all the work down by Dowding and the scientists to forge Fighter Command into a potent shield and simply repeated the mantra that the only means of defence was attack.

Chapter 29

Large Allowances Against Underestimate

As spring turned to summer in 1938, the chances of peace in Europe shrank almost daily. There was widespread recognition that after the bloodless triumph of the *Anschluß* Hitler would move onto his next objective, the Sudetenland region of Czechoslovakia, arbitrary relic of the Versailles settlement, which appeared an affront to German nationhood. Czechoslovakia's German-speaking population of rather more than three million people was a quarter of the country's total and the second largest language grouping, but they had lost the position they enjoyed in the Bohemia and Moravia provinces of the Hapsburg empire up to 1918 when the German-speaking aristocracy controlled the region. Czechoslovakia was dominated by Czechs who accounted for a little more than half the population, with the support of the Slovaks, who comprised around 15 per cent of the total. Protecting the Sudetens was Germany's ostensible target, but Hitler privately craved the destruction of the Czechoslovakian state. He had a particular detestation of the Czechs. It looked as though German aggression against Czechoslovakia was the most likely outcome, which would trigger a French declaration of war in keeping with its treaty with the victim and, in turn, drag Britain into war.

The risk of war moved on from being a rather abstract possibility to an acute, immediate danger. The RAF's rearmament was now a topic of immense concern. Parity was no longer a distant goal; it was the measure of how the air forces of Britain and Germany might match up in actual battle. Slessor's paper was incorporated into COS755, the last full-scale Chiefs of Staff appreciation before the crisis broke out in full. The paper juggled Trenchardian doctrine and the admission that the RAF was still going to be short of war readiness even if war did not break out until April 1939.[1] The six months' extra time to prepare for war lent an element of unreality to the analysis, but there was little indication that it prompted any unwarranted hopes for what might be done in this time. The paper began the air force section with a sturdy restatement of Trenchardian dogma: 'An immediate offensive by our own air striking force and those of our allies is the only measure which could affect the issue during the first weeks of a war on the assumption we have taken [that] the Germans may be concentrating all their resources either against France or Great Britain,' but the pessimistic view of how far Bomber Command had come was evident: '[t]he pressure which we could exert upon the German war effort as a whole in the initial stage of a war in April 1939 would be comparatively small.' The extra six months was clearly not expected to bring a decisive improvement. The report did admit that Fighter Command would serve some practical purpose, even if it remained resolutely Trenchardian in treating counter-bombing as the only real defence. It noted that the RAF would be able to field 558 fighters out of the 608 authorized, of which 100 would be obsolescent types, which would contribute to 'considerable opposition' to German bombers. The report mentioned that Britain would have five RDF stations, but made no comment as to how effective any of these measures would be in defending against a German knock-out blow. The report of Britain's defences did not inspire the planners to alter the estimate they had made in 1937 of the weight of the potential German attack on Britain: '600 tons of bombs a day ... sustained for some time.'

In parallel to the formal contingency planning of the COS report for the following year, Slessor set to work urgently to establish what would happen if war broke out in weeks. He wanted to know the damage that the Germans would be able to do to London or other centres and the fighter resources that the RAF would be able to deploy against this attack.

Here he encountered the nearest anyone within the Air Staff – admittedly at a fairly junior level – ever came to scepticism about the knock-out blow theory, which had shaped military and political thinking from the start, both in terms of it being the German strategy and Germany's ability to deliver it. Wing Commander Victor Goddard, the head of AI3 section charged with intelligence on the Luftwaffe, challenged fundamental tenets of the theory. He recognized that whatever the propaganda allure of the bomber, hard military logic counted for more in German practice:

> However much we may suspect that Field Marshal Göring would like to exploit the knock-out blow theory ... responsibility for war strategy rests at present upon General

Keitel who is a soldier and is believed to have the soldier's idea that the German Air Force exists primarily to enable the army by direct support to gain land – i.e. Czechoslovakia.

Large allowances against underestimate of bomb load and strength have been made in this assessment of maximum potential against England. A scaling down of 50% during the progress of war in Czechoslovakia seems, without analysis, reasonable and conservative ... A mere fifteen squadrons of short-range dive bombers will not satisfy the army requirements for the rapid conquest of Czechoslovakia and the holding of the French Army.[2]

Masked by the tortuous syntax of the second paragraph, Goddard was saying that estimates of the bomb tonnage the Luftwaffe might drop were excessive. He set to work on other shibboleths of the Air Staff. The increase in German squadron strength to 15 aircraft that had lain at the heart of the Newall's figure for his parity calculations in the budgetary battle over Scheme J, had never been proven and had been steadily undermined by 'convincing evidence'. Intelligence now put the Luftwaffe's total bomber strength at 1,197 all in or 897 excluding immediate reserves, compared to the 1,350 'morally sure' figure used to argue for a large bomber force for the RAF.

Goddard also queried German aircraft performance data from which the tonnage figures for the bombing attack on Britain had been calculated. He was concerned that recent 'concrete evidence' showed that past estimates for the Heinkel He 111 bomber had been too high. As this type accounted for 65 per cent of the estimate of Luftwaffe's bomb maximum lift capacity, this was critical.[3] In reality the He 111 did not have sufficient range to carry its maximum bombload for an attack on London or the Midlands.

The likely needs of the land war against Czechoslovakia and some action against France meant that the worst-case assumption that the Luftwaffe would immediately be directed in full against Britain, could be dropped. The ensuing 50 per cent reduction in the assumed rate of German sorties against Britain was brutal, but Fighter Command tools to oppose this effort were also weak. Target Fighter Command strength had been set at 688 aircraft to face 600 sorties so the actual figure of 406 fighters expected on 1 October should have been comfortable to face the 300 sorties now estimated.[4] However, the fighter force comprised only 84 Hurricanes or Spitfires, monoplanes with top speeds well above the German bombers', 342 Gauntlets, Fury and Gladiator biplanes with approximately the same speeds and 70 ancient Demon biplanes which were far slower. To dedicated Trenchardians the RAF's weakness in fighters should not have been a decisive disadvantage: it was the bomber counter-offensive that would thwart any attack by the Luftwaffe. Here, though, there was also disappointment. Ludlow-Hewitt, the head of Bomber Command, introduced a strong reason to be cautious as to what his force could achieve and one that should have been obvious all along. The vast majority of his aircraft were still Battles and Blenheims which simply did not have the range to penetrate very deeply into Germany and had poor defensive armament anyway. Ludlow-Hewitt claimed that even in January 1939, 80 per cent of his mobilizable bomber force would consist of Blenheims and Battles.[5] Bomber Command could muster seventeen squadrons of Battles, sixteen of Blenheims and only nine of Whitleys.[6] 'The counter-offensive against the German Air Force from England with existing aircraft does not promise decisive results within any measurable period of time.'[7] For Ludlow-Hewitt the North Sea and home air defence offered the most likely way to mitigate German air attacks.

Slessor set to work to find a way to get the RAF off the hook of having promised to defend Britain by bombing Germany. Throughout the summer he had been studying the question of what constituted a legal operation of war together with the Foreign Office's legal adviser and had become finely tuned to issues involved. He found salvation in a declaration that the prime minister had made some months before in a context quite different to that of what the RAF could or could not do which he passed on to Newall.[8] Chamberlain had suffered a severe mauling in the House of Commons over the government's supine reaction to attacks on British ships carrying supplies to the Republican side in the Spanish Civil War. The cause had united right-wing Conservatives, offended at the insult to the protection of the British flag, with the Republic's friends on the left. In a weak attempt to ward off accusations that the government was doing little or nothing to prevent the dictatorships from committing atrocities from the air, Chamberlain had claimed that Britain was working towards new proposals to regulate air warfare governed by three supposed principles of international law: bombing civilians was illegal, targets must be identifiable as military and care should be taken when attacking these targets that civilians were not hurt.[9] The Air Ministry salted these prime-ministerially enunciated principles with the warning that the Germans would make propaganda use of any civilian casualties and sent formal instructions to Ludlow-Hewitt that 'your action should be rigorously restricted to attack on objectives which are manifestly and unmistakably military on the narrowest interpretation of the term'.[10] In practice, the only action that was acceptable was bombing aerodromes, which Ludlow-Hewitt believed would cost heavy casualties and saw as 'futile and ineffective'[11]. In his memoirs Slessor quoted Chamberlain's principles as though the prime minister had intended them to apply to British options; he had not – they merely provided a convenient pretext for a course of action dictated overwhelmingly by the weakness of the RAF. They were not mentioned again.

Having manufactured a prime-ministerial ban on the kind of action which Trenchardian doctrine insisted offered the only protection against German air attack, the Air Staff now had the wiggle room to tone down severely its previous forecasts of what the Germans could do and confess to the RAF's own weakness. The threat of a knock-out blow was pushed firmly into the background; the Luftwaffe would be used in 'an overwhelming air offensive Czechoslovakia' and would refrain from attacking Britain unless attacked.[12] Newall now claimed: 'I cannot visualize the possibility of "a bolt from the blue".'[13] Newall did advise Wood that Fighter Command personnel should be called back from leave, albeit not for military reasons but to impress the Germans. Goddard's doubts had trickled up the hierarchy and the Air Staff now admitted to 'considerable doubt as to the range and capacity of the bombers with which the German squadrons are now equipped'.[14] The forecast of 600 tons of German bombs raining on London every day for months that had been advanced barely a month before was very severely qualified, even though it was not formally amended. The Germans might be weaker than first thought, but the allies were weaker still. The Air Staff calculated that the RAF would only be able to deliver 100 tons of bombs a day on Germany and that the French might just deliver a further 200 tons; it was highly sceptical of the value of the French air force. Against this unfavourable balance of force, the British planners argued that the temptation to take advantage of a fleeting opportunity to attack the 'Achille's heel' of our enemy. Apart from the considerations mentioned above [political objection to initiating bombing and the likely scale of German retaliation], our main reason is that the weight of the attack which we and the French could deliver is, in our opinion, inadequate to produce decisive results.[15]

Despite the unargued priority accorded to developing the RAF's striking force for more than three years and the resources devoted to the effort, it still fell far short of an effective weapon of war. The Chiefs of Staff were formally asked for advice on whether Britain should refrain from 'initiating any particular form of offensive action' if war broke out and their answer was emphatic:

> We consider it essential to refrain from provocative action, such as bombing Germany, at least until we are definitely ready both to defend ourselves and to strike effectively. ...
>
> To attempt to take offensive action against Germany until we have had time to bring our naval, military and air forces and also our passive defence services to a war footing would be to place ourselves in the position of a man who attacks a tiger before he has loaded his gun.[16]

This had been toned down from the rather more vivid phrasing of one draft: 'To attempt to take offensive action against Germany until we have had time to bring our military, naval and air forces and also our passive defence services on to a war footing, would be to place ourselves in the position of a man who tries to show how brave he is by twisting the tail of a tiger, which is prepared to strike before he has loaded his gun.'[17]

This meant that much of the contingency planning within the Air Staff was largely redundant and would only acquire practical importance if the Germans launched their own air offensive against British (and perhaps French or Czech) towns. Then the 'gloves would come off' and the RAF would be in a position to unleash its full potential. This was not an immediate risk. Moreover, whilst it is possible to detect a note of relish at the prospect in the internal RAF discussion, realism was creeping in.

Chapter 30

The Utmost Limit Compatible

The Chiefs of Staff did not give the government advice as to whether to risk war during the crisis – it does not seem that they were asked – but war seemed imminent; the day after Newall's letter to Ludlow-Hewitt, Colonel Hastings Ismay, who had taken up Hankey's mantle as the military face of the Committee of Imperial Defence and Cabinet Secretariat, circulated a brief paper: 'Note on the question whether it would be to our military advantage to fight Germany now, or to postpone the issue.'[1] It was distributed within the narrowest of circles but this included two men at the heart of Britain's political and military decision-making: Inskip and Wilson, Chamberlain's intimate and, in some judgements, dominating adviser. Ismay was sufficiently honest to imply that war was inevitable but supposed that Britain had some option as to when it would come. The Air Staff might have rowed back a good distance from its core projection of a massive attack on London as Germany's natural and inevitable opening move, but it was far too late to do away with the psychosis of fear that it had cultivated since early days of rearmament and Ismay's calculation was dominated by the same scenario that had ruled for at least two years:

> the greatest danger to which we would be exposed, and equally Germany's only chance of obtaining a quick decision, would lie in the possibility of a Knock-Out Blow from the air.

This was the vision that Chamberlain and Wilson took to the Bad Godesberg meetings on 23 and 24 September 1938 when Hitler turned the screw on the British and seemed to tear up everything that had been agreed before with demands for an entirely new set of concessions. As Chamberlain flew back to Britain through clear skies, looking out over the vast expanse of London's houses, he put himself in the place of German airmen approaching the capital on a bombing mission. Then as now, the bends in the River Thames provide the perfect guides for anyone navigating a plane towards the centre of London and practically any significant objective at its centre. Acutely conscious that the building blocks for a proper expansion of the Royal Air Force had only recently been put in place, he saw the capital as a practically undefended target. It was a chilling vision he shared with Wilson on the plane and, later that day, with the Cabinet: 'what degree of protection we could afford to the thousands of homes which he had seen stretched out below him, and he felt that we were in no position to justify waging a war.'[2]

Newall was determined to avert war with any means at his hand. As the prime minister was flying back from Germany to brief the Cabinet on the failure of his talks at Bad Godesberg he begged his minister, Wood, to remind the Cabinet of the Air Staff's defeatist advice when it met to decide on peace or war.[3] The French leaders were due imminently in London and he extended his plea to cover Britain's putative allies. He had dark fears that the French might start bombing Germany and wanted the British government to head them off from any such action. Wood did not heed the CAS's pleas directly and did not repeat to the Cabinet any of this cautious advice, but he was one of the three ministers (Inskip was another) who recommended accepting the humiliating terms that Hitler had set out at Bad Godesberg.[4] There was, anyway, little need for Wood to remind Chamberlain of the threat from the air.

The choice between peace and war now lay with the politicians, but whatever came, the RAF's striking force was not going to play any serious part in it; unless the Germans, against the Air Staff's expectations, 'took the gloves off' and attempted a knock-out blow, Bomber Command would have little to do. Even if they did, Newall was studiedly ambiguous as to how intensely Ludlow-Hewitt was supposed to operate his forces. Newall reminded Ludlow-Hewitt of the 'very serious shortage of reserves' and instructed him

> to conserve your energy and resources to the utmost limit compatible with those operations which it will be essential to undertake in defence of this country, or to fulfil our obligations to France.[5]

Newall did not specify whether this applied under any particular scenario for German operations. Twice elsewhere in the letter Ludlow-Hewitt was told to 'conserve your resources' or 'conserve your strength'[6] In practice, Bomber Command would only be going through the motions of fighting a war. His subordinate had similarly modest ambitions for his command. The same day, Ludlow-Hewitt wrote to Newall stating that the combination of the restrictions imposed by the Air Ministry and the limited range of his bombers meant that he could not 'devise an effective air bombardment role for our bombers immediately on the outbreak of hostilities'.[7] Dropping propaganda leaflets by night and converting his Blenheims into extempore fighters was the best he could come up with. As and when the gloves did come off, Bomber Command's Fairey Battles could begin to access French bases and 'it may be possible to attack far more profitable objectives', in other words the Ruhr.[8]

***

Chamberlain surrendered at Munich because he believed that the Germans could annihilate London by bombing. His vision of London under the bombs was the same one that Churchill had set out to the House of Commons in 1934. Few would have argued with it. Only the RAF would have been in a position to say flatly that this vision was an exaggeration, but its commanders could never do so. The German air menace and the Trenchardian solution to dealing with it had fused inextricably. The RAF did not have the bombers that the Air Staff believed it needed to deal with the threat, therefore the threat was still there. When Chamberlain's apologists claim that the year of peace which he bought at Munich saved Britain from defeat, they should bear in mind that this defeat existed first and foremost in the mind of the Air Staff.

Chamberlain's persistent commitment to seeking every possible avenue to a peaceful settlement and Hitler's last-second decision to take what he was being importunately offered on a plate, rather than fighting for it, meant that it was never put to the test whether the RAF could conserve its forces. Much though Hitler would have liked to destroy Czechoslovakia by military action, he could comfort himself with the thought he had shone a harsh light on the powerlessness of Britain and France. Reliving his victory with his propaganda minister and possibly closest collaborator, Joseph Goebbels, Hitler particularly relished the fact that he had flatly refused Chamberlain's proposal of a general ban on bombing civilians as part of the programme for the general betterment of the world that the British prime minister fondly imagined would flow from 'peace for our time'.[9] Hitler simply assumed that Chamberlain had asked for this because Germany's bomber arm was far (*haushoch*) superior to Britain's. The RAF's expansion had not merely failed to give the Air Staff a viable weapon, it had not even dented Hitler's conviction that Germany dominated in the air.

The RAF did not formally mobilize during the Munich crisis but it went to a level of alert that came very close to full activation. Inevitably this brought to light a whole series of deficiencies. Some of these were the ordinary growing pains of an organization in the midst of a dramatic expansion phase. Some raised the question as to whether this growth had been pushed too fast. Far more disturbing for the leaders of the RAF was the possibility that difficulties had arisen because of matters that should have been addressed long before given a modicum of foresight and imagination. The overall conclusion was stark. The RAF had been unable to do its job when the dictators began their latest round of aggression and was still falling short, 'In each crisis [Abyssinia, Austria and Czechoslovakia] our air defence was insufficient to provide security against the threatened air attack.'[10]

Reading between the lines, a rather more nuanced picture emerged. The different components of the RAF had performed differently in the crisis. The defensive parts of the service had put up a more impressive showing, whilst its striking force – the embodiment of its Trenchardian mission – had lagged noticeably.

All but one of Fighter Command's entire home force of thirty squadrons were brought onto on a war footing, seemingly without major complications. The command had also deployed seven army cooperation squadrons in an improvised interceptor role, with no prior preparation.[11] At least in terms of numbers, Fighter Command would have been able to field a significant defence. Dowding was prepared to throw everything available into battle.

The picture was less happy when it came to the quality of the aircraft as Slessor had been warned. Only five of the squadrons were equipped with Hurricanes so only seventy of Fighter Command's aircraft met the test for 'efficient modern Fighters'.[12] Of the remainder, fourteen squadrons had 'obsolescent' biplanes: five Gladiators and nine its predecessor, the Gauntlet. The Air Staff reckoned that these were, 'Nevertheless capable of giving a good account of themselves'. Indeed, Gladiators remained in front-line war service into 1941, scoring successes against Axis bombers over Norway, Greece and Malta. The older biplanes would have been capable of little more than showing the flag and the value of the army cooperation squadrons would have been entirely speculative, although two of them did have the modern Lysander monoplane, which did achieve isolated successes in the French campaign of 1940.[13]

The picture of the RAF's new technological defence aids was similar to that in the fighter aircraft themselves. The modernization programme was far from complete but there was dynamic approach to using what was available. Only about one-third of Fighter Command's planned new command and control system was operating: five RDF stations of the eighteen planned. Three mobile stations were also brought into operation to fill gaps in the coverage and proved helpful, 'While this improvisation was crude and elementary it did in fact provide a considerable and valuable augmentation of the Air Defence resources in a remarkably short space of time.'[14] Overall, the Air Staff put the shortfall in RDF coverage at a 72 per cent gap and 65 per cent for the direction-finding stations which were the other, often forgotten component of the system. Seventeen of forty-eight direction-finding stations were functioning.

The control system's showing in the crisis fed a move of urgency in the aftermath. Its contribution to Britain's defence resources was beyond argument and there was a distinctly bullish mood amongst its promoters to complete what had been begun. Robert Watson-Watt, the architect of the RDF system, believed it would be possible to bring the bulk of the outstanding RDF chain, fifteen sites, on line by April 1939 and it could be practically completed with a further three sites if compulsory purchase powers were used to acquire the land. There would also be two or three more mobile units. The constraints were administrative and financial, not technical. Watson-Watt insisted that finance must be released.[15] He understood just how important the work was. In order to meet Watson-Watt's schedule, 'The principle should be accepted that the interests of National security outweigh financial considerations and that the financial and contractual aspects of details be left to the judgement of the Directors and others responsible for the execution of the work.'[16]

Fighter Command had done the maximum to bring its resources into action should they have been needed. Bomber Command's watchword seems to have been 'conserve the bombers'. Even before this doctrine was enunciated, only forty-two out of sixty-eight squadrons were brought up to readiness. This was the 'maximum effort which could be achieved with reasonably efficient aircraft after due consideration had been given to the question of forming a small aircraft reserve'.[17] The Air Staff was being less than honest here as the reserve was closer to half of available aircraft.[18] The modernization of Bomber Command's inventory was much further advanced than Fighter Command's, but the conservative-minded instinct to build up reserves is striking. In its overall assessment of the force's showing in the crisis, the Air Staff did not mention Fighter Command specifically, but did state bluntly that, 'Our Air Striking Force was insufficient to act as a counterpoise to the air threat against us and could not ensure freedom of action for our diplomacy'.

There was a similar gulf in how far the two commands had progressed in putting into place the final element in the modern command and control system that the RAF wanted: operations rooms for the fighting units. The broad picture across the service was bleak and 'Urgent action' was required but here again Fighter Command was ahead of Bomber Command where 'nothing has yet been done'.[19] Fighter Command had put in operations rooms at sector stations – the lowest level of command. Work had begun on the operation room for 11 Group, the most important of the fighter groups. The commercial orders for the Fighter Command and one other group headquarters operations rooms were out to tender. Apart from any difference in the determination of each command to advance, there was a strong hint that they were both having to fight a powerful force of inertia within the Air Ministry. It was recommended that a 'firm line' be taken with the Air Ministry's directorate of works, which operated under the powerful personality of Colonel 'Conky Bill' Turner.

Chapter 31

A Weapon We Can Use Very Effectively

When Trenchard was battling to establish the RAF as a permanent part of the British military establishment, he spotted that an air force could make a cost-effective contribution to policing the far-flung corners of the Empire. The task was immense. The First World War had inflicted huge damage on the country – the death or maiming of a large percentage of the adult male population – but it had led to an enormous expansion of the British Empire. In the competitive frenzy of the peace-making process that centred on the Versailles Conference Britain pursued claims to the Ottoman Turkish Empire which was dismantled entirely and the colonial possessions that the new German Empire had built up in the space of a few decades. In 1921, the British Empire reached its greatest size; the only pre-1914 possession it lost was Ireland. The newly obtained territories were held under mandates from the League of Nations, which gave the process a fig-leaf of democratic respectability, but few in the British government establishment took this seriously. It was a land-grab just like any other. Competitive diplomacy and military strategic priorities were the order of the day; there was no room for other voices, including that of economic self-interest. Much of the new territory had hung at the fringes of the collapsing Ottoman empire in a state of de facto autonomy from ineffectual and light-touch rule by Istanbul. No serious thought had been given as to how an impoverished nation, which had lost a large part of its adult male population, was to sustain this huge expansion. Only Tanganyika in south-east Africa seized from Germany offered a significant and viable agricultural colonial economy; the oil reserves of Iraq were barely suspected and exploiting them did not feature in the British gameplan. If Britain had a strategy at all, it was to protect the route to India from putative future enemies. Much of what had been acquired at Versailles was not going to lend itself to either of the internal control systems used by Britain in most of the Empire: unchallenged autocratic rule in Africa and its dominant participation in partnerships with servile local elites in the body of the Indian sub-continent. Britain's gains at Versailles expanded the requirement for the kind of constant, violent self-assertion that the Empire had long conducted on the North-West Frontier of India, long the most problematic boundary of its possessions.

The British Raj in India had failed catastrophically to conquer Afghanistan on its North-West Frontier in 1842 and had learned enough of a lesson not to repeat the attempt in 1879 when relations were strained with the kingdom of Afghanistan. A British invasion forced a change in regime but the relationship between independent Afghanistan and the Raj remained problematic. An independent Afghanistan provided a useful buffer against much-feared Russian encroachment into the north of India but left the British authorities with what was, in their eyes, a significant internal security problem. The frontier was ill-defined and largely irrelevant to the local, more-or-less autonomous communities, whose lives were organized in age-old tribal structures. The areas were so large and inaccessible that permanent garrison by security forces was practically impossible as well as being questionably effective. The only way to project British authority was by military expeditions, usually columns of several hundred troops. The tribesman harassed the columns and camps from a distance but only very rarely engaged in set-piece battles, so they could not be defeated conventionally. Nor was it possible to capture individual leaders or fighters with any regularity. The only practical target for action was the tribesmen's villages and livestock. Refusing to submit meant your home would be destroyed and your animals killed. Harming women and children was never an objective, so active steps were taken to minimize the risk of this occurring, typically by sending warnings that a village was to be bombarded. These were never fool-proof and what we now euphemize as collateral casualties inevitably occurred. Down the years the British army developed elaborate practices and controls to conduct these operations in cooperation with civilian political officers.

One of Trenchard's inspirations as he fought for the RAF's status was to recognize that a few aircraft could do the same work as a punitive column at a fraction of the cost. The RAF simply applied the new technology of flight to an old challenge that had grown even larger. There was no significant difference in the direct effects. One of the RAF's earliest operations manuals, CD22, included a chapter entitled, 'Aircraft in Warfare against an Uncivilised Enemy'.[1] The Air Staff set out how the RAF could use different methods to achieve the same effects as ground troops in clear, tabular form.[2] Just as army columns had sent warning ahead that villages would be destroyed, so did the RAF drop leaflets. Before British aircraft bombed, warnings were to be issued 'whenever practicable'. Over time the doctrine evolved; definitely hostile tribes could be bombed without notice, but in case of doubt, target villages were to be told in advance of action.

The psychological warfare dimension was recognized from the start: violent control and propaganda worked hand in hand. Dropping leaflets became almost a goal in its own right as a means of disrupting normal life for enemies by forcing or inciting them to flee their villages. Humanitarian and economic considerations could happily merge if cheap leaflets could produce the same result in the opening operations as expensive bombs would have done in subsequent operations. The next stage was to divide leaflets into two classes. Firstly 'ultimata' warned villagers that unless they complied with government demands, say by releasing hostages or stolen livestock or desisting from whatever breach of *pax Britannica* had brought them into disfavour, they would be bombed. If these were disregarded, 'bombing notices', announcing that the community was to be duly punished, would be dropped, setting a specific deadline for villagers to evacuate and remain away for a set time. The 'preliminary warning notices' were printed on white paper and the subsequent 'final bombing notices' on red paper. In a further refinement, in areas where unrestricted bombing was permitted, leaflets could be dropped on the expected line of advance of hostile tribesmen telling them that any movement in that area could be attacked: a method that was known unofficially as proscription. If British aircrews were captured, the manual set down that leaflets should be used to tell the enemy that air action would not be suspended and that the tribesmen would be held responsible for any harm to their captives. The aircrew themselves would be provided with what were colloquially known as 'goolie chits', promising cash rewards for any downed airman returned to the British authorities in a fully intact state. The womenfolk habitually castrated non-Muslim captives. In a further variation the RAF developed a special airborne loudspeaker and amplifier system to broadcast oral warnings to villages. One overblown and rather patronizing argument advanced for the technique was that listeners would believe that this would be like the voice of God, but an assessment of local levels of literacy provided a more solid justification.

The propaganda dimension to air control was firmly understood by one of the RAF's outstanding figures of the interwar period, then Air Vice-Marshal Edgar Ludlow-Hewitt. As AOC Iraq between 1930 and 1932 he had been responsible for one of the most important regions where the RAF was the dominant force and then, as AOC India from 1935 to 1937, he was in charge of air operations on the North-West Frontier. Ludlow-Hewitt understood that tribesmen could be sustained in their opposition to British authorities by religious leaders, national level politicians with their own agendas or foreign powers and recognized how important it was to set the message of the British or Raj government against these.[3] These messages should include the carrot of offering light-touch control and the stick of threatening bombardment from the air. Ludlow-Hewitt saw loudspeaker aircraft as an effective tool in delivering these messages. In keeping with his reputation as one of the more intellectual air marshals, his vision embraced a holistic approach to air control that verged on a French *mission civilatrice* where the tribes would garrison themselves. Ludlow-Hewitt believed that using air control involved less bloodshed than land operations.

Ludlow-Hewitt's next job after India was the service's premier command as the AOC-in-C of Bomber Command, but this saddled him with the thankless task of steering Bomber Command through the long fallow years until the Air Staff's chosen large bomber strategy translated itself into a viable military weapon. As the Czechoslovakia crisis built, he was acutely aware of how much Bomber Command needed to do to become an effective fighting force and the RAF became as anxious to avoid war as Neville Chamberlain. With Britain's supposedly decisive striking force against Germany forced to sit on the side-lines, Ludlow-Hewitt searched for some more active task in which it could demonstrate such power as it had in a form that would be acceptable to his ultimate political masters. He suggested that Bomber Command might drop propaganda on Germany if war broke out. The idea was enthusiastically taken up by Newall's powerful assistant, Slessor, who had also recently returned from service in India where he had acquired first-hand experience of the propaganda dimension of air control.[4] If the Germans bombed British cities, he saw the possibility of 'issuing some warning, on the lines of bombing notices issued in Frontier warfare' that the RAF would retaliate. This would play well with American opinion. Slessor himself drafted the text of a leaflet which distinguished between the misdeeds of the Nazi leaders which were being punished and the German people itself who were implicitly invited to divest themselves of a regime which persisted in such wickedness.

With Newall's mighty right-hand man convinced of the plan, Bomber Command was ready to reinvent itself as a propaganda weapon. In turn, the RAF officers found an enthusiastic partner in the project in the shape of Sir Stephen Tallents, the Director General designate of the embryonic Ministry of Information, euphemism for propaganda, which was to come into being when war broke out. Tallents was a skilful and enthusiastic publicist who had pioneered many of the techniques commonplace today but were then at the cutting edge. His pamphlet *The Projection of Britain* of 1932 attracted widespread interest with its call to use the full range of modern media to promote British goods and values throughout the world. He had moved to the BBC where Sir John Reith, its autocratic Director General, rapidly spotted a potential challenger to his authority and was happy to steer him towards the Ministry of Information project in 1936, where he was the only full-time employee. He also found himself distinctly underemployed; the Ministry of Information existed purely as a piece of contingency planning and the powers that be in Westminster and Whitehall were determined to prevent it growing beyond this.

Preparing a massive propaganda offensive that the RAF would deliver offered the perfect project for the RAF officers and the publicist trapped in frustrating inactivity at the height of the Czechoslovakia crisis. In the space of days, they organized the composition, printing and delivery to airfields of millions of leaflets to be dropped on Germany if war broke out. The Munich settlement put a swift end to the project but Slessor still had the propaganda bit between his teeth. He began to sound positively evangelical in arguing the possibilities for propaganda: he saw 'possibilities of most valuable propaganda results' and even let Tallents persuade him that

> propaganda is a weapon of which the Nazi leaders are especially afraid. It is a weapon which we have shewn in the past we can use very effectively, and in the use of which the Germans are particularly inept.[5]

Joseph Goebbels and anyone familiar with his work might have raised an eyebrow at the last assertion. Slessor began angling to push the Air Staff to an alliance with Tallents as promoters of a high-profile, well-resourced and proactive propaganda policy in contrast to the minimalist approach pre-Czechoslovakia. A full-scale propaganda department should be established and begin operations forthwith. He was even prepared to push the Air Staff into 'departing from the usual procedure' (Whitehall-speak for rebellion) in short-circuiting the set process for shuffling paper from one sub-committee to another.[6]

Perhaps fortunately for Slessor's career, events in Whitehall moved too fast for Slessor's propaganda plan to be put to the acid test of combat in the corridors of power. Tallents had severely overreached himself and had fallen victim to a savage intrigue launched by another figure who entertained great ambitions in the field of propaganda.[7] Sir Campbell Stuart was a businessman with close, but obscure, links to the government, who had played a part in Britain's First World War propaganda efforts. He enthusiastically promoted the notion that these had made a major contribution to defeating the Kaiser's Germany, recirculating at face value self-serving postwar attempts to blame the defeat on anything but Allied military victory on the battlefield. Stuart also had access to the top levels of power in Whitehall and knew the right buttons to push there. He had been instrumental in arranging radio broadcasts to Germany by Neville Chamberlain over Radio Luxemburg, in which the prime minister tried to capitalize on his supposed reputation as a bringer of peace. Stuart viewed propaganda as a form of secret service which should be shrouded in the same cloak of impenetrable mystery as MI6 was at the time. This had a double benefit: Sir Horace Wilson, Neville Chamberlain's dominant adviser and the most powerful man in government, despised propaganda in its own right and was desperately anxious to keep to a minimum anything that might appear to be a preparation for war and thus a provocation to Hitler; strict confidentiality also allowed Stuart to begin to build his own propaganda empire out of sight and immune to his many potential rivals.

Once Tallents had been eliminated, Stuart was in the driving seat on propaganda. Wilson moved ruthlessly to reduce the Ministry of Information to even greater insignificance than its position before the Czechoslovakia crisis. Stuart could thumb his nose at anyone unwise enough to attempt to use it as a platform for their own ambitions, up to and including a senior Cabinet minister, Sir Samuel Hoare. Slessor's task shrunk to acting as the liaison between Stuart and the Air Staff. His remit was no more than coordination and logistical with the opportunity to superintend the RAF's efforts to develop free-flying balloons as a delivery mechanism for propaganda. He was allowed glimpses of a more exciting world, such as the 'Currency idea', where forged banknotes were to be used to cause inflation and destabilize the enemy's economy.[8] By a remarkable coincidence the same idea occurred in the German propaganda ministry at the time, although it was the SS who put it into practice as Operation *Bernhard* in 1942.[9]

The final crisis of peace in the summer of 1939 put airdropped propaganda back near the top of the Air Staff's agenda. The same imperative to 'conserve the bombers' that had dominated RAF war planning during the Czechoslovakia crisis was revived, giving a further lease of life to propaganda as the mission for Bomber Command. Even before war actually broke out the Committee of Imperial Defence instructed the RAF to begin dropping leaflets irrespective of what Germany might do with its air force.[10] These leaflets were drawn as personal messages from Chamberlain to the German people; once again the prime minister exaggerated his reputation as a man of peace in Germany. The curtailment of the actual bombing operations that the RAF was allowed to undertake against German coastal targets after huge losses, meant that dropping leaflets was almost the RAF's only active contribution to the war effort under the codename Nickels. For a short while the RAF's propaganda role rode a high crest of optimism, which one army officer described:

> I found some quite fantastic optimism regarding the effects from propaganda. The dropping of leaflets was considered almost a major military victory and I remember excited propagandists rushing into my office asking how long I thought the Germans could hold out against them.[11]

The Air Staff took a calmer view and the operations were labelled as 'reconnaissance missions'. Bert Harris, then commanding a bomber group, claimed afterwards that airmen 'never had the slightest faith' in the operation and wrote off the whole exercise: 'the only thing we achieved as to supply the Continent's requirement for toilet paper for the five long years of war.'[12] A senior air marshal was only fractionally more positive, 'though quite valueless as an attack on German morale, did raise the standard of training of the bomber crews during their long flights over enemy country'.[13]

The Nickels were emblematic of the embarrassing and delusional months of the Phoney War in which the statesmen of Britain and France imagined that Nazi Germany would somehow collapse of its own accord. They were part of wider farce of the early phase of the wartime Ministry of Information that was so humiliating that it led to the only significant parliamentary challenge to Chamberlain's government before May 1940.[14] The Nickels themselves provided the government with an opportunity to bring deserved ridicule upon itself when it refused to disclose to Parliament the content of the leaflets, millions of which were being delivered to the enemy.[15] The leaflets were even treated as secret documents at the RAF stations from which they were dispatched to Germany.[16]

The RAF's leaflets did attract the attention of Joseph Goebbels, Germany's master propagandist, who was alert to anything that might undermine domestic morale. He had nothing but contempt for what he saw as the unimaginable stupidity of the first versions and held back from issuing any kind of reply as he did not want to signal to the British where they were going wrong in their propaganda.[17] He monitored successive editions of the leaflets and conceded that the later ones did show some improvement, which made him redouble his vigilance.[18] The only practical step he took was to calm public fears aroused by the leaflets by persuading the Germans that a leaflet was a long way short of a bomb.[19] Goebbels was not especially concerned about the risk from leaflets; at no point did he see the need for the kind of drastic punishment that he meted out to Germans caught listening to enemy radio stations, which he saw as the most powerful weapon in the battle for morale supremacy.[20]

Chapter 32

Per Astra Ad Ardua

In the practically unanimous view of anyone who looked at the question, one of the most acute faults of Bomber Command as it entered was the Second World War was the low level of navigational ability. Even the official popular history of the RAF in the Second World War, which is usually uncritical, managed to rank the shortage of navigation skills as a 'gross and palpable fault' and one for which 'the Air Ministry may be charged with lack of foresight'.[1] A well-placed Air Ministry civil servant, Sir Maurice Dean, afterwards described navigation methods as 'primitive in the extreme' and the official history of the bomber offensive devotes a number of pages to the topic.[2]

This failure is extraordinary and rather hard to explain. Navigation is a key aspect of flying and the RAF was supposed to be a professional air force and recognized fully its importance. It was understood that the increase in aircraft sizes and the move from simple two-man machines with a trained pilot and a largely untrained observer, changed how aircraft could be navigated. When the specification for a new night heavy bomber was being written in 1934, a key feature was to provide the navigator with an adequate work station.[3] As the mission of Bomber Command switched to attacking targets deep in Germany, by both night and day, no thought seems to have been given to whether this would involve navigational skills and techniques that went beyond those current in the RAF.

The question of the specific task that aircraft navigators would have to perform may have been neglected in a furious debate that broke out about their status in the crew. One of the most bitterly debated topics that arose in Ludlow-Hewitt's agonized discussions with the Air Staff in 1938 and 1939 over whether Bomber Command was ready for war, was that of aircraft navigation. Ludlow-Hewitt was dogmatic and old-fashioned on the question of the navigation function. Ludlow-Hewitt proceeded from a traditionalist, almost nautical stance, that the aircraft captain should have full charge of all aspects of its operation, in particular navigation, although he accepted that the captain might see fit to delegate some of these responsibilities. Lurking in the background seemed to be a British, class-driven judgement that commissioned pilots were a distinct and superior race. Ludlow-Hewitt was appalled when the Air Staff planned to reduce the standard of navigational training for pilots, confronted by the need to train huge numbers of new crew.[4] Worse, the observer would 'normally' carry out the navigation of the aircraft, albeit under the direction of the captain. Experience proved Ludlow-Hewitt wrong on both counts. Navigators came to be recognized as a distinct specialization, recruited according to stringent criteria closer to that of pilots and trained *ab initio* for the job and for longer than other aircrew.

Ludlow-Hewitt did call for officers to be given dedicated training in 'modern' navigation methods without going into what these were, but this seems to have been limited to the use of up-to-date instruments to perform traditional dead reckoning and astral navigation.[5] Dead reckoning remained the dominant method of air navigation until well into the war.

The insistence on competence in the skills of traditional navigation may well have contributed to the greatest flaw in the RAF's practices: the complete absence of any interest in, still less of application of, radionavigation aids. This is all the more remarkable as a high-level committee under Air Marshal Brooke-Popham set up in 1934 as rearmament got under way, reported that Britain lagged behind European countries in the development of radionavigation aids and might thus be at a disadvantage to enemy bombers attacking Britain.[6] Just as new technology was transforming the aircraft themselves, new technology was also transforming navigation methods. The Lorenz blind-landing system from Germany was very widely adopted and the US installed the national Low Frequency Radio Range infrastructure of beacons. These were for civilian use, but the potential for military applications was manifest. Germany developed the highly effective long-range *Knickbein* system which was to become the cornerstone of the night Blitz in the autumn of 1940.

The British did recognize that there might be potential but fell woefully short in exploiting their resources. RDF has gone down in legend as a great British scientific success, but there was no corresponding achievement in navigation. The Tizard Committee for the Scientific

Survey of Air Defence did have a counterpart to cover the needs of Bomber Command also led by Tizard, the Committee for the Scientific Survey of Air Offensive, but it achieved almost nothing. Without the kind of political and military support that RDF got from Swinton and Dowding respectively, the scientists faced an institutional brick wall. In Tizard's words:

> the defence committee works quite well. We know what is going on and we have some effect, at least I hope we do. I cannot say the same for the Offence Committee ... But the fact is that no one seems very anxious to get our advice on these subjects, or to follow it, if offered. We have had no meeting for a long while and there seems no anxiety on the part of the Air Ministry that we should meet.[7]

Without the support of the airmen, the scientists had little chance. R. V. Jones, one of Tizard's assistants who had worked closely on the early development of radar in 1938, conceived a radio navigation system for aircraft, which was rejected.

> I was, incidentally, astonished at the complacency that existed regarding our ability to navigate at long range by night. The whole of our bombing policy depended on this assumption, but I was assured that by general instrument flying, coupled with navigation by the stars Bomber Command was confident it could find pinpoint targets in Germany at night, and that there was therefore no need for any such aids as I had proposed. I was not popular for asking why, if this were true, so many of our bombers on practice flights in Britain flew into hills.[8]

Tizard understood enough of the way that new technologies were going to shape the aerial battlefield to recognize that the RAF's bombing operations would be just as deeply affected by new developments as Fighter Command's would be by the advent of RDF and other new technology. For a brief moment he found an ally on the Air Staff. In conversation with Assistant CAS Sholto Douglas soon after the Czech crisis, he volunteered the services of his committee to help Bomber

Command. Sholto Douglas and Tizard had worked closely on the build-up of the RDF network and Sholto Douglas clearly understood the potential for new technologies elsewhere in the RAF. The bombers of the RAF and the Luftwaffe would be facing the same problems and Tizard had been devoting considerable thought as to how the German bombers would operate. Sholto Douglas suggested a number of areas where Tizard might be able to help Bomber Command that went to the very roots of its mission and how it was going to carry them out:

> Location and identification of targets by day and night, navigation, and problems connected with night bombing.[9]

Tizard and Sholto Douglas were in practice proposing a complete rethink of how Bomber Command worked. They suggested a small meeting to open the debate.

Ludlow-Hewitt was too skilled a bureaucrat to refuse point-blank but set up a series of roadblocks behind which to fight the rearguard action. The first was a list of no fewer than twenty-one mostly unrelated topics that the scientists might be set upon. None was remotely as fundamental as the ones raised by Sholto Douglas and Tizard. Most looked for solutions to relatively trivial questions, but they ran the gamut from the old chestnut of the quest for some kind of beam that would interfere with motor ignition from a distance, which had no special relevance to Bomber Command anyway, to a special casing which would explode and scatter propaganda leaflets over a precise area from 1,000 feet. The author of the list seemed not to appreciate that there was a difference between ingenious engineering solutions and fundamental scientific research. Tizard refused to be diverted and insisted that scientists could not be of real help unless the airmen explained clearly what they were trying to do by bombing and the difficulties that they foresaw.[10] Sholto Douglas remained ostensibly helpful, but was starting to hedge his bets. He was prepared to countenance the need for further assistance in night bombing, but was moving to close down any broad debate on navigation.[11] Indeed Sholto Douglas had one of his juniors draft a paper on the general topic of navigation to present to the meeting. This left Ludlow-Hewitt in a position to silence any debate on the point with the statement that 'Bomber Command's ... navigational problems were not serious, the main point being to make the navigators' work as simple as possible'.[12] Bomber Command's struggles to find its targets in Germany in the first three years of the war show just how nonsensical and complacent this claim was.

Tizard came dangerously close to suggesting that it might be worth putting Bomber Command's navigational abilities to a practical test. He floated the idea of dummy raids over friendly foreign countries or on long flights over the North Sea, which would entail less diplomatic preparation. Ludlow-Hewitt found an objection to putting any such scheme into rapid operation as it would be essential to provide adequate air–sea rescue arrangements for the crews of any bombers forced to ditch. As if the proposal to test Bomber Command's navigational skills were not bad enough, Tizard compounded his offence to RAF decencies by suggesting that the bombers returning from the dummy missions over the North Sea might then be used in experiments to test fighter interception and RDF detection techniques. They would, of course, be following the same track that Luftwaffe bombers operating from Germany would have followed. The last thing Bomber Command wanted was anything that might contradict the mantra that 'the bomber will always get through'.

After what Ludlow-Hewitt admitted was a rambling discussion, Tizard did get as far as persuading the RAF to accept that there could be an investigation into what help RDF might give to bomber navigation and that a bomber station might be set to the work in the same way that Biggin Hill had worked on integrated RDF and fighter defence. The suggestion was endorsed by Ludlow-Hewitt, but this was simply an exercise in kicking the can down the street. Tizard was full of praise for the work done at Biggin Hill, but might not fully have appreciated that different rules applied at Fighter Command, the despised junior in the RAF's defence force, to Bomber Command, the premier component of the RAF and the vector of its holy mission of offence. It was unwise to imagine that Bomber Command would take kindly to outside moves to improve its performance. The bomber station at Feltwell was duly selected for the work, but here the scientists began to encounter the full force of military obstructionism. A demarcation dispute got under way as to how work should be allocated between Tizard's operation and Ludlow-Hewitt's project for a Bomber Development Unit (BDU). Purely military tasks, such as the actual bombing or identifying targets by means of flares, would go to the BDU.[13] When Tizard's assistant, A.

P. Rowe, visited Feltwell in early March 1939 almost four months after Tizard had first raised the idea, he was nonplussed to discover that the station knew nothing of the work it was supposed to be doing and he felt strongly enough to take the matter up at ministerial level.[14] Here the story of Feltwell fizzles out of the record apart from spasmodic attempts to interest Bomber Command in scientific solutions. It was to take two years of futile and costly campaigns to bomb Germany accurately before science could be enlisted on behalf of Bomber Command and to start to surmount a complacent confidence in traditional methods.[15] As an internal RAF report described the RAF's practice before the war starkly long afterwards as 'in general[,] navigation consisted of D.R. [dead reckoning] unassisted in any way'.[16]

Well into the war senior officers sniffed at radionavigation tools dismissed as 'adventitious aids'.[17] Rather as Ludlow-Hewitt opposed non-commissioned airmen taking a senior role in the operation of bombers, the RAF seemed to see mere scientists as unfit to assist in the higher mysteries of navigating military aircraft. Bert Harris even decried attempts to interfere with German navigation beams:

> We use no beams ourselves but we bomb just as successfully as the Germans bomb, deep into Germany ... They are simply aids to navigation, and it is within our experience that such aids are not indispensable to the successful prosecution of bombing expeditions. I would go further and say that they are not even really useful.[18]

Had Bomber Command been two years further advanced in re-equipping its force with heavy bombers in 1940, it would merely have dropped a greater tonnage of bombs on open countryside deeper in Germany and even further from the intended targets as the greater distance travelled would have magnified the errors in navigation.

The turning point arrived in the middle of 1941 when it was becoming increasingly clear that Bomber Command was achieving very little. Frederick Lindemann, who had become hugely powerful as Churchill's scientific adviser, forced through an objective study of Bomber Command's bombing accuracy. The Butt Report, named after the civil servant who undertook it in the summer of 1941, revealed a dire picture in which only a small minority of bombs fell anywhere near the intended targets. The way was clear for reform, but there was a mountain to climb:

> Up to this time [summer 1941] it had been difficult to persuade Bomber Command to take science seriously. The contrast with Fighter Command had been remarkable. If, as a scientist you visited Bentley Priory, Fighter Command's Headquarters, you were likely to be bombarded with questions from officers at all levels up to the Commander-in-Chief. The Command knew it was up against desperate odds and was therefore keen to try new ideas. Bomber Command was still nearly as complacent as it had been when Tizard had tried to help it.[19]

Ultimately the British developed highly effective radio and radar aids to navigation and bombing, but only in 1943 did such equipment and techniques for using it reach a point that the RAF was able to get full use out of the large bombers that had been the core of its strategy since 1937. Tizard resented this failure long afterwards and took to task the authors of the official history of the air offensive against Germany – usually considered to be highly critical of the Air Staff – for being, 'too tolerant of the Air Staff's neglect of the problems of navigation in the interwar period'.[20]

***

At least someone was aware of the RAF's failings in navigation, but there is no sign that anyone at all was concerned about or even aware of another major failing: the deficiencies in its bombs. The service was dedicated to a strategy of dropping as great a tonnage of bombs on the enemy but took astonishingly little interest in the bombs as weapons. The Air Staff noted with minimal discussion that 500lb bombs were the smallest ones capable of damaging modern buildings and that supply arrangements were being revised accordingly.[21] In reality, when the RAF began to bomb in earnest in 1940, three times more 250lb bombs were dropped than 500lb bombs.[22] It also turned out that RAF bombs often failed to detonate, which might have come to light in better time had Ludlow-Hewitt been provided with his BDU more promptly.

Per Astra Ad Ardua

Considering the Air Staff's obsession with matching German bomb tonnage, RAF intelligence was guilty of a major omission. It failed to detect that German bombs carried almost twice the weight of explosive as a percentage of the total bomb weight – 50 per cent compared to 27 per cent – until war began.[23] Unwittingly, the British were allowing the Germans to deliver twice as much explosive power as they were planning to deliver in return. It was not until war had started that a newly appointed Royal Air Force member of the Ordnance board put in hand realistic tests of the effectiveness of bombs.[24]

As with navigational aids, it was only under the Harris regime as AOC-in-C Bomber Command that things began to improve. The heavyweight super-bombs designed by Barnes Wallis and famously dropped by 617 Squadron, the 'dambusters', lay far in the future.

Chapter 33

By This Means Alone – Scheme M

In the summer of 1938 as Europe lurched towards the Czech crisis and battle raged in Whitehall over Scheme L, undeterred by such mundane questions as current finance, the Chief of the Air Staff, Sir Cyril Newall, launched a new campaign to expand the RAF that culminated in a visionary bid to have it established as the most important of the armed services with a claim on the resources of the state to match. He also set out to alter what had been the government's established policy for some years.

The opening move in the campaign was defensive. The removal of Swinton, Winterton and Muirhead had not closed the political controversy over air rearmament and the opposition obtained another debate on the topic barely a fortnight after the ministerial bloodbath. The threat to the RAF came, though, from the government itself. Newall was alerted to the possibility that Chamberlain was trying to distance himself from Baldwin's commitment to parity, which had provided such a convenient justification for increasing bomber numbers to compete with Germany. Sir Horace Wilson, the prime minister's civil service adviser and éminence grise, had drafted a speech labelling it as a mistake to 'model ... our air force on the air force of some other country differently situated from ourselves'.[1] The draft was not used, but the threat was clear: the government was considering backing away from shaping the RAF to match the Luftwaffe exactly. The Air Ministry's new set of politicians might succumb to this heresy too. Following the age-old formula for the best means of defence, Newall went on the attack, apparently using what appears to have been the final Christie/X intelligence report on German plans, that was already almost a year old, as his point of departure. The relevant file is marked, '"X" Papers' and covers what would be needed to meet German expansion plans for early 1940; the Christie/X report set out Germany's new plan set for completion by the end of 1939.[2] This featured total Luftwaffe strength of 5,400, of which 2,430 were to be heavy bombers. On the RAF's basis of calculation this translated to a total first-line strength of 3,240. These Christie/X figures had already been used in drawing up Scheme J; this time Newall tried to show how far short this fell of attaining parity with the Germans. He left the way open for even darker forebodings by admitting that his figures were an 'instructed guess'.[3] Newall never made a formal expansion scheme of this and there is no sign that it was followed through, although the suggestion that a Treasury representative should be included on the Air Council Committee on Supply to speed up the procedure of approval for expenditure, did produce a happy result.[4]

Newall's next step in protecting the cherished goal of parity was to slip the statement that this was Britain's 'traditional policy' into an Air Staff paper.[5] Palming off a four-year-old political commitment as an immutable part of Britain's heritage helped set the base for an even bolder drive that Newall launched in the summer of 1938, to take on the Royal Navy and its centuries old mission of 'command of the seas'. He stretched Trenchard's doctrine far further than anyone had attempted ever before; compared to Newall's efforts, Trenchard's swansong paper was a model of balance and compromise. The cornerstone of Newall's argument was that the Royal Navy should lose its historic status as Britain's principal defender and the source of national power. He came up with the argument that German bombers posed a threat to British shipping comparable to that of submarines and that the Germans were fully alert to this strength. As the ports of western Britain were out of the range of existing German bombers, this was already an invention, even leaving aside the assessment of German strategy which was every bit as false as the RAF's faith that the Luftwaffe had been built to deliver a knock-out blow to London. Göring had even less intention of cooperating with the Kriegsmarine than the Air Staff had of helping the Royal Navy. Newall advanced the most aggressive claim made for the unique value of the counter-offensive bomber force:

> By this means, and this means alone, we can expect to reduce the enemy's air attack on this country to a scale at which our close defences [fighters and anti-aircraft artillery] can deal with them. By this means, and this means alone, we can hope adequately to deal with the menace of enemy attack by air on our shipping.[6]

Just as the Trenchardians had never explained in detail how British bombers would defeat German bombers over the cities of Britain, Newall did not explain how this would happen over the sea-lanes to British ports.

In practical terms, Newall's goal was to go beyond the target of parity with Germany in bombers. 'We thus require as a minimum for any sound system of national defence, air superiority no less than naval superiority … Of bombers we shall require sufficient to ensure that we possess a margin of strength over the enemy Air Striking Force.' Only this offered the prospect of winning a future war because the German policy of autarky made it invulnerable to blockade and no large British army would be sent to the continent again. If the Striking Force were restricted in size, Newall admonished, this could not be achieved. Anything except an overwhelming commitment to bombers was a high-risk strategy: 'There is in fact only one safe course to follow.'

Newall's wild, one-man strategy for establishing the RAF as Britain's premier fighting service inspired deep misgivings even amongst his natural allies, however much they might have endorsed its goals. When Newall circulated the paper setting out his vision in July 1938, they recognized that it would need to be significantly redrafted before it was fit to see the light of day outside the RAF.[7] Replacing the policy of air parity with Germany with one of outright superiority was a political impossibility and Newall was told this very directly. It was not a claim that the air minister, Sir Kingsley Wood, disputed intellectually; he just knew that it would take so much even to achieve parity that it was futile to ask for more. Newall must have known he was going out on a limb and did not take Slessor, normally his trusted lieutenant, into his confidence beforehand. Slessor tried to persuade the DCAS AVM Richard Peirse to try to bring him to his senses.[8] The episode shook Slessor's faith in Trenchardian doctrine so much that he admitted that the experience of actual air combat in Spain threw Newall's more aggressive assertions into doubt. Sir Edgar Ludlow-Hewitt, who was confronted with the immense if mundane realities of putting Newall's vision into practice as AOC-in-C of Bomber Command, told the CAS bluntly that if he claimed that the RAF could bomb Germany as easily as the Luftwaffe could bomb Britain, he would lose credibility. For good measure he made plain to Newall that he resented not having been consulted on the question.

Perhaps fortunately for Newall, the Czechoslovakia crisis intervened and pushed his vaulting vision for the service's future as Britain's premier armed service far down the in-tray and from there into the further recesses of the archives. He no longer needed some doctrinal justification – and certainly not one so confrontational – to underpin the policy that the future of the RAF lay in an all big bomber force, which the air staff had already decided. There was a much more important, strictly practical question to be addressed: this policy had yet to be accepted by the politicians, or even explained to them, still less to be fully costed out. The abortive Scheme H had been a step in that direction but nearly a year had gone by since it was formulated and the day was coming closer when the 1936-generation bombers would have to be brought into the budgetary equation as the moment loomed to buy them. Even at the time of the discussions over Scheme H, it was known in Adastral House that '[t]he rise in cost will be colossal'.[9] The move to intermediate bombers foreseen under Scheme H had stepped up the RAF's financial wants considerably; the move to the truly heavy bombers would swell them even further. As the RAF adopted the big-bomber model, it was practically inevitable that it would go even further than it had done with Scheme H and ask for the largest slice of the defence cake by some measure. Newall's open and specific claim to put the RAF ahead of the Royal Navy was being quietly forgotten, but the amount of money that would be needed to implement fully the big-bomber strategy meant that the junior service would want a lot more money than the senior service.

Once the Czech crisis had settled down, Newall and his colleagues returned to the question of how the future RAF was to be equipped. He shared none of Chamberlain's blind confidence that he had brought peace to Europe for the foreseeable future. At the end of the crisis when Chamberlain told the nation that he had secured 'peace for our time', Newall gathered his staff and told them that Britain had suffered a national humiliation and that they had to work night and day to prepare for a likely war.[10] Newall could now advance a much more solid case for expanding the bomber force than warmed-over year-old intelligence or the assertion that the RAF ought to displace the Royal Navy: Czechoslovakia could be added to the woeful list of crises in which Britain's inferiority in 'Air Defence' had left the country powerless to respond to challenges from the dictators.[11] The ministers responsible for defence were no more optimistic. A few weeks after Munich, Wood joined his fellow service ministers in preparing new and ever higher bids for finance. Wood understood the political dynamic and knew that his Cabinet colleagues would not cause difficulties. He instructed the airmen to open their mouths wide and do it quickly. Propelled by post-Munich panic, the Air Staff needed neither Newall's attempt to displace the Royal Navy nor Wood's dubious Canada-based financing scheme to get its all large bomber force. Under the RAF's new post Munich Scheme M its demands ratcheted up even further to £650 million although it was getting very hard to make precise estimates and it was clear that there was every risk that the actual figure would be substantially higher.[12]

The main cause was the big bombers whose estimated cost had started at £30,000 each, but had climbed to no less than £50,000. The total capital cost alone for the bombers was £175 million and it was a near-complete mystery what it would it would cost to keep the force in operation. By contrast, the new fighters were expected to cost only £45 million. The Treasury was naturally fully alert to the financial cost of the big-bomber scheme, but it also recognized that its implications went far further. The civil service money men identified a string of ways in which the Treasury was being asked to fund major decisions of policy: they knew that this marked a significant change in the Air Ministry's programme; that it was a different strategy from the ones that the Germans were following; perhaps most important with the threat of war imminent, they knew that the supposed benefits of the new step in re-equipment would not come through immediately. The civil servants had picked up a vital consideration that the air marshals simply did not include in their equations: how long it would take to fulfil their dreams. None of the new bombers had even flown in prototype and were not to do so for some months; the Stirling's maiden flight was in May 1939, the Manchester's in July and the Halifax's in October. The Treasury spotted an opportunity to intervene in the debate on strategy and challenge the Air Ministry's love of the big bomber in the unfamiliar realm of popular politics.

> I do not myself believe that the great mass of people in this country are primarily concerned with the degree of security which may be attained in four years hence. Surely what they want to know is what progress is going to be made between now and Christmas and next summer in amending the very high degree of unpreparedness which was suddenly exhibited to them on the 30th September last.[13]

The Treasury was coming perilously close to invoking Trenchard's hated 'ignorant masses' to contradict the Air Staff's expert opinion. They even allowed themselves an access of humanitarian scruple over a strategy whose uglier implications they were prepared to confront in a way that the Air Staff refused to contemplate:

> Incidentally, it seems a strange result of the Prime Minister's policy of appeasement that we should be devoting so enormous a sum to the slaughter of civilians in other countries.[14]

The gigantic scale of what the RAF wanted was clear to the Treasury: 'The new scheme represents not so much an expansion of the striking force as its replacement by a new Striking Force of the same number but of vastly larger, more powerful and more expensive machines.'[15] They also spotted that the Air Staff had come up with a novel argument for opposing investment in fighters: there was a danger of putting so many into service that the defence would be saturated by its own resources.

The Treasury civil servants spoke to their opposite numbers at the Air Ministry with the goal of swaying their spending plans back into less visionary territory. They hoped that Sir Kingsley Wood, the air minister, might be persuaded to give priority both publicly and in the detail of his scheme to fighter production at the expense of the new, costly bombers. But they knew that even if Wood fell in with their thinking, he would face opposition from the Air Staff on the question of giving priority to fighters. As the budgetary debate over Scheme M gathered pace, relations between the Air Ministry and the Treasury resumed the traditional adversarial pattern of finance ministry versus spending ministry; the goodwill that had underpinned the creation of the Air Council Committee of Supply had been exhausted. Under the pretext that the immediate emergency had passed, the Treasury withdrew its representative. This would deprive the committee of its spending firepower at a stroke, but the Treasury was willing to risk the wrath of Bruce-Gardner, still in high favour at 10 Downing Street, whose members had been major beneficiaries.[16]

Wood was willing to make pro-fighter statements in public but in private he was every bit as resolutely Trenchardian as his service advisers on practicalities and the Treasury's hopes were dashed. The formal scheme that Wood submitted to the Cabinet a few weeks after the Munich deal abounded in verbiage to the effect that fighters were being prioritized, but a glance at the detail showed that bombers stood as usual at the head of the list. Scheme M foresaw almost the same number of bombers as fighters – 3,500 bombers to 3,700 fighters – but the bombers were all to be 1936-generation big aircraft, which would cost more than three times what the fighters would. When Wood defended this approach to ministers, he adopted the traditional Air Staff metaphor of a football team composed solely of goalkeepers to decry a fighter-heavy strategy.[17] When Lord Stanhope, First Lord of the Admiralty, whose service would most likely be expected to make sacrifices to bankroll the big bombers, gently asked if 'we might concentrate more on defence and less on retaliation', Wood told him that the prime minister had delivered a definitive statement of what the public commitment to parity meant and it meant equality of striking force.

Wood was overstating the support he could expect from Downing Street. Chamberlain and his adviser Wilson were far less attached to Baldwin's commitment and bridled at the attempt to resurrect the doctrine. Wood's most heinous crime was to suggest that parity with the Luftwaffe should once again be the 'overriding consideration'.[18] This was doubly objectionable to Wilson. It threatened to skewer Chamberlain with the same futile and dangerous commitment that had opened Baldwin to Churchill's criticism, when air rearmament first became a hot political topic in 1932: 'parity … in at least as dangerous form as it has ever been stated.'

Wood might have been determined, but his case was weak and he faced a Chancellor of the Exchequer, who was also one of the most effective courtroom lawyers of his day. Sir John Simon understood full well how important the big bomber was and knew that the Air Staff was proposing to put the bulk of its resources into a machine that could perform only one task.[19] He was also aware that none of the new types had yet flown. Before they even got onto the question of bomber sizes, Wood opened a flank to Simon by giving figures for the proposed size of front-line strength and reserves together with the figure for the total number of aircraft it was proposed to order which was much higher. Simon remorselessly exposed Wood's inability to reconcile the figures. Even Lord Stanhope, who was not noted for his intellectual gifts, then spotted a clumsy attempt by Wood to palm the 1936 bombers off on the ministers as the Air Staff's notion of an 'ideal' bomber. No one was put off the scent by Wood's attempt to present his scheme as a form of rationalization as it involved producing only three types of bombers.

As the moment approached for the politicians to decide, Newall was terrified that they might give serious priority to fighters:

> I am afraid that we may be pressed into turning over further bomber capacity to the production of fighters, which may well result at a later date in our having to accept vast output of obsolescent, if not obsolete fighters and at the same time deferring the re-equipment of the service with really powerful bombing aircraft.[20]

Newall was alarmed that a factory slated to make Wellingtons had been switched to Hurricanes. He was genuine – if misguided – in his concern that the Hurricane and, perhaps, the Spitfire as well would soon be of little value in combat. They belonged to the same design era as Battle and Blenheim, which had long been left behind as the Air Staff's notion of useful bombers.

In the end, it was the prime minister himself who delivered the coup de grâce to Scheme M in a full Cabinet meeting.[21] Still relishing his 'triumph' at Munich, Chamberlain was hostile to anything that might compromise the friendly and mutually respectful relationship that he deluded himself that he had built up with Hitler. 10 Downing Street verged on paranoia in its hostility to anything that the Germans might see as evidence that the British wanted to 'sabotage the Munich Declaration'.[22] The specific reference to the declaration rather than the four-power agreement that dismembered Czechoslovakia is telling. It was the personal document signed by Hitler on Chamberlain's initiative that inspired his 'peace for our time' boast. Chamberlain's contribution to the Cabinet discussion of the big-bomber policy combined a statement of the obvious, which should have been made long before, and one that has been ruthlessly turned against him. Chamberlain told his colleagues that it 'was rather difficult to represent [bomber strength] as in any way defensive', because he thought the news that Britain was spending more money on bombers would upset Hitler. This does rather beg the question as to why no one had queried the Air Staff's highly questionable insistence that bombers were defensive weapons before. This was a far more important consideration for Chamberlain than something else that he said which demonstrated his unerring ability to provide quotations which would harm his later reputation. He repeated Simon's point that bombers cost four times as much as fighters, which has gone down in history as a proof of his feeble tight-fistedness.[23]

Chamberlain's attitude to the big-bomber scheme was shaped by three distinct factors: political desire to bury the parity commitment, fear of annoying Hitler and the cost of bombers compared to the cost of fighters. Only the last of these is remembered today and is cited ad nauseam as the sole reason for Chamberlain's choice. Moreover, an unaccountable supposition has recently developed in military history circles that Chamberlain was a long-standing champion of fighters against bombers in the teeth of Trenchardian orthodoxy.[24] In reality, as Chancellor he had fully supported the RAF's bomber strategy, signing off the substitution scheme which set in stone the migration to big bombers.

Chamberlain's intervention is sometimes presented as bringing a radical change in RAF policy but it fell well short of this.[25] In the game of bomber versus fighter, the decision was at best a draw. The Cabinet authorized Wood to order the fighters specified in Scheme M but only sufficient bombers to maintain production capacity. The ministers did not, though, close the door on Wood's case for the big bombers. Wood was to re-examine the question of what aircraft were right for the RAF. In practice, the apparent clipping of the Air Staff's wings on the bomber question was more apparent than real. Firm pilot orders had already been placed for the heavy bombers to allow the manufacturers to gear up for production. It would be two years anyway before production in volume would be possible. Wood's concession to the pro-fighter sentiment of his colleagues came cheap.

Newall was dismayed at the Cabinet's decision to withhold full approval from Scheme M and even more by the way policy was presented to the public. Days after the Cabinet meeting. Wood announced that spending on the RAF would jump from some £120 million that year to £200 million in the next, but in Newall's ears Wood poisoned the implicit affirmation of the RAF's importance with his hint as to where the money was to go:

> the Prime Minister has already emphasised the fact that our rearmament is essentially defensive, and I propose to give the highest priority to the strengthening of our fighter force.[26]

The press was told that the programme was going to include 5,000 or 6,000 fighters. There was no mention of bombers, medium or heavy.

Newall showed again his naivety as to how politics operates and was so enraged by the apparent suggestion that Trenchardian orthodoxy was being ditched that he sent a circular to all RAF stations insisting that Wood's statement should not

> lead to some erroneous deductions that a change of policy is thereby implied in the direction of a defensive strategy at the expense of our capacity for counter-offensive action. It is therefore thought desirable to reaffirm that no such change is implied by the measures ... or is in any way contemplated.[27]

Newall ought not to have worried. Wood was merely playing his political hand astutely. A few days later he was openly swinging back towards the path of Trenchardian righteousness in a publicly reported speech, using phrases lifted directly from Newall's circular and telling his listeners that the bomber force was being expanded.[28] Wood stuck to the Air Staff line in the review of RAF aircraft needs that the Cabinet had imposed on him. He reported back that he was even more committed to the big bomber plan than before.[29] He claimed that big bombers were the cheaper means of delivering bombs to Germany, backed by an unsupported estimate that it would cost £50 million more to equip the RAF with Wellington medium bombers to deliver a given bombload than the heavy bombers that would be needed to deliver the same load. Wood heartily recommended the plan as it 'would offer substantial advantages in all respects'.[30]

Wood's pitch arrived first on Wilson's desk and he was not convinced. He lined Chamberlain up to challenge Wood. His main concern was money and not military strategy: 'In view of the appalling sums which anyway it is proposed to spend on bombers none of the alternatives seems to be "cheap"!'[31] Wilson was suspicious of the pseudo-management jargon rolled out by the Air Staff such as 'total bomber lift', but he rejected the thought of finding some tame expert outsiders to torpedo the plan. Both Chamberlain and Wilson were deep in a fog of ignorance as to how air forces and the minds of air marshals worked. They were not dubious of the big bomber on military (still less on ethical) grounds, but because they saw it as a device to manipulate and circumvent budgetary constraints in the traditional struggle between a spending department and the Treasury. Wilson came up with a wildly false analogy with the Royal Navy's first Dreadnought battleships, and warned that 'we shall presently be told that in order to safeguard the very large bomber it will be necessary to accompany it by the appropriate number of very fast fighters so as to protect so large and costly a machine from enemy attack'. He was entirely wrong; the air marshals worked under the firm delusion that bombers could defend themselves, until the Luftwaffe demonstrated their mistake in the early days of the Second World War. Wilson secured the prime minister's authority to set the Chancellor of the Exchequer and, if necessary, the prime minister, loose on Wood to explain the error of his ways.

By this point Wood spotted that Downing Street was bringing up the heavy artillery and knew that tactical retreat was the safest option. He conceded that things could be left where the Cabinet had wanted with orders for bombers restricted to a level to keep the factories ticking over.[32] Downing Street, though, still wanted to find out what the Air Staff were up to and asked for more detail.[33] This was enough for Newall to detect an opportunity to sell the Air Staff's cherished big bomber strategy to the highest level. This centred on a wholly artificial cost comparison for dropping an arbitrary 4,000 tons of bombs on Germany between a feasible force of 958 Stirling four-engine heavy bombers and an unattainably large force of 3,584 Wellington twin-engine bombers.[34] The elementary description of the types of aircraft makes plain that the document was prepared for a non-specialist readership, in practice Chamberlain and Wilson. The political dynamics were plain and the staff officer who forwarded the paper to Wilson made a point of informing him that his air industry czar, Sir Charles Bruce-Gardner, was being kept well in the loop.[35]

Predictably enough, Newall's paper was a vehement reaffirmation of Trenchardian orthodoxy. It wildly overstated the capacities of the Stirling, which it presented as better than the Wellington in practically every respect. On one score his arguments contained an outright lie. He claimed that it would be possible to arm the Stirling with defensive cannon, even though he had just attended a meeting which had been told that it was practically impossible to install cannon in any of the established gun turrets of any of the 1936-generation bombers.[36] Worse, it was already recognized that .303-calibre machine guns did not provide effective defence against fighters, so the picture he painted of lone Stirlings bombing Germany almost immune to attack was a demonstrable fantasy. Newall's figure for the Stirling's cruising speed of 265 mph also proved a wild exaggeration; in its acceptance trials in early 1941, it was only capable of a top speed of 218 mph.[37]

Newall did not need to win the argument to get his big bombers. Wood had managed to keep the door open a crack when he got approval for orders for enough bombers to keep factories going and the Air Ministry set out to drive a horse and cart through it. When a Treasury delegation discussed the detail of implementing the modified scheme with the Air Ministry, they were told that that the Air Ministry wanted to give definite orders for 1,350 bombers, as this was the smallest number that could be ordered to attain the production potential that had been accepted.[38] This was only a quarter fewer than originally asked for in Scheme M. The airmen had outflanked the bean-counters and Sir Warren Fisher, whose hopes had been built up by an order for 1,000 Hurrricanes, was left to inquire plaintively, 'What is happening, I wonder, about fighters?'[39] The big bombers cost at least four times each what fighters did, so the RAF would still be spending three times as much on bombers as fighters.

The tactical landscape in Whitehall was also shifting in favour of the Trenchardians as the prominent sceptics of the big-bomber policy fell by the wayside. Hankey had clung on to the secretaryships of the Cabinet and the Committee of Imperial Defence well past the official retirement age but finally stood down in the middle of 1938. His schemes to find a full-blooded successor to his own unique status failed. Fisher, too, was fading from the scene, partly in disgust at the government's surrender at Munich, partly because he knew that he had long been out-distanced in power and influence by his former protégé, Sir Horace Wilson. Fisher treated himself to a year's leave prior to his official retirement as Head of the Civil Service due in September 1939. Sir Thomas Inskip, the loudest pro-fighter voice in the Cabinet, earned the disfavour of Downing Street because he championed the creation of a Ministry of Supply, which was read as casting doubt on the durability of 'peace for our time'. He was sacked as Minister for the Coordination of Defence in January 1939.

Chapter 34

Saturation Point – Fighters and Scheme M

Amongst the many potent legends that surround the RAF in the run-up to the Second World War is that of the dramatic switch in priority to fighters from bombers after Munich. The most cynically dishonest mouthpiece here is Newall's lieutenant, Slessor, who wrote: 'we were too strong [for the Germans to attempt a knock-out blow] thanks to our belated recognition in Scheme M of the importance of fighter defence.'[1] It meshes neatly with the argument that the Munich deals secured for Britain a 'year's breathing space' in which it was able to rearm properly and prevent an abject defeat by Germany the moment war broke out and so is popular amongst apologists for appeasement. This year's grace supposedly allowed Fighter Command to prepare itself for the Battle of Britain.

The raw numbers that Air Minister Sir Kingsley Wood presented to Cabinet for Scheme M certainly did show an increase in fighters. The big headline number was that fighter strength would rise to 800 aircraft from 640 before. This would involve adding 'the equivalent' of ten new fighter squadrons. Immediate orders would be given for 1,850 fighters compared to 1,750 bombers, although no mention was made of the cost. The detail of Scheme M began by asking for more than three times the amount of money to be spent on bombers than fighters. There was no clearly costed budget for the fudge that emerged from Chamberlain's dialogue with Wood in December 1938 but the fact that the RAF remained on track to switch to an all big-bomber fleet meant that Bomber Command was keeping by far the largest claim on resources.

Fighter Command was certainly stronger at the outbreak of war than at the time of Munich, but this had very little to do with any political or budgetary decisions. It was overwhelmingly because existing problems were overcome rather than because of any single, heroic factor. Fighter Command was short of modern aircraft at the time of the Munich crisis because only a few of the modern fighters that it had ordered in 1936 had been delivered. The first production orders for Hurricanes and Spitfires had been granted on the same day, 3 June 1936. As at 26 November 1938, 167 Hurricanes out of 600 ordered had been delivered and twenty-nine Spitfires out of 510. This was not even the full extent of the gap in Fighter Command's inventory. Because it was to prove such a failure in combat, it is easy to overlook the Boulton Paul Defiant turret-equipped fighter, but the Air Staff, notably Newall, had pinned great hopes on it and it was supposed to make up one-fifth of Fighter Command. Not one was in service at the time of Munich even though the type had also been due to enter service in 1938. The first batch of Defiants had been ordered in 1937 before the prototype first flew in August of that year and the order total had been increased in stages to 450 aircraft, not much short of the total number of Spitfires on order in the autumn of 1938. It is fortunate for the Air Staff's future reputation in aircraft type selection that development and delivery delays meant that only two squadrons of Defiants were in service in the summer of 1940. When battle experience showed they were unfit for combat and they were withdrawn, it did not leave as gaping a hole in Fighter Command's order of battle that it would have done if the original plans had come to fruition.

The problem with Spitfire production was particularly acute; practically every aspect of its early manufacturing history went wrong in a sorry tale of ineptitude, dishonesty and disorganization.[2] The Supermarine company had been taken over by the immense Vickers arms conglomerate in 1928 but it was still handicapped by an almost artisan organization. Supermarine's waterside works at Southampton suffered from inconsistency in producing parts to fine tolerances due to variations in tide levels which fed through to fluctuations in the workshop floor level. The Spitfire was a relatively complex design and its stressed-steel wing structure confronted manufacturers with quite unfamiliar techniques. Vickers was less than honest in informing the Air Ministry about the scale of the problems and indulged in widespread scapegoating to shift blame elsewhere. The death of R. J. Mitchell who had dominated the technical side of Supermarine as well as designing the Spitfire in June 1937 just as the Spitfire was supposed to be entering full-scale production was also blamed.[3] Output also suffered from a heavy reliance on contracting work to a good number of small sub-contractors

Slowly but surely these problems were overcome and the RAF could start to equip squadrons with Spitfires. At the beginning of February 1939 only sixty-eight Spitfires had been delivered compared to eighty-one scheduled, but as the year progressed the shortfall on planned figures narrowed. By the beginning of March 106 Spitfires had been delivered, nine fewer than planned. Weekly deliveries had, though, hit the planned level of six aircraft.

The RAF did make one key decision to boost fighter production during the Czechoslovakia crisis, but this was well before Scheme M came under discussion. A thousand Hurricanes were ordered from Hawkers to allow the former Gloster aircraft plant at Hucclecote originally slated to make Wellingtons to be jigged up to go into production, much as the Castle Bromwich shadow factory project had been based on an order for 1,000 Spitfires.[4] The order was passed as an emergency measure during the Czech crisis taken without reference to Treasury.[5] Because the RAF had been let down so badly on Spitfire production the Hurricane was the only dependable modern fighter available. The driving force appears to have been Sir Wilfrid Freeman, the Air Member for Supply and Production; there is no sign that the order was discussed by the Air Staff. The first mention of it is when Freeman apologized to the Treasury seeking retrospective approval. Sir Warren Fisher, head of the Civil Service and the Treasury who had been one of the small numbers of senior figures pushing for more fighters, approved willingly. He mistakenly saw the order as a sign that Air Staff were 'seriously reconsidering the relationship between bombers and fighters'.[6] The order was duly rubber-stamped a few days later at a meeting of the Air Council Committee on Supply.[7] This was a major setback for Newall in his campaign to devote resources to big bombers and he complained that capacity was being turned over to fighters that he saw as outdated; he considered the Hurricane to be practically obsolete.[8] Wood implicitly claimed credit for the order when he told his instinctively pro-fighter Cabinet colleagues that two 'special orders' for 1,000 fighters each had been placed when he presented the plan for Scheme M. Hucclecote has attracted far less attention than Castle Bromwich, but it made a far greater contribution to equipping Fighter Command for the Battle of Britain. The first Hurricane left the Hucclecote works in October 1939 and a year afterwards the first 1,000 aircraft had been delivered.[9] The plant was also intended to make the next generation of Hawker fighters. Its importance was recognized by a visit from King George VI in February 1939 although publicity for this was minimal and misleading, probably a sign of how much the importance of security had grown since the fanfare that surrounded the announcement of Castle Bromwich.[10]

This was not the only instance of Freeman driving policy that ran counter to the prejudices of Newall or the Air Staff. He resisted Newall's preference for the Westland Whirlwind fighter and, most famously, signed off the first order for the de Havilland Mosquito in defiance of Air Staff hostility to the 'speed bomber' concept.

Nor did RAF Fighter Command have an exclusive claim on the modern fighters. Diplomatic considerations also played a part. Even in January 1939, the Air Ministry accepted that modern fighters – twenty Hurricanes and twenty-four Spitfires – would be exported to countries seen as key targets for favourable treatment.[11] Their diplomatic importance was in almost direct proportion to their irrelevance in the balance of force against the Luftwaffe. Belgium, the only client whose air force was likely to come up against Germany's, was still doggedly neutral in the futile hope that Hitler would leave it alone. Germany posed no immediate direct threat to Estonia or Greece; it was the USSR and Italy respectively that they had to worry about.[12]

The legend that Fighter Command was decisively strengthened after Munich takes a further knock from the fact that some of the extra aircraft added to Fighter Command were ineffective modifications of Blenheim bombers. The questionable idea of converting bombers to a fighter role had been floating around for some time. In the course of discussion of Scheme J in late 1937, Hankey had advanced what he accepted the Air Staff would consider heresy, that bombers could be used directly to reinforce fighters in the defence of London.[13] Hankey had returned to the charge and almost a year before Munich had suggested that 'types of medium bombers might reinforce fighters initially'.[14] The idea had been firmly squashed by the RAF at the time, but in 1938 the political and military imperatives had moved on and the project received a fillip from a perhaps unlikely quarter.

Ludlow-Hewitt reacted to the strategic bankruptcy of Bomber Command that was revealed by the burgeoning Czech crisis by thrashing around to find some use for his aircraft. He lit on the idea of converting Blenheim bombers to a fighter role.[15] The numbers-driven production strategy had saddled Bomber Command with too many types which did not fit into the Air Staff's big-bomber strategy and the hunt was on for some use for them. The Blenheims were to be armed with a pod containing six standard Browning .303-inch machine guns fitted over the space used for the bomb bay. He did not think that this would involve undue difficulty. Wood took up the running when he presented Scheme M with the claim that these would be 'formidable fighters'.[16] This tells us much about Wood's grasp of aircraft technology or, perhaps, his assessment of his colleagues' gullibility; he also claimed that Lysander army cooperation aircraft had 'definite value' as a fighter. In the blind drive to accelerate what was then still Scheme L this idea was enthusiastically adopted even though it overrode elementary military and technical practicalities. The committee overseeing the process recommended that three Blenheim bomber squadrons were to be converted to fighters.[17] This 'diversion' was acceptable as it would not hurt the bomber reserves. By April 1939 there would be more Blenheims available than crew to fly them. By this stage the number of machine guns in the pod had shrunk to four, but the committee calculated that together with the single fixed machine guns in one wing and the gun turret, this would give them a total of six machine guns, fewer than Hurricane or Spitfire single-seat fighters. No thought seems to have been given to removing the gun turret with its attendant weight and drag so as to increase the type's speed which was already inadequate for an effective interceptor. At that stage only one experimental conversion had been undertaken and there were very significant technical question marks over the conversion. The Air Staff was wildly overconfident how easy it would be to convert the bombers in 'simple blacksmith's work'.[18]

By November the Air Staff had got the bit firmly between its teeth. Newall was jockeying along the process with the statement that a commitment had been made to the Cabinet to have at least three squadrons of Blenheim fighters by March 1939 and a declaration that he wanted to go even further.[19] As many as sixteen squadrons could be converted to Blenheim fighters: four or five regular bomber squadrons; the three Auxiliary Air Force (AAF) light bomber squadrons; two Fighter Command squadrons; two army cooperation squadrons; four of the fighter squadrons designated to accompany the army Field Force to France.[20] The following spring, as the question of how to organize the RAF in France had become a matter of great importance, the Blenheim fighter was being discussed as though it were part of the RAF's regular inventory. The scheme had the added attraction that it seemed to solve elegantly the question of what to do with the remaining AAF bomber squadrons which Newall was keen to eliminate.[21] It would be easier to retrain the crews for fighter operations than bring them up to scratch on modern, larger – and of course, more vital – bombers.

Doubts came quickly on the feasibility of the scheme; it was 'not such a simple job as we were originally given to understand'.[22] It was unsure whether the guns could operate without heating or whether the Blenheims could be fitted with the radio systems that were standard on single engine fighters and crucial to the effectiveness of Fighter Command's interception system. No one seems to have consulted Dowding as to whether he actually wanted the planes at all.[23] Ludlow-Hewitt's initial optimism about the ease with which Blenheims could be converted began to be proved excessive. The practicalities took on an ever more daunting aspect and even by March 1939, months later, manufacture of the gun-pack had not started and was not expected to start until the middle of the following month.[24] This was despite the visible relics of the high-level political commitment, which gave scheme 'extreme importance.[25] The project was also losing popularity at the highest levels of the RAF. Ludlow-Hewitt performed a smart, but complete, about-face against the project and labelled it as a 'diversion' and part of a 'serious interference with bomber efficiency'.[26] He added this complaint to a doleful litany of difficulties that Bomber Command was facing which he presented to the Air Staff. But by then Newall too had developed second thoughts and he was able to give his subordinate the happy news that his 'statement is now incorrect. I have recently decided to abrogate the decision by which five Blenheim squadrons were to be re-equipped and trained in the alternative role of fighters'.[27] Quite how or why the decision was taken is mysterious but the seven-week gap between complaint and reply, together with the needless and pompous verbiage, points to an arbitrary decision. The Cabinet's enthusiasm for the project appeared to have evaporated if it had ever truly existed.

The Blenheim fighter was never more than an improvisation. All of the seven squadrons that were scheduled to operate Blenheim fighters in April 1939 were set to be operating Defiants a year later.[28] Those Blenheims that were fitted with the gun-pack lingered on at the fringes of Fighter Command's inventory with a couple of squadrons operating the version. They were used in the Battle of France briefly, but in one operation lost five out of six planes to Bf 110s, which were hardly the Luftwaffe's premier air superiority fighter.[29] Perhaps, fortunately, they do not appear to have been committed in the Battle of Britain where they would have been easy meat for Luftwaffe fighters and only marginally capable against unescorted Luftwaffe bombers, even if they had been put into action in daytime. They served briefly and mostly ineffectually as night fighters during the early phases of the Blitz when the RAF's desperate shortage of any aircraft suitable for the role led to desperate expedients.

***

The declared switch in favour of fighters was not popular amongst the Air Staff. The die-hard Trenchardians at the top saw it as a wrong turning. Slessor, one of the most vocal and effective spokesmen of the school, at least recognized that the bomber lobby had fallen into a trap, which they had played a large part in constructing:

> It is unfortunate that our quite natural and proper obsession with a Knock-Out Blow against this country has forced us to concentrate on a type of fighter and a static fighter defence organization, at the expense of our capacity to assist easily in resistance to a Knock-Out Blow against France.[30]

The Air Staff moved swiftly to draw a line in the sand to ward off the danger that fighters might gain further ground on the bombers. The Deputy Director of Operations, Group Captain Donald Stevenson, was set to work drafting a lengthy paper explaining that Scheme M was going as far as needed – implicitly too far – in providing fighter protection. Despite taking a series of worst-case assumptions in favour of the Luftwaffe, he claimed that a force of 800 fighters would be able to inflict prohibitive losses on the attackers. He concluded with a ringing assertion of accepted doctrine that only a counter-offensive by bombers could do any further damage to the German effort and that the Air Staff regarded '50 squadrons … as all that can usefully done with Fighters in the defence of this country'. This read rather too obviously as a direct manifesto for Trenchardianism of the kind that the Air Staff had been bombarding all and sundry with for years, so the next iteration of the paper was a far more subtle production. It retained the projection that the 800 fighters would severely maul the Luftwaffe despite a worst-case scenario in favour of the attackers, but insidiously undermined the dangerous Dowdingian optimism of the first version. It inserted the truism that no fighter force could stop every single bomber. The first version had foreseen the risk that it might occasionally be needed to institute wasteful standing patrols of fighters; in the second version, this became a firm forecast that would require a fighter force 'so colossal as to be impracticable'. The clunky Trenchardian slogan was dropped, an ostensibly contingency scenario was inserted in which counter-bombing was the only form of defence: Luftwaffe raids being maintained at night or in cloudy or foggy conditions. The only risk taken here was expecting that a reader would not spot the false implication that RDF would be ineffective in poor visibility. The paper rounded off the work of undermining faith in fighter defence by coming up with the notion that the scheme might actually lumber Fighter Command with too many fighters which would 'saturate' the RAF's ability to control them from the ground.

In the event Dowding was never burdened by the task of managing such an embarrassment of wealth. The Air Staff's true order of priorities meant he would have to stand at the back of the queue for extra aircraft. The fighter force with which he had to fight the Battle of Britain in the summer of 1940 was approximately 600 aircraft. This was around the figure for 640 fighters authorized before Scheme M was launched more than a year and a half before. In the year to March 1940 the fighter force was set to show a net expansion of precisely two aircraft, admittedly more modern types. The one concrete move to improve the fighter force in the wake of Munich was a comparatively modest order for 200 extra Spitfires placed in November 1938.[31] In total, the RAF at home was set to expand by one-third, but bombers, above all heavy bombers, would account for the vast bulk of the increase. Only in 1941 would fighter strength reach the magic figure of 800.

Chapter 35

A Gross Misuse of Air Forces

Rivalry between armed services is as old as warfare though relations between navies and armies up to the twentieth century were contained by the limited scope for it to affect operations of war. The history of Britain's imperial campaigns is littered with tales of failure and mutual recrimination (and some stunning successes). The advent of military aviation moved the rivalry onto new planes. At the simplest level, the addition of a third party multiplied the complexity of the relationships. Military aviation had the flexibility to affect both the land and the sea battles. Britain was several decades in advance of anywhere else in the world in having an independent air force as an armed service separate to navy and army so there was no foreign experience to offer guidance. Conflict between the RAF and the older services was likely to have happened under any circumstances, but personalities lent it an especially nasty edge. There is little excuse for the tactics of Admiral Beatty in his campaign to hobble the RAF in the 1920s. Trenchard's aggressive fights for pre-eminence in colonial policing were bound to create ill-will. The Trenchard doctrine that subordination to either of the older services was wasteful and inefficient became the unshakable orthodoxy in the Air Staff. The Air Staff was ever alert and hostile to any attempt to encroach on the independence of the RAF. Any practical discussion of how the RAF might coordinate its work in wartime with the other services had to be conducted in the shadow of this wider question of principle.

It is one of the mild curiosities of the way in which the RAF came into being that there was very little indication that the relationship between Royal Naval Air Service (RNAS) and the Royal Flying Corps (RFC) with their parent services caused serious problems. To begin with there was no pressure for independence from the operational level. The RNAS was peripheral to Royal Navy operations in the First World War. The turf fights between the Royal Navy and the army over the role of their air services were as much an extension of their traditional disputes and precursors to the turf fights between the independent RAF and the older services. The RFC and Trenchard himself made their reputations providing services to the army. It was only after the divorce that the younger partner began to assert that such a relationship was structurally abusive. In the words of Air Ministry mandarin Sir Maurice Dean, 'Between 1918 and 1939 the RAF forgot how to support the Army.'[1]

In the First World War advances in aviation technology had been driven by military applications. New technology was shaped by the requirements of the battlefield and applied immediately to it. Impractical innovations and techniques could be discarded instantly if they failed the acid text of combat. As the RAF rearmed it faced a quite different paradigm. Aircraft technology made gigantic strides in the 1930s and this was applied to both military and civil aircraft but it was overwhelmingly in the civil sphere that it could be tested in practice. Relations between major industrial nations were tense but there was practically no warfare. The RAF could not but acknowledge that only limited data was available and that its strategy had to be devised on the basis of theory not experience. It was thus of immense interest when the Spanish Civil War broke out in 1936. Nazi Germany, Fascist Italy and the Soviet Union quickly sent their air forces to assist their ideological clients – respectively Franco's conservative insurgents and the ever-more Communist-dominated Republicans – only very lightly disguised as idealistic volunteers or mercenaries. Each side sent its latest aircraft designs into action; the Germans, at least, were aware that this was giving valuable direct experience of combat.

The British authorities were equally interested in studying the lessons from a war between major industrialized powers, all making extensive use of air forces. The Joint Intelligence Committee set up a special sub-committee to investigate the topic, which yielded four reports on specific aspects of air war in Spain. These were put to a high-level meeting in October 1937, ostensibly of the Chiefs of Staff, but the presence of three Cabinet ministers shows the importance attached to the discussion.[2] The meeting was chaired by Sir Thomas Inskip and was attended by the two of the service ministers: Lord Swinton, the air minister, and Leslie Hore-Belisha, the war minister; only Duff Cooper, the First Lord of the Admiralty, was not there.

One of the reports dealt in detail with 'Low Flying Attacks on Ground Forces' and cannot have made agreeable reading for Newall. It gave ample evidence of how effective aircraft were in influencing the ground battle and concluded:

> In every report of mobile military operations stress has been laid on the positive effects of aircraft operating in conjunction with the successful forces or on the negative and demoralizing effects of the absence of aircraft and/or A.A. artillery.[3]

The report quoted examples of aircraft operating successfully in both attack and in defence or counter-attack. Hore-Belisha pointed these sections out with the implicit suggestion that the RAF might consider adopting such tactics. This earned him the stinging rebuke from Newall that this would be 'a gross misuse of air forces'. Newall clearly believed that using air forces to support ground operations was not merely wrong-headed but actively damaging as he went on to express the hope that the Italians had indeed succumbed to the temptation of committing such an error.

The controversy over using air forces in support of ground forces stifled the development of a clear picture of Britain's potential enemies. When an army intelligence officer learned that the Luftwaffe was in practice subordinated to the German army – notably because well-placed Luftwaffe officers complained about this – he mentioned this in lectures that he gave to the Imperial Defence College, which had students from all three services.[4] He was ordered to stop making any comment on how the German air force might be used in war. Giving publicity to a heretical strategy was tantamount to endorsing it.

The debate between army and RAF was venomous but had little practical significance for most of the interwar period. Even as rearmament got under way the relationship between the junior services lay in the realms of theory and hypothesis. The army was the least important of the three services in the process. It was taken for granted that the British army would never again participate seriously in a full-scale European war, so the question of army/air force inter-operation was moot anyway. Its principal task was seen as providing anti-aircraft artillery and searchlights to defend Britain against the Luftwaffe. Much of the widespread visceral anti-war sentiment that dominated public and political thinking up to the end of 1938 was rooted in horror at the mass slaughter on the Western Front and it was inconceivable that Britain would once again send a mass army to fight on the battlefields of Europe. There was provision for a token field force of a handful of divisions; in late 1935, the army and RAF had agreed informally on the size of the RAF force that would accompany it on a foreign deployment. In December 1935, the government formally authorized a field force that was even smaller than the original project which implied a corresponding reduction in the call on RAF resources. In early 1939, the Air Staff was expecting to send only four squadrons of fighters to France with the Field Force.[5] The RAF did acknowledge the army's need for aircraft support but attached little priority to it. As the army cooperation derivative of the versatile Hawker Hart, the Audax, reached the end of its useful life, the RAF designed a replacement. The Westland Lysander's chief role was low-level reconnaissance and, as though to remove temptation from the army's reach, had minimal ground-attack capacity. It proved an abject failure in the Battle of France in May 1940, although its short take-off and landing capacity later gave it a quite unexpected role flying resistance and intelligence personnel and supplies into and out of occupied France.

Things changed dramatically in March 1939 when Germany flagrantly breached the Munich agreements by invading the rump of Czechoslovakia, swiftly followed by Mussolini's invasion of Albania. The hollowness of Chamberlain's triumph in securing 'peace for our time' and his policy of appeasing the dictators was pitilessly exposed and his political survival depended on a display of resolution and he was driven to a series of panic measures. Britain guaranteed Poland and Rumania against German aggression and the government bowed to long-standing pressure to create a Ministry of Supply, a totemic reincarnation of the First World War's Ministry of Munitions. Chamberlain went one step further and, with minimal planning or strategic calculation, announced that the volunteer Territorial Army was to be doubled in size. Peacetime conscription was then introduced for the first time ever to meet the crippling manpower shortage of the army. The size of the Field Force authorized for dispatch overseas soared to sixteen divisions in the first six months of a war, doubling to thirty-two divisions in the next six months. In the space of weeks Britain had been committed to full-scale participation in a European land war. A fundamental assumption that had governed British military policy since the end of the First World War was discarded overnight to keep the prime minister in Downing Street.

To meet its new mission the army proceeded to scale up its demands for RAF support and did so in a way that might have been carefully calculated to provoke the Air Staff to the maximum. It had already given advance warning that the Chief of the Imperial General Staff, General Ironside, did not 'altogether agree' with Slessor's publicly stated contention that the 'aircraft is not a battlefield weapon.' Under the title 'Services Required from the Royal Air Force for the Field Force', the army presented a comprehensive shopping list in June 1939.[6] Even worse, Ironside explicitly called for aircraft to be available for close support operations, citing the example of Spain as proof of their value in this role. He also touched on the fundamental issue of control of air forces and sought to amend a legacy of the air force's divorce from the army: the proposition that 'the Army has no established right to assistance in war from any Royal Air force resources other than the Royal Air Force component of the Field Force'. He cited a questionable precedent in a public commitment that Sir Samuel Hoare had made in 1923 when he was air minister that the

> The Admiralty will demand what they require from the Air Ministry and the Air Ministry will provide it.

Ironside went even further in asking that the commander of the Field Force should have a 'recognised call on the Air Striking Force'; in other words, a single local army commander was to have a claim over the RAF's entire bomber strength. Ironside was seeking little less than the position that ruled before the RFC was removed from army control and injected into the RAF.

The Air Staff responded with predictable fury. It was Slessor, Newall's closest adviser, who led the charge with a combination of contempt for soldiers, intellectual dishonesty and enthusiastic bureaucratic turf fighting. Slessor admitted that he was adopting a lecturing tone but insisted that this was what was required with soldiers and a vital point of principle was at stake.[7] His first complaint was the scale of the army's demands for aircraft: 'they have opened their mouths as wide as possible quite regardless of practical considerations and, indeed of tactical requirements.'[8] He returned to the Air Staff's old stamping ground of manipulating statistics on the German armed forces to support the RAF's case. He contrasted unfavourably the British army's requirements for air support per division with what he calculated as far lower figures for the German army, but he quite ignored the fact that Luftwaffe bombers were tasked to support the army even if they had no formal linkage. He addressed the complaint that the army would have no call on the RAF's by simply denying this was the case. The issue of control was fundamental; only the Air Staff could know how bombers could be 'of the most decisive importance'. The Air Staff claimed it had plans to use them in conjunction with the Field Force and the French army to resist a German invasion through the Low Countries. There is no sign that these plans for the RAF to become involved in the ground war had ever been discussed with the army, assuming they existed at all in anything more than the most rudimentary form. Predictably, he accused the army of having 'absorbed false lessons from recent campaigns in Spain and China'. In his solution only army cooperation (reconnaissance) aircraft would be directly affiliated to army units. Fighters could serve in France but as part of an integrated, autonomous air defence organization responsible for covering defined geographical sectors not the Field Force. Any bomber requirements were to be met by Bomber Command via the British Air Mission in France, a purely RAF body.[9]

Slessor lay at the extreme Trenchardian end of the spectrum of views that were kicked around inside the Air Staff as it prepared its response to the army's demands. In Slessor's words there were to be 'negotiations' with War Office over, 'Many points with which we cannot agree'.[10] Others were more inclined to compromise. Perhaps reflecting his background from outside the RAF's bomber inner circle, Sholto Douglas took a more generous view, and even embraced the heresy that the evidence from Spain might 'raise a doubt' as to the belief that the aircraft was not a battlefield weapon. 'Not in my mind,' pencilled Slessor on Douglas's comment.[11] The airmen had to steer a careful path to avoid leaving the army with so little that it might seek an organic air arm of its own on the pattern of the Fleet Air Arm.[12] Another ball to juggle was that the RAF's strategic shift towards ever-larger bombers meant it would have even fewer aircraft suitable for battlefield operations.[13]

Slessor spotted an opportunity to turn the situation to the RAF's advantage: 'it is sometimes possible in practice to obtain money for one purpose which could not be obtained if it were to be applied to another purpose. In other words, we might get an addition to our total strength for this purpose [supporting the army] which we could not get for purposes which we approve.'[14] Army demands for battlefield support might be parlayed into extra bombers for strategic missions. If the Germans allotted 450 aircraft to army support, the RAF had a claim on the same number 'in addition to our strategical bomber force'.

Slessor had set the scene for another statistical swerve. When the two services sat down to discuss the issue, the RAF took the offensive and outflanked the army's claim to have a say in how the air force was used with the promise that more planes would be available to help the army without committing itself to delivering this help. The army representatives might thus have been taken aback when the RAF began to talk up the number of German aircraft that would have to be reckoned with. Having previously ignored short-range Luftwaffe bombers - dive-bombers in other words - they now had to be taken into account. The War Office figure for a close support force requirement of 288 aircraft should thus be increased to 488. As the RAF's future long-range bombers might not be suitable for the work, the Air Staff said it was working on a specification for a short-range light bomber. This might refer to a short-lived project that was also used to fob off Bomber Command's requests for a dedicated reconnaissance aircraft or the freakish F.11/37 turret fighter and ground-attack plane; nothing came of either.[15] The crucial issue of who would control the bombers was fudged in two ways. The RAF proposed a supreme commander for all British forces in France with a joint staff at the top level of command and beneath this – implicitly co-equal – an army commander of the Field Force and two RAF officers commanding the bombers and air defence respectively. Next, the nitty-gritty of each aspect of air operations was to be addressed by a dedicated sub-committee. As the RAF team on the key bombing sub-committee was to include Slessor, the prospects for a harmonious outcome were not great. It was going to have to deal with 'some very controversial issues'.[16]

The matter was not treated with any great urgency and on the last day of July 1939, a month later, the bombing sub-committee had not met, nor, apparently, had a specific date been set for a meeting. There is no sign that it had met before war broke out and the Field Force was dispatched to France with no more air support than had been originally planned. The formal directive issued to the Advanced Air Striking Force (AASF) after the start of the war was signed by Slessor and shows his concept firmly in the ascendant.[17] The AASF was 'entirely independent, as regards command and control, of any British or French land or air formations in France'. Any call on its services by the Field Force would normally have to be routed back to London and the Chiefs of Staffs. In time of 'real crisis involving critical danger to the land forces in France' the Head of the British Air Mission was permitted to use his own discretion. In the event the Fairey Battles of the AASF were committed to try to halt the German breakthrough in May 1940 and were slaughtered to no avail. This has helped leave a legacy of confusion over the intended role of the AASF, fuelled by an inexplicable error in the Official History.[18]

There was little change in this position until the Germans attacked in May 1940. Newall told Ludlow-Hewitt that the Battles of the AASF might be used 'prudently' against an assault on the Maginot Line with the theoretical possibility that a 'critical situation' such as a German breakthrough might justify the use of British heavy bombers.[19] When practicalities were discussed with the army, it was clear that this was not a welcome possibility:

> [The] Air Ministry and especially Slessor are trying to get out of the task [air action against advancing Germans] at every turn, reserving themselves as much as they can for the Ruhr attack.[20]

The Battles were duly massacred in futile attacks on the advancing Germans, losing half their strength in two days, whilst the remainder of Bomber Command was conserved for the supposedly decisive operations against the Ruhr of WA5.

Chapter 36

You Can Stand up to Hitler Now

In the ears of Downing Street Sir Charles Bruce-Gardner remained the most powerful voice on the question of air rearmament. Apart from brief forays into the detail of policy such as the big-bomber battle, Chamberlain was content to work on the simplistic picture that Bruce-Gardner supplied him via Wilson. Bruce-Gardner remained very much in favour with Wilson, feeding him a detailed account of developments at the Air Ministry, together with a French journalist's estimate of French and German aircraft output as though normal Civil Service channels and the British intelligence machine were somehow unreliable.[1] Bruce-Gardner also supplied Wilson with ammunition to use against Churchill's demand that a Ministry of Supply should be established. He spun his evidence to suggest that the creation of a Ministry of Supply would lead the air marshals to practise the heresy that he had detected in Lord Swinton, of putting the production of modern planes ahead of the output of large numbers of older types. Bruce-Gardner recognized the overwhelming force of crude numbers even if they had been dumped as a formal commitment: 'I do not believe Parliament will allow Baldwin's parity formula to go away.'[2]

The raw numbers finally delivered the result that Wilson had striven for on Chamberlain's behalf. In early April 1939, Bruce-Gardner reported that monthly output had nearly quadrupled from the levels of early 1938 and was set to rise further.[3] Delightedly, Wilson passed this on to Chamberlain with the rider, 'If you want to stand up to Hitler now, you can do so.'[4] This casts an important light on Chamberlain's policy in other areas afterwards. It is debatable whether he would have taken steps such as the introduction of conscription if the air picture had not given him confidence. By the summer of 1939 Bruce-Gardner was cheerfully telling his patron, Montagu Norman, Governor of the Bank of England, that he was now 'well satisfied' with aircraft production.[5] Both Wilson and Bruce-Gardner were correct as far as crude, total numbers went, but there were still ample grounds for concern when the detail was examined.

Bruce-Gardner spread his new confidence in Britain's air might widely and claimed personal credit for the rise in production.[6] He went even further than Wilson in overstating the extent to which his work was altering the balance of power in Europe to a group that included the press baron Lord Rothermere and Professor Lindemann: 'our curve of preparation is rising so swiftly that if there is no war before September, the Axis will not risk it.' His confidence in the superiority of the new British plane types surpassed even Newall's optimism for the Stirling and its stablemates in that they were 'infinitely superior to anything the Germans have'.

It was not just Downing Street that had reason to be grateful to Bruce-Gardner. The level of profits that the plane-makers would earn on all this new business was a topic of great interest since rearmament got under way in 1934. Much of the Labour Party objection to rearmament of any kind was rooted in elemental hatred of all business profits, magnified by visceral anti-military sentiment. The unilateralist pacifist MP Frederick Pethick-Lawrence was one of the industry's sternest parliamentary critics. Enthusiastic stock market promotion of newly floated plane-making companies injected an unpleasant atmosphere of spivvery into the whole process, although as usual in such equity booms, it was the bankers and brokers who did better than the speculators.[7] The Treasury, with so notably hawkish a Chancellor of the Exchequer as Neville Chamberlain at the helm, was also determined to obtain value for the taxpayers' money. The Air Ministry itself was keen to keep costs down. Control of profitability through the terms of the contracts through which the companies dealt with the Air Ministry featured a series of tortuous negotiations between government and industry in which the latter was represented by the iconic Scottish chartered accountant Sir William McLintock. The resulting deals were known as the McLintock Agreements and they were no more successful than any such exercise before or since in keeping both sides happy.

As in all commercial arrangements, it is normal for participants not to brag openly of how beneficial these agreements might be, but there are good signs that the SBAC's members had every reason to be happy with what Bruce-Gardner had achieved on their behalf. The most conspicuous winner appears to have been Fairey Aviation, which casts an amusing sidelight on a furious letter that Richard Fairey wrote to *The Times* in 1936 complaining of comments in the House of Commons by Pethick-Lawrence and a colleague in which the plane-makers were accused of being rogues. This was in Fairey's view an ignorant 'appeal to prejudice'. In the event, between 1935 and 1938 the profits of Fairey Aviation multiplied tenfold to £395,000 and for 1938 the shareholders received an extra bonus of twice the regular dividend. Fairey cheerfully informed his shareholders of the deal to produce Battles at the Nuffield shadow factory and assured them that the payments the company received under the arrangements would not be set off against the company's revenue from regular plane delivery contracts to the Air Ministry. Right at the start of the shadow factory scheme, Fairey had made sure that it would be paid royalties for Battles produced by the shadows and was now reaping the benefit.[8] Shadow production of Blenheims also featured in the happy picture painted to shareholders of Bristol Aviation as its profits doubled to £378,000 between 1936 and 1938, although they had to be content with a rather more niggardly dividend policy.

The Handley Page company was more astute in keeping its declared profits more or less unchanged at 1937 levels for the two succeeding years. The Air Ministry was especially alert to Handley Page's profit margins and saw 'strong political objections' to allowing the firm to increase what were already viewed as high profits. The ministry acknowledged that Handley Page had high profit margins because it was efficient but was deeply reluctant to grant it a fixed price on a batch of Hampdens, which would have been particularly lucrative.[9] Publicly the firm blamed its flat profits on government limitations on profitability, but did point out this was the highest level profits had reached since the company was listed on the London Stock Exchange. It could also be noted that the company's balance sheet improved dramatically, going from an overdraft of £53,000 in 1936 to cash plus investments of £446,000 two years later, which suggests a healthy trading environment. In the time-honoured dictum of investment analysts, profit is an opinion but cash is a fact.

The Hawker Siddeley group was the most important single plane-making company of the period and it arose from a series of mergers and takeovers in the early 1930s. Eventually it owned Hawkers of Hurricane fame; Gloster who made the RAF's last biplane fighter, the Gladiator; Sir W. G. Armstrong Whitworth, maker of the Whitley; and A. V. Roe, most famous for the Avro Lancaster and its unhappy parent, the Manchester, but also the maker of the RAF's unspectacular but dependable maid-of-all-work the Anson, which stayed in production until 1952, by which time no fewer than 11,000 had been made. Its fortunes provide a bellweather for the industry but in keeping with the practice of the time did not publish full consolidated accounts for all its businesses. What it did reveal, though, shows a very healthy picture. The first annual meeting of the company in its final, expanded form took place in 1936 and the shareholders were told that the company had taken in £503,000 from its subsidiaries from which they were being paid a healthy dividend of 30 per cent plus a one for ten bonus issue of new shares. The financial picture brightened further over the next two years' trading with income rising to £783,000 in 1936/7 and then to £822,000 the following year; the loss on a contract to supply civil aircraft to Imperial Airways held back results in 1937/8. The shareholders were rewarded with an increase in the dividend to 32 per cent and another 10 per cent bonus, this time in cash and not just shares. Supposedly for security reasons few details were published of the operating businesses, but in 1938 it did give figures for the aggregated stock and work in progress at all the companies owned by Hawker Siddeley as a once-off disclosure which gave a snapshot of the progress. The figure was up by about half to £6.4 million which points to a similar increase in turnover. The company cheerfully admitted that government controls – which it willingly endorsed – meant that profit margins had fallen but still allowed profits to rise in the absolute. The company was especially proud to have been chosen to operate two shadow factories, being built at a cost to the government of more than £2 million. This was, however, less lucrative than raking in royalties for the production of designs at shadow factories owned by other companies such as Fairey and Bristol were doing which entailed no cost. In Hawker Siddeley's case these factories manufactured aircraft designed by group companies: Hurricanes at Hucclecote and Avro bombers at Manchester. Nothing was said of the fact that Hawker was still selling Hind biplanes to Irak on a purely commercial basis, which held back output of Hurricanes for the RAF.[10]

All told, 1938 was something of an annus mirabilis for the planemakers with every major firm in the business expanding its capacity to meet government orders, mostly financed wholly or in part by the government itself. Rates of production had doubled and were still accelerating. And this was translating itself into improved profitability because the Air Ministry had done away with the old system of piecemeal orders by the middle of the year. In turn, the key influence here was the establishment of Committee on Supply in the spring of 1938 where the Treasury flourished a, for once, open chequebook as well as the appointment of Sir Charles Bruce-Gardner, officially as chairman of the plane-makers trade association, the SBAC, and unofficially as the government's plane-making czar with a direct line to Downing Street. It was Bruce-Gardner's pro-business approach that had spelt the end for Swinton with his preference for quality over quantity as air minister.

Chapter 37

The Result of Overexpansion

The furious circular that Sir Cyril Newall wrote in response to the air minister's public comments in November 1938 denying that there had been a shift in policy in favour of fighters duly arrived at the headquarters of Bomber Command in Hillingdon, along with the all the major units of the service. The letter reaffirmed Trenchard's hallowed doctrine that bombing was the only means of defence and insisted that this had been in no way changed by Scheme M's concession to fighter defence. It provoked a surprising reaction considering that it was a document that spelled out Bomber Command's unique and special status in the service as the arm which was dedicated to fulfilling the RAF's historic role as the vector of its offensive mission.

Newall's resounding letter rang hollow to Sir Edgar Ludlow-Hewitt, the man charged with the practical reality of giving the RAF the offensive capacity. He fully endorsed the mission as set out by Newall, but was enraged at the gulf between the complacent theory emanating from Adastral House and the routine struggles to make a reality of the Air Staff's vaulting visions, which he had been fighting since he took command more than a year before, and which he had set out often and clearly. Whilst Ludlow-Hewitt was stuck in the morass of welding into combat-ready shape a force that had been vastly expanded, and completely re-equipped, Newall was telling the RAF that the new programme would create 'a bomber force at least comparable in striking power' with the Luftwaffe's bomber arm.[1] This would form 'an essential component in any system of air defence'. Ludlow-Hewitt might have asked himself what he was supposed to be working on with the previous programme. He had begged for expansion to be paused to allow the measures already undertaken to be properly digested, but now Newall was signalling that he was driving on remorselessly with a fresh programme.

Ludlow-Hewitt drafted a letter of bitter complaint, which practically accused the Air Staff of sabotage. It threw the goals set out in Newall's letter back in the face of his commander:

> I now feel compelled to express my grave anxiety at the manner in which this policy as expressed by the Air Staff appears to be progressively neglected in principle and threatens to be abandoned in effect.[2]

He proceeded to enumerate the specific points on which he felt that his command was being hurt by the decisions of the Air Staff. The 'real value' of Bomber Command was far adrift of the CAS's grandiose vision. Ludlow-Hewitt appears to have held his hand and not to have sent the letter to the Air Ministry, but over the succeeding months a blizzard of paper did fly from Hillingdon to Adastral House on Kingsway which had the same intent. Relations between the commander of the RAF's most important operating unit and the RAF's staff practically broke down into outright hostility. Ludlow-Hewitt had no confidence in the effectiveness of the force he commanded and felt that the Air Staff was not merely failing to help him improve this, but making decisions that actively damaged his force. The squabble showed both sides at their worst: Ludlow-Hewitt inconsistent, querulous, sunk in detail, poorly focused and ineffectual; the Air Staff, including its chief, complacent, high-handed, dilatory and unwilling to face unpleasant realities. Writing long afterwards in his memoirs Slessor accepted that Ludlow-Hewitt had good reason for his concerns even if he was sometimes 'unduly pessimistic'; crucially Slessor admitted that 'he did not err as much on that side [pessimism] as much as we did in the Air Ministry on the side of optimism'.[3]

Ludlow-Hewitt's litany of complaints embraced almost every aspect of Bomber Command, naturally including the points set out in his 1937 annual report and the after-action analysis that followed Munich. At the top of the list came the availability of competent personnel and deficiencies in training, amplified by the obstacles that Ludlow-Hewitt saw in the way of an effective training regime. He was also increasingly concerned about the ability of the types of aircraft that equipped Bomber Command to perform their missions. The 'inadequate armament and ineffective performance' of the Fairey Battles meant that they were not fit to be counted in the strength of the RAF to set against the Luftwaffe.

Ludlow-Hewitt touched on another fundamental issue in crew training when he recognized that it was costly and inefficient for bomber crews to move directly from simple, basic, elementary trainers to the first-line aircraft.[4] Yet again, this was not something that had been thought about when the move to big bombers was mandated. The Air Staff accepted the principle of needing an intermediate trainer aircraft but there was still an active debate as to what types would be suitable for the task.[5] Perhaps, fortunately, the stalwart Avro Anson utility aircraft, which was no longer fit for front-line combat, was available in large numbers to be pressed into service.

The practical flying experience of even middle-ranking officers in the Air Staff had been obtained in the easy and simple days of one- or two-man biplanes. Pilots were invariably commissioned officers and the man in the rear cockpit was often as not an untrained junior aircraftman whose main job was aircraft maintenance on the ground from whom little was expected beyond shooting skills appropriate for a fairground range; the air gunners were 'drawn from a comparatively uneducated class of society'.[6] This policy was still current in the middle of 1938 and was vigorously criticized by Ludlow-Hewitt.[7]

Ludlow-Hewitt was increasingly anxious about the ability of his bombers to defend themselves. The Battles and Blenheims that made up the bulk of his force carried only two machine guns each. Worse, he had doubts about the effectiveness of the powered gun turrets which had become a cornerstone of bomber design. He and colleagues recognized that air gunnery had become a far more skilful task and demanded a correspondingly professional approach: 'It seems poor economy to spend vast sums of money on expensive aircraft and on the training of pilots and mechanics to a high standard of skill if the air gunners, on whom the safety of the aircraft will depend in war, are half trained and inefficient.'[8] Ludlow-Hewitt came perilously close to recognizing that the entire defensive armament thinking that had dominated bomber design was flawed. He saw the value of what was otherwise the best bomber in his inventory, the Vickers Wellington, as compromised by the poor field of fire of its tail turret.[9] With a remarkable humane sentiment, he felt that tail turrets generally were impossibly exposed and terrifying stations. The Air Staff did share one of Ludlow-Hewitt's concerns: the desirability of installing cannon with their far greater hitting power in defensive turrets. Detailed studies of the practicality of cannon turrets revealed almost insuperable difficulties, but the Air Staff was blandly confident that they would soon feature on bombers.[10] When Bomber Command actually entered combat, Ludlow-Hewitt's doubts proved to be more than valid. They were to be proved again when the US Eighth Air Force launched its daylight raids on Germany: unescorted bombers were simply unable to defend themselves against faster and more manoeuvrable fighters.

A new theme for 1939 was the erosion of numbers of aircraft available to Bomber Command for its primary mission. Ludlow-Hewitt amply showed the truth of the charge of inconsistency levelled against him, by reversing the enthusiastic stance he had taken on the conversion of Blenheims to fighters at the time of Munich. A short-lived project to deploy more Blenheims in another air defence role – dropping small bombs on attacking German formations ('scatter bombing') – also attracted his ire. Having clamoured for months for the Bomber Development Unit to be established, he now complained that one of his squadrons of Wellingtons was to be allocated to it. Ludlow-Hewitt was even willing to challenge long-held shibboleths of the Air Staff on the kinds of aircraft that were needed. He asked for the question of long-range fighters, in other words escorts for bombers, to be investigated. Ludlow-Hewitt broke with the Air Staff's all big-bomber policy by asking as matter of urgency for a 'speed bomber' which could also carry out vitally needed target reconnaissance.

Ludlow-Hewitt's campaign got under way properly with his Bomber Command efficiency report for 1938, circulated in March 1939. One section addressed the root cause of the challenges that he faced. It was headed bluntly, 'Results of Over Expansion'. When it arrived at Adastral House, more junior members of the Air Staff recognized that it raised urgent and important questions that deserved to be handled at high level, up to and including bringing in the air minister, but as the debate moved up the hierarchy towards the CAS, the enthusiasm for serious action dwindled sharply.[11] Newall disapproved of precipitate action. A committee composed exclusively of staff officers from Adastral House discussed the report, agreed to address a few minor practical issues, firmly told Ludlow-Hewitt that the RAF had long ago decided against escort fighters and passed some unspecified questions up to the Air Council.

The Air Staff did not merely more or less ignore Ludlow-Hewitt's complaints, it also made a move that upset him deeply on a topic of policy very dear to his heart: aircraft navigation. The level of training of pilots was to be lowered steeply and that of observers improved so that they would be able to carry out the navigation of the aircraft.[12] The move had been under discussion but the official circular setting out the new arrangements was dated three days before the handwritten date of Ludlow-Hewitt's new letter, so this might have been the straw that broke the camel's back, prompting him to launch an updated version of the missile that Newall's letter had provoked months before. The new letter did not refer specifically to the new training regime so Ludlow-Hewitt might have written it weeks before. He stopped short of reviving his claim that the Air Staff's actions were positively harmful to his command, but stated that the solution to his problems lay in 'higher policy', a light code for the decisions of the Air Staff. He did include an unvarnished statement that Bomber Command was hopelessly unready to fulfil the vision set out by Newall:

> I am, however, far from satisfied with the progress toward the attainment of this aim and I am bound to confess my conviction that under existing conditions we will not attain, within any predictable period, either to the strength or to the efficiency necessary to reach the standard envisaged.[13]

The ACAS Sholto Douglas made a gentler attempt to use the letter to jog the Air Staff into action with no greater effect.[14]

There the matter might have rested but somehow Ludlow-Hewitt's letter came to the attention of the air minister Sir Kingsley Wood in early July, six weeks after it was written. It did not take the most finely tuned political antennae to spot that Newall's policy of trying to ignore Ludlow-Hewitt's complaints was untenable. Wood declared himself 'astonished' at the delay in replying to 'an extremely important document containing as it did an indictment of the Air Council and the Air Staff which demanded urgent and serious consideration'.[15] Newall accused Ludlow-Hewitt of taking an unrealistically pessimistic view of the inevitably consequences of expansion and re-equipment and tried to fob his minister off with the claim that Ludlow-Hewitt was merely writing 'for posterity' and to 'clear himself in the event of a catastrophe', but Wood would not be deterred and pressed for an answer to be sent to Ludlow-Hewitt with a minimum of delay.[16]

The only substantial piece of positive news for Ludlow-Hewitt was hardly a major concession by the Air Staff which had never liked the scheme: the number of Blenheim squadrons converting to the fighter role was being cut back sharply. The Air Ministry accepted Ludlow-Hewitt's argument for the creation of the BDU but pointed to the huge practical difficulty of finding an area of country suitable for the project and which did not attract apparently insuperable opposition from local landowners and organizations dedicated to the protection of rural England. Otherwise, the Air Ministry blankly refused to accept Ludlow-Hewitt's contention that it was impossible to see when Bomber Command would be ready for war.[17] The Air Ministry expressed sympathy for Ludlow-Hewitt's position but he would just have to carry on. Even though Ludlow-Hewitt was in practice echoing the fears which had prompted the then CAS Ellington to resist major expansion in 1934, his views received no support from that quarter.[18] Ellington, who was filling the more-or-less honorary role of Inspector General of the RAF, was more concerned to defend his own legacy and was anxious to rebut the suggestion that 'forethought or energy' might have been lacking. A distinct hint of uneasiness can be detected in Ellington's response which mentioned that Ludlow-Hewitt had been DCAS and should share the blame for any weaknesses arising from the specification of the now current generation of bombers. He advanced a decidedly defensive argument that these had been specified at a time when powered gun turrets were at an early stage of development, which suggests that he recognized that the system was imperfect.

Ludlow-Hewitt was anything but mollified and issued a veiled threat that he might refuse to take Bomber Command into war in its present state.[19] This was enough to panic the Air Staff into action. Ludlow-Hewitt was invited to attend what was practically a peace conference and the various directorates of the Air Ministry were set to work to provide answers for his detailed points, which were entered in a long and imposing table.[20] The RAF establishment was accusing Ludlow-Hewitt of trying to cover his back but this was an instinct that the organization appreciated to the full.

Ludlow-Hewitt attended the Air Council meeting almost exactly a month before war broke out. The encounter was a damp squib. Ludlow-Hewitt ducked the opportunity to insist that Bomber Command was not ready for war and produced an almost entirely new topic for concern: whether bombing should be conducted from high or low altitude and how pilots should train for this. He was invited to come up with his

The Result of Overexpansion

suggestions for a site for the BDU and he was promised in the vaguest terms some action on the questions of air gunnery and the availability of reserve personnel to make good the anticipated combat losses.

***

Ludlow-Hewitt's message appears to have made some impact on the Air Staff's recognition of how far the RAF's bombers had to go to deliver on the RAF's promises. At the start of April 1939, the Air Staff issued a detailed paper on the form that air war with Germany might take.[21] The picture it painted was barely different to the one that had ruled during the Czechoslovakia crisis six months before:

> It is thus doubtful, in view of our present inferiority in air strength whether a counter-offensive, although directed against objectives ultimately vital to Germany's war effort, would cause any great reduction in the scale of German air attack on this country during the early weeks of a war.

This was rubbing the Air Staff's nose in the messy reality of implementing its previous expansion schemes, but in the middle of 1939, they were also confronted with growing evidence that their visionary heavy bomber scheme had built in excessively optimistic projections for what the new bombers would be capable of and how quickly they would be available.

In April 1939, Slessor confronted Newall with the bad news that the RAF was not going to be able to deliver on the promises of parity with Germany even with its treasured Stirlings, Halifaxes and Manchesters.[22] In part, Slessor's analysis featured a dubious intelligence picture of what the Germans were up to. On the basis of a single intelligence report, he believed that they were developing their own four-engine bomber and that these would make up a considerable part of the German bomber force by 1941. This was completely inaccurate. More realistically, Slessor expected the Germans to continue to expand the Luftwaffe beyond the 2,050 long-range bombers that had been predicted for April in the autumn to reach 2,500 or more by the summer of 1941. Just as he seemed to be crediting the German aircraft industry with extraordinary powers of new type development production, he seemed to expect that they would be able to bring the Czech industrial infrastructure that they had seized a month before into productive use.

Under the Newall regime intelligence on Germany had been used to support demands for an ever-larger RAF bomber force, but it was now being used to relativize a British failure that could be laid at the door of the Air Staff. The true substance of Slessor's paper was that the performance of the British big bombers was well below what had been expected. The bombload that the Stirling and Halifax could carry for the 2,000 round-trip needed to attack the heart of Germany was about a quarter less than originally thought. The cruising speeds of the Stirling was 10 per cent less than thought and the Manchester's 6 per cent down. This was blamed on the decision to fit extra equipment, notably armour, since the autumn.

Newall summoned all the top officers of the Air Staff to a crisis meeting to address the problems which came up with a blend of complacency and an instinct to see silver linings. Even though Germany's industrial resources now stretched into what had been Czechoslovakia, the air marshals decided that a range of only 1,5000 miles was adequate. Orders could be focused on the Halifax, the least disappointing new bomber. In time, more powerful engines would dispose of the performance question. A shopping list of extra bombers was duly prepared.

The question would not, however, go away. The air marshals found themselves floundering at an EPM which discussed it a few weeks later.[23] The junior air minister, Harold Balfour, smelt a rat. He could not believe that the reduced performance figures were entirely due to new equipment. Freeman, the Air Member for Development and Production, had to confess that the deliveries of the extra bombers might be pushed back to December 1941 from June. Another air marshal came up with a uniquely feeble claim that the extra equipment made the bombers more survivable and thus able to carry out more missions.

***

When the air staff drew up Bomber Command's rules of engagement as war became imminent, it displayed no greater enthusiasm for the prospect of committing the striking force to a significant offensive than it had the previous year during the Czechoslovakia crisis even though it was noticeably better equipped. The percentage of short-range Battles and Blenheims practically incapable of attacking Germany had fallen; of thirty-three fully operational squadrons in Bomber Command, sixteen were equipped with Battles and Blenheims and seventeen with longer-range Hampdens, Whitleys and Wellingtons.[24] The insistent instruction to 'conserve the bombers' did not reappear, but its spirit still dominated. Newall told Ludlow-Hewitt that, whilst things were better than at the time of Munich, 'It would be manifestly unwise to expend a high proportion of our best aircraft and crews at the very beginning when there are so many factors in air warfare of which we have to gain experience.'[25] The RAF was going to fight the Phoney War and nothing more adventurous. The same insistence on limiting objectives to purely military targets with no risk of civilian casualties was repeated. The Air Staff understood that that this meant that the RAF's ability to relieve pressure on the Poles was going to be limited.[26] The Foreign Secretary Lord Halifax complained that the 'severe restrictions' would upset Britain's allies.[27] A mere declaration of war without even a statement of what military action might be undertaken would neither awe the Germans nor comfort France or Poland. Halifax observed that it was unclear whether the RAF would be allowed to attack German air bases or the Siegfried Line (as the British called the *Westwall*) and asked for a formal mechanism to be put in place to soften the rules.

Chapter 38

The Miracles Proposed for Them

The gulf between the Air Staff and the operational commands almost had the flavour of the gulf observed in the First World War between the fighting units and the higher command installed safely in chateaux remote from the front. The balance of power lay clearly with the staff and the commands spoke with only a weak voice. It is easy to believe that Ludlow-Hewitt felt that no one was listening to his warnings as to the state of Bomber Command and the relationship between Sir Hugh Dowding at Bentley Priory and Adastral House was no better.

One of the weaknesses that Dowding detected early on in his tenure at Fighter Command was that the RAF's policy of using unpaved grass runways left his command exposed to the vagaries of British weather, with the risk that his aircraft would be unable to take off from waterlogged ground to intercept German bombers. This became painfully obvious in the very wet winter of 1936/7 which left all but one of his stations out of action, some for weeks.[1] Dowding launched a long and arduous campaign to secure all-weather runways for all or almost all his stations. Here he encountered a determined opponent in the shape of the Air Ministry's director of works, Colonel 'Conky Bill' Turner, who appeared to operate the works department as a state within a state. It was a telling illustration of the balance of power between the operational commands and the bureaucrats of Adastral House.[2] Predictably enough, Turner objected to the cost of runways and believed that improving drainage would solve the problem. He went further and decided that he was competent to judge questions of operational policy. He opposed hard runways as he felt that they would be difficult to camouflage, as far as can be told, entirely without reference to anyone else. Turner's instincts and ambitions went beyond mere facilities provision and management. He went on to make a wartime career as a builder of fake aerodromes and other deceptive schemes.[3] Even within the Air Staff it was recognized that Turner needed firm handling.[4]

There the matter rested until the end of 1938. The importance of all-weather surfaces for fighter airfields had become clear during the Czechoslovakia crisis when as an emergency measure clinker was distributed to improve surfacing in wet weather.[5] The opposition to Dowding's recommendation was also spotted at the top of the Air Staff and the question was asked as to what lay behind it.[6] This seems to have been sufficient to break the deadlock and the Deputy Chief of the Air Staff, Sholto Douglas, decided that the time had come to 'lay down a clear policy' for Turner, who had decided to go over to France to investigate a system of metal grilles as an alternative to hard surfaces.[7] Newall finally signed off the equipment of fighter stations with hard runways, but Dowding still had to lay down the law to Turner at a meeting to discuss implementing the scheme that operational efficiency was of more importance than camouflage.[8]

Newall's bias towards turret fighters permeated the Air Staff and a good number of senior officers were convinced that they enjoyed distinct advantages over single-seat fighters. As the Defiant had yet to enter service, the arguments in favour of the class were of necessity purely theoretical and even one of the proponents of turret fighters accepted that practical trials would be desirable. When the correct proportion of turret fighters in Fighter Command was discussed at Adastral House, the consensus was that they should equip almost one-quarter of squadrons. This ratio had not been arrived at in any scientific fashion: it merely reflected the number of Defiants that were on order. Group Captain Donald Stevenson, the turret fighter's most enthusiastic advocate, wanted to lift the ratio to one-third should Fighter Command expand further or if it turned out that the Germans were armouring or upgrading the defensive armament of their bombers.[9] Experience with the 20mm cannon turret fighter – still only a project – might be another reason for the ratio to increase.

Dowding was given a perfunctory opportunity to object and to produce some counter-suggestions.[10] As 450 Defiants had already been ordered Dowding had little scope to do any such thing and he replied in a letter dripping with sarcasm.[11] He insinuated that the Air Staff was exercising 'dictatorial powers' over Fighter Command's equipment policy, by the old rhetorical trick of disclaiming any such intention on his own part. He was sorry to hear of the order for Defiants and begged that no more should be ordered. Dowding knew that speed was a fighter's most important asset and pointed out how slow the Defiant was even compared to the mediocre Dornier 17 bomber. The idea of the 20mm turret fighter filled him with horror. He doubted the hitting power of the 20mm compensated for the smaller supply of ammunition and spotted the huge difficulties in a 20mm ammunition feed to a turret (which were never resolved). He was fully aware that unless he made his opposition plain, there was every risk that 'I shall wake up in a year's time and be told that I am "committed" to have 15 squadrons of something with a 20 mm gun'.

Faced with Dowding's implacable (and well-founded) objections to the turret fighter, the Air Staff simply tried to ignore the question. Four months and a reminder later he was still waiting for a substantial answer in late October 1938.[12] The officers of the Air Staff tried to shuffle responsibility for dealing with such a pointed question onto each other. Dowding's concern went beyond the discrete issue of turret versus fixed-gun fighters and touched the wider question of the balance of power between Fighter Command and the Air Ministry on choice of equipment. Eventually, the question of two-seat fighters was broached amongst a number of other topics in a meeting between Dowding and a group of Air Staff officers.[13] Stevenson's note of the meeting gives a more hard-line pro-turret fighter account of the Air Staff's views than the formal minutes.[14] According to Stevenson, Dowding was told bluntly that Fighter Command already had a voice in new designs under the existing system as it could send a representative to the Operational Requirements Committee drawing up the specifications for a new aircraft. Stevenson also asserted that the expansion of Fighter Command to fifty squadrons, which had been decided since the discussion began, meant that the ratio of turret fighters was to be re-opened.

The argument over turret fighters was emblematic of the tensions between the Air Staff and the commands. Dowding was confronted with a highly theoretical scheme for the distribution of his squadrons that seemed to take no account of the availability of aerodromes or how quickly they could shift bases and assumed that every fighter would be able to make six sorties every twenty-four hours: 'fighter squadrons are very mobile, but they cannot work the miracles proposed for them.'[15] Coincidentally this scheme was authored by Stevenson. Even a comparatively junior officer such as a wing commander could plague Dowding with schemes to intercept German bombers over the sea, sacrificing the advantages of fighting over land, as well as the 'scatter bombing' proposal for attacking German formations with bombs from aircraft flying above them.[16]

Air Staff oversight of the dangerously independent-minded commander of Fighter Command was not confined to questions of equipment and tactics. Newall was horrified when he read a newspaper report of a speech to Air Raid Precaution workers in Coventry in which Dowding was quoted as putting the odds in favour of British fighters against German bombers as sixty to four and demanded an urgent explanation from his subordinate.[17] Dowding knew that the quoted ratio was an erroneous mishearing of the common phrase from bookies' odds of six to four meaning better than evens, but took the opportunity to ram home to the CAS that he did not subscribe to the Trenchardian doctrine that only bombers provided adequate defence. Dowding said he would actually put the chances of fighters higher than six to four and was confident that Fighter Command could inflict sufficient losses on the Luftwaffe to halt an attack in a month or less.[18]

Dowding's vision of Fighter Command as Britain's defence against Luftwaffe bombers was set to face a more dangerous challenge than Newall's scepticism and slavish adherence to Trenchardian doctrine. The Air Staff began to view the fighter squadrons as a pool of assets that could be drawn on to serve other purposes. Having spent years presenting the risk of a German knock-out blow as the principal threat that Britain would face if it went to war against Germany, the importance of home defence was quietly being scaled back. The basis on which Fighter Command and its system of centrally controlled defence had been built up since 1923 was unceremoniously written off as an unfortunate aberration. In an arguably even greater reversal of established Air Staff policy, the new thinking was motivated by a desire to help the French directly to repel a German invasion. Slessor set the ball rolling, acting apparently on his own initiative shortly after the German occupation of the rump of Czechoslovakia ratcheted up yet again the risk of war:

> unless we can make some arrangements for operating fighters from French bases, we might be faced with the spectacle of five or six hundred good short range fighters sitting in England unable to contribute at all to the issue of the struggle in the Low Countries ...

> It is unfortunate that our quite natural and proper obsession with the danger of a "Knock-Out Blow" against this country has forced us to concentrate on a type of fighter and a static defence organization, at the expense of our capacity to assist easily in resistance to a Knock-Out Blow of a different kind against France – which, if successful would only be a first stage of a Knock-Out Blow against England.[19]

The possibility that Britain might help France with bombers was mentioned but almost instantly discarded. Fighters were expendable, bombers were not. It would, though, have been a highly sensitive issue to run down Britain's fighter defences to support a commitment on the Continent and Slessor put tight limits on the circulation of his minute. Slessor had sown the seed. When war broke out the Air Staff was broadly sympathetic to French requests to send more fighters to France, which sparked a battle royal between Dowding and Adastral House. Dowding was shocked that the four Hurricane squadrons earmarked for France were to be dispatched immediately despite assurances that had been made to him that this would not happen until the security of the 'home base' was assured.[20] He was incensed that he had been asked to make a radio broadcast to the nation in which he assured his listeners that he had enough fighters to bring a German attack on Britain to a standstill. More ominously, a further six Hurricane squadrons were to be placed on a mobile basis and thus capable of being sent abroad at short notice. Dowding feared that the commitment to France 'has opened a tap through which will run the total Hurricane output', leaving the home-based Hurricane squadrons to dwindle though wastage. Newall was put firmly on the back foot and pleaded that he was not 'preparing to sell Fighter Command to the French'. Dowding supported his case with a direct rejection of the Trenchardian doctrine:

> The best defence of the country is the Fear of the Fighter. If we were very strong in Fighters we should probably never be attacked in force. If we are moderately strong, we shall probably be attacked, and the attacks will gradually be brought to a standstill.[21]

The dispute intensified and Dowding expressed the ultimate heresy, not just putting fighters above bombers in the list of Britain's defences, but putting the navy there as well:

> the Home Defence Organization must not be regarded as co-equal with other Commands, but ... should receive priority to all other claims until it is firmly secured, since the continued existence of the nation, and all its services, depends on the Royal Navy and Fighter Command.[22]

Ultimately the number of Hurricane squadrons sent to France was limited to six, with two less valuable Gladiator squadrons as well. Dowding's battles to keep fighters for the defence of Britain in the autumn of 1939 prefigured his similar and far more famous appeal at the height of the Battle of France in May 1940, when Churchill wanted to accept a desperate plea from the French government to send more fighter squadrons to help stem the German invasion. This too features in Guy Hamilton's *The Battle of Britain* movie although here it is entirely historical, unlike the discussion of relative German and British strengths. In 1940 Dowding had the support of Newall, which was not the case in 1939. Dowding's success in keeping his squadrons at home intact is widely regarded as a key contributor to the British victory. It is the 1939 clash, though, that illustrates the philosophical collision between the perceptive military pragmatist and the doctrinaire theorists who had shaped the RAF which entered the Second World War. The theorists had saddled Britain with a bomber force that was incapable of contributing much to the war effort for the first three years of the war and done their best to limit the number of fighters that Dowding had to defend the country.

Endnotes

Introduction: Why the Few Were so Few
(notes to pages xvi–xxiv)

1. Churchill *Their Finest Hour* p. 643
2. Wood & Dempster *The Narrow Margin* p. 248f; Murray *Luftwaffe: Strategy for Defeat* p. 84
3. Churchill *Their Finest Hour* p. 641, AIR 22/33 gives daily returns
4. A.J. P. Taylor 'Brummagen Statesmanship' in *From the Boer War to the Cold War*
5. AIR 8/243 Dowding to Hankey 14 February 1938
6. Terraine Introduction to Carrington *Soldier at Bomber Command* p. viii
7. Terraine 1984 Address to the Western Front Association in *Stand To!* 1985 No. 13 pp. 4–7
8. Harris *Bomber Offensive* pp. 42f
9. For Bomber Command's work during the Battle of Britain, www.iwm.org.uk/history/how-bomber-command-helped-win-the-battle-of-britain
10. Murray *Luftwaffe: Strategy for Defeat* p. 428
11. A. J. P. Taylor 'Boom and bombs' in *From the Boer War to the Cold War*

Chapter 1: A Modern Major-General
(notes to pages 1–9)

1. Hanson *First Blitz* p. 43; Fredette *The First Battle of Britain* pp. 36f
2. CAB 23/3 Appendix II
3. Overy *RAF The Birth of the World's First Air Force* p. 11
4. *Evening Post* 5 October 1917

5. *The Times* 15 December 1917
6. Boyle *Trenchard* p. 240 quoting Weir
7. Baring *Royal Flying Corps Headquarters* pp. 274f
8. Rose *The Later Cecils* pp. 258–62
9. Boyle *Trenchard* p. 293
10. Trenchard to Lord Weir 23 June 1918 quoted at Boyle *Trenchard* p. 295
11. '*Notes sur les sujets de discussion proposés par le représentant français à la 3eme session du Comité Interallié, par le général commandant la Force Indépendante d'aviation britannique, à Ochey*', 9 July 1918, annex Y to the *procès-verbal*, '*3e reunion du Comité Interallié d'Aviation tenue à Versailles*', cited in 'Strategic Bombing and Restraint in "Total War", 1915–1918' Author(s): Andrew Barros Source: *The Historical Journal*, June 2009, Vol. 52, No. 2 (June 2009), pp. 413–31

Chapter 2: The Prophet (notes to pages 10–15)

The main sources for this chapter are Andrew Boyle's biography of Trenchard, written with extensive assistance from the subject, Hyde's *British Air Policy Between the Wars* and Stephen Roskill's *Hankey Man of Secrets* Vol. II.
1. Boyle *Trenchard* p. 372

Chapter 3: Who Squeals First? (notes to pages 16–24)

1. AIR 2/1267 Minutes of a conference 10 July 1923
2. AIR 9/69 The composition of the air defence of Great Britain n.d.
3. Hoare *Empire of the Air* frontispiece and chapter 'The Prophet and his Interpreter'
4. Slessor *The Central Blue* p. 204
5. Douhet & Ferrari (1943). *The Command of the Air* ... Translated by Dino Ferrari
6. Slessor *The Central Blue* p. 41; Murray *Luftwaffe: Strategy for Defeat* p. 425
7. CAB 53/14/12
8. Roskill *Hankey* Vol. II p. 447

9. Roskill *Hankey* Vol. II p. 447
10. CAB 21/314
11. CAB 24/207 CP332(29)

Chapter 4: Rabbits (notes to pages 25–35)

1. AIR 9/69 memorandum by Air Staff, The Proportion of fighters to bombers ... in the Home Defence Air Force, July 1923
2. AIR 9/69 The Composition of the Air Defence of Great Britain n.d. but post 1923
3. AIR 9/69 The Composition of the Air Defence of Great Britain n.d. but post 1923
4. Boyle *Trenchard* p. 311
5. AIR 9/69 Air Staff memorandum, Reasons for Having Fighting Squadrons 8 March 1923
6. Russell Miller *Trenchard* p. 279
7. Boyle *Trenchard* p. 520
8. AIR 9/69 Lecture by the DCAS [Steel] to the Naval Staff College 10 March 1924
9. AIR 9/69 Lecture by the DCAS [Steel] to the Naval Staff College 10 March 1924
10. AIR 9/69 memorandum by Air Staff, The Proportion of fighters to bombers ... in the Home Defence Air Force, July 1923
11. AIR 9/69 memorandum by Air Staff, The Proportion of fighters to bombers ... in the Home Defence Air Force, July 1923
12. AIR 9/69 Air Staff memorandum, Reasons for Having Fighting Squadrons 8 March 1923
13. AIR 9/69 The Composition of the Air Defence of Great Britain n.d. but post 1923
14. AIR 6/69 Air Staff memorandum, Reasons for Having Fighting Squadrons 8 March 1923
15. AIR 9/69 loose paper undated quoting Trenchard before the C.I.D. Home Defence Committee in May 1923
16. AIR 9/69 memorandum by Air Staff, The Proportion of fighters to bombers ... in the Home Defence Air Force, July 1923
17. AIR 20/40 Air Staff Memorandum No. 11 of 1923

18. AIR 20/40 Air Staff Memorandum No. 11A
19. AIR 9/69 DCAS comments on air exercise report 27 November 1927
20. AIR 9/69 Note on the proportion of fighter and bomber Aircraft [illegible] November 1927
21. CAB 24/256/4 Sub-committee on the re-orientation of the air defence system of Great Britain interim report
22. AIR 20/243 Note on the relation between bomber strength and fighter strength in a balanced defence system n.d.
23. AIR 20/33 FO1 Draft Note on the Fighter Strength 21 June 1935
24. AIR 8/1113 Notes on the S. of S.'s minute
25. AIR 8/1113 Newall to Swinton 4 October 1937
26. AIR 8/226 Note on aide memoire ... 11 December 1937
27. AIR 6/35 EPM 133
28. AIR 6/34 EPM 130
29. AIR 8/244 Fighters or Bombers

Chapter 5: Evasion of Responsibility (notes to pages 36–47)

1. Sinnott's PhD thesis provides an invaluable guide to the steps that each project went through
2. AIR 20/84 FO1 to CAS 14 March 1933
3. AIR 20/220 Newall minute, Orders for New Types 3 December 1938
4. Sinnott PhD thesis pp. 68f
5. Weir quoted at Ritchie *Industry and Air Power* p. 33
6. AIR 16/108 Dawson to AO i/c Administration 30 March 1939
7. AIR 16/108 AO i/c Administration to C. in C. 7 April 1939
8. Ritchie *Industry and Air Power* pp. 54f
9. AIR 6/30 EPM90
10. AIR 14/412 Note by Wing-Commander Ops. 1 (c) 30 October 1939
11. AIR 2/279 Dowding minute 16 August 1934
12. AIR 20/84 21 August 1933 FO1 to DCAS
13. AIR 20/32
14. AIR 2/279 Ellington minute 17 June 1934
15. AIR 2/279 Dowding to Ellington 2 August 1934

16. AIR 8/8111 Scheme L aircraft programme Note on decisions 23 March 1938
17. Sinnott PhD thesis Chapter 5 disentangles the true narrative from legends

Chapter 6: Protection from the Slipstream (notes to pages 48–56)

1. AIR 20/84 DCAS to A.M.S.R February 1931
2. C. H. Keith *I Hold My Aim* p. 111
3. AIR 20/9 OR to DCAS and DTD 10 January 1935
4. AIR 2/279 Ludlow-Hewitt to Brooke-Popham 16 June 1934, Brooke-Popham to Ludlow-Hewitt 3 July 1934
5. AIR 2/279 Brooke-Popham to Ludlow-Hewitt 18 June 1934
6. The story of RAF weapons development is entertainingly told in C. H. Keith's memoir *I Hold My Aim*
7. AIR 9/88 ACAS to DCAS 21 December 1938
8. Harris *Bomber Offensive* p. 42
9. AIR 20/9 OR to DTD 2 March 1935
10. AIR 8/247 Brief for the Secretary of State
11. AIR 20/84 Ellington to Swinton 3 September 1935
12. AIR 6/31 EPM97
13. AIR 6/31 EPM97
14. AIR 20/167 Paper Prepared for the Canadian Government ... 13 March 1938
15. AIR 9/77 The gun armaments for bombers, CAB 63/95 Considerations affecting the Design of the ideal bomber aircraft for the RAF
16. *Le Fana de l'Aviation* November 2020 p. 65
17. AIR 20/220 Note on increase in fighter strength and re-equipment
18. CAB 63/95 para 35, AIR 9/77 The gun armaments for bombers
19. AIR 20/9 DDOR to DDTD II 31March 1937
20. Hinsley et al *British Intelligence in the Second World War* Vol. 3 Pt. 2 pp. 567f
21. AIR 20/9 OR to DTD 2 March 1935
22. AIR 20/84 DCAS to AMSR Feb 1931, AIR 20/220 Newall minute Orders for new types 3 December 1938.

23. KV 2/2780
24. AIR 2/2964 Dowding to Douglas 25 June 1938
25. AVIA 46/97 144 EPM Cannon Gun Fighters
26. AIR 9/77 Minutes of Operational Requirements Committee 11 August 1938
27. AIR 20/220 Newall minute, Orders for New Types 3 December 1938
28. AIR 20/245 Liaison meeting between DCAS and DGRD 16 February 1939
29. McKinstry *Lancaster* pp. 429–36

Chapter 7: Incalculable Potential (notes to pages 57–62)

1. Hansard 28 November 1934
2. Powers *Strategy Without Slide-Rule* pp. 121ff
3. AIR 9/69 Lecture by the DCAS to the Naval Staff College 10 March 1924
4. Phillips *Fighting Churchill, Appeasing Hitler* passim
5. Streat diaries 26 July 1935

Chapter 8: The Air Defence of Great Britain (notes to pages 63–69)

1. Boyle *Trenchard* pp. 701f
2. AIR 2/8877 Reorganisation of Home Commands 14 September 1935
3. AIR 2/8875 Dowding to Ellington 4 October 1935
4. AIR 9/50 War requirements in aircraft January 1935
5. Joubert *The Third Service* p. 106
6. V. Orange. 'Dowding, Hugh Caswall Tremenheere, first Baron Dowding (1882–1970), air force officer'. *Oxford Dictionary of National Biography*. Retrieved 31 July 2021, from www.oxforddnb.com/view/10.1093/ref:odnb/9780198614128.001.0001/odnb-9780198614128-e-32884.
7. Quoted at Orange *Dowding of Fighter Command* p. 11
8. Dean *The Royal Air Force and Two World Wars* p. 142

Chapter 9: No Longer in a Position Inferior (notes to pages 70–76)

1. C. Thorne (1970). 'The Shanghai Crisis of 1932: The Basis of British Policy'. *The American Historical Review*, 75(6), 1616-1639. doi:10.2307/1850758
2. CAB 24/230/2
3. 27 April 1935 AIR 8/196 quoted Hyde *British Air Policy Between the Wars* p. 338
4. Hansard 10 November 1932 col. 632
5. Roskill *Hankey* Vol. III p. 87
6. *The Times* 5 February 1934
7. Hansard 8 March 1934

Chapter 10: A Pretty Bad Half Section – Scheme A (notes to pages 77–86)

1. Hyde *British Air Policy Between the Wars* p. 233
2. Hyde *British Air Policy Between the Wars* p. 494
3. AIR 75/157 Recollections of the Air Ministry 1923–1953
4. Pownall diaries p. 34
5. CAB 53/4/14 130 meeting
6. J. Sweetman. 'Ellington, Sir Edward Leonard (1877–1967), air force officer'. *Oxford Dictionary of National Biography.* Retrieved 31 July 2021, from www.oxforddnb.com/view/10.1093/ref:odnb/9780198614128.001.0001/odnb-9780198614128-e-67138.
7. Dean *The Royal Air Force and Two World Wars* pp. 54 & 88
8. AIR 20/84 Ellington to Londonderry 3 September 1935
9. Terraine *The Right of the Line* pp. 16f
10. Rhodes James *Memoirs of a Conservative* p. 405
11. Hyde *British Air Policy Between the Wars* p. 332
12. Chamberlain letters, Chamberlain to Hilda 12 May 1935
13. Pownall diaries p. 36
14. T172/1830 Fergusson to Chamberlain 27 April 1935
15. Channon diaries Vol. I p. 554, Vol. II pp. 134f

Endnotes

16. Roskill *Hankey* Vol. III p. 104
17. CAB 16/111 fols 145–166
18. Kershaw *Making Friends with Hitler* pp. 84f
19. CAB 16/111 fol 139
20. CAB 16/111 DC(M)(32)115
21. AIR 9/69 Estimate of the requirements for the security of Great Britain against air attack from Germany 29 May 1934
22. AIR 9/69 Estimate of the requirements for the security of Great Britain against air attack from Germany 29 May 1934
23. CAB 53/24/2 JCS. 341
24. CAB 16/111 fol 165
25. AVIA 46/210 Freeman to Postan 29 October 1943
26. AIR 2/1269 Ellington to DCAS 30 July 1937
27. AIR 2/279 Ellington 7 June 1934
28. AIR 2/279 Dowding to Ellington 2 August 1934
29. CAB 24 C.P. 193(34)
30. Self *Neville Chamberlain* p. 238 quoting CAB16/111 paper 120
31. CAB 24/250/18 CP 193(34)
32. Self *Neville Chamberlain* p. 238 quoting CAB16/111 paper 120
33. Hyde *British Air Policy Between the Wars* p. 319; AIR 2/907 16 June 1937
34. Hyde *British Air Policy Between the Wars* p. 320
35. Roskill *Hankey* Vol. III p. 119

Chapter 11: A Malay Running Amok (notes to pages 87–93)

1. Hansard 13 July 1934 col. 671
2. Hansard 30 July 1934 col. 2339
3. Hankey to Baldwin 23 August 1934 quoted at Roskill *Hankey* Vol. III p. 122
4. Wark *The Ultimate Enemy* p. 38
5. Wark *The Ultimate Enemy* p. 42
6. CAB 4/23 1150 and 1152
7. Gilbert *Churchill* Vol. V pp. 554f & 570f
8. https://almostchosenpeople.wordpress.com/2014/02/19

9. Hansard 28 November 1934 col. 882
10. Brett Holman. "The Air Panic of 1935: British Press Opinion between Disarmament and Rearmament'. *Journal of Contemporary History*, Vol. 46, No. 2, 2011, pp. 288–307; JSTOR, www.jstor.org/stable/41305313. Accessed 14 February 2021
11. CAB 24/254/41
12. CAB 24/254/41
13. CAB 27 511 DC(M) (32) 139 25 April 1935
14. Wark *The Ultimate Enemy* p. 47
15. CAB 27/508 Minutes of Ministerial Committee on Defence Requirements 30 April 1935

Chapter 12: An Air Minister Bypassed – Scheme C (notes to pages 94–100)

1. CAB 24/254/41
2. CAB 24/254/41
3. CAB 24/254/41
4. CAB 24/254/41/1 Memorandum by the Secretary of State for Air
5. Cross *Swinton* p. 137
6. CAB24/255/15 and CAB 24/255/18
7. CAB 23/81/28
8. Hansard 22 May 1935 col. 367

Chapter 13: The Man for Push and Go (notes to pages 101–107)

1. Reader *Architect of Air Power* pp. 59f & 71
2. *Daily Express* 24 May 1935 quoted at Reader *Architect of Air Power* p. 204
3. Roskill *Hankey* Vol. III p. 209
4. Amery diaries pp. 284 & 288
5. Quoted at Hyde *British Air Policy Between the Wars* p. 387
6. Hyde *British Air Policy Between the Wars* p. 359
7. Reader *Architect of Air Power* p. 207

8. AVIA 46/210 Freeman to Postan 29 October 1943
9. AIR 6/24 EPM29
10. Swinton *I Remember* p. 111

Chapter 14: A Striking Force of Such Power – Scheme F (notes to pages 108–114)

1. AIR 2/1270
2. AIR 20/67 CAS to AMSO 10 February 1936
3. CAB 24/259/27
4. CAB 24/257/27 Swinton memorandum, Air Striking Force 10 February 1936
5. CAB 23/83/10
6. AIR 2/1270 RAF Expansion Scheme F
7. AIR 20/67 Summary of aircraft required 29 January 1936
8. AIR 20/67 Provisional allocation of orders for aircraft 6 March 1936
9. AIR 20/67 RAF Programme 11 March 1936
10. AIR 6/26 EPM45
11. Hyde *British Air Policy Between the Wars* p. 363
12. Para. (n) p. 8 of CAB 23/83/10
13. Reader *Architect of Air Power* p. 226f
14. Churchill papers 2/266 Rothermere to Churchill 23 February 1936
15. Reader *Architect of Air Power* pp. 230–3
16. Chamberlain to Hilda 9 February 1936
17. CAB 23/83/10

Chapter 15: An Ideal Scheme of Defence (notes to pages 115–123)

1. Roskill *Hankey* Vol. III pp. 201–6
2. Roskill *Hankey* Vol. III pp 51f & 180f
3. Pownall diary p. 102
4. CAB 24/26/17

5. CAB 3/6 CID paper 255-A
6. AIR 16/160 Notes marked 24B undated
7. CAB 3/6 CID 255-A
8. Roskill *Hankey* Vol. I pp. 356ff
9. CAB 63/19 Some suggestions for anti-submarine warfare 12 February 1917
10. CAB 54/1/4 DCOS meeting 19 November 1936
11. AIR 16/161 Hankey to Dowding 10 February 1938
12. CAB 64/6 ADGB undated
13. CAB 64/6 Weir to Chamberlain 30 September 1937
14. CAB 64/6 Swinton to Inskip 22 October 1937
15. CAB 64/9 Most Secret n.d.
16. CAB 23/93/8

Chapter 16: Horrors in the Most Intense Form (notes to pages 124–133)

1. CAB 55/7 Paper JP137
2. CAB 53/27/6
3. Wark *The Ultimate Enemy* pp. 52–5
4. AIR 40/2012 Ellington to Swinton 13 February 1936 with note by Swinton
5. Quoted at Wark *The Ultimate Enemy* p. 54
6. CAB 53/29/5 COS401
7. CAB 27/508 Ministerial Committee on Defence Requirements 27 May 1935
8. Hollis *One Marine's Tale* p. 51; Leasor *War at the Top* p. 38
9. CAB 54/1/4
10. CAB 53/30/6
11. CAB 53/30
12. AIR 2/2731 Ismay to DCAS 5 August 1937
13. AIR 20/2070 Possible German courses of action …
14. Irving *The Rise and Fall of the Luftwaffe* p. 64; *Luftwaffe: Strategy for Defeat* p. 42
15. AIR 9/50 unheaded sheet marked B
16. Slessor *The Central Blue* pp. 151f

Endnotes

Chapter 17: A Striking Bomber Force Not Inferior – Scheme H (notes to pages 134–139)

1. Wigram quoted at Wark *The Ultimate Enemy* p. 56
2. CAB 24/267/19 Plan for the further expansion of the Royal Air Force
3. CAB 23/87/6
4. AIR 6/28 EPM64
5. CAB 23/87/7
6. Irving *Rise and Fall of Luftwaffe* pp. 51f
7. CAB 23/90B/11
8. CAB 23/87/7

Chapter 18: Maximum Offensive Potential (notes to pages 140–149)

1. AIR 14/81 Note on preliminary discussion of Air Staff requirements 4 October 1935
2. AIR 2/716 Ludlow-Hewitt
3. AIR 2/1402 DCAS to AMSR 5 December 1934
4. AIR 2/1402 DDTD to AMSR 14 December 1934
5. Sinnott PhD thesis pp. 235
6. AIR 9/37 Harris to DCAS November 1935
7. AIR 20/84 DDOI 13 July 1933
8. AIR 9/77 Operational Requirements Committee minutes 29 July 1936
9. AIR 6/29 EPM73
10. AIR 6/29 EPM77
11. AVIA 46/97 EPM meeting 13 July 1937
12. Tedder *With Prejudice* pp. 9f
13. AIR 8/222 D of O Memorandum on the completion of the Royal Air Force Programme – Prepared to meet the requirements of CP 165(37) 5 July 1937
14. AIR 6/28 EPM64
15. AIR 6/28 EPM64
16. AIR 9/77 Operational Requirements Committee minutes 29 July 1936

17. AIR 9/77 Operational Requirements Committee minutes 22 June 1936
18. Webster & Frankland *Strategic Air Offensive Against Germany* Vol. I p. 137
19. AIR 6/28 EPM64
20. AVIA 46/97 Order for B12/36 Heavy Bomber (EPM 84)
21. McKinstry *Lancaster* p. 35
22. CAB 53/7/2 COS meeting 17 February 1937
23. AVIA EPM meeting 9 March 1937
24. AVIA 46/97 EPM meeting 9 March 1937
25. AIR 9/37 Air Staff note on the size of bomber aircraft 22 December 1938
26. AVIA 46/97 EPM 73

Chapter 19: Swinton's Hobby
(notes to pages 150–158)

1. Zimmerman *Radar* pp. 25–50
2. CAB 54/1/4 Deputy Chiefs of Staff Sub-Committee meeting 24 November 1936
3. AIR 2/4484 Installation of direction finding stations 2 August 1935
4. AIR 2/4484 Note of conference on RDF organisation
5. AIR 2/4484 Rowe memorandum 11 November 1935
6. T161/1319 Air Ministry memorandum, Treasury Inter Services Committee Radio Direction Finding Stations 10 August 1937
7. Joubert *The Third Service* p. 93
8. AIR 16/53 Tysson to HQ Fighter Command 18 February 1937
9. AIR 2/4484 Dowding to Air Ministry 2 December 1936
10. AIR 2 4488 Watson-Watt to DSR and DSS 9 May 1937
11. AIR 2/4484 Air Defence Research Sub-Committee Memorandum by Deputy CAS (draft n.d.)
12. CAB 16/81 Defence Plans (Policy) Sub-Committee 23 July 1937
13. AIR 20/435 Report on the home defence exercise 1938
14. *Sunday Times* 14 September 1947
15. Gordon Scott Smith. 'RAF War Plans and British Foreign Policy: 1935–1940'. PhD thesis p. 95

Endnotes

16. Roskill *Hankey* Vol. III p. 144
17. Joubert *The Fated Sky* p. 110
18. AIR 20/250 Peirse(?) to Anderson 23 February 1939
19. AIR 20/2070 Possible German courses of action …
20. AIR 8/222 Swinton to Inskip 26 November 1937
21. AIR 6/30 EPM87
22. AIR 2/4484 Saundby to DCAS 13 October 1937
23. AIR 16/677 Newall to Dowding 25 May 1938
24. Irving *The Rise and Fall of the Luftwaffe* p. 58
25. Terraine *Business in Great Waters* pp. 176ff
26. AIR 2/3323 Pye to Dowding 31 May 1938, Dowding to Pye 1 June 1938

Chapter 20: Striking a Careful Balance – Scheme J (notes to pages 159–166)

1. Hyde *British Air Policy Between the Wars* p. 404
2. Dean *The Royal Air Force and Two World Wars* pp. 142f
3. Hyde *British Air Policy Between the Wars* p. 404
4. Boyle *Trenchard* p. 690
5. AIR 6/36 EPM146
6. AIR 6/33 EPM119
7. Ismay memoirs p. 166; Richardson *From Churchill's Secret Circle to the BBC* p. 34
8. V. Orange. 'Newall, Cyril Louis Norton, first Baron Newall (1886–1963), air force officer'. *Oxford Dictionary of National Biography*. Retrieved 23 July 2021, from www.oxforddnb.com/view/10.1093/ref:odnb/9780198614128.001.0001/odnb-9780198614128-e-35208.
9. Lockhart diaries Vol. II p. 65; Colville *Fringes of Power* pp. 145 & 216
10. AIR 75/175 Slessor memoir
11. Frankland *History at War* p. 99
12. Slessor *The Central Blue* pp. 45–51
13. Boyle *Trenchard* p. 580
14. Slessor *Air Power and Armies* pp. 64–9
15. AIR 40/2043 AI3(b) memorandum 3 June 1937

16. AIR 40/2043 Ellington to Hankey 11 June 1937, Newall to Hankey 24 November 1937 and draft
17. AIR 40/2043 Minute by DCAS 3 June 1936
18. AIR 20/37 Air Staff memorandum 10 September 1937
19. AIR 20/37 DCAS to CAS 13 September 1937
20. CAB 24/273/41 CP 316(37)
21. CAB247/273/41 DP(P)12
22. AIR 8/237 Newall to Swinton 6 May 1938
23. AIR 20/37 fol 15b Old draft – return to plans
24. CAB 24/243/41

Chapter 21: The Interpreter (notes to pages 167–173)

1. Self *Neville Chamberlain* p. 267
2. AIR 20/67 Set-back or Reduction of Strength of the Metropolitan Force by 20 Squadrons at 31March 1937
3. Ritchie *Industry and Air Power* p. 77
4. Ritchie *Industry and Air Power* p. 78
5. AIR 20/37 Slessor memorandum, The Bomber Strength of Great Britain 2 September 1937
6. AIR 20/37 DCAS to CAS 13 September 1937
7. Ritchie *Industry and Air Power* p. 90
8. Ritchie *Industry and Air Power* p. 86
9. Ritchie *Industry and Air Power* p. 87
10. AIR 6/29 EPM 75 and AIR 6/40 EPM 184
11. AIR 6/29 EPM75
12. AIR 6/31 EPM96
13. Ritchie *Industry and Air Power* p. 88.
14. Ritchie *Industry and Air Power* p. 88
15. PREM 1/236 Statement on aircraft production, 1938–1939

Chapter 22: Morally Sure – Scheme K (notes to pages 174–181)

1. AIR 8/226 Inskip to Swinton 4 November 1937; Hyde *British Air Policy Between the* Wars p. 408

Endnotes

2. T161/855 Inskip Aide-Memoire 9 December 1937
3. T161/855 memorandum by Fisher 18 December 1937
4. T161/855 Air Staff note on Aide Memoire 11 December 1937
5. AIR 2/246 The Strength of the Bomber Force in Relation to the Principle of Parity 2 November 1938
6. CAB 24/273/41 CP316(37)
7. Phillips *Fighting Churchill, Appeasing Hitler* pp. 87–93
8. AIR 20/3575 note on conversation between Swinton and Inskip December 22 1937
9. AIR 20/3575 Bomber Requirements January 1 1938
10. Wark *The Ultimate Enemy* p. 59
11. AIR 20/3575 Newall to Swinton December 31 1937
12. AIR 20/3575 Swinton to Newall January 2 1938
13. AIR 8 /8111 EPM 111 Minutes
14. AIR 8/8111 Aircraft orders for Scheme K
15. AIR 20/3575 Slessor memorandum 28 December 1937
16. CAB 24/274/24 CP 24(38)
17. AIR 8/237 Newall to Swinton 6 May 1938
18. CAB 24/272/3 CP257(37)

Chapter 23: No Reflection on Swinton's Administration – Scheme L (notes to pages 182–189)

1. PREM 1/236 Wilson to Bruce-Gardner 18 March 1938
2. Ritchie *Industry and Air Power* p. 50
3. PREM 1/238 Cleverley to Chamberlain 11 January 1938
4. PREM 1/238 Syers memorandum 29 January 1938
5. PREM 1/238 Wilson minute 11 February 1938
6. PREM 1/238 Wilson minute 10 March 1938
7. PREM 1/238 Wilson minute 10 March 1938
8. Lyth Peter. 'The Empire's Airway: British Civil Aviation from 1919 to 1939' in *Revue belge de philologie et d'histoire*, tome 78, fasc. 3–4, 2000; *Histoire medievale, moderne et contemporaine – Middeleeuwse, moderne en hedendaagse geschiedenis* pp. 865–87
9. *The Times* 12 March 1938
10. PREM 1/251 Wilson to Chamberlain, Notes for Meeting with TUC General Council Mar 23 1938

11. PRO *The Rise and Fall of the German Air Force* p. 19
12. AIR 20/3572 F4 to Second DUS 5 April 1938
13. AIR 8/237 Newall memorandum (drafted by Slessor) 4 April 1938
14. AIR 8/237 Newall to Swinton and Winterton 8 April 1938

Chapter 24: A Wave of Uneasiness
   (notes to pages 190–196)

1. AIR 8/237
2. Irving *The Rise and Fall of The Luftwaffe* p. 54
3. PREM 1/236 Bruce-Gardner to Wilson 17 March 1938
4. PREM 1/236 Bruce-Gardner to Swinton 14 April 1938
5. *Daily Telegraph* 22 April 1938 'M.P. Criticises Air Ministry's Policy'
6. PREM 1/236 Bruce-Gardner to Swinton 23 April 1938
7. Wilson to Chamberlain n.d. but c. 24 April 1938
8. PREM 1/236 Wilson to Chamberlain n.d. (after 14 April 1938) 17 March 1938
9. AVIA 46/93 Minutes of Special Progress Meeting 25 April 1938
10. AVIA 46/93 Minutes of Special Progress Meeting 25 April 1938
11. Dean *The Royal Air Force and Two World Wars* p. 97
12. CAB 23/93/8
13. PREM 1/238 Churchill memorandum on aircraft types 12 March 1938
14. PREM 1/237 Churchill to Chamberlain 18 April 1938
15. PREM 1/237 Chamberlain to Churchill 26 April 1938
16. Chamberlain letters, Chamberlain to Ida [misdated] 10 May 1938
17. *The Times* 13 May 1938 p. 16 The Debate and After
18. Swinton *Sixty Years of Power* p. 119
19. Amery diaries p. 504
20. Channon diaries I p. 510

Chapter 25: From Telephones to Warplanes
   (notes to pages 197–201)

1. McKinstry *Spitfire* pp. 89 & 87
2. Hyde *British Air Policy Between the Wars* pp. 370–5

3. McKinstry *Spitfire* pp. 90f
4. AIR 6/34 EPM125
5. AIR 6/38 EPM165
6. AIR 20/167 DOR to ACAS 9 May 1939
7. Ritchie *Industry and Air Power* p. 51
8. CAB 24/277/24
9. CAB 24/277/29
10. CAB 23/94/3
11. AIR 20/3572 Scheme L Rough Estimate of cost 1 July 1938
12. Chamberlain letters, to Hilda 30 July 1939

Chapter 26: The Doubts of Sir Edgar Ludlow-Hewitt (notes to pages 202–209)

1. Slessor *The Central Blue* pp. 165f
2. CAB 21/517 Newall to Swinton 12 March 1938
3. Slessor *The Central Blue* pp. 170f
4. Lee *Never Stop the Engine When It's Hot* pp. 256f
5. Harris *Bomber Offensive* pp. 35f
6. CAB 53/4/11 Chiefs of Staff Sub-Committee 17 April 1934
7. M. Hastings. 'Hewitt, Sir Edgar Rainey Ludlow (1886–1973), air force officer'. *Oxford Dictionary of National Biography*. Retrieved 21 July 2021, from www.oxforddnb.com/view/10.1093/ref:odnb/9780198614128.001.0001/odnb-9780198614128-e-31380.
8. Joubert *The Third Service* p. 131
9. AIR 14/296 Ludlow-Hewitt covering letter Annual Report of Bomber Command 1937 19 March 1938
10. AIR 14/296 Ludlow-Hewitt Annual Report of Bomber Command 1937 March 1938
11. AIR 14/296 Ludlow-Hewitt Annual Report of Bomber Command 1937 March 1938
12. AIR 14/296 Manuscript note on Air Ministry to Ludlow-Hewitt 26 July 1938
13. AIR 20/245 Liaison meeting between DCAS and DGRD 17 April 1939
14. Frankland *History at War* p. 31

15. AIR 2/3306 Committee of Expansion ... Agenda for first meeting
16. AIR 2/2731 Ludlow-Hewitt to Air Staff 19 March 1938
17. AIR 2/3078 Minutes of conference 6 April 1939
18. AIR 14/179 Bomber Command notes on deficiencies affecting the readiness for war
19. Dean *The Royal Air Force and Two World Wars* p. 267
20. AIR 14/225 Ludlow-Hewitt to Air Ministry 28 July 1938
21. AIR 14/225 Ludlow-Hewitt to Air Ministry 14 July 1938
22. AIR 9/102 Bomber Command to Don 30 September 1938
23. AIR 9/102 Pilot Officer to OC 76 Squadron 27 September 1938
24. AIR 8/222 Notes of the proposals contained in the memorandum entitled 'A new standard of air strength'

Chapter 27: An Ideal of Bombing
(notes to pages 210–214)

1. AIR 8/257 manuscript note marked 'Keep'
2. CAB 63/95 Considerations affecting the design of the ideal bomber aircraft for the RAF
3. CAB 63/95 Newall to Hankey 25 September 1939
4. CAB 21/902 Extract from the conclusions of the meeting of committee on defence programmes and acceleration 31 October 1938
5. Joubert *The Third Service* pp. 94 & 134
6. AIR 2/2958 ACAS to ADMP and DGRD 13 August 1938 quoted Sinnott PhD thesis p. 319
7. Sinnott PhD thesis pp. 319–21 & 324–7

Chapter 28: As Much Damage as Possible on the Attackers.
(notes to pages 215–223)

1. AIR 16/161 Dowding to Ellington 16 March 1937
2. AIR 16/161 Peirse to Dowding 12 April 1937
3. AIR 16/161 Peirse to Dowding 12 April 1937
4. AIR 8/243 Dowding to Peirse 13 April 1937
5. AIR 9/86 Slessor memorandum Revision of JP 155

6. CAB 53/33/6 HDC memorandum 33-M
7. CAB 55/33/6 COS 621
8. AIR 16/161 Hankey to Dowding 10 February 1938
9. AIR 16/161 Dowding to Hankey 14 February 1938 and Newall to Dowding 18 February 1938
10. AIR 16/161 Newall to Dowding 18 February 1938
11. AIR 9/89 Enc 5A February 1938
12. AIR 9/89 Revision of JP155 February 1938
13. AIR 9/86 Slessor minute JP155 Re-draft
14. AIR 2/2948 Slessor to Sholto Douglas 11 March 1938
15. AIR 2/2948 Sholto Douglas to Slessor 23 March 1938
16. AIR 2/2948 Dowding manuscript note on questionnaire
17. AIR 2/2948 Answers to questions raised by DD Plans
18. AIR 9/86 Maintenance of the scale of attack
19. CAB 53/40/3 COS 747 (J.P.)

Chapter 29: Large Allowances Against Underestimate (notes to pages 224–229)

1. CAB 53/40/6 COS 755
2. AIR 9/90 AI3 memorandum August 24 1938
3. AIR 9/90 AI3(b) paper 23 August 1938
4. AIR 9/90 Fraser to DCAS 29 August 1938
5. AIR 14/225 Ludlow-Hewitt to Air Ministry 30 August 1938
6. Terraine *The Right of the Line* p. 67
7. AIR 14/225 Ludlow-Hewitt to Air Ministry 30 August 1938
8. AIR 9/251 Simon to Newall 9 September 1938
9. Hansard 14 June 1938 col 937
10. AIR 20/22 Air Ministry to Ludlow-Hewitt 15 September 1938
11. AIR 14/225 Ludlow-Hewitt to Air Ministry 19 September 1938
12. CAB 53/41 COS 764 13 September 1938
13. AIR 8/248 Newall to Wood 10 September 1938
14. CAB 53/41/1 COS 764
15. CAB 53/41/1 COS 764
16. CAB 53/41/1 COS 770
17. CAB 53/41 draft report

Chapter 30: The Utmost Limit Compatible
(notes to pages 230–235)

1. CAB 21/544
2. CAB 23/95/6
3. AIR 9/90 Newall to Wood 24 September 1938
4. CAB 23/95/7
5. AIR 14/225 Newall to Ludlow-Hewitt 19 September 1938
6. AIR 14/225 Newall to Ludlow-Hewitt 19 September 1938
7. AIR 14/225 Ludlow-Hewitt to Air Ministry 23 September 1938
8. AIR 14/225 Newall to Ludlow-Hewitt 19 September 1938
9. Goebbels diaries 2 October 1938
10. AIR 20/228 Note on the difficulties experienced in the September 1938 crisis
11. AIR 20/228 Note on the difficulties experienced in the September 1938 crisis
12. AIR 20/228 Note on the difficulties experienced in the September 1938 crisis
13. www.tangmere-museum.org.uk/aircraft-month/westland-lysander & www.classicwarbirds.co.uk/british-aircraft/westland-lysander.php
14. AIR 20/228 Note on the difficulties experienced in the September 1938 crisis
15. AIR 20/228 Note of meeting October 1938
16. AIR 20/228 Note on the difficulties experienced in the September 1938 crisis
17. AIR 20/228 Note on the difficulties experienced in the September 1938 crisis
18. AIR 20/22 Ludlow-Hewitt to Air Ministry 25 September 1938
19. AIR 20/228 Stevenson to DCAS 15 October 1938

Chapter 31: A Weapon We Can Use Very Effectively
(notes to pages 236–243)

1. AIR 10/1197
2. AIR 9/28 Air staff memorandum 19
3. AIR 5/1323 Air Staff memorandum 52
4. Slessor *The Central Blue* p. 132

5. AIR 75/121 Draft Propaganda as a weapon of war against Germany n.d. but Oct/Nov 1938
6. AIR 75/121 Draft Propaganda as a weapon of war against Germany n.d. but Oct/Nov 1938
7. Phillips *Fighting Churchill, Appeasing Hitler* chapter 17
8. AIR 75/121 Slessor to DCAS 19 January 1939
9. Goebbels diaries 6 September 1939
10. CAB 2/9 Minutes of the 374th meeting of the Committee of Imperial Defence
11. Strong *Intelligence at the Top* p 54
12. Harris *Bomber Offensive* p. 36
13. Joubert *The Third Service* p. 129
14. Phillips *Fighting Churchill, Appeasing Hitler* pp. 345–8
15. Hansard 10 October 1939 cols. 196–7
16. Harris *Bomber Offensive* p. 37
17. Goebbels diaries 5 September 1939
18. Goebbels diaries 27 September and 28 October 1939
19. Goebbels diaries 29 September 1939
20. Goebbels diaries 19 December 1939

Chapter 32: Per Astra Ad Ardua (notes to pages 244–251)

1. Richards *The Fight at Odds* pp. 27f
2. Dean *The Royal Air Force and Two World Wars* p. 68; Webster & Frankland *Strategic Air Offensive Against Germany* Vol. I pp. 111–14
3. AIR 2/279 Brooke-Popham to Ludlow-Hewitt 18 June 1934
4. AIR 2/3078 Air Ministry Navigation – General Policy 22 May 1939
5. AIR 2/3078 Ludlow-Hewitt to Air Staff 25 May 1939
6. Hyde *British Air Policy Between the Wars* p. 319
7. Tizard to Freeman 8 Nov 1938 quoted at Webster & Frankland *Strategic Air Offensive Against Germany* Vol. I p. 114
8. Jones *Most Secret War* pp. 45f
9. AIR 2/3494 Sholto Douglas to Ludlow-Hewitt 16 November 1938
10. AIR 23494 Tizard to Sholto Douglas 30 November 1938
11. AIR 2/3494 Sholto Douglas to Tizard before 6 December 1938
12. AIR 2/3494 Minutes of a Conference … 8 December 1938

13. AIR 2/3494 Sholto Douglas to Ludlow-Hewitt 25 February 1939
14. AIR 2/3494 Rowe to Balfour 10 March 1939
15. Jones *Most Secret War* pp. 36, 45f & 210
16. AIR 20/3672 Appendix B
17. Jones *Most Secret War* p. 217
18. Harris to Joubert 1 February1941 quoted at Jones *Most Secret War* p. 169
19. Jones *Most Secret War* pp. 217 & 210
20. Frankland *History at War* p. 99
21. AIR 6/33 EPM118
22. Webster & Frankland *Strategic Air Offensive Against Germany* Vol. IV fn. 1 p. 32
23. Webster & Frankland *Strategic Air Offensive Against Germany* Vol. IV p. 31
24. MacBean & Hogben *Bombs Gone.* p. 46

Chapter 33: By This Means Alone – Scheme M (notes to pages 252–263)

1. AIR 8/227 Wilson draft n.d.
2. AIR 8/241 Cover sheet, AIR 40/2043 Notes on Germany's air force programme
3. AIR 8/241 Note on air parity
4. AIR 8/241 Draft Some notes on Scheme L and any further expansion
5. AIR 8/227 The policy of parity c. 11 June 1938
6. AIR 8/243 The Role of the Air Force in National Defence 5 July 1938
7. AIR 8/243 Wood to Newall 28 July 1938, Slessor to DCAS 11 August 1938
8. AIR 8/243 Slessor to DCAS 11 August 1938
9. AIR 20/3575 Manuscript notes of CAS's meeting 29 December 1937
10. Dean *The Royal Air Force and Two World Wars* p. 89
11. AIR 20/228 The difficulties experienced in the September 1938 crisis
12. PREM 1/236 Hopkins to Simon 29 October 1938
13. PREM 1/236 Hopkins to Simon 29 October 1938

14. PREM 1/236 Hopkins to Simon 29 October 1938
15. T161/923 Barlow note 28 October 1938
16. T161/923 Sanctions for Air Force Programme, note of meeting on 30 November 1938
17. CAB 21/902 Extract from Conclusions of Committee on Defence Programmes and Acceleration 31October 1938
18. PREM 1/236 Wood memorandum n.d. (November 1938)
19. CAB 21/902 Extract from Conclusions of Committee on Defence Programmes and Acceleration 28 October 1938
20. AIR 8/250 Newall to Wood 4 November 1938
21. CAB 23/96/5 meeting of 7 November 1938
22. PREM 1/236 Wilson to Woods 1November 1938
23. A. J. P. Taylor 'Brummagen Statesmanship' in *From the Boer War to the Cold War*, p. 362; Leo McKinstry 'Did Neville Chamberlain create the conditions for the RAF to win the Battle of Britain?' *New Statesman* 24 April 2018
24. Holland *The Story of the RAF, 1918–2018* pp. 50 & 53; McKinstry 'Did Neville Chamberlain create the conditions for the RAF to win the Battle of Britain?' in *New Statesman* 24 April 2018
25. Self, Robert. 'Neville Chamberlain and Rearmament: Did the Treasury Win the Battle of Britain?' *20th Century History Review* September 2007
26. Hansard 10 November 1938 col. 351
27. AIR 8/243 The composition and strength of the Royal Air Force Air Staff policy
28. *The Times* 19 November 1938
29. T161/923 Wood to Chamberlain 9 December 1938
30. PREM 1/236 Wood to Chamberlain 9 December 1938
31. PREM 1/236 Wilson to Chamberlain 13 December 1938
32. PREM 1/236 Wilson memorandum 14 December 1938
33. PREM 1/236 Wilson to Sandford 14 December 1938
34. AIR 9/82 Air Staff memorandum 22 December 1938
35. AIR 9/82 Sandford to Wilson 23 December 1938
36. AIR 20/220 Orders for new types 5 December 1938
37. Sinnott PhD thesis p. 95
38. T161/923 BWS to Barlow 10 January 1939
39. T161/923 Fisher manuscript note on The Air Ministry Programme 11 January 1939

Chapter 34: Saturation Point – Fighters and Scheme M (notes to pages 264–271)

1. Slessor *The Central Blue* p. 204
2. McKinstry *Spitfire* pp. 70–87
3. AVIA 10/151 Committee on Supply afternoon session 5 May 1938
4. T161/923 Freeman to Fisher 30 September 1938
5. T161/923 Freeman to Fisher 30 September 1938
6. T161/923 Fisher to Freeman 30 September 1938
7. AIR 6/55 Decisions of the Air Council Committee on Supply reached at the meeting held on 5 October 1938
8. AIR 8/250 Newall to Wood 4 November 1938
9. James *Gloster Aircraft Since 1917* p. 41
10. AIR 19/2 Visit to the Gloster Aircraft Company Limited; *The Times Court Circular* 11 February 1939
11. AIR 6/56 1. Aircraft
12. AIR 6/56 1. Aircraft
13. CAB 54/1/4 12 fol. 83
14. T161/855 Minutes Review 7 Meeting 2 December 1937; CAB 54/1/3 Deputy Chiefs of Staff meeting 12 November 1936
15. AIR 20/20 Ludlow-Hewitt to Air Ministry
16. CAB 24/279/18
17. AIR 8/250 Acceleration of expansion scheme L recommendations of a conference on 18 October 1938
18. AIR 14/225 Group Captain Plans to Ludlow-Hewitt 28 September 1938
19. AIR 8/250 Newall to Freeman 25 November 1938
20. AIR 20/220 FO1(a) to DDOps 23 November 1938
21. AIR 20/220 minutes of DCAS conference on 18 November 1938.
22. AIR 8/250 Newall to Freeman November 25 1938
23. AIR 20/250 minutes of conference on L scheme acceleration
24. AIR 6/56 EPM 153
25. AIR 20/245 Liaison meeting between DCAS and ADRGD 23 March 1938
26. AIR 2/3078 Ludlow-Hewitt to Air Ministry 25 May 1939
27. AIR 2/3078 Newall memorandum 7 July 1939
28. AIR 20/220 hand drawn diagrams accompanying FO1 to DDOps 5 December 1938
29. Richards *The Fight at Odds* p. 114

Endnotes

30. AIR 20/220 Slessor to D of O 6 April 1939
31. T161/923 EPM 175 1 December 1938

Chapter 35: A Gross Misuse of Air Forces
(notes to pages 272–279)

1. Dean *The Royal Air Force and Two World Wars* p. 151
2. CAB 53/8/6
3. CAB 53/33/8/33
4. Strong *Intelligence at the Top* pp. 17f
5. AIR 20/252 Notes of a discussion held on 19 April 1939
6. CAB 53/50/4
7. AIR 20/252 Covering note by Slessor to Newall 8 May 1939
8. AIR 20/252 note by Slessor on COS 924 undated
9. AIR 20/252 Slessor's solution
10. AIR 20/252 Slessor to ACAS DoO DCAS 16 June 1939
11. AIR 8/272 pencil note on Sholto Douglas memorandum 30 May 1939
12. AIR 20/252 DDops notes
13. AIR 20/252 Note of conference on 12 June 1939
14. AIR 20/252 minute to DCAS, D of Ops views
15. AIR 2/3708 Conference held in DCAS's room … 6 April 1939
16. AIR 20/252 D. of Ops. to ACAS
17. AIR 20/253 Air Staff Directive 23 September 1939
18. Holland *The Story of the RAF, 1918–2018* p. 79, Webster & Frankland *Strategic Air Offensive Against Germany* Vol. IV p. 402
19. AIR 14/81 Notes on discussion between Chief of the Air Staff and Air Commanding-in-Chief Bomber Command
20. Pownall diary p. 253 10 November 1939

Chapter 36: You Can Stand up to Hitler Now
(notes to pages 280–284)

1. AVIA 46/93 Bruce-Gardner to Wilson 22 October & 4 November 1938
2. AVIA 46/93 Bruce-Gardner to Freeman January 9 1939
3. AVIA 46/93 Bruce-Gardner to Wilson 3 April 1939
4. Mosley *On Borrowed Time* p. 221fn. Mosley confuses Bruce-Gardner with a financial antique Lord Crewe who played no part.

5. Norman papers diary 30 August 1939, Bank of England, London
6. Brooks journals pp. 247f
7. Ritchie *Industry and Air Power* pp. 184–190. Shute *Slide Rule* chaps 7–9 for the insider story of one such promotion; the book is the only one known to the author in which the boss of a company honestly admits to flagrant overstatement of its profits.
8. AIR 6 EPMs 31 and 43
9. AIR 6/35 EPM131
10. AIR 6/35 EPM 134

Chapter 37: The Result of Overexpansion (notes to pages 285–293)

1. AIR 8/243 the Composition and Strength of the Royal Air Force- Air Staff Policy
2. AIR 14/105 Ludlow-Hewitt to Air Ministry Draft n.d.
3. Slessor *The Central Blue* pp. 208f
4. AIR 2/3306 Committee of Expansion … Agenda for first meeting
5. AIR 2/3306 Committee of Expansion … Minutes of first meeting
6. AIR 6/39 EPM 179 meeting
7. AIR 2/3308 Committee of Expansion … Agenda for first meeting
8. AIR 2/3306 Douglas to AMP 16 July 1938
9. AIR 2/1964 Ludlow-Hewitt to Air Ministry 8 May 1939
10. AIR 2/1964 Sholto Douglas to Ludlow-Hewitt 18 May 1939
11. Air 2/3078 S6 to ACAS 23 March 1939, ACAS to S6 24 March 1939, ACAS to CAS 30 March 1939
12. AIR 2/3078 Air Ministry, Navigation – General Policy 22 May 1939
13. AIR 2/3708 Ludlow-Hewitt to Air Ministry 25 May 1939
14. AIR 2/3708 ACAS to CAS 23 June 1936
15. AIR 6/39 EPM 176
16. AIR 2/3708 Newall to Wood 5 July 1939 and AIR 6/39 EPM176 Meeting 18 July 1939, AIR 2/3708 PS to S of S. to PUS (through CAS) 24 July 1939
17. AIR 2/3708 Street to Ludlow-Hewitt 24 July 1939
18. AIR 2/3078 Ellington to Newall 27 July 1939
19. AIR 2/3708 Ludlow-Hewitt to Air Ministry 2 August 1939
20. AIR 2/3708 Report on action taken …

Endnotes

21. AIR 20/250 Germany's object
22. AIR 8/250 Striking power of the metropolitan bomber force on completion of scheme 'L' accelerated (CP 218 (38)) 15 April 1939
23. AIR 6/39 EPM174
24. Webster & Frankland *Strategic Air Offensive Against Germany* Vol. IV p. 402
25. AIR 20/22 Newall to Ludlow-Hewitt 23 August 1939
26. AIR 2/3222 Draft paragraphs … 29 August 1939
27. AIR 2/3222 Ashton-Gwatkin to Committee of Imperial Defence 18 August 1939

Chapter 38: The Miracles Proposed for Them (notes to pages 294–299)

1. AIR 2/2067 Dowding to Air Ministry 18 May 1937
2. AIR 20/20 FO1 to DDOps 16 February 1939
3. Cruickshank *Deception in the Second World War* pp. 4–7, 66f & 77f
4. AIR 20/228 Stevenson to DCAS 13 October 1938
5. AIR 8/248 Newall to AMSO 16 September 1938
6. AIR 2/2067 marginal note on Dowding to Peirse 28 November 1938
7. AIR 2/2067 Dowding to Newall 23 February 1939
8. AIR 2/2067 Minutes of Conference 28 April 1939
9. AIR 2/2964 Stevenson to Sholto Douglas 20 June 1938
10. AIR 2/2964 Sholto Douglas to Dowding 22 June 1938
11. AIR 2/2964 Dowding to Sholto Douglas 25 June 1938
12. AIR 2/2964 Dowding to Sholto Douglas 22 October 1938
13. AIR 2/2964 Notes of a meeting on 16 November 1938
14. AIR 2/2964 Stevenson note 22 November 1938
15. AIR 2/3034 Air Staff note on fighter strength …. Dowding to DCAS 12 October 1939
16. AIR 16/180 Dowding to Whitworth-Jones 20 June 1938
17. AIR 16/261 Newall to Dowding 23 February 1939
18. AIR 16/261 Dowding to Newall 24 February 1939
19. AIR 20/220 Slessor to DoO 6 April 1939
20. AIR 2/3127 Dowding to Air Staff 16 September 1939
21. AIR 2/3127 Dowding to Air Staff 25 September 1939
22. AIR 2/3127 Dowding to Air Staff 13 October 1939

Selected Bibliography

Archival Material

National Archives Kew documents listed as AIR, AVIA, CAB, KV, PREM and T.
Swinton papers at the Churchill Archives, Cambridge.

Memoirs and Diaries

Babington Smith, C. *Evidence in Camera: The Story of Photographic Intelligence in World War II*. Newton Abbot: David & Charles, 1974.
Balfour, H. H. *Wings over Westminster*. London: Hutchinson, 1973.
Baring, Maurice. *Flying Corps Headquarters, 1914–1918*. London: W. Heinemann, 1930.
Brooks, C. *Devil's Decade: Portraits of the Nineteen-Thirties*. London: Macdonald & Co. Ltd, 1948.
Barnes, John & David Nicholson (eds). *The Empire at Bay: The Leo Amery Diaries*. London: Hutchinson, 1988.
Bond, Brian (ed). *Chief of Staff: The Diaries of Lieutenant-General Sir Henry Pownall*. London: Leo Cooper, 1972.
Carrington, C. *Soldier at Bomber Command*. London: Leo Cooper, 1987.
Chatfield, Alfred Ernle Montacute, *The Navy and Defence: The Autobiography of Admiral of the Fleet Lord Chatfield*. London: William Heinemann, 1942.
Channon, Henry & Simon Heffer (ed.). *Henry 'Chips' Channon : The Diaries. Volume 1, 1918–38*. London: Hutchinson, 2021.
Channon, Henry & Simon Heffer (ed.). *Henry 'Chips' Channon : The Diaries. Volume 2, 1938–43*. London: Hutchinson, 2021.
Colville, John Rupert. *The Fringes of Power: Downing Street Diaries 1939–1955*. London: Phoenix, 1985.

Selected Bibliography

Crowson, N. J. (ed). *Press Barons and Politics: The Journals of Collin Brooks, 1932–1940*. Cambridge: Cambridge UP for the Royal Historical Society, 1998.

Douglas, Sholto & Robert Wright. *Years of Command: The 2nd Volume of the Autobiography of Sholto Douglas, Marshal of the Royal Air Force, Lord Douglas of Kirtleside, G. C. B., M. C., D. F. C.* London: Collins, 1966.

Dupree, M. (ed). *Lancashire and Whitehall: The Diary of Sir Raymond Streat*. Manchester, 1987.

Fröhlich, Elke (ed). *Die Tagebücher von Joseph Goebbels*. Munich: K. G. Saur, 1998.

Frankland, N. *History at War: The Campaigns of an Historian*. London: Giles de la Mare, 1998.

Harris, A. T. *Bomber Offensive*. London: Collins, 1947.

Hoare, Sir Samuel (Lord Templewood). *Empire of the Air: The Advent of the Air Age, 1922–1929*. London: Collins, 1957.

Hollis, Leslie. *One Marine's Tale*. London: André Deutsch, 1956.

Hooker, Sir Stanley. *Not Much of an Engineer*. Ramsbury: Airlife, 1984.

Ismay, Hastings. *The Memoirs of General the Lord Ismay*. London: Heinemann, 1960.

Jones, R. V. *Most Secret War*. Ware, Hertfordshire: Wordsworth Editions, 1998.

Joubert de la Ferté, P. B. *The Fated Sky: An Autobiography*. London: Hutchinson, 1952.

Keith, C. H. *I Hold My Aim*. London: G. Allen & Unwin, 1946.

Leasor, James & Hollis, Leslie *War at the Top: Based on the Experiences of General Sir Leslie Hollis*. London: Joseph, 1959.

Longmore, Arthur. *From Sea to Sky, 1910–1945*. London: Geoffrey Bles, 1946.

Lee, David. *Never Stop the Engine When It's Hot*. London: Thomas Harmsworth, 1983.

Marshall-Cornwall, James. *Wars and Rumours of Wars: A Memoir*. London: Leo Cooper, 1984.

Panton, Alastair & Panton Bacon, Victoria. *Six Weeks of Blenheim Summer: An RAF Officer's Memoir of the Battle of France, 1940*. London: Penguin 2014.

Rhodes James, Robert. *Memoirs of a Conservative: J.C.C. Davidson's Memoirs and Papers, 1910–37*. London: Weidenfeld & Nicolson, 1969.

Rowe, A. P. *One Story of Radar*. Cambridge: Cambridge University Press, 1948.

Self, Robert. *The Neville Chamberlain Diary Letters Volume Four: The Downing Street Years, 1934–1940*. Aldershot: Ashgate, 2000.

Shute, Nevil. *Slide Rule: The Autobiography of an Engineer*. London: Mandarin, 1990.

Simpson, William. *I Burned My Fingers*. London: Puttnam, 1958.

Slessor, John. *The Central Blue: Recollections and Reflections*. London: Cassell, 1956.

Strong, Kenneth. *Intelligence at the Top: The Recollections of An Intelligence Officer*. London: Cassell, 1968.

Swinton, Lord, previously Cunliffe-Lister, Philip. *I Remember*. London: Hutchinson, 1948.

Swinton, Lord, previously Cunliffe-Lister, Philip. *Sixty Years of Power*. London: Hutchinson, 1966.

Tedder, Arthur. *With Prejudice: The War Memoirs of Marshal of the Royal Air Force, Lord Tedder*. London: Cassell, 1966.

Vigors, Tim. *Life's Too Short to Cry*, London, Grub Street, 2007.

Watson-Watt, R. A. *Three Steps to Victory*. London: Odhams Press, 1957.

Young, Kenneth (ed). *The Diaries of Sir Robert Bruce Lockhart, 1915–1938*. London: Macmillan, 1973.

Young, Kenneth (ed). *The Diaries of Sir Robert Bruce Lockhart, 1939–1965*. London: Macmillan, 1980.

Secondary Works

Baughen, Greg. *The Rise and Fall of the French Air Force: French Air Operations and Strategy, 1900–1940*. Stroud: Fonthill, 2018.

Baughen, Greg. *The Fairey Battle*. Stroud: Fonthill, 2017.

Baughen, Greg. *The Rise of the Bomber*. Stroud: Fonthill, 2016.

Bialer, Uri. *The Shadow of the Bomber*. London: Royal Historical Society, 1980.

Beevor, Antony. *Crete: The Battle and the Resistance*. London. John Murray, 1991.

Biddle, Tami Davis. *Rhetoric and Reality in Air Warfare*. Princeton NJ: Princeton UP, 2002.

Selected Bibliography

Bishop, Patrick. *Air Force Blue: The RAF in World War Two: Spearhead of Victory*. London: William Collins, 2017.

Boyle, Andrew. *Trenchard*. London: Collins, 1962.

Bungay, Stephen. *The Most Dangerous Enemy: A History of the Battle of Britain*. London: Aurum, 2001.

Churchill, Winston. *The Second World War* Vol. II *Their Finest Hour*. London: Cassell, 1949.

Clark, Ronald. *Tizard*. London: Methuen, 1965.

Collier, B. *Leader of the Few: The Authorised Biography of Air Chief Marshal the Lord Dowding of Bentley Priory*. London: Jarrolds, 1957.

Collier, B. *The Defence of the United Kingdom*. London: HMSO, 1957.

Colvin, I. G. *The Chamberlain Cabinet: How the Meetings in 10 Downing Street, 1937–9, Led to the Second World War, Told for the First Time from the Cabinet Papers*. London: Gollancz, 1971.

Cross, J. A. *Lord Swinton*. Oxford: Clarendon Press, 1982.

Cruickshank, Charles. *Deception in World War II*. Oxford: Oxford UP, 1979.

Dean, Maurice. *The Royal Air Force and Two World Wars*. London: Cassell, 1979.

Douhet, Giulio & Dino Ferrari. *The Command of the Air*. London: Faber & Faber, 1943.

Flint, Peter, *Dowding and Headquarters Fighter Command*, Shrewsbury: Airlife, 1996.

Franks, Norman L. R. *RAF Fighter Command 1936–1968*. Sparkford: Patrick Stephens, 1992.

Fredette, R. H. *The First Battle of Britain, 1917–1918 & the Birth of the Royal Air Force*. London: Cassell, 1966.

Furse, Anthony. *Wilfrid Freeman: The Genius Behind Allied Survival and Air Supremacy, 1939 to 1945*. Staplehurst: Spellmount, 1999.

Gilbert, Martin. *Winston S. Churchill: Volume V, the Prophet of Truth, 1922–39*. Hillsdale, MI: Hillsdale College, 2009.

Gilbert, Martin. *Winston S. Churchill: Volume VI, Finest Hour 1939–1941*. Hillsdale, MI: Hillsdale College, 2011.

Gough, J. *Watching the Skies: A History of Ground Radar for the Air Defence of the United Kingdom by the Royal Air Force from 1946 to 1975*. London: HMSO, 1993.

Hanson, N. *The First Blitz: The Secret German Plan to Raze London to the Ground in 1918*. London: Doubleday, 2008.

Hastings, Max. *Bomber Command*. London: Pan, 1981.

Hinsley, F. H. et al. *British Intelligence in the Second World War: Its Influence on Strategy and Operations Vol. 1*. London: HMSO, 1979.

Hinsley, F.H. et al. *British Intelligence in the Second World War: Its Influence on Strategy and Operations Vol. 3, Pt 1*. London: HMSO, 1984.

Holland, James. *Royal Air Force. RAF 100: 1918–2018: The Official Story*. London: André Deutsch, 2018.

Holman, Brett. *The Next War in the Air: Britain's Fear of the Bomber, 1908–1941*. Farnham: Ashgate, 2014.

Hyde, A. *The First Blitz: The German Bomber Campaign Against Britain in the First World War*. Barnsley: Leo Cooper, 2002.

Hyde, H. Montgomery. *British Air Policy between the Wars, 1918–1939*. London: Heinemann, 1976.

Irving, David. *The Rise and Fall of the Luftwaffe: The Life of Luftwaffe Marshal Erhard Milch*. London: Futura Publications, 1976.

James, Derek N. *Gloster Aircraft Since 1917*. London: Putnam, 1971.

James, T. C. G. *The Growth of Fighter Command, 1936–1940*. London: Whitehall History, 2002.

Jones, Neville. *The Beginnings of Strategic Air Power*. London: Cassells, 1987.

Joubert de la Ferté, Philip. *The Third Service: The Story Behind the Royal Air Force*. London: Thames & Hudson, 1955.

Kershaw, Ian. *Making Friends with Hitler: Lord Londonderry and Britain's Road to War*. London: Allen Lane, 2004.

Maiolo, Joseph A. *Cry Havoc: How the Arms Race Drove the World to War, 1931–1941*. New York: Basic, 2010.

MacBean, John & Arthur Hogben. *Bombs Gone: The Development and Use of British Air-dropped Weapons from 1912 to the Present Day*. Wellingborough: Patrick Stephens, 1990.

McKinstry, Leo. *Lancaster: The Second World War's Greatest Bomber*. London: John Murray, 2009.

McKinstry, Leo. *Spitfire: Portrait of a Legend*. London: John Murray, 2007.

Mason, Francis K. *Battle over Britain*. London: McWhirter Twins, 1969.

Middlebrook, Martin. *The Nuremberg Raid*. London: Allen Lane. 1973.

Miller, Russell. *Boom: The Life of Viscount Trenchard: Father of the Royal Air Force*. London: Weidenfeld & Nicolson, 2016.

Selected Bibliography

Mosley, Leonard. *On Borrowed Time: How World War II Began.* London: Weidenfeld & Nicolson, 1969.

Mosley, Leonard. *The Battle of Britain: The Making of a Film.* London: Weidenfeld & Nicolson, 1969.

Murray, Williamson. *Luftwaffe: Strategy for Defeat.* London: Grafton, 1988.

O'Halpin, Eunan. *Head of the Civil Service: A Study of Sir Warren Fisher.* London: Routledge, 1989.

Orange, Vincent. *Dowding of Fighter Command: Victor of the Battle of Britain.* London: Grub Street, 2008,

Overy, R. J. *Göring.* London: Phoenix, 2000.

Overy, R. J. *The Birth of the RAF, 1918: The World's First Air Force.* London: Penguin, 2018.

Overy, R. J. *The Bombing War: Europe 1939–1945.* London: Penguin, 2013.

Peden, G. C. *British Rearmament and the Treasury.* Edinburgh: Scottish Academic Press, 1979.

Phillips, Adrian. *Fighting Churchill, Appeasing Hitler: How a British Civil Servant Helped Cause the Second World War.* London: Biteback, 2019.

Postan, M. M. *British War Production.* London: HMSO, 1952.

Postan, M. M., D. Hay & J. D. Scott. *Design and Development of Weapons: Studies in Government and Industrial Organisation.* London: HMSO, 1964.

Powers, Barry Douglas. *Strategy Without Slide-Rule.* London: Croom Helm, 1976.

Probert, Henry. *Bomber Harris: His Life and Times: The Biography of Marshal of the Royal Air Force, Sir Arthur Harris, the Wartime Chief of Bomber Command.* London: Greenhill, 2001.

Public Record Office. *The Rise and Fall of the German Air Force, 1933–1945.* London: Arms & Armour Press. 1983.

Reader, W. J. *Architect of Air Power: The Life of the First Viscount Weir of Eastwood 1877–1959.* London: Collins, 1968.

Richardson, Charles. *From Churchill's Secret Circle to the BBC: The Biography of Lieutenant General Sir Ian Jacob.* London: Brassey's, 1991.

Ritchie, Sebastian. *Industry and Air Power: The Expansion of British Aircraft Production, 1935–41.* London: Frank Cass, 1997.

Rose, K. *The Later Cecils.* London: Weidenfeld & Nicolson, 1975.

Roskill, S. W. *Hankey: Man of Secrets.* 3 volumes. London: Collins, 1970.

Saunders, Hilary Aidan St. George. *Royal Air Force, 1939–1945. Volume 1 The Fight at Odds*. London: HMSO, 1974.

Self, Robert C. *Neville Chamberlain: A Biography*. Aldershot: Ashgate, 2006.

Shay, Robert P. *British Rearmament in the Thirties: Politics and Profits*. Princeton: Princeton UP, 1978.

Sinnott, Colin. *The RAF and Aircraft Design, 1923–1939: Air Staff Operational Requirements*. London: Frank Cass, 2001.

Slessor, J. C. *Air Power and Armies*. London: Oxford University Press, 1936.

Smith, Malcolm. *British Air Strategy between the Wars*. Oxford: Clarendon, 1984.

Taylor, A. J. P. *From the Boer War to the Cold War: Essays on Twentieth-century Europe*. London: Penguin, 1996.

Terraine, John. *Business in Great Waters*. London: Mandarin, 1990.

Terraine, John. *The Right of the Line: The Royal Air Force in the European War, 1939–1945*. London: Hodder & Stoughton, 1985.

Thorburn, Gordon, *Bomber Command 1939–1940*, Barnsley, Pen & Sword, 2013.

Wark, W. K. *The Ultimate Enemy: British Intelligence and Nazi Germany, 1933–1939*. Oxford, 1986.

Webster, C. K. & N. Frankland. *The Strategic Air Offensive Against Germany, 1939–1945*. 4 volumes. London: HMSO, 1961.

Wood, Derek and Derek Dempster. *The Narrow Margin: The Battle of Britain and the Rise of Air Power 1930–40*. London: Hutchinson. 1961.

Wykeham, Peter. *Fighter Command: A Study of Air Defence, 1914–1960*. London: Putnam, 1960.

Zimmerman, David. *Radar: Britain's Shield and the Defeat of the Luftwaffe*. Stroud: Amberley, 2013.

Periodicals

Daily Telegraph
Evening Post
Hansard
Le Fana de l'Aviation
Sunday Times
The Times

Articles

Barros, Andrew. 'Strategic Bombing and Restraint in "Total War", 1915–1918'. *The Historical Journal* 52.2 (2009): pp. 413–31.

Bialer, Uri. 'Elite Opinion and Defence Policy: Air Power Advocacy and British Rearmament during the 1930s'. *British Journal of International Studies* 6.1 (1980): pp. 32–51.

Holman, Brett. 'The Air Panic of 1935: British Press Opinion between Disarmament and Rearmament'. *Journal of Contemporary History* 46.2 (2011): pp. 288–307.

Layne, Christopher. 'Security Studies and the Use of History: Neville Chamberlain's Grand Strategy Revisited'. *Security Studies* 17.3 (2008): pp. 397–437.

Lee, Gerald. '"I see dead people": Air-raid Phobia and Britain's Behavior in the Munich Crisis'. *Security Studies* 13.2 (2003): pp. 230–72.

Lyth, Peter. 'The Empire's Airway: British Civil Aviation from 1919 to 1939'. *Revue Belge de Philologie et d'histoire* 78.3 (2000): pp. 865–87.

McKinstry Leo. 'Did Neville Chamberlain create the conditions for the RAF to win the Battle of Britain?' *New Statesman* 24 April 2018.

Redford, Duncan. 'Inter- and Intra-Service Rivalries in the Battle of the Atlantic'. *Journal of Strategic Studies* 32.6 (2009): pp. 899–928.

Self, Robert. 'Neville Chamberlain and Rearmament: Did the Treasury Win the Battle of Britain?' *20th Century History Review* 3.1 (2007): p. 13.

Smith, Malcolm. 'Planning and Building the British Bomber Force, 1934–1939'. *Business History Review* 54.1 (1980): pp. 35–62.

Terraine, John. 1984 Address to the Western Front Association in *Stand To!* (1985) No.13 pp. 4–7.

PhD Theses

Scott Smith, Gordon. 'RAF War Plans and British Foreign Policy, 1935–1940'. MIT, 1966.

Sinnott, Colin. RAF Operational Requirements, 1923–1939. King's College London, 1998.

Acknowledgements

My biggest thanks go to my wife Sheila and these go far beyond the customary gratitude for home support and tolerance. The restricted hours and limited availability of documents at the National Archives when they reopened after the end of strict covid lockdown curtailed hugely what a single researcher could achieve, so Sheila stepped into the breach and had a crash course in the craft of history. She unearthed many gems at Kew amongst the vast volumes of material she examined. But for her help this book would just not have been possible.

Neil Chamberlain and Liz Deery of the RAF Air Historical Branch did not stint of their time and effort in helping me find answers to the recondite queries with which I presented them. David Hassard of the Hawker Association provided me with vital information on Hawker's Hucclecote works.

All the staff at the National Archives in Kew deserve the deepest respect for their courage, efficiency, tolerance and good humour in delivering the maximum level of service possible during the pandemic. Andrew Riley and his colleagues at the Churchill Archives Centre deserve similar praise.

David Heath of the Bawdsey Radar Trust and Sophie Jeffrey of the Shuttleworth Collection were generous in the valuable help they gave with photographs.

The family of the late James Holland very kindly traced and allowed me to use the artist's cartoons for the murals at the Castle Bromwich shadow factory.

Jake Denton of Hachette made available to me a copy of an elusive article.

Dave Sharruck gave me the benefit of his huge experience in setting out the difference between modern practices of procuring major military

Acknowledgements

systems and those of the RAF in the 1930s. Mark Lubienski leapt to my assistance to supply a missing reference.

Lastly, thanks to Claire Hopkins and Alan Murphy of Pen & Sword for their enthusiasm and support. My editor Chris Cocks deserves every praise for his patience in bringing to book to print, as well as sharing his grandfather's stories of the RAF in India during the late 1920s.

Index

20mm cannon, 53–56, 295–296

Adam, Sir Ronald, 126, 221
Albermarle, Armstrong-Whitworth, 192
Anderson, Sir John, 126
Attlee, Clement
   criticizes government air policy, 184–185
   mentioned, x, 69, 69, 88

Baldwin, Stanley
   'bomber will always get through', 71–73
   parity pledge, 75–76, 89, 92
   willing to push for rearmament, 84–85, 95
   declares Rhine is Britain's frontier, 88–89
   claims Britain has 50% margin over Germany in the air, 90–91
   admits to underestimation of German strength, 99–100
   annoyed by JP, 155, 129
   mentioned, x, 61, 62, 79, 80, 87, 91, 101, 102, 103, 107, 108, 115, 116, 117, 130, 135, 152, 155, 186

Balfour, Harold, unconvinced by Air Staff explanation of poor bomber performance, 291 mentioned, x, 196
Battle, Fairey, ix, xxiii, 41–43, 45, 46, 84, 106, 110, 140, 148, 149, 168, 188, 192, 198, 227, 232, 259, 282, 286, 287, 288, 292–293
Beatty, Lord, underhand campaign to regain control of naval aviation, 12–13, 272
Beaverbrook, Lord, 91, 161, 198
Blenheim, Bristol, ix, xxiii, 41–43, 45, 46, 106, 110, 140, 149, 168, 188, 192, 227, 232, 259, 267–270, 282, 286, 287, 292–293
Bonar Law, Andrew, 14
Bottomley, Horatio, 4
Brandenburg, Ernest, 4
Bridges, Edward, low opinion of Ellington, 78, position on Air Council Committee on Supply speeds up orders, 184
Brooke-Popham, Sir Robert, x, 50, 64, 245
Bruce–Gardner, Sir Charles picked as Downing Street's air rearmament czar, 172–173

position undermines Swinton's, 182–183
scheme to boost aircraft production numbers, 190–193
feeds optimistic picture of aircraft production to Downing Street, 280–281
enthusiast for Stirling, 281
policies boost plane-makers' profits, 281–284
mentioned, x, 184, 198, 257, 262

Bullock, Sir Christopher, x, 80, 80, 156, inflated opinion of his role, 102–104

Butt, David, 249

Cadman, Lord, 185

Cecil, Hugh, on Trenchard's staff, 5–6

Chamberlain, Neville
fears German bombing of London, xxii, 186
low opinion of Londonderry and Ellington, 79
favours spending on RAF and bombing strategy, 84–86, 89, 113–114, 149
uninterested in detail of rearmament, 167–168
knows he is politically vulnerable to Churchill's criticism, 171, 183
alarmed at slow delivery of new aircraft, 171–173
retreats from support of bombing strategy, 177–178
takes confrontational approach to Churchill, 184–186, 194
shares Hitler's purely numerical view of air strength, 190–193
dismisses Swinton and Winterton, appoints Wood as air minister, 195–196
true reason for call for rules on bombing, 227–228
believes strength of Luftwaffe means Britain weaker, 230–232
backs away from parity commitment, 252, 258
opposes Scheme M, 259–260
misconceptions about big bombers, 261–262
expands British land commitment in Europe, 275–276
mentioned, x, xi, xiv, 62, 92, 102, 107, 116, 122, 155, 165, 175, 182, 199, 233, 239, 241, 242, 243, 255, 264, 280, 281

Channon, 'Chips', 80, 196

Chatfield, Sir Ernle, only member of DRC to impress, 35
mentioned, 80, 148

Christie, Malcolm, 134, 134, 162–163, 216, 252

Churchill, Winston
appoints Trenchard for his second term as CAS, 9
enthusiasm for turret fighters, 52
speech on havoc air attack could wreak on London, 59–60

criticises government's air rearmament policy, 75–76, 87–88, 89–90, 171, 184, 194–195
ambitions for Tizard committee, 96
Arms and the Covenant campaign, 129–130
supports Lindemann's campaign, 151–152
contrast with Chamberlain's approach to defence questions, 167
expected to call for inquiry into air policy, 185
mentioned, xi, 61, 61, 80, 91, 115, 117, 118, 128, 161, 192, 193, 232, 258, 249, 280, 299
Courtney, Christopher, 130–131, 138, 146, 154, 159
Cunliffe-Lister, Sir Philip see Swinton, Lord

Davison, J. C. C., 79
Dean, Maurice, low opinion of Ellington, 78, describes RAF navigation methods as primitive, 244, writes that RAF forgot how to support army, 273, mentioned, xi, 69, 84
Defiant, Boulton Paul and turret fighters, ix, 47, 52–54, 133, 160, 192, 214, 269, 295–296
Dornier Do 17, 292
Douhet, Giulio, 21
Dowding, Sir Hugh
in *Battle of Britain* movie, xviii–xix, 299
understands that budgetary debate reflects economic reality, xx
Whitley specification, 44–45
sceptical of 20mm cannon, 55, 296
opposed to split into Bomber and Fighter Commands, 65
background and appointment as AOC-C Fighter Command, 67–69
wants hard runways for fighter aerodromes, 69, 181, 294–295
ambition to become CAS, 69–70, 216
resists impractical expansion projects, 120–122
promotes RDF, 151, 153–154
confident that fighter defence effective, 155, 220–222, 297–299
helps bring women into RDF operation, 158
challenges Trenchardian dogma, 215–223
not consulted about Blenheim fighters, 269
sceptical of value of Defiants, 295–296
struggles with plans by Air Staff, 296–297
resists move of fighter squadrons to France, 298–299
mentioned, xi, 158, 201, 233, 246, 271

Index

Eden, Anthony, 92, 97
Ellington, Sir Edward
   poor reputation, 24, 77, 77–79, 161, 175
   blames delay in rearming RAF on disarmament conference, 44, 72
   advocate of turret fighters, 52
   Trenchard despises for his failure over FAA, 64, 77, 77–78, 119, 159
   appointed as CAS, 77
   advocate of large bombers, 79, 84, 111–112, 146, 148
   dissents from DRC report, 80, 86
   drags feet over air rearmament, 81–84
   believes Nazi regime will be short-lived, 83
   poor presentation of Scheme B, 98–99
   complacency towards Luftwaffe, 125, 133–135, 162–163
   challenges Swinton's account of his scepticism towards RDF, 155–156
   challenged by Dowding, 216–218
   put on defensive by Ludlow-Hewitt's concerns, 290
   mentioned, xi, 69, 87, 113, 131, 138, 159, 163, 203, 204
Evill, Douglas, 138

Fairey, Richard, xi, 170, 281–282
Fisher, Sir Warren
   and DRC, 74
   questions competence of Air Staff, 175–176
   still hopes for genuine switch to fighters, 263, 266
   withdraws, 263
Freeman, Sir Wilfrid
   willing to challenge Newall, 55, 267
   low opinion of Ellington, 78
   accuses Swinton and Weir of putting quantity before quality, 106, 107
   initial confidence in Vulture, 145
   combined responsibility for aircraft design and production, 184
   order for 1,000 Hurricanes, 262, 266
   mentioned, ix, xii, 196, 196, 198, 292

George VI, 49, 267
Gladiator, Gloster, 47, 104, 191, 203, 227, 233–234, 282, 299
Goddard, Victor, scales back estimate of Luftwaffe bombing potential, 225–226
Goebbels, Joseph, contempt for British propaganda, 243
   mentioned, xii, 61, 232–233
Goering, Herman, xii, xiii, 61fn, 83, 176, 190, 223
Groves, Percy, 17–18, 91

Haig, Sir Douglas, 5, 10, 21, 25, 84
Halifax, Handley Page, 143, 144, 145, 176, 200, 213, 256, 291–292
Halifax, Lord, complains at Air Staff restrictions on bombing, 293 mentioned, 177, 193
Hampden, Handley Page, xxiii, 9, 43–44, 45, 46, 84, 140, 187, 192, 292–293
Handley Page, Frederick, xii, 170
Hankey, Sir Maurice
  challenges Trenchard's claim RAF could win war on its own, 23–24
  advocates ban on bombing, 72–73
  driving force behind early rearmament moves, 74
  dominant force in Whitehall, 77
  and DRC, 80
  dismisses Scheme A as window-dressing, 86
  believes German air threat not imminent, 89
  and defence review, 109
  co-opts Weir, 112–113
  and appointment of Minister for Defence Coordination, 116–117
  overcomes Admiralty hostility to convoys, 121–122
  challenges pessimism of JP155, 129–132
  promotes RDF, 152
  tries to revive Ideal defence scheme, 220
  retires, 263
  proposes conversion of bombers to fighter role, 267
  mentioned, xii, 103, 118, 119, 148, 162, 182, 212, 217, 230
Harris, Arthur 'Bert'
  claims never to have heard of Douhet, 21
  advocates gun turrets, 49–50, 51
  tries to improve defensive armament of bombers, 56
  and JP155, 126–130
  advocates big bombers, 142, 146
  contempt for propaganda dropping, 242–243
  disparages radio navigation aids, 249
  mentioned, xii, xxii, xxiii, 133, 161, 189, 204, 251
Hart, Hawker and derivatives, 37, 41, 105–106, 110, 105–107, 203, 227, 275, 283
Heinkel He 111, 51, 226
Henderson, Sir David, 3, 6
Hindenburg, Paul, 4
Hitler, Adolf
  claims Germany has parity with Britain, 92
  derides Chamberlain's desire to limit bombing, 232–233
  mentioned, xi, xii, 37, 70, 75, 80, 83, 96, 97, 99, 80, 104, 106, 109, 115, 124, 134, 135, 171, 186, 190, 224, 231, 241, 259
Hoare, Sir Samuel, xii, 20, 175, 241
von Höppner, Wilhelm, 4

Index

Hore-Belisha, Leslie, points to successful use of aircraft on battlefield in Spain, 273–274
Hurricane, Hawker, ix, xxiii, 47, 52, 55, 107, 110, 192, 200, 220, 222, 227, 259, 263, 266, 267, 282, 283, 298–299
Hyde, Montgomery, 159

Inskip, Sir Thomas
  appointed as minister for defence coordination, 117–118
  rules on FAA dispute, 118–119
  'Ideal' defence scheme, 119–123
  sees danger of knock-out blow, 164
  opposed to Scheme J, 174–178
  clash over Scheme L, 188
  dismissed, 263
  mentioned, xii, 156, 165, 169, 178, 180, 181, 199, 201, 204, 211, 216, 217, 220, 230, 231, 263, 273
Ironside, Sir Edmund, demands sharp increase in RAF support for army, 276

Jones, Dr. R. V., 246, 250
Joubert de la Ferté, Philip, 67, 151, 213
Junkers 52, 104
Junkers 87, xix
Junkers 88, 214

Kendall, Dennis, 55, 156, 213

Lancaster, Avro, ix, 145, 200, 282
Lansbury, George, 74, 88

Lemon, Ernest, brings knowledge of production techniques into Air Ministry, 184
Lindeman, Professor Frederick
  and committee to promote use of science in air defence, 95–96
  malign influence on scientific planning, 151–152
  forces through study of bombing, 249, 281
Lloyd George, David, xiii, 4, 6, 11, 13, 14, 101, 103, 115, 122
Londonderry, Lord
  slow to recognize swing in favour of rearmament, 75
  background to appointment and weakness as air minister, 79–81
  political position weakens, 84–85
  side-lined in favour of Cunliffe-Lister, 94–96
  poor presentation of Scheme B, 98–99
  dismissed, 100
  mentioned, xiii, 83, 87, 90, 96, 102, 103, 125, 159, 186, 195
Ludlow-Hewitt, Sir Edgar
  lack of confidence in Bomber Command, xxi, xxii, 204–208, 227–228, 285–291
  doubts over gun turrets, 49
  drags feet over air rearmament, 81
  character and background, 204

343

supports Air Staff WA5 plan,
    208–209
supports use of bombers to
    drop propaganda,
    232, 239
advocates conversion of
    Blenheims to fighters, 232,
    267–269
traditionalist stance on aircraft
    navigation, 244–245, 249
resists offer of scientific
    assistance from Tizard,
    247–249
unconvinced by Newall's bid
    for RAF primacy, 254
changes mind on Blenheim
    fighters, 288
mentioned, xiii, 56, 230, 231,
    250, 279, 293, 294
Lysander, Westland, 40,
    234, 275

Macdonald, James Ramsay, xiii,
    79, 80, 85, 84, 93, 94, 100
Macmillan, Harold, 58
Manchester, Avro, ix, 143, 144,
    145, 176, 211, 213, 256, 282,
    291–292
Margesson, David, 185, 186
McLintock, William Sir, 281
Messerschmitt Bf 109, 47
Messerschmitt Bf 110, xix, 47,
    214, 270
Milch, Erhard
    manipulates estimates of
        Luftwaffe size, 138
    asks British about their
        progress in radar, 157

comments on size of Luftwaffe
    squadrons, 178–179
mentioned, xiii
Mitchell, R.J., 147, 265
Morton, Desmond, 90, 134
Mosquito, de Havilland, 53,
    214, 267
Muirhead, Anthony, 185, 252
Murray, Williamson, xxiii

Newall, Sir Cyril
    commands VIII Brigade RFC,
        4–5, 7
    faithful to minimum fighters
        doctrine, 33–35
    intelligence on German
        bomber defensive
        armament, 51
    advocate of turret fighters, 52,
        265, 295
    favours Westland Whirlwind,
        55, 160, 198, 267
    wants to arm bombers with
        20mm cannon, 56
    chosen as CAS, 69, 159–160
    advocate of large bombers, 148
    exaggerated opinion of
        Stirling, 160, 261, 263, 281
    bad judge of aircraft, 160
    politically illiterate,
        160–161, 261
    sees RAF expansion as
        urgently necessary, 163–164
    sees bomber/fighter ratio of
        Scheme J as 'balanced',
        165, 180–181
    Scheme J claims pre-eminence
        for RAF, 174

Index

insists parity in bombers vital to save British civilization, 188–189
Slessor convinces of need for pause in expansion, 202–203
sees Ideal bomber as expression of doctrine, 212
tries to restrain Dowding, 220–221
no longer visualizes 'bolt from the blue', 228
begs Wood to sway Cabinet against war, 231
instructs Ludlow-Hewitt to conserve bomber resources if war breaks out, 231–232, 293
bids to displace Navy as premier fighting service, 252–254
push to expand RAF in wake of Munich, 255–256
opposed to any shift in favour of fighters, 259–261, 266
false claim to Downing Street, 262
promotes big bomber strategy to Downing Street, 262–263
promise of Blenheim fighters to Cabinet, 268–269
rebukes war minister for suggesting aircraft could be used for battlefield support, 273–274
Battles might be used 'prudently' against German advance, 279
accuses Ludlow-Hewitt of unreasonable pessimism, 289
weak response to poor performance data of big bombers, 291–292
horrified by Dowding's optimism on fighter performance, 297
claims that he is not 'selling Fighter Command to the French', 298
mentioned, ix, xiii, 31, 46, 133, 162, 169, 179, 216, 226, 227, 229, 230, 240, 264, 276, 285, 286, 288, 293, 299
Norman, Montagu, 172–173, 280
Nuffield, Lord, Castle Bromwich shadow factory, xiii, 197–198

Oxland, Robert, 147

Peirse, Richard, tries to restrain Dowding, 217–218, unconvinced by Newall's bid for RAF primacy, 254
mentioned, ix, xiii, 164, 169
Pethick-Lawrence, Frederick, 281–282
Phillips, Tom, 126, 221
Pownall, Henry, low opinion of Ellington, 79

Radar/RDF, xiv, xv, xix, xxiv, 19, 33, 67, 96, 130–131, 150–158, 181, 188, 214, 222, 223, 225, 234, 245, 246, 247, 248, 271
Reith, Sir John, 240

Rothermere, Lord, alarmist press campaign on German air strength, 91, 101, 113, 137, 281 mentioned, xiii, 4, 6, 8, 13, 14, 17, 41–42
Rowe, A. P., 248–249

Salmond, Geoffrey, xiv, 24, 64
Salmond, John, xiv, 7, 16, 22, 24, 54, 64, 69
Samuel, Herbert, 88
Sassoon, Sir Philip, 80, 185
Scarff, F. W., 48
Seely, Hugh, 194
Sholto Douglas
   knows Ideal bomber unrealistic, 213
   confident that fighter defence effective, 222
   supports Tizard's initiative but backs away, 246–247
   open-minded on aircraft as battlefield weapon, 277
   tries to make Air Staff take Ludlow-Hewitt's concerns seriously, 289
   wants to bring Colonel Turner under control, 295
   mentioned, ix, xiv, 161, 161
Simmonds, Oliver, 191
Simon, Sir John
   on Trenchard's staff, 5–6, 175
   Berlin visit, 75, 92, 92, 97–98
   says Scheme B inadequate, 98
   approves RDF scheme, 154
   supports Inskip's opposition to Scheme J, 175–177
   clash over Scheme L, 188
   attempts to impose budgetary discipline on Wood, 200
   attacks flaws in big bomber scheme, 258, 259
   mentioned, xiv
Slessor, John
   admits belief in bomber was matter of faith, 20
   Air Power and Armies advocates strategic bombing, 21, 162
   low opinion of Ellington, 78
   Newall's *éminence grise* and disciple of Trenchard, 161–162
   blames production shortfalls on plane-makers, 169
   manipulates statistics to exaggerate strength of Luftwaffe, 179–180
   insists parity in bombers vital to save British civilization, 188–189
   pleads for consolidation pause in expansion, 202–204
   revises JP155 in belief that value of fighter declining, 220–223
   tries to assess Luftwaffe bombing potential, 225
   uses Chamberlain's words as pretext for restrictive rules on bombing, 227–228
   enthusiasm for propaganda, 239–241
   unconvinced by Newall's bid for RAF primacy, 254

Index

pretends that Munich led to switch in priority to fighters, 264
admits obsession with knock-out blow was damaging, 270
leads resistance to army demands for air support, 276–279
admits Ludlow-Hewitt's pessimism justified, 286
briefs Newall on disappointing performance of big bombers, 291–292
promotes transfer of RAF fighters to France, 297–298
mentioned, xiv, 133, 233

Smuts, Jan Christian, 3
Sorley, Ralph, 39
Spitfire, Supermarine, ix, xxiii, 47, 55, 106–107, 110, 160, 192, 196, 197–198, 220, 222, 227, 259, 266, 267
Stanhope, Lord, detects fraudulence of Wood's claim that 1936 generation aircraft are Ideal bombers, 212, 258
Steel, Sir John, 65
Stevenson, Donald
drafts paper challenging increase in fighter numbers, 270–271
advocates turret-fighters, 295–296
composes ambitious plan for Fighter Command, 296
Stirling, Short, ix, 144, 148, 160, 206, 211, 213, 256, 262–263, 291–292

Streat, Raymond, 61
Stuart, Sir Campbell, 241–242
Swinton, Lord, formerly Sir Philip Cunliffe-Lister
Baldwin's choice to drive air rearmament, 95–96, 98–99
and Scheme C, 99, 103–107
becomes air minister, 100
partnership with Weir, 102–103
and Scheme F, 109–110
resists Inskip's proposals, 122–123
challenges Ellington's complacency towards Luftwaffe, 125
and Scheme H, 135–139, 216
promotes RDF, 152–155, 246
accuses Ellington of opposing extension of RDF chain, 155–156
selects Newall as CAS, 159
warns Luftwaffe might double in size, 166
Scheme J claims pre-eminence for RAF, 174
falls in with Slessor's exaggerated figure for Luftwaffe strength, 179
loses ground politically, 182, 184–186
uneasy relationship with Bruce-Gardner, 183
innovations to accelerate aircraft production, 183–184
clash over Scheme L, 188
attempts to resist drive for mere numbers of aircraft, 191–193, 280, 284

347

blames his dismissal on
   Chamberlain's lack of
   interest in rearmament, 195
knows pause in expansion
   politically impossible,
   202–203
mentioned, xi, xiv, xv, 108,
   111, 141, 177, 182,
   191, 194, 196, 197, 198,
   252, 273
Sykes, Frederick, 7, 9, 10, 14,
   17, 52

Tallents, Sir Stephen, and
   propaganda, xiv, 240–241
Taylor, A. J. P., xx, xxiv
Terboven, Josef, 176
Terraine, John, xx
Tizard, Sir Henry
   and committee to promote use
      of science in air defence,
      95–96, 158
   tries to help Bomber
      Command use science,
      245–248
   resents Air Staff's neglect of
      navigation, 250
   mentioned, xiv, 152
Trenchard, Sir Hugh
   does not believe fighters
      provide defence against
      bombers, xix, 19–20,
      26–27, 32–33
   calls Henderson 'Father of the
      RAF', 3
   first term as CAS, 4–6
   political skill, 6, 13
   commands IAF, 7–8

Southampton mutiny, 8–9
Churchill appoints for second
   term as CAS, 9
marriage and enhanced status,
   10–11
fights for RAF's interests,
   11–15, 18–19
puts his mark on RAF, 15
origin of 'air control', 16–17
press campaign against, 17
develops bombing doctrine,
   18–20
vision of air war as duel
   between bombing forces,
   19–21
held in reverence, 20, 161
defends 'air control'
   against accusations of
   inhumanity, 22
circulates papers to bolster
   RAF's standing, 22–24
status as 'Father of the RAF', 25
despises popular pressure for
   fighter defence, 25, 26
sees investment in fighters as
   wasteful, 26–28, 31–33, 68
believes air superiority
   unattainable, 28–29
sees role of fighters as boosting
   morale of 'ignorant
   masses', 29–30
fighters will only deter weak-
   spirited bomber pilots,
   30–31, 223
grotesque over-statement of
   anti-fighter case, 31
little involved in aircraft
   design, 38

348

shapes RAF's command structure, 62–64
choice of successors, 64, 159
despises Ellington for his failure over FAA, 64, 77, 77–78, 119, 159
intrigues against Hankey, 117
invites Newall to intrigue against Swinton, 160
mentioned, xii, xiv, xv, xxiii, xxiv, 2, 67, 69, 77, 83, 101, 102, 103, 118, 175, 215, 218, 221, 236, 237, 253, 256, 272, 273, 285
Turner, 'Conky Bill', 235, 294–295

Vansittart, Sir Robert, and DRC, 74, warns of German air menace, 92–93, mentioned, 135

Wallis, Barnes, 251
Watson-Watt, Robert, urges rapid extension of RDF chain, 234
mentioned, xv, 153
Weir, Lord
  patron of Trenchard and strategic bombing, 7
  criticises RAF's aircraft design procedures, 39
  background to appointment, 101–103
  advocates ordering off drawing board, 103–104
  accused by Freeman of putting quantity before quality, 106
  Shadow factories, 106
  proposes extra capacity for Blenheims, 111
  brought onto Defence Policy and Requirements committee, 112–114
  appointment of Inskip puts end to his ambitions, 113–116
  nearly resigns over FAA, 119
  believes bombload of striking force key, 136
  resigns when Swinton dismissed, 195
  mentioned, xv, 9, 108, 117, 122, 136, 159, 168, 170, 195, 198, 202
Wellington, Vickers, ix, xxiii, 43–44, 46, 84, 140–141, 149, 187, 188, 192, 259, 261, 262, 266, 286, 288, 292–293
Wells, H. G., 57
Whitley, Armstrong-Whitworth, ix, xxiii, 44–45, 46, 107, 110, 140–141, 145, 149, 227, 282, 292–293
Wilson, Sir Henry, 15, 16, 22
Wilson, Sir Horace
  fears German bombing, 61–62, 186
  move to accelerate slow pace of aircraft deliveries, 171–173
  undermines Swinton, 182–183, 186, 195
  handles political response to criticism of air policy, 184–185, 194
  discusses rearmament with union leaders, 186–187

scheme to boost aircraft
production numbers,
190–193
belief Britain weaker
than Germany due to
exaggerated fear of
Luftwaffe, 230–231
strives to minimize
propaganda, 241
backs away from parity
commitment, 252, 258
misconceptions about big
bombers, 261–262
mentioned, x, xv, 263,
280–281
Wimperis, Harry, and committee
to promote use of science in air
defence, 95
Winterton, Lord, curious choice
to present air policy, 185–186,
disastrous parliamentary
performance, 194–195, 252
Wood, Sir Kingsley
appointed as air minister, 196
instinct for publicity, 197, 201
Nuffield shadow factory,
197–198
project to manufacture
bombers in Canada,
199–200, 255
tries to pass 1936 generation
aircraft off as Ideal
bombers, 212–213
votes to accept Hitler's Bad
Godesberg demands, 231
unconvinced by Newall's bid
for RAF primacy, 254
push to expand RAF in wake
of Munich, 255–256
represents Scheme M as
switching priority to
fighters, 257, 260–261,
264, 266
supports Air Staff's big
bomber scheme, 257–262
keeps budgetary door open for
big bombers, 262–263
praises Blenheim and
Lysander in fighter role to
Cabinet, 268
forces Air Staff to pay attention
to Ludlow-Hewitt's
concerns, 289
mentioned, xv, 228